THE MEMOIRS OF CATHERINE THE GREAT

RULES* FOR
THE BEHAVIOR OF ALL ENTERING THESE DOORS

1.

Leave all ranks outside, likewise hats, and particularly swords.

2.

Orders of precedence and haughtiness, or anything however similar, must be left at the door.

3.

Be merry, but neither damage nor break anything, nor gnaw on anything.

4.

Be seated, stand, walk, as you see fit, regardless of others.

5.

*Speak with moderation and not too loudly, that those present not have
an earache or headache.*

6.

Argue without anger or passion.

7.

Do not sigh or yawn, and do not bore or fatigue anyone.

8.

Others should join in any innocent fun that someone thinks up.

9.

*Eat well, but drink with moderation, that each can always find his legs
upon going out the door.*

10.

*Disputes shall not be taken outside the izba;† and what goes in one ear should
go out the other before one steps through the doors.*

———

*Whoever infringes the above, on the evidence of two witnesses, for any crime each guilty
party must drink a glass of cold water, ladies not excepted, and read a page of the*
Tilemakhida‡ *out loud.*

Whoever infringes three articles in one evening is sentenced to learn six lines from the
Tilemakhida *by heart.*

And whoever infringes the tenth article will no longer be admitted.

* Catherine's rules for behavior in her hermitage are in Russian. See Mikhail B. Piotrovsky, ed., *Treasures of Catherine the Great* (London: Thames & Hudson, 2000), 17.

† An izba is a peasant hut.

‡ The *Tilemakhida* (1766) by Vasily Trediakovsky (1703–69) is about Odysseus's son Telemachus, based on François Fénelon's *Les Aventures de Télémaque* (1699). Trediakovsky's experiment with ancient Greek hexameters in Russian was considered pedantic and difficult to read or appreciate.

THE MEMOIRS OF CATHERINE THE GREAT

A new translation by

Mark Cruse and Hilde Hoogenboom

MODERN LIBRARY

NEW YORK

2006 Modern Library Paperback Edition

Translation copyright © 2005 by Mark Cruse and Hilde M. Hoogenboom
Preface, Note on the Translation, Note on Noble Families, Table of Ranks
and Chivalric Orders copyright © 2005 by Hilde M. Hoogenboom

Published in the United States by Modern Library, an imprint of
The Random House Publishing Group, a division
of Random House, Inc., New York.

MODERN LIBRARY and the TORCHBEARER Design are registered
trademarks of Random House, Inc.

Originally published in hardcover in the United States by Modern Library,
an imprint of The Random House Publishing Group, a division of
Random House, Inc., in 2005.

Pages lxxxix–xc constitute a continuation of this copyright page.

ISBN 978-0-8129-6987-0

www.modernlibrary.com

146122990

TO OUR PARENTS

Monsieur Diderot... In all your plans for reform you forget the difference between our two positions: you work only on paper, which tolerates everything; it is smooth, supple, and offers no resistance to either your imagination or your pen; whereas I, a poor Empress, work on human skin, which is much more irritable and ticklish.

COMTE DE SÉGUR,
Mémoires ou Souvenirs et anecdotes,
2nd ed., vol. 3 (Paris, 1826), 42–43.

Preface

Catherine the Great and
Her Several Memoirs

Catherine the Great's memoirs are exceptional as a literary work and as a historical document. Yet, over the two hundred years since Catherine wrote them, they have been judged both infamous and marginal. While biographers have mined them for details about her sex life and court gossip, historians have dismissed them as blatant self-justification for her seizing the throne. These approaches underestimate the memoirs' significance. Catherine's autobiographical writings occupy a central place in her extensive, varied oeuvre, which unquestionably shaped her thinking and reign in fundamental ways.[1] Catherine ruled as an absolute monarch in a century of growing ambivalence about the concentration of power in the hands of one individual. Well aware of European criticism of Russian rule as innately tyrannical and of herself as an enlightened despot, Catherine used her writings to demonstrate that she was indeed enlightened but not a despot. Through numerous memoirs, Catherine attempted to portray herself as just, wise, and merciful, and thereby justify her use of absolute power.

During some of the most challenging years of her long reign (1762–96), Catherine secretly wrote, revised, and recommenced memoirs about her life under the rule of her predecessor, Empress Elizabeth I (reigned 1741–61). This first half of her life might appear irrelevant to the second half of her life as Empress, but Catherine wrote three such memoirs that all reflect her immediate difficulties in the periods when she was writing. Catherine wrote her first memoir around 1756 before she became Empress, during a period of ruthless court politics in preparation for the succession struggle that would occur when the ailing Elizabeth died. Although she does not write about her role in these politics, her letters from this period to the British Ambassador, her friend and mentor Sir Charles Hanbury-Williams (1709–59), for whom she most likely wrote the memoir, explain her difficult position in the Russian court. She writes:

> I would like to feel fear, but I cannot; the invisible hand that has guided me for thirteen years along a very rough road will never allow me to falter, of that I am very firmly and perhaps foolishly convinced. If only you knew all the perils and misfortunes that have threatened me, and that I have overcome. You will have a little more faith in arguments that are too hollow for someone who reasons as solidly as you.[2]

Catherine's sense of her destiny sustained her both as Grand Duchess and later, during her reign. With similar confidence in her ability to successfully confront challenges as Empress, she wrote her middle memoir from 1771 to 1773, while Russia fought a war against Turkey and partitioned Poland, Moscow suffered a serious outbreak of plague, and Catherine overcame two threats to her rule.

In her last decade, during several critical turning points over which she had only limited control, Catherine returned to her memoirs to write about past difficulties overcome. She made revisions to her middle memoir in 1790, and then began her final memoir in 1794, the fiftieth anniversary of her arrival in Russia, a period in which she began to feel old and alone. She had written her epitaph in 1778, and in 1792 she wrote her will. In 1791, Catherine lost her closest confidant, who was for several years her lover and most likely her secret husband, Prince Grigory Potemkin (b. 1739), viceroy for all of Southern Russia and one of Russia's greatest military statesmen.[3] As she looked to the future, the French Revolution and the execution of Louis XVI in 1793 struck fear in the hearts of Europe's monarchs. Afraid for Russia's stability after her death, she tried unsuccessfully to bypass the rightful succession of her son Paul in favor of her grandson, Alexander.[4] Her final memoir, translated here, indirectly responded to these future challenges to her legacy.

In all her memoirs, but especially in the last memoir, we see the perils of power through the eyes of an intelligent woman who was a consummate political animal. Her fundamental concern—political power—never changed.[5] In this final memoir, contemplating her death and place in history, Catherine recounts her brilliant but unhappy marriage to the heir to the Russian throne, and gives the fullest account of the events leading up to the most dangerous year of her career. On December 25, 1761, Empress Elizabeth I died, and her nephew and heir designate, Catherine's husband, became Emperor Peter III. Pregnant by her lover Count Grigory Orlov (1734–83), Catherine found herself at risk of arrest, exile, or worse, as Peter hinted at plans to install his mistress, Elizabeth Vorontsova (1739–92), as his consort, and did not declare his and Catherine's son as his heir. Six months later, Catherine seized the throne and declared herself Empress Catherine II, while Peter abdicated and was killed a week later by members of her political faction, though without her approval. Catherine's last memoir never explicitly addresses her coup or her husband's murder, but it has long been understood as an exercise in implicit self-justification. Her unstated premise is that although she had no claim to the throne, by virtue of her character and actions she nevertheless deserved, and was even meant, to rule.

The final memoir builds up to the crisis provoked in 1758 by the arrest and exile of her ally, Chancellor Count Alexei Bestuzhev-Riumin (1693–1767), who was in charge of foreign affairs.[6] This overthrow of Empress Elizabeth's senior statesman serves as a dress rehearsal for the dangers of Catherine's coup of 1762. Catherine writes about the day of his arrest: "A flood of ideas, each more unpleasant and sadder than the next, arose in my mind. With a dagger in my heart, so to speak, I got dressed and went to mass."[7] Bestuzhev-Riumin's arrest implicated her in his plans for the succession after Elizabeth's death, which were to have Catherine rule either alone or jointly with her husband, Peter. Her enemies hoped to force her into exile abroad instead. Catherine saved herself, her position, and her children through an extended, brilliant appeal in a letter and two conversations with Empress Elizabeth. In a calculated display of humility, she turned her enemies' threat to her advantage and in fact asked to be sent home to the German state of Anhalt-Zerbst, a dramatic step that Elizabeth, known for her indecisiveness, rejected. With a nod toward her situation four years hence, Catherine concluded her outline for the final memoir with the point of her story: "Things took such a turn that it was necessary to perish with him, by him, or else to try to save oneself from the wreckage and to save my children, and the state." In the memoir, she placed this conclusion after citing her husband's remark in 1758: "God knows where my wife gets her pregnancies. I really do not know if this child is mine and if I ought to recognize it." In 1762, her rights and safety would hinge on precisely the recognition of her son's, and thus her, legitimacy.

Though the idea that Catherine was a nymphomaniac is pure speculation, one thing is sure: she was a graphomaniac. Catherine wrote about herself from the time she arrived in Russia, in 1744, at the age of fourteen, until her death, in 1796, at age sixty-seven. The memoirs are not one but three main documents in French. She wrote her first full memoir around 1756; her middle memoir (in three parts) dates to 1771–73, a text she revised in 1790–91; and she began the final memoir (in two parts) around 1794. In addition, there are two early, short verbal self-portraits, two extensive outlines for the middle and final memoirs, numerous sketches, notes, and anecdotes for the memoirs, and autobiographical letters. These autobiographical writings in French and Russian add up to seven hundred pages, forming the last and largest of a dozen volumes of her works, which the Russian Imperial Academy of Sciences published in 1907, the first time this archival material was made public in Russia.[8] Under Catherine's successors—her son and his male descendants—the memoirs remained a state secret because they indicate that Paul was perhaps illegitimate and thus he and his offspring were not Romanovs. Moreover, Catherine's unflattering picture of life at court and in the royal family, not to mention her and Peter's affairs, were an embarrassment to the wholesome image of the nineteenth-century Russian royal family. Before 1907, scholars knew about the existence of only the final memoir, which circulated after her death in several handwritten copies. A copy was used for their first publication, in London in 1859, by the Russian radical Alexander Herzen (1812–70), in English, German, French, Russian, Swedish, and Danish.

This is the fourth English translation of her final and also fullest and longest memoir, and only the second complete translation; moreover, we are the first translators to study Catherine's original manuscript.[9] We also translated her outline for the memoir, noting what she crossed out and added as she was writing. Our goal has been an accurate, readable translation that conveys her voice, which combines a well honed art of plain speaking with a vigorous style of thought. In fact, Catherine tells us that how she writes is essential to her rhetorical purpose: "Besides, this writing itself should prove what I say about my mind, my heart, and my character."[10] Catherine appears to have sought and found a profound connection between herself and her writing. For more than fifty years, she used her autobiographical writing to understand herself as a human being, a woman, and an Empress. She wrote to take stock of her life and reign. Catherine also wrote to persuade future readers, for each memoir contains a different overall rhetorical purpose related to her concerns at the time she was writing.

This preface traces Catherine's autobiographical impulse over the course of an extraordinarily rich, accomplished, and controversial life. She expected her readers to be familiar with the history of her reign, which she does not recount in the memoir. Those eager to encounter Catherine and her memoir directly with no further introduction should have a sufficient overview of her reign and her memoirs from the preceding few pages. The remainder of this preface illuminates in detail the historical context, legacy, and uniqueness of Catherine's memoirs. It addresses the importance of writing to Catherine's rule and reputation abroad, the influence of the memoirs on Catherine scholarship since her death, and the genesis and unusual structure of this significant, original document. It brings together literary and historical analyses of the memoirs in a contribution to Catherine scholarship that is meant to be informative for those encountering Catherine for the first time and for experts alike.

A SHORT BIOGRAPHY OF A GREAT LIFE

Born on April 21, 1729, Princess Sophie Auguste Frederike von Anhalt-Zerbst died of a stroke on November 6, 1796, as Empress Catherine II of Russia. The space between her birth and death is divisible into three parts; with each transformation of her identity, Catherine acquired a different title and name to match her new role. From 1729 to 1744, she was Princess Sophie, the daughter of German nobles; from 1745 to 1762, she was Grand Duchess Ekaterina Alekseevna, wife of the heir to the Russian throne and mother of his son and successor; and finally, from 1762 to 1796, she was Empress Catherine II. The opening of her last memoir indicates that her mother's family connections—more than Catherine's personality, experiences, or desire for glory—paved the way for her marriage to Peter III, who was Catherine's second cousin. Catherine's mother,

Princess Johanna Elisabeth (1712–60), came from the same German family as Peter III, the house of Holstein Gottorp (1544–1773).[11] Peter's father, Karl Friedrich (1700–39), was Princess Johanna's paternal first cousin and married Anna Petrovna (1708–28), the eldest daughter of Peter I, "the Great" (1672–1725).[12] In addition to her cousin's marriage, Princess Johanna had another connection to the Russian royal family: her brother Karl August had been engaged to Anna's sister, the future Empress Elizabeth, but had died before the wedding.[13] These ties to the Russian royal family assumed great importance for Catherine when Elizabeth succeeded to the throne in 1741 and brought Anna's orphaned son Peter to Russia as her heir. A year later, when Elizabeth sought a wife for her nephew and heir, she chose her dead fiancé's niece Catherine.

According to Catherine's early and middle memoirs, Princess Johanna performed her job as mother and aristocrat well, and did everything to arrange a prestigious royal match for her daughter. Two presentation portraits of Catherine were sent to Elizabeth.[14] Elizabeth in turn performed kind gestures for Catherine's family. In 1742, Elizabeth became the godmother for Catherine's new sister, Elisabeth (1742–45), named after her, and sent a portrait of herself set in diamonds that were worth 25,000 rubles. She also provided an annual pension to Catherine's maternal grandmother, Princess Albertine Friederike (1682–1755) of Baden-Durlach.[15] To please Elizabeth and potentially further his own interests in Russia, the Prussian King Frederick II, "the Great" (1712–86, reigned 1740–86), promoted Catherine's father to Field Marshal. Frederick the Great and Princess Johanna also intrigued in the Russian court, where other factions favored a French or Saxon bride. Aside from Peter, Princess Sophie's only other serious suitor was her mother's brother, Georg Ludwig (1719–63), who proposed and was accepted by the young Princess, but not her parents, who had greater aspirations for her. In late 1743, Elizabeth invited the fourteen-year-old Princess Sophie and her mother, but for reasons unknown, specifically not her father, Prince Christian August (1690–1747), to Moscow.

On February 9, 1744, Princess Sophie arrived in Moscow. As her early and middle memoirs make clear, although Catherine was born into a minor German noble house, her mother had prepared Catherine well for life at a royal court. In fact, Catherine shows her disappointment in the quality of Russian court life. Thanks to her mother's godmother, the dowager Duchess Elisabeth Sophie Marie of Brunswick-Wolfenbüttel (1683–1767), she and her mother had spent several months each year at one of the most brilliant courts in Germany, where she met and played with some of the future royalty of Europe. While her mother traveled in Europe to keep up family contacts, Princess Sophie stayed with her grandmother in Hamburg and visited, among other places, the Prussian court of Frederick the Great in Berlin. Her governess, Elisabeth Cardel, a French Huguenot and professor's daughter, introduced her to the customs of French society and to French classical literature. This education allowed her to aspire to a royal marriage.

As Grand Duchess, Catherine's position depended on producing a male heir and cultivating political supporters at court. She was under constant scrutiny—no part of her life at court, nor anything in the memoirs, most especially her love life, was private. Catherine had innate political instincts that guided her well during and after her introduction to life in the Russian court. By contrast, even such a successful veteran of court politics as her mother nearly caused her and her daughter's dismissal before the wedding.[16] Princess Sophie willingly learned Russian, and on June 28, 1744, she converted from Lutheranism to Orthodoxy and became Ekaterina Alekseevna, in honor of Elizabeth's mother, Catherine I; the next day, she was betrothed and became Her Imperial Highness Grand Duchess.[17] Married on August 21, 1745, the sixteen-year-old bride and seventeen-year-old groom, according to Catherine's middle memoir, failed to consummate their marriage until 1754, when each was having an officially sanctioned affair in the hopes that experience would encourage them.[18] After two miscarriages, Catherine gave birth, on September 20, 1754, to Grand Duke Pavel Petrovich, the future Paul I (d. 1801), perhaps fathered by Sergei Saltykov (1726–1813).[19]

The significance for Catherine of the long-awaited birth of a male heir constitutes the underlying plot of her early memoir, written around 1756. Her son made Catherine's position at court much more secure, for she was now not only the wife of the heir apparent but also the mother of the future heir. Catherine's personal security became especially important as Elizabeth's health worsened and a succession struggle loomed.[20] Thus in 1756, in a letter to her mentor, Hanbury-Williams, Catherine planned ahead. "After being informed of her death and making sure that there is no mistake, I will go straight to my son's room."[21] Her son and timely information through her allies were crucial to her political and even physical survival. The Empress countered Catherine's intrigues by isolating her—from her son, friendly courtiers, and bad news about Elizabeth's health to make her less of a threat. As the memoirs make clear, the Empress also carefully kept Catherine on a limited budget of 30,000 rubles per year and watched what Catherine spent. However, Catherine ran up a debt of six hundred thousand rubles by 1762, money she used to buy the loyalty of courtiers and of her husband, as well as dresses.[22] After another miscarriage, she had two more children, a daughter, Anna Petrovna (1757–59), by a future King of Poland, Count Stanislaw August Poniatowski (1732–98), and by Count Grigory Orlov, a son, Count Alexei Grigorevich Bobrinsky, born on April 11, 1762 (d. 1813), without any of the usual fanfare. On June 28, Catherine seized power, aided by forty supporters, including Orlov and his four brothers, and became Catherine II, Empress of Russia. This pragmatic mixture of love and politics affected her relations with her son, Paul, and with Orlov, and would reach its apogee with Prince Potemkin. Catherine's personal relations had serious political consequences for her and others due to the concentration of power in individuals and the intimate, familial nature of rule in Russia at this time.[23]

In all her memoirs Catherine balances her relationships with her husband and with Elizabeth, for although her ultimate future depends on Peter, her immediate future is in Elizabeth's hands. This central double thread in the memoirs reflects a system of inheritance in which Elizabeth could choose and, equally important, dismiss her chosen successor. Having disinherited his eldest son, Alexei, on February 3, 1718, in a manifesto, on February 5, 1722, Peter the Great issued the Law of Succession to the Throne, in which he concluded: "We deem it good to issue this edict in order that it will always be subject to the will of the ruling monarch to appoint whom he wishes to the succession or to remove the one he has appointed in the case of unseemly behavior."[24] He nevertheless died in 1725 without naming a successor, and his second wife, born Martha Skavronska, a Livonian peasant, became Catherine I (1684–1727). Surely it was no more fantastic for a well-connected German Princess, not only married to Emperor Peter III but also related to him and Empress Elizabeth, to become Empress.

Much has been made of Catherine's ominous desire for the throne, which she does not hide in the memoirs. For example, on the eve of her wedding, filled with foreboding, Catherine consoles herself: "My heart did not foresee great happiness; ambition alone sustained me. At the bottom of my soul I had something, I know not what, that never for a single moment let me doubt that sooner or later I would succeed in becoming the sovereign Empress of Russia in my own right." Catherine's correspondence with Hanbury-Williams gives some idea of her machinations to promote her husband, her son, and by extension herself during an uncertain succession. This all seems quite damning evidence of excessive ambition, except that it was in fact possible, though unlikely, for Catherine to rule legitimately—if Elizabeth named her as heir. According to the early and middle memoirs, Catherine's mother urged Procurator General Prince Trubetskoi to ask the Empress whether her title should include Heiress to the Throne, and Elizabeth declined (50, 453). Yet the final memoir ends with a very important conversation between Catherine and Elizabeth that hints at the possibility that Elizabeth might disinherit Peter III, which reinforces Catherine's case for her legitimacy.

While Catherine's legitimacy was questioned in Russia, in the eyes of public opinion in Europe her coup and the consequent murder of her husband reflected badly on the stability of Russia and its government, which undermined her credibility.[25] Catherine's final memoir addresses her ability to create a stable government by stressing her good judgment, even temper, fairness, and ultimately, her genius for rule. Catherine's long rule broke a pattern. In eighteenth-century Russia, coups were the rule, not the exception. In the absence of male heirs of the right age, the practice of naming an heir appears to have led to a series of coups by unmarried female rulers and their favorites.[26] In 1727, Catherine I was succeeded by the last direct male heir of the Romanov line, Peter II (1715–30), Peter the Great's grandson by his son Alexei (1690–1718).[27] Before her death, Catherine I had signed a will naming first Peter II and then her daughters, Anna and Elizabeth, as heirs.[28] After the sudden death three years later of Peter II at age fifteen, Elizabeth was pushed aside for Anna Ivanovna (1693–1740), the widowed Duchess of Courland and daughter of Peter the Great's half brother and co-czar, Ivan V (1666–96). On her deathbed, Empress Anna designated her grandnephew, the infant Ivan VI (1740–64), as heir, and her German favorite, Ernst Johann Bühren (1690–1772), Duke of Courland, as regent.[29] Bühren lasted twenty-two days before being ousted by the infant's parents, Anna Leopoldovna of Mecklenburg and Prince Anton Ulrich of Brunswick-Bevern. In November 1741, Elizabeth seized power and imprisoned Ivan VI for life; unfortunately for Catherine, he was killed on her watch in 1764. Later, the

French *philosophe* Denis Diderot (1713–84) advised Catherine to reinstate primogeniture as a check on the ruler's power, which she of course could not do without making her own rule illegitimate.[30] But her son, Paul, in his rejection of all things Catherinian, had three sons, and upon his coronation, he immediately returned to a system of primogeniture and the ideal of a proper royal family. However, as Catherine feared, this did not prevent Paul, who behaved as a tyrant, from being overthrown and killed in a coup. Ironically too, if the memoirs are accurate and Catherine in fact knew, Paul was perhaps biologically a Saltykov, and so despite all the male heirs, the Romanov bloodline ended not with Nicholas II (1868–1918) but with Peter III and Ivan VI.

Because of the fundamental weakness of her position, Catherine's success depended on her political skills, her policies, and her personality. Her memoirs paint an unflattering picture of Elizabeth's personality and style of rule, and Catherine thus implies that she has done things differently.[31] For example, under Elizabeth, allies could become enemies overnight, and such elder statesmen as Bestuzhev-Riumin were humiliated, stripped of all privileges, condemned to death, and exiled. Elizabeth thus continued her predecessors' method of midnight arrests, torture, and imprisonment of her enemies, which one historian has termed "mini-coups."[32] In contrast, Catherine carefully promoted and rewarded opponents until they were no longer in a position to harm her. Like Elizabeth, Catherine depended for support on family clans, political factions, ministers, favorites, and the elite guards, who formed a complex network of alliances. Throughout her early reign, Catherine relied extensively on the clan of Grigory Orlov (her favorite from 1760 to 1772), who with the Chernyshev extended family and the elite guards supported her coup.[33] Her opponents, the faction around her son's governor, Count Nikita Panin (1718–83), favored making Paul the Emperor and Catherine his regent until his majority in 1772, and generally tried to limit Catherine's power. As 1772 approached and Panin agitated for transferring rule to Paul, Catherine's son became a double-edged sword in her career, important for her legitimacy on the one hand and a potential (though never actual) threat to her power as he grew older and became independent. Catherine quashed several conspiracies, and after she put down Pugachev's armed revolt in 1774, her hold on power became reasonably secure.

Catherine was above all a working ruler, unlike Elizabeth. In the memoirs, Catherine criticizes Elizabeth, who let her advisers and favorites write up papers based on what she said, and often did not follow through on matters. In contrast, Catherine did her own writing, had a good memory for details, delegated well, and expected things to get done. As Empress, Catherine wrote and read every day, adapting her ideas, which she acquired through reading classical, French, German, and English political philosophy, to what was possible in Russia. She inherited a country that Peter the Great had dramatically turned in the direction of modern European statehood at the beginning of the eighteenth century. Reforms, however, had remained incomplete. After Peter's death, in 1725, the six rulers who followed did not build significantly or systematically on his reforms. Intelligent, well-read, energetic, and ambitious, Catherine, like Peter, applied herself to all aspects of Russian politics, society, history, and culture, and had a profound and lasting impact on Russia and Europe.

Histories of her reign and biographies tend to mention Catherine's writing separately from her life and rule. Though as Grand Duchess she had written, and could write safely, relatively little, with her coup, Catherine unleashed a sudden deluge of what she called "scribbling."[34] From the very beginning of her reign, Catherine's writing was everywhere intertwined with her reading, her thinking, and her reign. Barely a month after the coup, having written manifestos proclaiming her rule, she sent one to the French *philosophe* and celebrity Voltaire (1694–1778) to initiate a literary, political, and philosophical correspondence of mutual flattery and usefulness that lasted until his death. Throughout her reign, she corresponded constantly with statesmen and women, the *philosophes,* her ministers, historians, and favorites. Aside from letters and state business, her daily writing included extensive notes on her reading and marginalia in her books. To the leading Enlightenment *salonnière* Madame Geoffrin (1699–1777), Catherine elaborates on her routine:

> I regularly get up at six A.M., I read and I write all alone until eight; then someone comes to read the news to me, those who have to speak to me come in one by one, one after the other, which can take until eleven or later, and then I dress. On Sundays and feast days I go to mass, on other days I go into my antechamber, where a crowd of people usually awaits me, and after a half- or three-quarter-hour conversation, I sit down to lunch ... and I bring my papers. Our reading, when it is not interrupted by packets of letters or other hin-

drances, lasts until half past five, when I either go to the theater, or play cards, or else chat with the early comers until dinner, which ends before eleven when I go to bed, to do the same thing tomorrow, and this is as fixed as the lines on a sheet of music.[35]

The emphasis on the regularity of her day, in contrast to her description in the memoirs of Empress Elizabeth's bohemian lifestyle, reflects Catherine's perception of regulated time as European and enlightened.[36] Like her favorites, writing and reading were a daily part of her life and rule.

To treat Catherine's writing as either a personal or a cultural or a literary or an intellectual exercise diminishes the breadth and context, not to mention the significance, of her work. As one Soviet literary historian starkly summarizes the paradox her writings present, "Her work rarely meets the standard even of the average literary output of the time.... But everybody was interested in everything the Empress wrote and published."[37] The didactic tone of her writings has aged poorly, but in her day, together with most writers in a variety of genres, Catherine actively published in what Cynthia Whittaker has termed the literature of justification and advice between the monarch and her elite.[38] Catherine never claimed to be a literary writer, a position that was socially beneath her. Although she wrote in many genres, her memoirs and letters, especially to Voltaire, are among Catherine's best writing, lively and polished. The integration of her writings with her life and rule ideally ought to address not only their literary quality and policy significance at the time but also their quantity, variety, and complex political, historical, and cultural functions, the sum of which she meant to transcend her era.[39] However, we still lack a comprehensive account, a complete collection, or even a complete bibliography of her writings.[40]

Catherine wrote on politics, Russian history, education, economics, and linguistics; she wrote thousands of letters, more than two dozen plays and operas, the first Russian children's literature, memoirs, and journalism. Fluent in Russian, French, and German, she published a good deal in Russia and abroad, in French and in translations, often "anonymously." In this way, Catherine promoted an enlightened Russia and its monarch together, and defended them against their many foreign critics, on a European historical, political, social, cultural, and intellectual stage.

In 1767, in a direct challenge to the largely negative opinions about

Russia in Europe, she opened her most influential work, the *Great Instruction*, to the Legislative Commission, with the pronouncement that "Russia is a European power." By this she meant that she was a monarch subject to natural laws, rather than an absolute, Asiatic despot, as Russia's critics maintained. For this compilation of her recommendations on the proper government of Russia, she borrowed extensively from her reading of the best and latest in European political thinking: *Spirit of the Laws* (1748) by Baron de Montesquieu (1689–1755), a comparison of relations between the state and the people in various nations, and *On Crimes and Punishments* (1764) by Cesare Beccaria (1735–93), a critique of penal systems. Like her predecessors, Catherine failed in the long overdue codification of Russia's laws, last done in 1649. But she published her ideas for all of Europe to read: in Russian and German parallel texts, and also in Russian, Latin, German, and French in one volume, and by 1780, in English, Dutch, Italian, Polish, and Greek translations. In her lifetime, the *Instruction* went through seven Russian editions and eight French editions, though it was banned in France.

The scholarship that exists on her writings places a premium on publication and readership that makes the memoirs, never published or read in her lifetime, marginal to her writing.[41] This is to misunderstand what writing meant to Catherine and her contemporaries in the eighteenth century. Catherine's writing was as much an activity as a concrete result, as much a verb as a noun. In a letter to her erstwhile correspondent Baron Friedrich Melchior Grimm (1723–1807), she evokes the ambience of the French Enlightenment salon: "I have told you a thousand times that I never write to you, I chat with you."[42] Catherine wrote in an era that valued informal, as well as formal, writing and also reading aloud as social activities among society's leading arbiters of literary taste.[43] Thus, the first and second parts of Catherine's middle memoir begin with dedications that evoke social conversation. In another example, like many such letters between luminaries then and now, her correspondence with Voltaire was meant to be read in private and aloud by others and only eventually published, which it was in 1785 in France, in 1797 in Russia, and thereafter in many editions and translations.[44] Letters were closely allied with conversation and thus resembled a performance.[45] Catherine continues to project a somewhat protean, ambiguous image because she wrote in an era that valued the nuances of addressing an audience appropriately, as in the art of conversation, a topic of her memoirs. Catherine's real success as a writer in French and in Russian to addressees ranging from Voltaire, whom she never met, to Potemkin, in all his different roles, to future unknown readers of her memoirs reflects her reputed talent for both judging and pleasing her audience.

In the eighteenth century, many things were written and read without being published, but this did not diminish their importance or influence.[46] On the contrary, the aristocratic elite could substantially aid the careers of professional writers, who were usually of a lower social class, by admitting them to salons where their works could circulate socially. In this intimate literary life, writers might publish anonymously, as Catherine did, or under pseudonyms, and still generally be known as the authors of their works. Writers also worked collaboratively, and salons could produce novels. In 1767, while traveling on the Volga, Catherine translated into Russian Chapter 9 ("On the Ruler") of Jean-François Marmontel's *Bélisaire* (1766), which was dedicated to her and banned in France. She wrote Marmontel a description of the translation process that underscores its informal, unprofessional, and social aspects: who translated which chapters, that Count Shuvalov arrived too late and therefore had to write the dedication, and that they decided to keep the unevenness of the translation to indicate the desire to translate *Bélisaire*, even in "those who had never in their life worked as professional translators."[47] Her *Great Instruction* (1767) and *Antidote* (1770) were collaborative, as were her operas and her historical and her linguistic projects, and many of her writings were meant to be both read and heard.[48]

Even without an audience in her lifetime for her memoirs, Catherine wrote them in French for a future readership that she imagined as part of the literary tradition in which she worked. Catherine followed a French tradition of worldly writing of prose and poetry, fiction and nonfiction, by women as well as men, for educated readers in society.[49] At the same time, she recognized the classical hierarchy, articulated in Nicolas Boileau-Depréaux's *The Art of Poetry* (1674), which ranked poetry as more serious than prose and praised the imitation of the classics and translations. For this reason, she tried hard, unsuccessfully, to learn to write poetry.[50] In the eighteenth century and earlier, literature was a more capacious concept than it is today; it embraced such nonfiction genres as speeches, sermons, and pamphlets. For example, Catherine's *Great Instruction*, a compilation of political theory by others that includes almost exact copies of 294 of Montesquieu's 526 articles in his *Spirit of the Laws*, was long considered her greatest literary achievement.[51] In a remarkably fluid and dynamic literary era, Catherine wrote constantly in many genres, and paradoxically claimed not to take her writing seriously, even though she greatly valued her time. In a letter in 1789 that serves as one of her several verbal self-portraits, she manages both to emphasize and dismiss her writings: "As for my writings, I consider them trifles, I enjoyed attempting different genres, it seems to me that all I have done is rather mediocre, moreover I have never attached any importance to them, except as amusement."[52] In the social context of worldly writing for which she wrote, it would have been unseemly to appear to take herself seriously. Thus the memoirs entertain as they instruct, and hide the fact that Catherine planned, researched, wrote, revised, rewrote, and edited them.

In Russia, the private circulation of memoir manuscripts, practiced until quite recently, assured the influence of these works among the political, social, and literary elite without publication.[53] In fact, the impossibility of publishing these memoirs, combined with the identity of their author, made them even more important. Upon Catherine's death in 1796, the last memoir was found in an envelope addressed in Russian: "To his Imperial Highness, Tsesarevich and Grand Duke Paul Petrovich, to my beloved son." Although the other memoirs were found in her bureau, Emperor Paul I showed the memoir addressed to him to only one other person, his friend Vice Chancellor Prince Alexander Kurakin (1752–1818), who made himself a copy. In 1818, Alexander Turgenev (1785–1845) made a second copy from Kurakin's, from which all subsequent copies were made. In 1824, at least two more copies were made, and Kurakin's brother gave his copy to Paul I's widow, Empress Maria Fedorovna (1759–1828). With Alexander I's death, in 1825, a small group of the elite attempted a coup, the Decembrist Rebellion, and upon his succession, Nicholas I instituted a repressive era lasting thirty years. He read and resealed the memoirs, and had all copies confiscated. Yet somehow Alexander Pushkin (1799–1837) himself managed to make a copy (in 1831–32), which Nicholas sealed upon the poet's death.[54] With his ascension in 1855, Alexander II read the memoirs, and again a couple of copies began to circulate. Their publication in London in 1859 was a major political coup for the radical writer and publisher Alexander Herzen, himself the author of the great nineteenth-century Russian memoir *My Past and Thoughts* (1852–68). For nearly fifty years, Russian scholars on Catherine quoted the memoirs from Herzen's edition as extensively as censors allowed, that Russians might at least taste some of this forbidden fruit, until after the 1905 revolution, when censorship was eased and all her memoirs were published. Yet Catherine had a larger audience in mind than just her elite Russian circle that read French, for in the final memoir, she writes Russian phrases and then translates them into French, one indication that she imagined her future audience as foreign.

Catherine had at her disposal an unusual array of genres, means, and opportunities to manage her reputation, from emissaries to salons to letters to publication, informal and formal, unsigned and signed, abroad and at home, in Russian, French, and German. But as with her memoirs, she also looked beyond her place and time. Central to her writing practice was an understanding of herself as making history, which made everything she did significant. Yet her daily schedule, conversations, and collective authorship could be appreciated by future historians only if written down. Publication was less important because historians would eventually find her manuscripts. Catherine's desire to leave a carefully designed personal record explains her great concern both with burning letters and papers and with preserving them.

Catherine was a prodigious writer in life, but in the middle and especially the final memoirs, she develops her reputation as a serious reader. The path her early reading took had important implications for the later variety, subjects, and genres of her writings. These memoirs contain several portentous scenes in her youth that predict Catherine's destiny, which is a standard feature of professional memoirs.[55] In her final memoir, Catherine constructs a striking and partially apocryphal prophetic moment when at the age of fifteen, in 1745, in St. Petersburg, for the first time everything—writing, reading, thinking, and ruling—comes together for her. Thus the Swedish Count Gyllenborg had recognized her talent and "very philosophical turn of mind," and recommended that she read the classics—Plutarch's *Lives,* Montesquieu, and especially Cicero—to steer her mind through the temptations and vicissitudes of court life. Catherine reassured him by ordering the books and writing a character sketch to demonstrate her self-knowledge, "Portrait of the Philosopher at Age Fifteen." A letter to her mother in 1750 reveals that Catherine took being a philosopher to heart and that to her it meant using her mind and being something of a stoic: "I am as philosophical as possible, no passion makes me act."[56] In 1766, now a philosopher-queen, she wrote to Gyllenborg that "the desire to accomplish 'great deeds' " had resulted from their conversations.[57] However, in the middle memoir, Catherine writes that she has difficulty getting the books and that they bore her, until two years later she finds and reads Plutarch. In her early memoir, from 1756, she never mentions any reading; instead she traces all the difficulties of her life at court, leading to an aborted suicide attempt. Perhaps, in the two memoirs that Catherine wrote after she was in power, it became important for her both to be, and to be seen to be, well-read, which added depth to her Enlightenment credentials.

The final memoir therefore carefully describes the path her reading took, from literature to political philosophy and history, as she educated herself. Once married, she reads novels for a year, beginning with the chivalric romance *Tiran the Fair.* She then happens on the letters of Madame de Sévigné (1626–96) to her daughter, considered the epitome of the epistolary art, before discovering Voltaire by the end of 1746. After 1749, when the kindly, learned Ivan Shuvalov (1727–97) became Elizabeth's favorite, Catherine had use of his excellent library.[58] She polished off the ten-volume *History of Germany* by Father Barre in two months and embarked on Plato. In 1753, she read the four-volume *Historical and Critical Dictionary* by Pierre Bayle, the most popular work among educated readers in the eighteenth century. It was central to the *philosophes'* (and Catherine's) practice of writing often, about diverse and current subjects, for the general reader, and "for a literary culture focused not on the production of 'great works' but on rapid exchange, on provocation and response."[59] With her foray into English-style satirical journalism in 1769, she encouraged this kind of give-and-take with journalist and publisher Nikolai Novikov.[60] In 1770, in *Antidote,* she aggressively sparred with Chappe d'Auteroche's negative portrait of Russia and Russians in his *Voyage in Siberia* (1768). Her plays, too, provided a means for portraying Russians as average, decent people. In their correspondence with one another, Catherine and the *philosophes* share their writings on current events, and she addresses the burning questions of the day. Given this shared Enlightenment practice of lively, frequent writing, it is less surprising that Catherine wrote several memoirs and many autobiographical jottings and letters than that she revised, rewrote, and edited them.

According to the final memoir, the next formative period of Catherine's education came in 1754, when she read her way out of postpartum depression after the birth of Paul, and acquired the historical and political cast of mind appropriate for an enlightened ruler. She read Voltaire's *Essay on Universal History*, Montesquieu's *Spirit of the Laws*, Tacitus's Roman history, Baronio's *Ecclesiastical History*, and more, in French and especially in Russian. She matured intellectually: "I began to see more things with a black outlook and to seek the causes that really underlay and truly shaped the different interests in the affairs that I observed." This reading proved formative for her *Great Instruction*. At the end of the memoir, in 1759, she is reading the first volumes of *A General History of Voyages* and the *Encyclopedia* (1751–72) by Diderot and Jean Le Rond d'Alembert (1717–83). Nine days after her coup, on July 6, 1762, she extended to Diderot an offer to publish the *Encyclopedia* in Russia at her expense, a grand gesture in a bid to gain friends by offending France, which had stopped its publication twice. Though he refused, Catherine's magnanimous gestures impressed the *philosophes* and established her reputation with them. In 1765 she purchased Diderot's library, and in 1778 that of Voltaire. Through intermediaries, in 1762 she invited d'Alembert to tutor her son, and in 1767, her lover, Orlov, invited Jean-Jacques Rousseau (1712–78) to live on his estate, most likely with Catherine's permission. The speed, consistency, and vision with which Catherine moved to claim her intellectual spoils once on the throne are stunning.

The "invisible hand" that guided Catherine in her letter to Hanbury-Williams in 1756 was history, or history as she had read it, especially as the *philosophes* understood and wrote the history of rulers. These rulers, and the histories of them, served Catherine as models for thinking about her own life and her memoirs as history. In 1762, in her first letter to d'Alembert, Catherine acknowledges his refusal to be her son's tutor and compares herself to Queen Christina of Sweden (1626–89, reigned 1632–54).[61] Catherine had read and annotated d'Alembert's *Mémoires et réflexions sur Christine, reine de Suède* (1753), which presents a model life for a woman ruler that attracted and challenged Catherine. One of the most noted learned women of Europe, Christina corresponded with the philosopher René Descartes (1596–1650) and invited him to Sweden. Doubtless, Count Gyllenborg had Christina in mind as he advised Catherine on her education. D'Alembert argues that despite Christina's abdication in 1654, her life is worthy, "not in her reckless love of glory and conquests, but in the grandeur of her soul, in her talent for rule, in the knowledge of men, in the expansiveness of her views, and in her enlightened taste for the sciences and arts."[62] Like d'Alembert, Voltaire emphasizes the individual and culture in his histories of great rulers—Henry IV (1553–1610), Louis XIV (1638–1715), Charles XII (1682–1718) of Sweden, and Peter the Great—and their contributions to the overall progress of mankind. Under Louis XIV, Voltaire connects the flowering of the arts and humanities with his rule and with the prominence of educated women in French society.

While Catherine purposefully and selectively published many of her writings during her lifetime, the continuous stream of the whole of her writing, including her unpublished memoirs, served the still larger purpose of the future professional history of her reign. When Catherine thanks Voltaire for *The History of the Russian Empire Under Peter the Great*, commissioned by Shuvalov in 1757, she discusses the business of writing history.[63] She writes that had she been Empress when he was writing, she would have given him "many other memoirs," and that she is collecting Peter's papers and letters, "in which he paints a picture of himself," for publication.[64] Catherine proposed materials to Voltaire for him to write *Le Siècle de Catherine II*.[65] Catherine's handwriting, in documents described as in "her own hand" and "written by herself," does more than ascertain authorship; it is fundamental to her overall historical project. Like Peter's letters, about which Catherine uses Horace's metaphor from the *Ars Poetica* for writing as painting, these writings would create her self-portrait as an individual and a ruler. From the very beginning of her reign, Catherine actively supported the collection and publication of Russian historical documents, and similarly thought about the future of her own papers.

Central to the mutual interests of Catherine and the *philosophes* were the mind and character of Catherine, precisely the declared subject of her final memoir in its opening maxim. This memoir in particular is therefore an Enlightenment document that reflects Catherine's nature as a ruler through her evaluations of Peter III and Elizabeth, and through her own actions as Grand Duchess. In his history of Peter the Great, Voltaire saw evidence for the tremendous difference one ruler could make in a nation as a lesson in reform for Europe. Despite disagreements among the *philosophes* about the dangers of a strong monarch, which was a necessary evil in their programs for reform, Catherine captured their imagination as a "great man" of her age, who might in their lifetime inscribe an enlightened government on the tabula rasa of the Russian state.[66] She read their works, and could bring to life their ideas—for rational, secular government and for natural laws, inalienable rights, and a social contract. She promoted Russia and herself shamelessly, but only Diderot accepted her invitation to visit Russia in 1773–74, and he left disillusioned, as Catherine later read in his posthumous memoirs.[67] Her famous response to his theories was that rulers must "work on human skin."[68] More successful was her extensive correspondence with Diderot's friend Grimm, who was in St. Petersburg in 1773; after many conversations, they began a relatively informal, wide-ranging exchange that lasted until her death. Her letters contain her responses to his biweekly newsletter, *Literary Correspondence* (1753–90), with new works and French news that was sent to fifteen royal subscribers, who like Catherine (who subscribed in 1764) were heads of state and nobles in central and eastern Europe. The French Revolution brought an end to Grimm's newsletter and to Catherine's support for the *philosophes*, whose radical ideas she held responsible for attacks on monarchy, and she banned their books. She of course disappointed them by not living up to their ideals. Yet, just as she balanced their theories with the exigencies of rule, the *philosophes* also made compromises to have the ear and generous support of one of Europe's most powerful rulers.

In practice, during her thirty-four-year reign, Catherine maintained absolute rule as she consolidated control over Russia's administration and vast lands by organizing them in a consistent manner. Although the memoirs take place before her reign, Catherine nevertheless carefully projects the ability and reasonable behavior necessary for an enlightened, absolute Russian ruler. She institutionalized Peter the Great's reforms, thus building a solid foundation for the Russia of the next two centuries. She continued his, Elizabeth's, and Peter III's secularization of Russia by subordinating the Orthodox Church's land and serfs to the state, in a decree she first published abroad in French (1764). Like her predecessors, Catherine attempted long-overdue legal reforms, including the codification of existing laws and the establishment of legal training, through the elected Legislative Commission (1767–68), a consultative process that allowed her to consolidate her position but also cost Catherine her ambition to undo serfdom.

Relations with her advisers and the nobility were central to her hold on power, and Peter III and the coup had raised their expectations. Catherine's reign has been referred to as "the golden age of the Russian nobility," and her memoirs indicate her willingness to please those upon whom she depended.[69] In particular, Peter III had freed the nobility from compulsory service to the state (1762), which Catherine agreed to only when she reorganized the nobility into a more independent, privileged body (1785). At the same time, Catherine used the nobility to institute a system of local administrative control over extensive, sparsely populated territory (1775). This problem became especially urgent after the plague in Moscow (1770–72) that killed 120,000, and which together with Pugachev's armed uprisings (1773–74) in the southern borderlands reaching up to Kazan challenged her authority. In this period she wrote her second memoir, of which parts 1 and 2 begin with cheerful dedications to friends. With much the same deceptively light tone, she wrote many letters to Voltaire concerning these problems, and in 1772 she wrote her first plays, five social comedies, beginning with *O These Times!*, where only the title hints at the situation in Moscow, where the play is set.

To implement her administrative reforms of the 1770s and 1780s and create more qualified civil servants and useful citizens, Catherine, with Ivan Betskoi (1704–95), promoted universal general education. They published the *General Plan for the Education of Young People of Both Sexes* (1764) abroad in French with Diderot's help, and the *Statute of National Schools* (1786). Her own pedagogical writings for young people included a Russian primer for reading, which was a bestseller and the first Russian work translated into English (1781); the first Russian children's literature, written for her grandsons, translated into German, French, and English (1781, 1783), one tale of which she then made into an opera (*Fevei*, 1786); a collection of Russian proverbs (many of which she composed) for children (1783); her *Notes Concerning Russian History* (1783–84); and her *Instruction* to Prince Saltykov on educating her grandsons (1784).[70]

Catherine inherited a country exhausted by the Seven Years' War against Prussia (1756–63), which forms the background to the conclusion of her final memoir. She took control of foreign policy from the outset of her reign, dispensing with a chancellor for foreign affairs, and built on Peter the Great's military legacy. She centralized the financial administration, which allowed for budgetary planning and a national debt to pay for the costs of wars. In pursuit of a Prussophile foreign policy, Peter III had ended the war by ceding Russia's gains back to Prussia, which Catherine used against him to justify her coup; nevertheless, she then maintained the alliance. Russia won new territories in two wars with Turkey (1768–74 and 1787–91), which, after her victory over Prussia in the Seven Years' War, cemented her reputation in Europe as a major power. Russia had long guarded itself in the north through alliances first with Austria (1746), then briefly with France while fighting Prussia (1756), and then with Prussia (1764), in the so-called Northern Alliance. But southern acquisitions played into Catherine's wish to regain Constantinople from Islam for Eastern Christianity, and she turned again secretly to Austria (1781).

The last expansion of Russia on this scope had happened in the sixteenth century, under the first Czar, Ivan IV, "the Terrible" (1530–84). Catherine expanded the Russian Empire to the south, adding Walachia and Moldavia (1770–74), and the Crimea (1783) and other lands north of the Black Sea, where she continued Peter the Great's priority of building a naval fleet. As part of the spoils of war, Catherine shared out Poland in three successive partitions (1772, 1793, 1795), and the rest of Ukraine, White Russia, and Lithuania. Catherine handed out conquered lands with serfs as rewards and she encouraged immigration because she believed that agriculture and an adequate farming population formed the basis of a successful economy. When she died, in 1796, her armies were poised to take over Georgia and Armenia, and she had ordered up 60,000 troops to join with Britain in an attack on France. Though Catherine was called "Great" during her reign in recognition of the above achievements, she always refused honorific titles in her lifetime.[71]

CATHERINE'S CULTURAL OFFENSIVE

It is hard to overestimate Catherine's attention and sensitivity to what was written abroad about Russia and herself, and her ceaseless work to influence foreign opinion through her writings and emissaries. Her middle and final memoirs certainly belong in this context, a genre of foreign writings that Russian scholars term "Russica," which partly explains her decision to write them in French.[72] Russia's enemies throughout the eighteenth century were Sweden, Turkey, and, behind the scenes, France. Catherine fought France in part through words—via her representatives, articles in the press, political and historical books, and her correspondence, especially with Voltaire.[73] As with everything Catherine wrote, the fact that she was a writer demonstrated her explicit argument that Russia and Russians were civilized and that she was an enlightened ruler.

Catherine persistently engaged her French critics from the very beginning of her reign. In her first letter to Voltaire, in 1763, Catherine wrote: "I will respond to the prophecy of Jean-Jacques Rousseau by giving him a most rude refutation, I hope, for as long as I live."[74] In *The Social Contract* (1762), Rousseau disagreed with Voltaire's hopeful assessment of Russia's future in the first volume of *The History of the Russian Empire Under Peter the Great* (1759). Rousseau saw no chance for progress in Russia because Peter the Great had crushed the desire for liberty, which had to develop naturally in the people. Yet even Voltaire thought that before Peter the Great, Russia had been a barbaric country. Encouraged directly by Shuvalov and indirectly by Catherine, Voltaire softened his negative assessments of Russia. Catherine's correspondence with Voltaire, which, after proceeding at the rate of a handful of letters each year, increased to about forty letters each in 1770 and 1771 during the war with Turkey, as she spread her version of the war. Her letters to Mme. Geoffrin promoted Russia too, as for example when she writes: "For the past two months I have been busy working three hours every morning on the laws of this empire. It is an immense undertaking. But people in your country have many incorrect ideas about Russia."[75] Throughout her reign, Catherine's *Great Instruction* served as her most important credential in Europe that she was indeed an enlightened ruler. Indeed, the existence of her *Great Instruction* and the Legislative Commission confirmed that laws governed her reign.

In Russia, Catherine banned accounts of her coup, and in France, she suppressed publication by Claude Carloman de Rulhière (1734–91), the former secretary at the French embassy, of his *History or Anecdotes on the Revolution in Russia in the Year 1762.*[76] Rulhière's portraits of Peter and Catherine, though sympathetic, had nuances that Catherine would vigorously dispute indirectly through her middle and final memoirs. Rulhière's *History* was well-known because of readings in the salons of Mme. Geoffrin and the Duc de Choiseul, the French foreign minister (served 1758–70), Catherine's outspoken opponent. To stop the readings, she turned to Voltaire, Diderot, and Mme. Geoffrin. Written in 1768, the work fed general European skepticism about Catherine's chances of staying on the throne, given the series of coups in Russia.

Catherine responded most energetically to Chappe d'Auteroche's *Voyage in Siberia*, about his voyage to Russia and Siberia in 1761–62 at the behest of the French Academy, which he published at the urging of Choiseul. Despite his positive references to Catherine's reforms, Chappe d'Auteroche, like Montesquieu, Rousseau, Voltaire, and Rulhière before

him, insisted on the barbaric nature of the Russian people. His account of
Catherine's coup, which could only be secondhand, as he left St. Petersburg in May 1762, coincided with Rulhière's *History* and thus angered
Catherine.[77] Catherine's *Antidote* makes more than a dozen references to
herself and her *Instruction,* and a rebuttal to Rulhière's assertion that she
did nothing as Grand Duchess finds its way into Catherine's final memoir.
The promised third volume of *Antidote* never appeared. Instead, in 1771
she began to write her middle memoir, as another kind of defense of herself and Russia against Rulhière as well as Chappe d'Auteroche. Her
autobiographical mode of writing continued in her lifelong literary, political correspondence (1774–96) with Grimm; the letters contain numerous autobiographical passages that echo her middle and final memoirs.
Other later French works that aroused Catherine's ire included *History of
the Two Indies* (1781) by Abbé Raynal (1713–96), an indictment of slavery
and despotism that influenced *A Journey from St. Petersburg to Moscow* (1790)
by Alexander Radishchev (1749–1802), for which the author was exiled.[78]
Catherine's constant vigilance against French historiography of Russia
shaped the polemical subtext of many of her writing projects, including
the memoirs.

At the same time, these foreigners' criticisms spurred Catherine on
with an enormous cultural and scientific agenda. With her eye on Voltaire,
France, and Europe, Catherine laid the institutional foundation for Russia's extraordinary cultural leap forward in the nineteenth century in literature, art, architecture, music, and theater. The memoirs often mention
the cultural amusements at Elizabeth's court, but Catherine aimed much
higher, and beginning with her coronation ceremonies, she immediately
established and publicized a brilliant court life as the center for Russian
culture.[79] While she rejected Chappe d'Auteroche's opinion that the lev-
els of Russian science, scholarship, and letters were low, in 1768 she ordered the Academy of Sciences to make expeditions, reports, illustrations,
and maps in a survey of Russia.[80] Surveys brought back accounts of different languages, and in the 1780s, when the British discovery of Sanskrit
made comparative linguistics fashionable, Catherine established a research project to assemble a comparative dictionary of all the languages,
not only in the Russian empire but worldwide, which she published.[81]

At home, historical debates coalesced against German historiography
of Russia. In response, Catherine first supported, and later wrote, Russian

history herself. While Catherine's historical writing has been uniformly dismissed as naïve plagiarism, her activity as a historian promoted the development of Russian historiography, in its infancy in the eighteenth century, and shaped the writing of her final memoir as a historical document. As *Antidote* makes clear, most eighteenth-century foreigners had little direct knowledge of Russia and relied on the accounts of travelers who spoke no Russian. Yet Russia had few scholars, and most of these were German. Their so-called Norman theory about the foreign origin of the Russian state provoked a nationalist backlash against the Germans and galvanized Russians to take up their history, which Catherine fully supported.[82] Under Catherine, publications included Peter the Great's correspondence, the chronicles of Russia's early history (1767–92), the first modern historical narrative of Russian history by a Russian, *Russian History from the Earliest Times* (1768) by Vasily Tatishchev (1686–1750), and more than eighty historical works that created the first public forum for Russian historiography. She bought historians' collections of books and documents; she ordered the systematic, statistical description of the Russian empire; and she had documents collected for an account of Russia's diplomatic history.[83]

Catherine was of course personally interested in Russian history, and her transition to writing history in the 1780s and subsequent return to her memoirs reflect that concern. In a letter to Grimm in 1778, she had written, "Who is this best poet or best historian of my empire? It is certainly not me, as I have never written either verse or history."[84] But as if to rectify this omission in her writing, in 1779 she created a commission to gather documents and prepare notes for her own use.[85] Catherine got no further than the fourteenth century; in letters to Grimm in 1794, for example, she mentions that "I've reached the year 1368 or 1369" and complains that Ivan Elagin's (1725–93) historical essay ends with 1389.[86] She wrote *Notes Concerning Russian History* (1783–84), based on Tatishchev's history, for her grandsons and the general reader, and rebutted Russia's critics: "These notes concerning Russian history were composed for youth at a time when books on so-called Russian history are being published in foreign languages, which should rather be called prejudiced works."[87] In the 1790s, Catherine continued to work on, along with her memoirs, her history, while overseeing its translation into German. In 1794, when she began the final memoir, she wrote to Grimm that "the passion for history has carried away my pen."[88] Thus this final memoir became much more a historical document than her previous memoirs.

CATHERINE'S HISTORICAL LEGACY

After Catherine's death in 1796, historians were not as fortunate as Voltaire had predicted they would be with Catherine's legacy because of political circumstances and the still underdeveloped nature of Russian historiography.[89] Under the repressive rule of her son, Paul I (reigned 1796–1801), and her grandsons Alexander I (reigned 1801–25) and Nicholas I (reigned 1825–55), historians did not have access to her papers.[90] Unable to write recent history, Russia's budding historians continued to work on history before 1700. Nikolai Karamzin (1766–1826), Russia's first imperial historiographer, left off at the year 1611 in his twelve-volume *History of the Russian State* (1818–29), recently reissued and still a bestseller.[91] In contrast, under Catherine, there had been a boom in Russian and translated biographies of Peter the Great, with twenty-four in all and eight in 1788 alone.[92] It was not until the second half of the nineteenth century, after the death in 1855 of the reactionary Nicholas I, that a handful of historians had the material, training, and skill to write full histories of Russia that reached Catherine's reign.[93] However, no full history of Catherine and her reign has ever been published in Russia. In the one major attempt, Vasily Bilbasov (1838–1904), due to problems with the censors, published only the first two volumes (covering 1729–64) of *History of Catherine II*, and volume 12 (on publications abroad about her) (1890–96).[94]

The void of information on her reign left by serious history was filled by European popular biographies that include such lurid titles as *The Secret History of the Loves and Principal Lovers of Catherine II, Empress of Russia* (1799), *The Romance of an Empress* (1892), *The Favorites of Catherine the Great* (1947), and *The Passions and Lechery of Catherine the Great* (1971). The most salacious representations of Catherine are primarily French and British. In France, the tradition of Salic law prohibited women rulers; moreover, the backlash against the beheading of Marie Antoinette in 1793 affected Catherine's European reception as a woman on the throne. Catherine's first two scholarly biographers set the tone and provided the material for later works. In his very negative *The Life of Catherine II, Empress of Russia* (1797), the French journalist Jean-Henri Castéra was most influenced by the recent publication of Rulhière's long-suppressed account of her 1762 coup and interviews with those who had been at Catherine's court. He portrays all of her actions as undertaken for the sake of trysts with her lovers rather than for politics and survival. His English translator, Tooke, doubled the size of the book by adding much scholarly material from German and Russian histories that substantially corrected Castéra's bias against both Russia and England; Castéra then retranslated it back into French with his own improvements. The biography was banned in Russia, but Russian translations circulated in manuscript.[95] Along with many false details, Tooke also describes secret, true events, such as Catherine's plans with Hanbury-Williams and Count Bestuzhev-Riumin, her decisive meeting with Empress Elizabeth after Bestuzhev's arrest, and Paul's uncertain parentage, that her unpublished letters and memoirs (to which he did not have access) corroborate.[96] In Russia, Catherine's posthumous supporters and detractors published biographies, memoirs about her reign, and some of her letters, that together with the circulation of manuscript copies of her final memoir ensured that the "whispering culture" of court life contributed to the consolidation of her reputation in the nineteenth century.[97]

However, already in 1859, when the publication of her papers could finally begin in earnest under Alexander II (reigned 1855–81), Herzen made clear in his introduction to her memoirs that the interest in Catherine would become irrelevant before the tide of history. "In perusing these memoirs, the reader is astonished to find one thing constantly lost sight of, even to the extent of not appearing anywhere—it is *Russia and the People*." Considered by some an enlightened despot in her time, Catherine was now condemned as a thorough hypocrite who cynically claimed to rule in the best interest of her people while actually expanding the institution of serfdom. The emancipation of the serfs in 1861 and Alexander II's reforms began a cycle of disappointed expectations for progressive political change, and an increasingly radicalized Russian intellectual life fomented the Bolshevik Revolution in 1917, when sixty years of Russian scholarship about Catherine effectively ended. Soviet Marxist historians rejected not only biographies but also the study of individual rulers, the nobility, and the eighteenth century, and instead studied class conflict.

Recent scholarship on Catherine and her reign has created fertile ground for a reassessment of Catherine's memoirs as more than the tale of a colorful life at court or an unwitting condemnation of the Russian autocracy. In the West, the publication of ten editions of two translations of the memoirs in English in the 1950s presaged the renewed scholarly interest in Catherine in the 1960s, as Western scholars gained access to Soviet libraries and archives for the first time. Isabel de Madariaga's *Russia in the Age of Catherine the Great* (1981) is an unsurpassed foundational study, the first in nearly one hundred years; her *Catherine the Great: A Short History* (1990) is for a general audience. In Russia, only with the fall of communism in the late 1980s did serious work on Catherine and her reign recommence, beginning with the publication of her memoirs in 1989 (last published in 1907), followed by four separate editions in 1990 alone. Drawing on her unpublished archival papers, scholars have written on modernity in the eighteenth century, Catherine's diplomacy in the Polish partitions, and her correspondence with Potemkin.[98] The international boom in studies of Catherine celebrated the 200th anniversary of her death in 1996 with conferences, essay collections, and performances.[99] Another handful of English translations of her writings, as well as studies of her court, the memoirs, her image and the arts, and an intellectual biography, are in progress. Several scholarly biographies that successfully integrate politics with her life have freed the memoirs from their role in novelized histories.[100] This translation and preface foreground her writing in her life and reign and balance literary and historical approaches to the memoirs. At the very least, these projects have cleared the way to write about the real issues of Catherine's reign, without reiterating the cynical eighteenth- and nineteenth-century ad feminam canards that disputed her command of French, authorship of her writings (especially the letters to Voltaire), her control over her favorites, her political acumen, and the importance of her intellectual life to her policies.

However, the perception of Catherine is not only an issue for scholars, but formed a central organizing focus for Catherine throughout her reign, especially in her writing. Ultimately, the memoirs raise questions about Catherine as a woman, as Empress, and as a writer, and about the problem of her image, which she projected and attempted to control in all the media of her day, from publications, coins, paintings, and her collections, to palaces, gardens, and spectacles. Recent feminist biographical studies of Marie Antoinette and women in nineteenth-century France eschew the story line of traditional biography, organized around defining personal characteristics, in favor of an approach that foregrounds the representations of women, their bodies, and femininity.[101] Catherine's life seems ideal for such an antinarrative—a rich, active, provocative life that refuses to cohere into a single story.[102] In fact, Catherine herself seems to have preempted her biographers by having written several different memoirs over fifty years that reflect her continuous attempts to explain the first half of her life. Just as there is no single memoir, there is no *one* Catherine. The memoirs represent different Catherines years apart. Larger than life, she made her mark in so many areas that any synthesis of Catherine as a woman, as Empress, and as a writer remains incomplete, in part because Catherine herself is elusive, despite, or perhaps because of, all she wrote—especially her memoirs. The urge to find the unguarded Catherine in her memoirs persists, not only because it makes her a more attractive person and less a cunning politician, but also because her pleasant, direct tone invites us to see her as honest and sincere.

THE VARIOUS MEMOIRS

As the first biographies of Catherine demonstrate, much in the memoirs was not news, and Catherine surely knew this. *How* she wrote turns out to be as important as *what* she wrote. Although she wrote some autobiographical notes in Russian, Catherine's decision to write her three main memoirs in French reflects practical and philosophical concerns. She wrote an early character sketch for a Swede and the first memoir for an Englishman; French was their common language. Later, as Empress, she constantly fought against her image in contemporary French historiography and hoped to influence future histories about her reign. French was the European and Enlightenment lingua franca, and the language of the major memoirs and biographies she read. She used French as a European polyglot.[103] Fluent in French, Russian, and German, mixing them for added effect, she adapted herself in language, style, and substance to her audience.

Aside from the significance of her choice of French, the literary aspects of the memoirs include their organization, especially at the beginning and end, unifying ideas and themes, and her use of autobiographical genres and of language. Each memoir presents a different kind of verbal portrait of Catherine. Over the course of fifty years of writing, she learned to write memoirs, transforming a static character sketch into a chronology of events with short stories and digressions set within an overall long narrative arc. Moreover, through the process of writing, her notions of her self and the memoirs in relation to history continued to evolve. The memoirs thus reflect a highly developed autobiographical consciousness.

She began writing about herself for others as an exercise in self-knowledge. The lifelong importance she attached to knowing oneself comes through in her self-portraits and criticisms of Peter III in the three main memoirs. Her first account of herself was her 1745 "Portrait of a Philosopher" written for Count Gyllenborg. In the middle memoir, she titles it "Rough Sketch of the Philosopher's Character at Age Fifteen," and explains:

> I found this document in 1757 and I confess that I was surprised that at the age of fifteen I already had such a deep understanding of the many facets of my soul, and I saw that this piece was profoundly reflective and that in 1757 I could not find a word to add to it, nor in thirteen years had I made any discovery about myself that I had not already known at age fifteen. [61]

This description is similar to her self-portrait in an undated one-page fragment that still exists. It begins with her birth, parents, governess, and education, and breaks off with the following sentences: "I was instructed in the Lutheran religion, I was horribly curious, quite stubborn, and most ingratiating, I had a good heart, I was very sensitive, I cried easily, I was extremely fickle. I never liked dolls, but quite liked any kind of exercise, there was no boy more daring than I, I was proud to be that and often I hid my fear, shame produced this impulse, I was quite secretive" (473).

In her later memoirs, Catherine incorporates such portraits of herself and others into her narrative. She draws out the central characteristics that motivate an individual's actions, what in the eighteenth century were called the springs of behavior, or one's character. Catherine here subscribes to the universalizing ideals of the Enlightenment, with its key words of "qualities," "character," and "mind" (*esprit*). Given her idea of human nature as unchanging, at age twenty-eight Catherine can claim to have understood herself fully at age fifteen. This is an Aristotelian notion of the individual who does not change with time and experience, but only reveals herself to be more thoroughly what she has always been. Education could significantly shape, but not change, someone's nature. This view of human psychology differs significantly from post-Freudian notions, which posit fundamental, erupting, conflicting forces that can be traced back to childhood and continually evolve. In Catherine's model, a child is in essence already a small adult. Thus in part, Catherine could start over each time she wrote a new memoir because as she understood herself, each memoir was the same portrait, only more so, no matter which particular incidents she chose to recount.

Catherine's first sustained autobiographical narrative, like her subsequent memoirs, is a political or court memoir. She includes information about Russia that a foreigner might not know, and thus most likely she wrote it for Hanbury-Williams, who arrived at court in June 1755 and left in June 1757; their letters indicate that she trusted him with personal information. Court memoirs revolve around access to the ruler. At the end of this memoir, she explains to Hanbury-Williams: "You will perhaps find it necessary to criticize me, since seeing myself so badly treated, I never spoke with the Empress personally to justify myself against the thousand calumnies, lies, etc. etc. Know then that a thousand thousand times, I have asked to speak with her alone but she has never wanted to consent to it" (467). All the memoirs recount whatever Catherine or Elizabeth say to each other, their meals together, gestures toward each other, presents (including their value) to each other, who notices their contact, and the greatest honor, time alone with Elizabeth.[104] Illnesses provide opportunities to show one's affection and esteem. They exchange compliments—Catherine praising Elizabeth's impressive appearance, Elizabeth commending Catherine's religious observance and her Russian. Access was also reflected in physical proximity to the ruler, hence the importance of the relative location of Peter's, Catherine's, and her mother's apartments in Elizabeth's palaces. For example, Catherine is never closer to Elizabeth's rooms than when she gives birth, a reflection of the importance of the event, though as Catherine learns, much to her chagrin, not of her own importance. Catherine's eye for detail not only makes for vivid storytelling, but these details are the heart and soul of court memoirs, representing the language of favor and disfavor at court. Once the reader appreciates the importance of these details, the memoirs become a gripping, timeless tale of the endless rise and fall of political fortunes.

Written before Catherine's coup, this first memoir, unlike the later ones, cannot be an attempt to justify herself on this question. Still, Catherine here deals with her Achilles' heel before the coup. In their first conversation alone, the Empress verbally, and nearly physically, assaults

Catherine for failing to produce an heir, which Elizabeth imagines as a plot against her at the behest of Catherine's mother and Frederick the Great. Frustrated in her attempts to defend herself against endless intrigues, in her hasty conclusion Catherine provides the greatest possible self-justification for her existence. The narrative arc of this memoir concludes with the birth of her son, Paul, who finally provides Catherine with the security she desperately needs, and Elizabeth with an heir. Thus Catherine concludes: "It is true that since November 1754, I have changed my attitude. It has become more regal. They have grown more considerate of me and I have more peace than formerly" (468). Catherine's greatly improved position increases her hopes for her political survival, with or without Peter, after Elizabeth's death.

Although Catherine wrote her three main memoirs years apart and to make different points, scholars have tended to interpret all her memoirs through the lens of the final memoir as a justification for her coup. Thus the memoirs continue to support historians' suspicions that Catherine is pulling the wool over their eyes. Simon Dixon suggestively proclaims, "Deafened by such self-justificatory overtones, we shall need something more than the memoirs if we are to penetrate the innermost recesses of her mind."[105] He sees the more vulnerable Catherine in her early correspondence, while Madariaga suggests that her more spontaneous voice can be found in her marginalia.[106] In contrast, Smith finds "some of the most honest, revealing glimpses into Catherine's heart and mind" in her letters to Potemkin.[107] Barbara Heldt has dismissed the memoirs because Catherine is too self-confident and unwilling to reveal her doubts, which is apparently unrepresentative of women's memoirs that are meant to document women's oppression in their own words.[108] Though these judgments actually relate to the final memoir, they have been taken to explain all the memoirs.

Based on the abrupt ending of the final, most comprehensive memoir, scholars have interpreted the earlier memoirs as lesser fragments of an incomplete whole. In fact, the preeminent German translator of her memoirs interpolated all of them together chronologically into one memoir.[109] However, the early memoir ends in December 1754, where the addressee ("you") knows what happens, and thus, unlike the later memoirs, Catherine basically brings them up to the time of writing. It makes the most sense to treat her memoirs together and also as separate and even as distinct subgenres of autobiographical writing. While they all cover her life as Grand Duchess, they end differently and thus really tell different stories. Rhetorically, in conversations, stories, and the memoirs, she tends to sum up her point at the end. While her memoirs are incomplete, they are not unfinished. Though they seem structured by chronology alone, they are also organized rhetorically from the beginning to the end.

The memoirs also seem like parts of a fragmented whole because they contain many similarities. Catherine engaged in self-plagiarism, recycling phrases from margin notes, letters, and published polemics. Although the Academy edition lists 156 parallel passages between the various memoirs and notes, there are no exact parallels (741–50). For the middle and final memoirs, Catherine may have consulted earlier versions, notes, and probably a diary as she made outlines, wrote, and revised. An outline for the middle memoir has two parts written at different times; with some overlap, the first covers 1745–51, and the second is for 1749–50. In her final outline (translated and appended here), which goes from 1756–59, she crossed out events in the outline as she incorporated them in the memoir. And later, after she had experience writing Russian history, Catherine did research, using the newspapers and court journals of the time. The final memoir even contains a footnote to Büsching's *Magazin.* Later, in the final memoir, in her account of her serious respiratory illness upon arriving in Russia in 1744, she elaborates on the circumstances, explaining that she became ill because of studying Russian at night while underdressed for the cold. This explanation derives from a story in the *St. Petersburg Gazette,* planted by her imperial supporters. These and other subtle textual differences nevertheless serve to distinguish the memoirs from one another as separate documents.

Most important, using similar subject matter, the memoirs tell different stories. Written many years apart, they subtly reflect Catherine's immediate concerns at the time of writing. However, knowing when the memoirs were written is problematic because most are undated. A. N. Pypin made an extensive description of Catherine's many autobiographical materials in the State Archives in the order that he found them, not how Catherine left them (731–41). Using dates and internal evidence, Pypin established their probable order. Based on internal evidence, Catherine most likely wrote the early memoir, covering 1729–54, around 1756. She probably began the final memoir around 1794; part 1 covers 1728–50, and part 2 continues with 1751 and ends in 1759.[110] The dating of the three parts of the middle memoir, which covers 1728–50, is problematic. Part 1 begins with a heading in her hand on the first page: "Memoirs begun on April 21, 1771." Catherine's papers also contain two separate sheets with later dates. On one she wrote, "Memoirs begun in 1790. Part One," which is followed by blank pages; on another she wrote, "Memoirs continued in 1791. Part Two," which is followed by part 2 of the middle memoir. Using internal evidence from part 3, the editors of the Academy edition conclude that all three parts of the middle memoir, begun on Catherine's birthday in 1771, must have been completed before the end of 1773. They suggest that Catherine somewhat revised this memoir in 1790–91, and then began the final memoir in 1794, in which she incorporated the middle memoir into a new part 1.[111]

Codicology sheds some light on how Catherine edited the memoirs and supports this chronological scenario. For the 1756 memoir, eighteen pages long, Catherine wrote on both sides of inexpensive paper, with a 1½-inch left margin, which was insufficient for additions. For the subsequent memoirs, she wrote on both sides of excellent, heavy gilt-edged English paper that came in bifolio sheets. She folded each folio (31.7 × 19.9 cm wide) in half vertically, then wrote on one half and made additions on the other half, while also making changes to her main text. The margins of the middle memoir contain extensive additions that sometimes cover the entire page in a patchwork of sections. She most likely made these additions in 1790–91. In contrast, the final memoir has few additions, but a number of insertions on smaller pages, usually single folios, and sometimes bifolios. These smaller folios resemble the lower quality paper she used in the 1756 memoir, which suggests that these added episodes had been written years earlier and were the notes from which she had written the middle memoir. The heavy editing of the middle memoir in 1790–91 indicates that Catherine's conception of the memoir had changed sufficiently to warrant another memoir with a new beginning and ending.

The middle memoir represents an expanded attempt to set the record straight for posterity in response to critical accounts of Russia and of Catherine's coup by Rulhière and Chappe d'Auteroche in 1768. In particular, she counters Rulhière's account of her background as a poor relation among German courts.[112] Thus part 1, while a court memoir, also contains the fullest description of her youth, family, and especially her brilliant match. It is the life of a successful German Princess, and it concludes with her marriage. She wrote it when she was looking for a similar spouse for her son, and after they had agreed upon Princess Wilhelmina of Hessen-Darmstadt (1755–76), Catherine wrote her a set of maxims about the "job," based on her own experiences.[113] The early memoir has four pages on her youth in Germany, which Catherine greatly expands in the middle memoir. In 1756, Catherine had reason to minimize her German background, given that her husband was too obviously Prussophile, but the return to her German years in 1771 allows her to evoke an alternative vision of court life to the one she had endured as Grand Duchess.

> The court of Brunswick was then a truly royal court, in the number of beautiful houses this court occupied and in the decoration of these houses, the order that reigned at court, the many people of all kinds that the court supported, and the crowd of foreigners who constantly came there, and the dignity and magnificence that went into the whole style of life. Balls, operas, concerts, hunting parties, carriage drives, and banquets followed one another daily. This is what I saw for at least three or four months in Brunswick each year, from my eighth to my fifteenth year. [14]

Thus, whereas Rulhière portrays Catherine's upbringing as poor and provincial, in her middle memoir Catherine counters with her ample experience of grand court life in Germany, which far outshone that of the Russian court. The memoirs are only one of the many ways that she attempted to repair the losses of those years in a dismal Russian court, which she summarizes in her epitaph (1778): "Eighteen years of tedium and solitude led her to read many books."[114]

The style in which Catherine wrote her memoirs amplifies her criticisms of Elizabeth's court and her vision of her own Russian court that combined splendor and familial congeniality. The dedication to part 1 of this memoir evokes the atmosphere of intimate conversation among her trusted inner circle at court. Catherine dedicates it to Countess Praskovia Alexandrovna Bruce (née Rumiantseva) (1729–85), her friend during all those years as Grand Duchess, "to whom I can speak freely without fear of consequences."[115] They had become close when Catherine first arrived in Russia in 1744 and remained thus through 1779, when Catherine learned that her friend was having an affair with her then favorite, Major Ivan Rimsky-Korsakov. Catherine's words to Grimm noting her death are typical of her gracious practicality. "It is impossible not to miss her when one has known her long, for she was very nice; it would have upset me much more six or seven years ago, but since then we have been somewhat distant and separated."[116] In her life and in her letters, Catherine practiced the art of unpretentious conversation, which she enshrined in her *Rules*. Conversation earns a place in her self-portrait in the final memoir: "My disposition was naturally so accommodating that no one was ever with me a quarter of an hour without falling comfortably into conversation, chatting with me as if they had known me for a long time." Catherine's skill at evoking the art of conversation in her writing reflected her early reading of Mme. de Sévigné's letters to her daughter during the opulent reign of Louis XIV, which were widely known and praised for their simplicity and vivid stories of a grand court life.

In this memoir, Catherine defends herself abroad implicitly as enlightened and worldly, and at home explicitly. In her domestic self-defense, she includes a self-portrait with her resolutions to perform her job to the best of her abilities; it comes on the heels of a reprimand from the Empress for her debts. She resolved to please (1) the Grand Duke, (2) the Empress, and (3) the nation. "I admit that when I despaired of succeeding on the first point, I redoubled my care to fulfill the last two, I thought I succeeded more than once on the second, and I succeeded on the third point to the fullest extent and without any reservations at any time, and therefore I believed that I had attained my goal sufficiently" (58). She later recycled this resolution for her epitaph. The end of the memoir restates her defense in the previous memoir against the Empress's accusation that she was at fault for not producing an heir: on their wedding night, her husband went to sleep, and this was "the state in which things remained for nine consecutive years without the least change."[117] She protests her innocence against rumors of her sexual appetite: "I knew nothing." At the time that Catherine was writing this memoir, she was between the two most important relationships of her life and career, having broken with Grigory Orlov in the fall of 1772 and moving toward making Potemkin her favorite, a process she put in motion with a letter in December 1773. On February 21, 1774, she wrote one of her autobiographical letters, "a sincere confession" of her love life to an often jealous Potemkin, defending herself against gossip of having had fifteen, rather than five, lovers.[118] Thus her autobiographical writings accomplished many purposes, only some related to her coup in 1762.

In fact, the complete middle memoir, dated to 1771–73, addresses an immediate threat to Catherine. During this period, aside from war, plague, and an armed revolt, Catherine had problems at home. This memoir ends with the arrival, on February 7, 1750, of the Ambassador from Denmark, Count Rochus Friedrich Lynar (1708–81), to negotiate for the exchange of the Grand Duke's territory of Holstein for Denmark's Oldenburg and Delmenhorst. This issue was relevant to Catherine's struggle with the threat to her legitimacy presented by the majority of her son, Grand Duke Paul, on September 20, 1772. His majority pitted Paul, the Panin party, and the Vorontsovs against the Orlovs and Chernyshevs, Catherine's supporters, in a last attempt to remove Catherine from the throne in favor of her son.[119] The Grand Duke's territory in Holstein, which he inherited from his father, Peter III, created an important potential foreign base for the power of both men at court. The restoration of Holstein to its former glory formed the whole of Peter's existence, as it had his father's; both men had allied themselves with Russia for this purpose. In her final memoir, Catherine says that she fills in for Peter to run Holstein because he cannot be bothered, but it is very much her problem, too.

Catherine took as great an interest in Holstein before as after her coup for the same reason: the external leverage and power it gave the two men with whom her political survival was inextricably linked. Before the coup, she wanted Peter to keep Holstein, and after the coup, she took steps to deprive her son of the territory. In 1767, Catherine made a preliminary agreement with Denmark to exchange Paul's inheritance, Holstein-Gottorp, for Oldenburg and Delmenhorst. Paul agreed on May 21, 1773, and then on July 14, 1773, signed these over to Catherine's maternal uncle Duke August Friedrich (1711–85) in exchange for a Russian treaty with Denmark against Sweden, effectively eliminating any foreign power base for himself. At the end of the middle memoir, Catherine promises a fourth part on this issue, but returns to it only at the opening of part 2 of her final memoir, which she begins with a monologue that shows her to be a brilliant politician. In effect, she argues that in 1751, Peter (like Paul in 1773) should keep Holstein and bargain it away only for the glory of Russia and his reputation. Thus her monologue in the final memoir that she will leave her son in effect justifies her actions against him as for his benefit.

Historians have only recently begun to appreciate the political significance of Catherine's actions in this situation. It was especially delicate for Catherine because at the very time she needed the support of the

Orlovs, she had learned on April 25, 1772, that her longtime favorite, Grigory Orlov, had been unfaithful. She replaced him as favorite with Alexander Vasilchikov on September 2, 1772, whereupon Orlov returned from negotiations with Turkey in early September, apparently at Catherine's secret request. Mikhail Safonov argues that Catherine, far from being just the hurt lover, used her break with Orlov to distract Panin (and Paul) with the potential real gain for Paul of greatly reducing Orlov's influence at court from the distant possibility of installing Paul as Emperor. To satisfy Panin and Paul, Catherine deprived Orlov of his honors; as soon as they signed away Holstein, she restored Orlov's honors to him.[120]

The middle memoir has a second dedication that pleasantly masks another of Catherine's important problems in the early 1770s: the plague in Moscow. Like her dedication to Countess Bruce at the beginning of part 1, this dedication, at the beginning of part 2, evokes an atmosphere of easy conversation among friends. "To Monsieur Baron Alexander Cherkasov, from whose body I pledge by my honor to extract at least one burst of laughter daily or else to argue with him from morning until evening because these two pleasures are the same for him, and I love to give pleasure to my friends" (73). Catherine had made a list of humorous causes of death of her friends: she would die trying to please others, Countess Bruce would die shuffling cards, and Cherkasov would die from suffocation by speech (653–54).[121] As with the previous dedication, Catherine creates a friendly, easy sphere that stands in vivid contrast to her withering attack on the stupidity and dangers of life at a court under Elizabeth.

> High stakes card games...were necessary in a court where there was no conversation, where people cordially hated one another, where slander passed for wit, and where the least mention of scandal was considered a crime of lèse-majesté. Secret intrigues passed for cleverness; one carefully avoided speaking of art or science because everyone was ignorant; one could wager that half the group could barely read, and I am not quite sure that a third knew how to write. [89]

In contrast with this picture of ignorance, Baron Alexander Ivanovich Cherkasov (1728–88) had studied at Cambridge University, spoke English perfectly, and enjoyed the pleasures of life, especially food and drink. She does not mention him in this memoir, and indeed he appears just once in all the memoirs, as the future husband of the Princess of Courland in the final memoir. His importance lies in her present, not the past, as she strove with his help to control a devastating outbreak of plague in Moscow. He founded and presided over the Medical Collegium (1763–75), which Catherine used to institute reform of medical education and public health and, more important, to train Russian doctors (rather than import German ones), especially for the military. As with her dedication to Countess Bruce, Catherine added this dedication to the memoir later; it is in a different color and thickness of ink on the first page in the column she used for additions. While Gyllenborg and probably Hanbury-Williams read the autobiographical pieces she wrote for them, there is no record that either dedicatee ever saw this memoir.

Beginning in the 1770s, Catherine appears to have circulated some autobiographical writings among her inner circle. In 1778, she wrote in Russian what she called a "sixteen year examination" of her reign since 1762.[122] She sent it to Grimm, and she mentions other readers, including Potemkin, Orlov, and Shuvalov, who found it a "chef d'oeuvre," "very nice," and "academic," respectively.[123] In 1789, she composed another epistolary self-portrait, this one for Dr. Johann Georg Zimmermann (1728–95), Swiss royal doctor and author of *On Melancholy* (1756), with whom she corresponded about literature and politics (1785–95).[124] It begins with a now familiar theme: "I have always thought that others have slandered me because they have not understood me." She concludes her portrait with a humorous change of tone that shows her sensitivity to her reader as a listener: "Here ends the dialogue of the dead, let us return to the living" (595). However, no surviving documents of her time contain any mention of her memoirs. Perhaps she followed the advice of an illustrious predecessor, the Duc de Saint-Simon (1675–1755), who in his *Memoirs* (1743) of the reign of Louis XIV warns that "he who writes the history of his times…would therefore have had to lose his mind even to let people suspect that he is writing. His work should ripen under the surest lock and key, thus to pass to his heirs."[125] In a letter to Grimm in 1790, she denies writing memoirs: "I do not know what Didot has heard about my memoirs, but one can be sure that I have never written any, and if it is a sin not to have done this, then I must admit my guilt."[126]

The explicit expectation in France that she would write her memoirs may have spurred Catherine on to try again in the 1790s. In addition, Catherine found reading and writing psychologically therapeutic in difficult times. For example, her dedication to Cherkasov in the middle memoir sounds like a prescription. In 1777, in a final letter to her anxious, jealous favorite Peter Zavadovsky (1739–1812), Catherine ends things on a dry note. "Most of all, calm your spirit and be healthy and merry, and I advise you to follow the advice of SRV [Semen Romanovich Vorontsov] to translate Tacitus or to practice Russian history."[127] After the untimely death of her favorite, Alexander Lanskoi (1758–84, favorite as of 1778), she embarked on her comparative linguistic project to allay her grief. Likewise, Potemkin's death, in 1791, reverberated, and Catherine took her own advice. Aside from writing her letters to Grimm and the memoirs, during this period Catherine was also composing her Russian history and corresponding (1790–92) with the French historian Gabriel Sénac de Meilhan (1736–1803), who had approached her to write a history of eighteenth-century Russia and her reign.[128] Sénac de Meilhan concludes an outline for his history of her with a comparison between Catherine and the one other enlightened European monarch with whom she was often compared, Frederick the Great.[129]

In the year before she began to revise her memoirs, Catherine read and responded to writings about and by Frederick, especially his posthumous memoir, *History of My Times* (1788), which helped shape her new conception for the final memoir.[130] Their writings are comparable, for like Catherine, Frederick was a voluminous writer, excelling in the one genre that eluded Catherine, namely poetry; he too corresponded extensively with Voltaire, Grimm, and others. In early 1789, Catherine wrote to Grimm about her "27 notes" on the first thirty pages of Frederick's works, which begin with his preface to his *History*, and concludes that "the witty bon mot often wins out over an exact account of the event, but there are many very good things in it."[131] In April 1789, she made critical notes in Abbé Denina's *Essay on the Life and Reign of Frederick II, King of Prussia* (1788). According to Denina, Bayle's dictionary was Frederick's favorite book, though his wife found it improper for a noblewoman; Catherine writes that she thinks it is "very philosophical," and mentions her own reading of this important work for the first time in her final memoir (675). Frederick's *History* begins with the state of Prussia at the beginning of his reign in 1740: "With the death of Frederick William, King of Prussia, the revenues of the state did not exceed 7,400,000 ecus."[132] Similarly, in 1794 Catherine began a largely financial memoir in Russian, though she dispensed with Frederick's classical use of the third person for himself: "In 1762, upon my ascension to the throne, I found a land army in Prussia of which two-thirds had not been paid" (517).[133] Frederick concludes his introduction to his *History* with a lesson in successful rule that sounds like his early study of Machiavelli (1740): "History is the school of Princes; it is up to them to instruct themselves in the mistakes of past centuries so as to avoid them, and to learn that one must design a plan and follow it step-by-step, and that only he who has best calculated his conduct can prevail over those who act less rationally."[134]

Catherine begins her final memoir with an unusual rhetorical maxim that hints at a moral reproach to Frederick and provides a further lesson in Enlightenment ideals and logic:

> Fortune is not as blind as people imagine. It is often the result of a long series of precise and well-chosen steps that precede events and are not perceived by the common herd. In people it is also more specifically the result of qualities, of character, and of individual conduct. To make this more concrete, I will make the following syllogism of it:
>
> Qualities and character will be the major premise.
> Conduct, the minor.
> Fortune or misfortune, the conclusion.
> Here are two striking examples.
> Catherine II.
> Peter III.

In 1794, in a letter to Grimm, Catherine echoes both this maxim and Frederick's lesson: "The good fortune and misfortune of each is in his character; this character lies in the principles that the person embraces; success resides in the soundness of the measures that he employs to arrive at his ends; if he wavers in his principles, if he errs in the measures that he adopts, his projects come to nothing."[135] During her reign, Catherine compared herself as a Russian ruler to Peter the Great; on the European stage, she vied for power with Frederick. In contrast to such worthy historical comparisons, in her final memoir Catherine instead draws an explicit comparison between herself and the inept Peter III.

In this memoir, the principle of comparison serves another larger historical purpose for Catherine. From the very beginning, Catherine's last memoir declares itself to be a biography in the tradition of Plutarch's *Parallel Lives* (100 A.D.). Plutarch pairs twenty-five individual biographies of illustrious Greek men with those of Romans, and for most pairs provides a summary comparison. Not only was Plutarch among the first serious works recommended to her by Count Gyllenborg, but he was very much a part of the vocabulary of ideas that Rousseau and Montesquieu used to discuss the merits of the legislator versus the monarch.[136] Until the end of the nineteenth century, Plutarch was standard reading for educated people, and many biographies of illustrious women as well as men use his comparative format.[137] Histories of monarchs have paired together Mary Stuart and Elizabeth I, Voltaire's Charles XII and Peter the Great, as well as, more immediately, Catherine and Peter the Great, and Catherine and Frederick the Great.[138] Catherine has also been compared with Princess Dashkova (1743–1810). Though not a monarch, Dashkova was the most accomplished Russian woman on the international stage, and from a young age her fate was everywhere intertwined with Catherine's political and literary life, beginning with the coup. She was Catherine's editor at the journal *The Companion of Lovers of the Russian Word* (1783–84), and in 1783 Catherine appointed her director of the Russian Academy of Sciences and president of the new Russian Academy of Language. In 1789, Catherine resorts to Plutarch to compare herself to Dashkova, who apparently did not get along with people: "I can adapt myself to all people. I am like Alcibiades in Sparta and in Athens."[139]

In 1790, Catherine appears to have been preoccupied with Plutarch while revising her middle memoir. She translated Plutarch's pair of Alcibiades and Coriolanus.[140] Catherine commented, upon reading several current biographical works in the style of Plutarch, that "one must never do that, because writers today are incapable of the ancients' tact," adding that "it resembles fake antiques."[141] Later that year, after the death of Prince Viktor Amadeus of Anhalt-Bernburg-Schaumburg in battle against the Swedes, she translated Plutarch and said, "This is such a comfort, this fortifies my soul."[142] Catherine, in fact, began her final memoir with her comparative maxim, which unlike her two dedications in the middle memoir, was not added later. Thus her thinking about Plutarch significantly shaped her memoir.

Catherine's new conception of this memoir as a classical biography explains some of the real differences, aside from the maxim, with her previous memoirs. She begins with a biography of Peter III, which integrates his genealogy. Thus, unlike the early and middle memoirs, which start with her birth in Stettin, the final memoir presents Catherine as she meets Peter for the first time, in 1739, at age ten. As in the beginning of Plutarch's biographies, Peter and Catherine are identified through their family. She eliminates her childhood, and her wedding happens in one sentence; her life does not begin until she arrives in Russia and starts her political career. Like Frederick the Great, she makes several references to herself in the third person, which is typical for autobiographies that imitate classical biography. Even at the semantic level, her conception holds. The phrase Catherine repeats most is contrastive, serving to distinguish her thoughts and behavior from those of another: "as for me" (*pour moi*).

An inveterate, eclectic, and opportunistic borrower, Catherine frames her revised court memoir with Plutarch's biographical structure to add historical weight, classical substance, and judicious distance. His biographical method allows her to generalize from part of Elizabeth's reign to the whole of Elizabeth's, Peter's, and her own reigns. He outlines his method in his biography of Alexander the Great:

> It must be borne in mind that my design is not to write histories, but lives. And the most glorious exploits do not always furnish us with the clearest discoveries of virtue or vice in men; sometimes a matter of less moment, an expression or a jest, informs us better of their characters and inclinations, than the most famous sieges, and the greatest armaments, or the bloodiest battles whatsoever.[143]

Everything that happens under Elizabeth's reign and the details of Peter and Catherine's stewardship of Holstein presage their different styles of rule and their relative merits as rulers. Thus Catherine's final conversation with Elizabeth, about Holstein and Peter, is meant to predict Peter's failure and Catherine's success as rulers. The final comparison is less between Catherine and Peter than between their respective good and bad relationships with Elizabeth. By implication, Elizabeth should prefer Catherine to Peter as her successor.

Catherine both applies and modifies Plutarch's principles of biography. Like Plutarch, who claims that "moral good is a practical stimulus," Catherine is a moralist, concerned with personal virtue.[144] Moreover, she shares Plutarch's view of character as static rather than evolving. Plutarch's great men combine good and bad qualities, none more than Alcibiades. Catherine depicts herself as fairly good, while Peter and Elizabeth are portrayed as having decidedly mixed qualities. In Plutarch's world, however, life often interferes with the best intentions. Catherine seems to agree with this in regard to her personal life alone. Here Catherine is purposefully inconsistent. In her maxim, Catherine transforms *la fortune,* the blind goddess Fortuna (the secular version of Providence), into carefully planned personal fortune, which the ancients thought depended as much on luck as virtue. Thus, in Catherine's interpretation, the virtuous individual ruler can transform fortune by the force of her personality.

Catherine's use of the Plutarchian framework of judicious comparison tempers her portrait of Peter III in the final memoir. The self-serving nature of Catherine's increasingly negative portrayal of her husband troubles scholars. Some even accuse her of destroying Peter's reputation posthumously in the memoirs and during her lifetime with her manifestos and the repression of any mention of him that might allow future historians a more balanced portrait.[145] The early memoir is in fact neutral on Peter, but, of course, it was written before Peter became Emperor and threatened to divorce her, when everything still hinged on Catherine's succeeding through Peter. After the coup, Catherine began to attack Peter in her manifestos, which reiterate that he acted against Russia's interests in the Seven Years' War, scorned the Russian Orthodox Church, and preferred Holstein to Russia.

The black portrait of Peter in the final memoir in fact appears consistently throughout her writings, thanks in part to Catherine's habit of repeating herself. There are various earlier permutations of the conclusion to her outline, written around 1794, "that it was necessary to perish with him, by him, or else to try to save oneself." Already in 1756, in a letter to Hanbury-Williams, she writes that after Elizabeth's death, "be assured that I will not play the quiet and weak role of the King of Sweden, and that I will perish or rule."[146] In *Antidote,* in 1770, she wrote: "Thus, seeing that she had only two paths before her, that of sharing the misfortunes of a husband who hated her, who was incapable of following good advice, and who had no greater enemy than himself, or of saving the Empire, the Grand Duke's son, age seven, and herself, Catherine no longer hesitated, she saved that Empire."[147] In her marginalia for Denina's *Essay on the Life and Reign of Frederick II* (1789), she writes: "Peter III had no greater enemy than himself; all his actions bordered on insanity.... He took pleasure in beating men and animals.... By ascending to the throne, Empress Catherine saved the empire, herself, and her son from the hands of a madman" (680–81). In the final memoir, by comparison, Catherine has "three paths" and is less explicit about his failings: "But to speak more clearly, it was a matter of perishing with him, or by him, or else of saving myself, my children, and perhaps the state from the disaster that all this Prince's moral and physical faculties promised" (399).

For the final memoir, using Plutarch's model, Catherine has developed a larger historical perspective that helps to moderate her individual assessment of Peter. By the 1790s, with the execution of Louis XVI and the destabilizing effects of the French Revolution on monarchs throughout Europe, and fearing Paul as a successor, Catherine more generally had hardened her feelings toward any further instability in the rule of Russia. For example, in the manuscripts of the middle memoir, Catherine later added one significant sentence about his inclination to drink. "It was there that I saw the Prince, who later would be my spouse, for the first time: he seemed then well raised and witty. *Meanwhile they already noticed his liking for wine and great irritation at everything that annoyed him;* he liked my mother, but could not stand me; he was jealous of the freedom I then enjoyed, while he was surrounded by teachers and all his steps were set and accounted for" (20, emphasis added). Nevertheless, if in the middle memoir Catherine urges pity for him, in the final memoir Peter himself is immune to this emotion, which Rousseau had praised as the greatest human feeling (118). Still, even in the final memoir, her biographical assessment of Peter makes quite clear that his education, "a clash of unfortunate circumstances," did him great harm, and that Elizabeth's unenlightened oversight made things worse.[148]

Overall, Catherine's treatment of Peter is contradictory. Over time, she adopted a moralizing tone, especially evident in her portraits, that interrupts rather than meshes with the flow of her tale, which chronicles the ups and downs of the royal couple. In particular, her descriptions of the Grand Duke's escapades, from drilling holes in the walls of Elizabeth's suite and setting up benches for the voyeurs, to his military games with pretend soldiers, dolls, and rats, constitute some of the liveliest, most memorable episodes. Catherine ultimately finished the memoir differently than planned, ending with Elizabeth rather than Peter. Something happens between her and the Grand Duke to trigger her permanent mistrust, which in the memoir she places before the birth of her daughter, but in the outline, after their relations improve, her daughter is born, and Poniatowski leaves.[149] This was to have been the ending of the memoir, according to her outline. Contradictions in her approach toward Peter in the memoir mirror those in life, when, on June 26, 1795, Catherine combined a requiem service in honor of Peter the Great's victory over the Swedes at Poltava in 1709 with, for the first time, one for Peter III.[150]

Catherine's use of Plutarch as a frame for the final memoir illustrates the increased importance of history and history writing for her. More immediate, the differences between Catherine's middle and final memoirs reflect two contrasting emphases for memoirs in French historiography at the time. The eyewitness account of her place and time, the *histoire particulière,* in the earlier memoir gives way in the later memoir to the admixture of the larger national and historical scope of the *histoire générale.*[151] Particular history simply relates what happened, while general history argues why things happened as they did. Thus Frederick calls his memoir a history, which was the more prestigious genre.[152] While Catherine's memoirs are eyewitness accounts with many overlaps, the final memoir contains conspicuous changes that make it more historical and general. Catherine summarizes her main points in the margins, frequently at first and then minimally, mainly noting a new year, a practice she developed in her writings on Russian history. The maxim provides a large general context and argument for the whole memoir, and like Frederick, she mentions documents in her archives. In particular, her account of Peter's childhood is not an eyewitness account, and she very likely researched it. In 1745, Elizabeth apparently instructed her ambassador to Denmark, Nikolai Korf, to learn about Peter's childhood, and Catherine may have used his report.[153] Her approach to her final memoir thus represents a significant shift in her autobiographical consciousness, from viewing her years as Grand Duchess as life at court to viewing that time as history. Catherine displays those larger historical ambitions elsewhere in 1794, in a sketch she commissioned by Johann-Baptist Lampi (1751–1830), titled "Portrait of Catherine II with Allegorical Figures of Saturn and History."[154]

Taken together, Catherine's various memoirs are sui generis. Catherine's concern for facts, her unpretentious frankness, and her difficult position as Grand Duchess under Empress Elizabeth make it possible to forget that the person writing the memoir was the most powerful woman in the world. Rulers' autobiographical writings, in various genres, were rare, and they tended toward military history and philosophy.[155] The only women who were rulers and writers were Queen Christina of Sweden and Queen Elizabeth of England (1533–1603), both more learned than Catherine.[156] Around 1681, Queen Christina wrote an unfinished autobiography that is sixty-nine pages and in French; it was published in 1759 in a collection of her works, about which Catherine had read d'Alembert's review essay, *Mémoires*.[157] While Catherine's reign coincided with the first significant amount of Russian memoir writing, much of this writing, including her own memoirs, remained unpublished (though rarely unread) until the nineteenth century.[158] In contrast, the publication of French memoir writing was well established by the latter half of the eighteenth century; by the seventeenth century, the number of published French memoirs already exceeded the number of Russian memoirs—published or unpublished—by 1800. Nevertheless, as the memoirs of a ruler, Catherine's work obviously has few peers; as those of a female autocrat, her memoirs stand alone.

Like other great memoirists, Catherine developed a unique language and structure. It took Catherine four decades and multiple memoirs, but in the final memoir, translated here, she succeeded in shaping the genre in an unusual way to suit her complex persona. The final memoir alone contains an important, unusual verbal self-portrait in which Catherine represents herself as exemplary, both as a woman and as a man. The memoir as a whole bears this out, for Catherine by her criticisms asserts that as a ruler she is superior to Elizabeth as well as Peter. Yet, the language of the self-portrait is unusual, with its universal Enlightenment terms for the self nevertheless delineated by gender. She writes: "If I may dare to use such terms, I take the liberty to assert on my own behalf that I was an honest and loyal knight, whose mind was infinitely more male than female. But for all that I was anything but mannish, and in me others found, joined to the mind and character of a man, the charms of a very attractive woman" (419). These tensions between masculine and feminine exist at the generic level too, as Catherine combined the classical biography of illustrious men with the general and individual histories of memoirs. Moreover, in this self-portrait Catherine for the first time calls her memoir a confession: "May I be pardoned this description in recognition of the truth of this confession, which my self-esteem makes without covering itself with false modesty" (419).[159] In a letter to Grimm in 1791, Catherine mentions both Plutarch and Rousseau, and, arguably, both influenced her final memoir.[160] Despite her dislike for Rousseau's political theories, Catherine acknowledges his sentimental aesthetic when she concludes her self-portrait with a revealing description of her heart, sensibility, and nature. Like Rousseau in his *Confessions* (1782), Catherine notes that feelings do not always obey "the finest moral maxims."

Catherine's portrait of herself is substantially more complex and nuanced than the overly feminized picture her critics paint of her. Rulhière gives a detailed physical portrait, from which he extrapolates:

> The softer characters of gentleness and goodness, which are likewise depicted there, appear, to a penetrating observer, only as the effect of an ardent desire to please; and those seductive expressions discover but too plainly an intention to seduce. A painter who was desirous of giving an allegorical representation of this great personage, proposed to exhibit her in the figure of a charming nymph, presenting with one hand, stretched forth, a wreath of flowers, and holding in the other, thrown behind her back, a flaming torch.[161]

In Catherine's verbal self-portrait she is a knight, the member of a royal order, not a naked nymph. Among the many painted portraits of herself that Catherine commissioned, only a handful lack the medals for the orders awarded her: St. Catherine, St. Andrei, St. George, and St. Vladimir. Empress first and foremost, Catherine sought forms and words to bring together and articulate an unorthodox personal life, a passion for ideas, and the ambition and talent to rule.

In a long writerly career, Catherine kept returning to the memoirs, writing, rewriting, and editing them. Of necessity and with real interest, Catherine studied language and languages throughout her life; moreover, she managed to make her idiomatic Russian, French, and German uniquely her own. Similarly, with the unusual opening structure of the final memoir, Catherine transformed her previous memoirs into something uniquely hers. As she wrote: "Besides, this writing itself should prove what I say about my mind, my heart, and my character" (419). To make this argument, Catherine, with her opening maxim and syllogism, forces the reader's attention away from her body and onto her mind. As with Peter's biography, the flow of her chronological narrative, which should begin with her physical birth, is interrupted. They present her intellect and her historical self where readers expect to find a more common opening, such as those of the early and middle memoirs: "I was born April 21 ..." This final memoir manifests her continued search for other narratives to represent the different aspects of Catherine—human being, woman, intellectual, and, above all, Empress of Russia.

NOTES

1. A recent study of her reign argues "how much it mattered that Catherine the Great was committed to the ideals of the European Enlightenment," a commitment she expressed primarily through her writings. Simon Dixon, *Catherine the Great* (New York: Longman, 2001), 17. In Russia, through her published writings and support for publishing, Catherine actively participated in an extensive public dialogue on the monarch that can be found in one fifth of all publications. Cynthia Hyla Whittaker, *Russian Monarchy: Eighteenth-Century Rulers and Writers in Political Dialogue* (DeKalb, Ill.: Northern Illinois University Press, 2003), 5, 8–9.

2. Catherine to Hanbury-Williams, August 27, 1756. *Correspondance de Catherine Alexéievna, Grande-Duchesse de Russie, et de Sir Charles H. Williams, Ambassadeur d'Angleterre, 1756 et 1757,* ed. Serge Goriaïnow (Moscow: 1909), 88. In English, *Correspondence of Catherine the Great with Sir Charles Hanbury-Williams and Letters from Count Poniatowski,* trans. and ed. Earl of Ilchester and Mrs. Langford-Brooke (London: Thornton Butterworth, 1928).

3. Douglas Smith, ed., *Love and Conquest: Personal Correspondence of Catherine the Great and Prince Grigory Potemkin* (DeKalb, Ill.: Northern Illinois University Press, 2004). This English edition of 464 letters is drawn from the 1,162 letters in V. S. Lopatin, ed., *Ekaterina II i G. A. Potemkin. Lichnaia perepiska, 1769–1791* (Moscow: Nauka, 1997). Simon Sebag Montefiore, *Prince of Princes: The Life of Potemkin* (New York: St. Martin's Press, Thomas Dunne Books, 2001).

4. Catherine apparently first approached Paul's wife and then his son with her proposal. John T. Alexander, *Catherine the Great: Life and Legend* (New York: Oxford University Press, 1989), 322.

5. On the meaning of political power in the eighteenth century and Catherine's approach to it, see Dixon, *Catherine the Great.*

6. On efforts since 1742 to overthrow Bestuzhev-Riumin and on his foreign policy, see Evgenii Anisimov, *Empress Elizabeth: Her Reign and Her Russia, 1741–1761,* trans. and ed. John T. Alexander (Gulf Breeze, Fla: Academic International Press, 1995), 101–9.

7. This and further such unattributed quotations are from the translation of the memoir and her outline in this volume.

8. *Sochineniia Imperatritsy Ekateriny II,* ed. A. N. Pypin, vol. 12 (St. Petersburg: Imperial Academy of Sciences, 1907). Volume 6 of this series, her *Great Instruction,* was never published. Please note that in the preface and notes to the translation, which is based on Pypin's definitive edition, all further references to volume 12, which contains her collected autobiographical writings with an introduction by Ia. Barskov, are given as page numbers in the text.

9. Catherine's other memoirs exist in one English translation, based on the German translation, *Memoiren der Kaiserin Katharina II,* trans. Erich Böhme, 2 vols. (Leipzig: 1913). *Memoirs of Catherine the Great,* trans. Katharine Anthony (New York: Alfred A. Knopf, 1927). See the translation note for a discussion of the three earlier translations and the original manuscript.

10. "Au reste cet écrit même doit prouver ce que je dis de mon esprit, de mon coeur et de mon caractère" (419).

11. Holstein-Gottorp was located in northern Germany and carved out of Schleswig-Holstein, with interests in Denmark, which were protected through two strategic marriages with Sweden in the seventeenth century.

12. Reversing a practice of not marrying off royal daughters, Peter the Great sought marriages for his two daughters to guard Russia's interests in the Baltic against Sweden, Russia's northern enemy, while Karl Friedrich wanted a powerful ally in order to regain territory his house had lost to Denmark. Karl Friedrich groomed his son, Peter III, as the potential heir not only to the Russian but also to the Swedish throne, because Peter's grandfather, Friedrich IV (1671–1702), Duke of Holstein-Gottorp, had married Princess Hedwig Sophia (1681–1708), sister of King Charles XII (1660–97) of Sweden, whose mother was Hedwig Eleonora (1636–1715) of Holstein-Gottorp.

13. In 1717, Peter the Great visited Paris in an unsuccessful attempt to arrange a marriage for Elizabeth to the future Louis XV and pry loose French support for a weakened Sweden, trounced by Peter at Poltava (in 1709). Peter tried again unsuccessfully in 1721. Rumor had it that in 1742 Elizabeth secretly married Count Alexei Razumovsky (1709–71); she had no children.

14. In 1742, Catherine's grandmother had one painting done by Balthasar Denner (1685–1749), who had painted many German royals, including Peter III (27). In 1743, according to the diary of Peter's tutor, Jacob Stählin, a second portrait of Catherine by Antoine Pesne (1683–1757), a French painter of German aristocrats, was delivered to Elizabeth at her request (Anthony, *Memoirs,* 77–78).

15. Catherine mentions 15,000 rubles in the early memoir (444), and 10,000 rubles in the middle memoir (30).

16. Princess Johanna was caught intriguing on behalf of Frederick the Great, and she was asked to leave after the wedding.

17. In the early memoir, she writes, "They forced the name I now bear on me solely because that which I had was horrible on account of the intrigues of Peter the Great's sister, who bore the same one" (451). Tsarevna Sophia Alexeevna was regent from 1682 to 1689.

18. Rumor had it that Peter had to be circumcised to enable him to have intercourse; although he had several mistresses, he appears to have fathered no children.

19. Saltykov was her lover from 1752 to 1755. As Empress, Catherine appointed him envoy to France in 1762, and then to Saxony in 1764; little is known about his fate. Alexander, *Catherine the Great,* 63.

20. She most likely had epileptic seizures.

21. Catherine to Hanbury-Williams, August 18, 1756, *Correspondance de Catherine,* 45.

22. In her middle memoir, it is 657,000 rubles (475–76).

23. See John P. LeDonne, *Absolutism and Ruling Class: The Formation of the Russian Political Order, 1700–1825* (New York: Oxford University Press, 1991).

24. Quoted in Lindsey Hughes, *Russia in the Age of Peter the Great* (New Haven, Conn.: Yale University Press, 1998), 411. Original in *Polnoe Sobranie zakonov Rossiiskoi Imperii, 1649–1913,* vol. 6 (St. Petersburg, 1830), 496–97. As a result of the ensuing dynastic instability, "four signs conferred legitimacy: designation, dynastic inheritance, worthiness, and election." Whittaker, *Russian Monarchy,* 63.

25. On Catherine's reputation in France at the time of her coup, see Voltaire's letters, and in Germany and England, see Ruth Dawson, "Perilous Royal Biography: Representa-

tions of Catherine II Immediately After Her Seizure of the Throne," *Biography* 27.3 (Summer 2004): 517–34. Whittaker argues that through her manifestos, Catherine inaugurated a new image of legitimacy, the legal sovereign, which she added to the existing images of the reforming czar and the elected monarch. *Russian Monarchy,* 9, 99–102.

26. The role of favorite was an unofficial position of a close friend or lover (though not necessarily) with direct access to the ruler. The ruler bestowed positions, titles, and great wealth on the favorite to legitimize the favorite's access and official duties; the favorite's family benefited enormously. Once she came to power, Catherine had ten successive favorites, but even after Potemkin was no longer her lover, he remained the most powerful favorite and vetted nearly every successor. For a recent informative discussion of favoritism under Catherine, see Smith, *Love and Conquest,* xxxii–xliii. Catherine's twelve lovers were: Sergei Saltykov (1752–55), Count Poniatowski (1755–58), Prince Grigory Orlov (1760–72), Alexander Vasilchikov (1772–74), Prince Grigory Potemkin (1774–76), Count Peter Zavadovsky (1776–77), Simon Zorich (1777–78), Ivan Rimsky-Korsakov (1778), Alexander Lanskoi (1778–84), Alexander Ermolov (1785–86), Count Alexander Dmitriev-Mamonov (1786–89), and Prince Platon Zubov (1789–96). *The Memoirs of Princess Dashkova,* trans. and ed. Kyril Fitzlyon (London: John Calder, 1956; reprint, with an introduction by Jehanne M. Gheith, Durham, N.C.: Duke University Press, 1995), 301–2.

27. Peter the Great had originally trained Alexei, his son from his first marriage, to succeed him, but then had him tried as unfit to rule, which led to his death during torture. Peter had his first wife, Evdokia Lopukhina (1669–1731), forcibly exiled to a convent.

28. To complicate matters only slightly, the daughters were illegitimate, as Peter and Catherine only married in 1712. On the history of Russian female rule, see Isolde Thyrêt, *Between God and Tsar: Religious Symbolism and the Royal Women of Muscovite Russia* (DeKalb, Ill.: Northern Illinois University Press, 2001).

29. Bühren became Duke of Courland in 1737. He Russified his name to Biren, and then Frenchified it to Biron when the French Dukes of Biron adopted him at the urging of Cardinal Fleury. The term for his unofficial reign was "Bironovshchina," indicating his excessive influence.

30. Isabel de Madariaga, "Catherine and the *philosophes,*" in *Politics and Culture in Eighteenth-Century Russia* (New York: Longman, 1998), 231, 234. The eighteenth-century *philosophes* included Voltaire, Montesquieu, Rousseau, Diderot, Grimm, and d'Alembert, popular intellectuals and social philosophers who argued for the systematic critique of society according to principles of reason and tolerance, pitting science against religious dogma.

31. On Elizabeth, see Anisimov, *Empress Elizabeth,* 167–81.

32. Eidel'man suggests that in the memoirs, Catherine implicitly condemns this aspect of Elizabeth's reign, and she established a more respectful working relationship with her courtiers. N. Ia. Eidel'man, "Memuary Ekateriny II—odna iz raskrytykh tain samoderzhaviia," *Voprosy istorii* 1 (1968): 156.

33. By 1762, Catherine had lost her parents and most of her immediate family. The eldest of five children, only she and her brother Friedrich August (1734–93), the last Prince of Anhalt-Zerbst, lived to maturity.

34. Catherine's correspondence as Grand Duchess exists in two nineteenth-century books: Ferdinand Sieliak, *Kathurina der zweiten Brautreise nach Russland 1744–1745. Eine historische Skizze* (Dessau, Germany, 1873); and *Sbornik Imperatorskogo russkogo istoricheskogo obshchestva*, vol. 7 (St. Petersburg, 1871), hereafter cited as *SIRIO*.

35. Catherine to Mme. Geoffrin, November 6, 1764, "Pis'ma Imperatritsy Ekateriny II, k G-zhe Zhoffren," *SIRIO*, 1:261–62.

36. Mme. Geoffrin "invented the Enlightenment salon. First, she made the one-o'clock dinner rather than the traditional late-night supper the sociable meal of the day, and thus she opened up the whole afternoon for talk. Second, she regularized these dinners, fixing a specific day of the week for them (Monday for artists, Wednesday for men of letters)." Dena Goodman, *The Republic of Letters: A Cultural History of the French Enlightenment* (Ithaca, N.Y.: Cornell University Press, 1994), 91.

37. Written in 1947 by Grigorii A. Gukovskii, "The Empress as Writer," in *Catherine the Great: A Profile*, ed. Marc Raeff (New York: Hill and Wang, 1972), 68.

38. Whittaker, *Russian Monarchy*, 9.

39. Isabel de Madariaga concludes, "In her literary as in her legislative production she was pragmatic in her approach, pedantic in her execution, and eclectic as regards her sources." *Catherine the Great: A Short History* (New Haven, Conn.: Yale University Press, 1990), 204. See also Isabel de Madariaga, "The Role of Catherine II in the Literary and Cultural Life of Russia," in *Politics and Culture in Eighteenth-Century Russia* (New York: Longman, 1998), 284–95.

40. A nearly one-thousand-page annotated bibliography of Catherine's writings catalogs accessible Russian publications and excludes rare books, archives, and Catherine's publications abroad in French and in translations. I. V. Babich, M. V. Babich, and T. A. Lapteva, eds., *Ekaterina II: Annotirovannaia bibliografiia publikatsii* (Moscow: ROSSPEN, 2004). See also Prince N. N. Golitsyn, *Bibliograficheskii slovar' russkikh pisatel'nits* (1889; reprint, Leipzig: Zentralantiquariat der Deutschen Demokratischen Republik, 1974), 92–109; and John T. Alexander, "Catherine II (Ekaterina Alekseevna), 'The Great,' Empress of Russia," in *Early Modern Russian Writers: The Late Seventeenth and Eighteenth Centuries*, ed. Marcus C. Levitt, Dictionary of Literary Biography, vol. 150 (Detroit: Bruccoli Clark Layman and Gale Research, 1995), 43–54.

41. Gukovskii, for example, writes that by 1790, when she stopped publishing and was working on her memoirs and a history of Russia, "she gave up her writing." "The Empress as Writer," 89.

42. "Je vous ai dit mille fois que je ne vous écris point, je jase avec vous." Catherine to Grimm, August 24, 1778, *SIRIO*, 23:100.

43. On this phenomenon in England and the role of women, see Margaret J. M. Ezell, *Social Authorship and the Advent of Print* (Baltimore: Johns Hopkins University Press, 1999). Ezell argues that scholarship on the growth of printing in the eighteenth-century based on outstanding work by Robert Darnton and Roger Chartier has created a progressive narrative of publication that overvalues the significance of publication for the purpose of creating a civil society. The idea that publishing is always better than not publishing, while true for scholars today, ignores the many other social and political relationships created by unpublished writing in the eighteenth century.

44. Catherine even left her "secret" correspondence with Potemkin to be read by her fa-

vorites, to foster trust between the men in her life; this correspondence also involved courtiers, couriers, and routes that pitted political factions against each other for influence, including the privilege of giving Catherine her mail. Smith, *Love and Conquest,* xxv–xxx.

45. Bruce Redford, *The Converse of the Pen: Acts of Intimacy in the Eighteenth-Century Familiar Letter* (Chicago: University of Chicago Press, 1986), 2.

46. In Russia's first biographical compilation of writers, *Attempt at a Historical Dictionary of Russian Writers* (1772), Nikolai Novikov (1744–1818) sometimes notes publication, along with knowledge of languages, the various genres used, and existence of manuscripts. But repeatedly, the most important fact about a writer is the esteem of "many knowledgeable people."

47. Catherine to Marmontel, 1767, *SIRIO,* 13:269.

48. On Catherine's notion of her audience as listeners as well as readers, see W. Gareth Jones, "The Spirit of the *Nakaz:* Catherine II's Literary Debt to Montesquieu," *Slavonic and East European Review* 76:4 (October 1998): 658–71.

49. Joan DeJean, "Classical Reeducation: Decanonizing the Feminine," in *The Politics of Tradition: Placing Women in French Literature,* ed. Joan DeJean and Nancy K. Miller, Yale French Studies, no. 75 (New Haven, Conn.: Yale University Press, 1988), 26–39.

50. She asked both Prince de Ligne and Count de Ségur to teach her; for their examples for her, see P. Pekarskii, *Materialy dlia istorii zhurnal'noi i literaturnoi deiatel'nosti Ekateriny II,* Prilozhenie k III-mu tomu *Zapisok Imperatorskoi Akademii nauk,* vol. 6 (St. Petersburg, 1863), 36–37, 68–70.

51. Isabel de Madariaga, "Catherine II and Enlightened Absolutism," in *Politics and Culture in Eighteenth-Century Russia* (New York: Longman, 1998), 198. For a literary analysis of the artistic structure of the *Instruction,* see Gareth Jones, "The Spirit of the *Nakaz.*"

52. Catherine to Johann Georg Zimmermann, January 1789 (596).

53. The special underground role of memoirs in Russian culture "as a form of autobiography with … a conscience" is the subject of Beth Holmgren, ed., *The Russian Memoir: History and Literature* (Evanston, Ill.: Northwestern University Press, 2003), x.

54. Eidel'man, "Memuary Ekateriny II," 157–59. In Soviet times, the memoirs were transferred from the Imperial Archives in the former Winter Palace, now the Hermitage Museum, to the Russian State Archive of Ancient Documents in Moscow.

55. For example, in the middle memoir she writes that "the first stirring of ambition that I felt was caused by M. Bolhagen … in 1736," as he read the announcement of her cousin's marriage to the Prince of Wales (15).

56. "D'ailleurs philosophe au possible, point de passion ne me fait agir." Catherine to Princess Johanna, 1756, *SIRIO,* 1:72.

57. Quoted in Vasilii A. Bil'bassov, "The Intellectual Formation of Catherine II," in *Catherine the Great: A Profile,* ed. Marc Raeff (New York: Hill and Wang, 1972), 22.

58. John T. Alexander, "Ivan Shuvalov and Russian Court Politics, 1749–63," in *Literature, Lives, and Legality in Catherine's Russia,* ed. A. G. Cross and G. S. Smith (Nottingham, England: Astra Press, 1994), 1–13.

59. Lionel Gossman, "Marginal Writing," in *A New History of French Literature,* ed. Denis Hollier (Cambridge, Mass.: Harvard University Press, 1989), 381.

60. Marcus C. Levitt, "Catherine the Great," in *Russian Women Writers,* ed. Christine D. Tomei, vol. 1 (New York: Garland Publishing, 1999), 3–27.

61. Catherine to d'Alembert, November 13, 1762, *Oeuvres et correspondances inédites de d'Alembert,* ed. Charles Henry (Geneva: Slatkine Reprints, 1967), 205. Veronica Buckley, *Christina, Queen of Sweden* (London: Fourth Estate, 2004).

62. Jean Le Rond d'Alembert, *Oeuvres complètes de d'Alembert* (Geneva: Slatkine Reprints, 1967), 2:148. *Mémoires* appeared in *Mélanges de littérature, d'histoire et de philosophie* (1753).

63. Voltaire first got the idea for a history of Peter the Great in 1737 from the future Frederick the Great, and in 1745 he first approached Elizabeth. Thus his relationship with Catherine had a precedent. P. K. Shchebal'skii, "Ekaterina II, kak pisatel'nitsa: literaturnaia perepiska Ekateriny, V," *Zaria* 8 (1869): 68–111.

64. Catherine to Voltaire, September 1763, *Voltaire's Correspondence,* ed. T. Besterman, 107 vols. (Geneva: Institut et Musée Voltaire, 1953–65), 53:30 (no. 10597).

65. Bil'bassov, "The Intellectual Formation of Catherine II," 27.

66. On Catherine's and the *philosophes'* ideas about the great man in history, see Dixon, *Catherine the Great,* 5–8.

67. Madariaga, "Catherine and the *philosophes,*" 215–34.

68. Quoted in Comte de Ségur, *Mémoires ou souvenirs et anecdotes,* 2nd ed., vol. 3 (Paris, 1826), 43.

69. John LeDonne, *Ruling Russia: Politics and Administration in the Age of Absolutism, 1762–1796* (Princeton, N.J.: Princeton University Press, 1984), viii.

70. An average print run was 600 books; Catherine's primer sold 20,000 copies.

71. To Grimm she wrote: "I beg you to no longer call me, nor to any longer give me the sobriquet of Catherine the Great, because *primo,* I do not like any sobriquet, *secondo,* my name is Catherine II, and *tertio,* I do not want anyone to say of me as of Louis XV, that one finds him badly named; fourthly, my height is neither great nor small." Catherine to Grimm, February 22, 1788, *SIRIO,* 23:438.

72. For a survey of 774 foreign publications about Catherine from 1744 to 1796 in the Russian Public Library's Russica collection, see Vasilii A. Bil'basov, *Istoriia Ekateriny vtoroi,* vol. 12 (Berlin, 1896).

73. Dr. Georg Sacke, "Die Pressepolitik Katharinas II von Russland," *Zeitungswissenschaft* 9 (1934): 570–79.

74. Catherine to Voltaire, September 1763, *Voltaire's Correspondence,* 53:31 (no. 10597). Catherine never forgot Rousseau's criticism, for in a letter to Grimm while she was revising her middle memoir, she cites a similar passage by Rousseau on Poland's loss of liberty. Catherine to Grimm, May 13, 1791, *SIRIO,* 23:538.

75. Catherine to Mme. Geoffrin, March 28, 1765, *SIRIO,* 1:266.

76. Claude C. de Rulhière, *A History, or Anecdotes of the Revolution in Russia, in the Year 1762* (1797; reprint, New York: Arno Press and *The New York Times,* 1970).

77. For a history of French writings about Russia, with both edited texts and correlated passages, see Hélène Carrère d'Encausse, ed., *L'Impératrice et l'Abbé: Un duel littéraire inédit entre Catherine II et l'Abbé Chappe d'Auteroche* (Paris: Fayard, 2003).

78. A revisionist view of much Russian historiography argues that "the dialogue between

ruler and ruled in Russia aspired to be nonconfrontational." Whittaker, *Russian Monar-chy,* 7.

79. On Catherine's coronation festivities, which took place for six months, Richard Wort-man writes that "their magnificence and scale reconfirmed the European character of the Russian court and stunned foreign visitors." *Scenarios of Power: Myth and Ceremony in Russian Monarchy,* vol. 1 (Princeton, N.J.: Princeton University Press, 1995), 118.

80. Richard Wortman, "Texts of Exploration and Russia's European Identity," in *Russia Engages the World, 1453–1825,* ed. Cynthia Hyla Whittaker (Cambridge, Mass.: Harvard University Press, 2003), 97.

81. She was influenced by the linguist Antoine Court de Gébelin's (1725–84) *Histoire na-turelle de la parole, ou Précis de l'origine du langage & de la grammaire universelle* (Paris, 1776), and was aided by Peter Simon Pallas (1741–1811), who published a two-volume edition of *Sravnitel'nye slovari vsekh iazykov i narechii, sobrannye desnitseiu vsevysochaishei osoby* (St. Petersburg, 1787 and 1789), and later by Jankevich de Mari-jevo, who published a revised and expanded four-volume edition, *Sravnitel'nyi slovar' vsekh iazykov i narechii, po azbuchnomy poriadku raspolozhenii* (St. Petersburg, 1791). See Shchebal'skii, "Ekaterina II kak pisatel'nitsa," *Zaria* 6:2 (1870): 17–27; and Friedrich von Adelung, *Catherinen's des Grossen verdienste um die vergleichende Sprachenkunde* (St. Petersburg, 1815).

82. Anatole G. Mazour, *Modern Russian Historiography* (Westport, Conn.: Greenwood Press, 1975), 33.

83. Shchebal'skii, "Ekaterina II kak pisatel'nitsa," *Zaria* 3 (1870): 10–14.

84. "Qui est ce meilleur poète et ce meilleur historien de mon empire? Ce n'est pas moi pour sûr, n'ayant jamais fait ni vers ni histoire." Catherine to Grimm, August 24, 1778, *SIRIO,* 23:100.

85. L. M. Gavrilova, "Istochniki 'Zapisok kasatel'no rossiiskoi istorii' Ekateriny II," *Vspo-mogatel'nye istoricheskie ditsipliny* 20 (1989): 167.

86. Catherine mentions Ivan Perfil'ievich Elagin, writer and Freemason, in her final memoir, for with his silence he supported her during Bestuzhev-Riumin's arrest in 1758. Her letter of January 12, 1794, to Grimm refers to Elagin's *Attempt at a Narrative on Russia. SIRIO,* 23:589.

87. *Sochineniia* 8 (1901): 5. Gavrilova, "Istochniki 'Zapisok,' " 164–74. Most history in the eighteenth century focused on the ruler, and, like Tatishchev, Catherine believed that because of its size, history, and culture, Russia needed an absolute monarch. In addi-tion to this empirical model, Whittaker also describes dynastic and antidespotic mod-els of history. *Russian Monarchy,* 119–40.

88. "J'en conviens, mais la rage de l'histoire a emporté ma plume." Catherine to Grimm, January 12, 1794, *SIRIO,* 23:589.

89. "Fortunate will be the writer who in a century compiles the history of Catherine II." Voltaire to Catherine, December 3, 1771, *Voltaire's Correspondence,* 80:169 (no. 16442). Voltaire here complains that the documents of history are unreliable and only great deeds will remain.

90. In *An Obsession with History: Russian Writers Confront the Past* (Stanford, Calif.: Stanford University Press, 1994), Andrew Wachtel traces Russian writers' (including Cather-

ine's) willingness to treat their history, long the exclusive turf of professional historians in other countries, as if there was a mystery to the problem of writing history in
Russia. Censorship and lack of access to materials still remain problems today.

91. Its value continues to lie in his discussion of many historical documents that were
burned during Napoleon's occupation of Moscow in 1812.

92. W. Gareth Jones, "Biography in Eighteenth-Century Russia," *Oxford Slavonic Papers* 22
(1989): 70–80.

93. These historians include Sergei Solov'ev (1820–79), Vasilii Kliuchevskii (1841–1911),
and Pavel Miliukov (1859–1943). Mazour, *Modern Russian Historiography*, 115, 138, 146.

94. On the story behind Bil'basov's history, see Simon Dixon, "Catherine the Great and
the Romanov Dynasty: The Case of the Grand Duchess Mariia Pavlovna (1854–
1920)," in *Russian Society and Culture and the Long Eighteenth Century: Essays in Honour of
Anthony G. Cross,* ed. Roger Bartlett and Lindsey Hughes (Münster, Germany: LIT
Verlag, 2004), 202.

95. This biography went through four editions and retranslations, as Castéra unwittingly
collaborated with an English translator, William Tooke. David M. Griffiths, "Castéra-
Tooke: The First Western Biographer(s) of Catherine II," *Study Group on Eighteenth-
Century Russia Newsletter* 10 (1982): 50–62.

96. For example, on Paul's parentage, Tooke writes: "In the mean time the grand duke co-
habited with his spouse; and thenceforward Soltikoff thought he had no longer any
danger to prevent; he now tasted without disturbance or remorse those pleasures from
the consequences of which he had nothing to dread." William Tooke, *The Life of
Catharine II, Empress of Russia*, 3rd ed. (London, 1799), 1:112.

97. Simon Dixon, "The Posthumous Reputation of Catherine II in Russia, 1797–1837,"
Slavonic and East European Review 77:4 (October 1999): 656.

98. Aleksandr Kamenskii, "*Pod seniiu Ekateriny*": *Vtoraia polovina XVIII veka* (St. Petersburg:
Lenizdat, 1992), *Zhizn' i sud'ba Imperatritsy Ekateriny Velikoi* (Moscow: Izdatel'stvo
Znanie, 1997), and *Rossiiskaia imperiia v XVIII veke: traditsii i modernizatsii* (Moscow:
Novoe literaturnoe obozrenie, 1999); P. V. Stegnii, *Razdely Pol'shi i diplomatiia Ekateriny
II: 1772, 1793, 1795* (Moscow: Mezhdunarodnye otnosheniia, 2002); Lopatin, *Ekaterina
II i G. A. Potemkin;* and Smith, *Love and Conquest*.

99. Claus Scharf, *Katharina II: Deutschland und die Deutschen* (Mainz, Germany: Verlag Phi-
lipp von Zabern, 1995); M. Fainshtein and F. Göpfert, eds., *Katharina II: Eine russische
Schriftstellerin,* FrauenLiteraturGeschichte, vol. 5 (Wilhelmshorst, Germany: Verlag F.
K. Göpfert, 1996); Hans Ottomeyer and Susan Tipton, eds., *Katharina die Grosse*
(Eurasburg, Germany: Edition Minerva, 1997); Piotrovsky, *Treasures of Catherine the
Great;* Lurana Donnels O'Malley, ed., *Two Comedies by Catherine the Great, Empress of Rus-
sia* (Amsterdam: Harwood Academic Publishers, 1998).

100. N. I. Pavlenko, *Ekaterina Velikaia* (Moscow: Molodaia gvardiia, 2003); Hélène Carrère
d'Encausse, *Catherine II: Un âge d'or pour la Russie* (Paris: Fayard, 2002); and Alexander,
Catherine the Great.

101. Dena Goodman, ed., *Marie-Antoinette: Writing on the Body of a Queen* (New York: Routledge, 2003); Jo Burr Margadant, ed., *The New Biography: Performing Femininity in Nineteenth-Century France* (Berkeley: University of California Press, 2000).

102. A first attempt was made by Mary Hays, "Catherine II," in *Female Biography; or, Memoirs*

of Illustrious and Celebrated Women, of all Ages and Countries (London, 1803), 2:247–404, 3:1–271. She recycles Tooke's *Life* and Masson's *Secret Memoirs*. She justifies Catherine's love life as no worse than Elizabeth's (her paraphrase of the above Tooke quotation leaves out that Catherine was sleeping with both her husband and her lover when Paul was conceived [2:266]) and like Masson, emphasizes her writings. On Hays, see Anthony Cross, "Catherine the Great: Views from the Distaff Side," in *Russia in the Age of the Enlightenment: Essays for Isabel de Madariaga*, ed. Roger Bartlett and Janet Hartley (New York: St. Martin's Press, 1990), 203–21.

103. Nobles, particularly those of the mostly minor German states, needed the entrée of French to arrange the international royal marriages they aspired to. For example, in addition to Russian and French, Empress Elizabeth knew German and Italian. Throughout the eighteenth century, the Russian court functioned in German and French as well as Russian, while government business was in Russian.

104. For example, for their betrothal: "The ring the Grand Duke gave me was worth 12,000 rubles, and the one he received from me, 14,000." Later: "From my betrothal to our departure, there was not a day when I did not receive presents from the Empress, of which the least was worth from 10,000 to 15,000 rubles, in jewels, money, fabrics, etc., everything that one could imagine. In sum, she manifested great tenderness" (452–53). These monetary details, less evident in the final memoir, were printed in the newspapers.

105. Dixon, *Catherine the Great*, 26.

106. Madariaga, *Catherine the Great*, 5.

107. Smith, *Love and Conquest*, xxxi.

108. Barbara Heldt, *Terrible Perfection: Women and Russian Literature* (Bloomington, Ill.: University of Illinois Press, 1987).

109. *Katherina II in ihren Memoiren*, ed. Dr. Erich Böhme (1920; Frankfurt am Main: Suhrkamp, 1972).

110. The last memoir really ends in 1758, because toward the end, Catherine was off by a year for such things as the birth of her daughter and Bestuzhev-Riumin's arrest. On the dating of this memoir, see also O. Kornilovich, "Zapiski Imperatritsy Ekateriny II," *Zhurnal Ministerstva narodnogo prosveshcheniia* 37 (January 1912): 37–74.

111. The editors note that in the middle memoir Catherine does not know the end of the Baturin affair (1749), but that a letter from her to the Procurator General in late 1773 makes clear that she has followed the matter closely and by then knows how it has ended; she recounts the entire matter in the final memoir (viii–ix). Monika Greenleaf's dating of Catherine's middle memoir is at variance with Pypin's dating; she dates part 1 to 1771 and parts 2 and 3 to 1791. The chronology of the memoirs is central to her argument that Catherine "refashioned her narrative images in response to the shifting literary practices, currents of political ideology, and attitudes to gender that prevailed in each decade" (425). "Performing Autobiography: The Multiple Memoirs of Catherine the Great (1756–96)," *The Russian Review* 63 (July 2004): 407–26.

112. "The princess Catherine d'Anhalt-Zerbst passed her earlier years in rather a middling condition. Her father, the sovereign of a petty state, and a general in the service of the King of Prussia, resided in a frontier town, in which, from infancy upward, she was ac-

customed to the military homage of a garrison; and if, now and then, on her ceasing to be a child her mother carried her to court, to attract a transient smile from some one of the royal family, an ordinary eye could not have distinguished her amidst the crowd which attend on such occasions." Rulhière, *A History, or Anecdotes of the Revolution in Russia,* 3.

113. *SIRIO,* 13:332–36.

114. Ibid., 23:77. She modeled her epitaph on one for her English greyhound, Sir Tom Anderson (Pekarskii, *Materialy dlia istorii,* 70–72).

115. In this memoir, Countess Bruce is mentioned only twice, as her friend and as a recipient of her gifts, and thus a cause of her debts.

116. Catherine to Grimm, April 14, 1785, *SIRIO,* 23:330.

117. "Mémoires commencés le 21 d'Avril 1771," fond 1 (Secret Packet), opis' 1, delo 21, fols. 73v–74, Russian State Archive of Ancient Documents (RGADA), Moscow.

118. Smith, *Love and Conquest,* 9–11.

119. Catherine had no celebration for Paul's majority; she further distracted him by arranging a marriage to Princess Wilhelmina of Hessen-Darmstadt on September 29, 1773, but then not giving the couple a separate court, which she knew from personal experience could be used to meddle against her. Alexander, *Catherine the Great,* 138, 166.

120. Safonov argues that by means of the surprisingly intimate ending of part 1 of the middle memoir, where Catherine writes that her marriage was unconsummated for nine years, she justifies depriving Paul of his inheritance and questions his right to rule by hinting that he is a bastard. However, it was common knowledge that her son might be illegitimate, and she had made the same point in her early memoir, and would make it again in the final memoir. Like Greenleaf (2004), Safonov overlooks the conclusion of the editors of the Academy edition that the middle memoir in its entirety dates to 1771–73, while the revisions date to 1790–91. When we redate the middle memoir, the ending of part 3 (about Holstein) nicely supports Safonov's argument that this memoir certainly relates to Paul's majority. Moreover, Catherine does not mention the Holstein issue in the first memoir, a further indication that the circumstances in which she wrote the middle and final memoirs raised the issue. M. M. Safonov, "'Seksual'nye otkroveniia' Ekateriny II i proiskhozhdenie Pavla I," in *Reflections on Russia in the Eighteenth Century,* ed. Joachim Klein, Simon Dixon, and Maarten Fraanje (Cologne: Böhlau Verlag, 2001), 96–111.

121. She concludes, "Two of the group will die from pleasure, but one does not say their names nor whether they are men or women" (654).

122. Later, she mentions that a secretary has prepared another such examination for her. Catherine to Grimm, July 5, 1779, *SIRIO,* 23:148.

123. Catherine to Grimm, August 24, 1778, *SIRIO,* 23:100.

124. Shchebal'skii, "Ekaterina II kak pisatel'nitsa," *Zaria* 9 (1869): 84–101.

125. *Mémoires complets et authentiques du Duc de Saint-Simon sur le siècle de Louis XIV et la régence* (Paris: Hachette, 1882), 1:xxxv.

126. Catherine to Grimm, June 22, 1790, *SIRIO,* 23:484. François Ambrose Didot (1730–1804) was a well-known printer in France. The editors of the Academy edition cite this passage too, but in an unusual mistake, claim it is Diderot, who had, however, died in 1784 (ix).

127. Alexander, *Catherine the Great*, 352. He was favorite from 1776 to 1777.

128. "Imagine the passion for writing about ancient events that no one cares about and that no one will read." Catherine to Grimm, January 12, 1794, *SIRIO*, 23:589.

129. "Histoire de la Russie au 18-me siècle," *Sochineniia*, 11:521–22. Catherine's response, "Réflexions sur le projet d'une histoire de Russia au 18-ième siècle," *Sochineniia*, 11:560–71. Sénac de Meilhan even compared Catherine to a building in his published booklet, "Comparaison de St. Pierre de Rome avec Catherine II. St. Petersbourg, 1791," *Sochineniia*, 11:543–44.

130. Frederick's first memoir, *Memoirs on the House of Brandenburg* (1751), goes up through the reign of his grandfather Frederick I (1657–1713).

131. Catherine to Grimm, January 23, 1789, *SIRIO*, 23:470.

132. Frederick II, *L'Histoire de mon temps*, vol. 1 of *Oeuvres posthumes de Frédéric II, Roi de Prusse* (Berlin, 1788), 25.

133. In English, Anthony, *Memoirs*, 299–307. Catherine concludes this memoir with her *Instruction* in 1767. Frederick wrote: "I will speak of myself only when necessity obliges me, and if one will allow it, as Caesar did, in the third person, to avoid the horror of egoism." In his opinion, *Commentaries on the Gallic War* (about 50 B.C.) by Julius Caesar (100–44 B.C.) was the last accurate history, in that it agreed with contemporary sources and "contained neither panegyrics nor satires." Frederick II, *L'Histoire de mon temps*, 10, 6.

134. Frederick II, *L'Histoire de mon temps*, 24.

135. Catherine to Grimm, February 13, 1794, *SIRIO*, 23:595–96. This letter and her financial memoir help date the beginning of the final memoir.

136. Numa ruled Rome by religion and culture, which disappeared with his death, while Lycurgus of Sparta ruled by laws that provided a model for Plato's *Republic*; on the *philosophes'* views, see Dixon, *Catherine the Great*, 75–77.

137. For example, Catherine may have read Brantôme's *Les vies des dames illustres de France de son tems* (1665), *Les vies des Dames galantes* (1666), and *Les vies des hommes illustres et grands capitaines étrangers* (1666).

138. On the political implications of pairing Catherine and Peter the Great, see Dixon, "The Posthumous Reputation of Catherine II in Russia."

139. July 31, 1789. A. V. Khrapovitskii, *Dnevnik A. V. Khrapovitskogo, 1782–1793* (St. Petersburg, 1874), 300.

140. Khrapovitskii, April 27, 1790, *Dnevnik*, 331. In 1790, Khrapovitskii copied her translation of Alcibiades on January 21–22, she thanked him on January 23, she gave him more to copy on February 2, and she was reading the companion life of Coriolanus on February 18, when she called in Khrapovitskii to discuss the use of the expression *hoc age*. *Dnevnik*, 323–25. This suggests that she may have been translating from a Latin translation of the original Greek into French.

141. Khrapovitskii, January 28, 1790, *Dnevnik*, 324.

142. Khrapovitskii, April 27, 1790, *Dnevnik*, 331.

143. *Plutarch's Lives*, trans. John Dryden (New York: Random House, 2001), 2:139.

144. *Plutarch's Lives*, 1:202.

145. Carol S. Leonard, *Reform and Regicide: The Reign of Peter III of Russia* (Bloomington, Ind.: Indiana University Press, 1993).

146. Catherine to Hanbury-Williams, August 12, 1756, *Correspondance de Catherine* 25. In 1755, the King of Sweden and his wife, Queen Luise, sister of Frederick the Great, had unsuccessfully attempted to seize more power for the Swedish throne from the Diet.

147. d'Encausse, *L'Impératrice et l'Abbé*, 436.

148. Here she contradicts Rulhière's assessment about the root of the problem, but not the mixed result: "The care of his childhood had been committed to two men of very uncommon merit, but who fell into a great mistake in attempting to form their pupil after the grandest models, attending rather to his fortune than to his capacity." Rulhière, *A History, or Anecdotes of the Revolution in Russia*, 19–20.

149. Rulhière offers two versions of this story, one in which only Poniatowski is detained by the Grand Duke, and the other in which he locks up Catherine too.

150. Alexander, *Catherine the Great*, 319.

151. Saint-Simon writes: "I call general history that which is indeed general, encompassing several nations or several centuries of church history, or one nation but many reigns, or one distant and far-reaching ecclesiastical act. I call particular history that of the time and country in which one lives. The latter, being less vast and occurring before the author's eyes, must be much more extensive in details and circumstances, and have as its goal to place its reader in the midst of those actors of what is told, so that the reader believes less that he is reading a history or memoir, than to be himself in on the secret of everything that is represented to him, and a spectator of everything that is told." *Mémoires*, xxix.

152. Faith Beasley argues that in seventeenth-century France, in the wake of the Fronde rebellion, which gave women a prominent political role, women especially turned to memoirs and fiction to argue for an alternative to official history that would include women. *Revising Memory: Women's Fiction and Memoirs in Seventeenth-Century France* (New Brunswick, N.J.: Rutgers University Press, 1990).

153. Anisimov mentions this report without a citation. Evgenii Anisimov, *Elizaveta Petrovna* (Moscow: Molodaia gvardiia, 1999), 379.

154. Saturn, one of the Titans, ushered in a golden age in Italy, where he fled after he was displaced by his son Zeus. The final portrait in the Hermitage Museum does not have the two allegorical figures; the sketch is in the Russian Museum.

155. Aside from Caesar's *Commentaries*, Marcus Aurelius's *Meditations*, and Frederick II's *Histoire*, there are Louis XIV's *Mémoires pour l'instruction du Dauphin* for his son. Catherine too wrote instructions for her grandsons.

156. Janel Mueller and Leah S. Marcus, eds., *Elizabeth I: Autograph Compositions and Foreign Language Originals* (Chicago: University of Chicago Press, 2003); and Leah S. Marcus, Janel Mueller, and Mary Beth Rose, eds., *Elizabeth I: Collected Works* (Chicago: University of Chicago Press, 2000).

157. "La Vie de la Reine Christine faite par Elle-même, dédiée à Dieu," in *Mémoires concernant Christine, reine de Suède*, ed. Johann Arckenholtz, vol. 3 (Amsterdam and Leipzig: P. Mortier, 1759); 4 vols. (1751–60).

158. Russian memoirists wrote in French as well as Russian, calling their writings "notes" (*zapiski*). Tartakovskii identifies 700 documentary writings in Russian and other languages in the eighteenth century, with 250 memoirs and diaries by Russians and for-

eigners who had lived in Russia for a long time. The latter documents include travel memoirs, ethnographic reports, memoirs of the French Revolution, and family memoirs. A. G. Tartakovskii, *Russkaia memuaristika XVIII-pervoi poloviny XIX v.* (Moscow: Nauka, 1991), 22–23. The main source is P. A. Zaionchkovskii, *Istoriia dorevoliutsionnoi Rossii v dnevnikakh i vospominaniiakh,* 5 vols. (Moscow, 1976).

159. Catherine titled her autobiographical letter of February 21, 1774, to Potemkin "A Sincere Confession." Smith, *Love and Conquest,* 9–11.

160. Catherine mentions both together in a letter to Grimm, May 13, 1791, *SIRIO,* 23:538.

161. Rulhière, *A History, or Anecdotes of the Revolution in Russia,* 6.

ACKNOWLEDGMENTS

This new translation of Catherine the Great's last memoir reflects the generous, timely support of several institutions, and collaboration over many years with teachers, colleagues, friends, and students. In 1989, in his seminar at Columbia University on Russian memoirs, Robert L. Belknap introduced Catherine's memoirs as part of a rich literary tradition. At Columbia too, Irina Reyfman counseled a new rather than revised translation. The project became a reality in 2000-1, during a leave from teaching at Stetson University and a residency as the Jesse Ball DuPont Fellow at the National Humanities Center, where former NHC trustee Lloyd Cotsen awarded the project a grant for scholarship to strengthen college teaching. Another trustee, the late Kirk Varnedoe, encouraged a trip to Catherine's archives. A Wallace Travel Grant from Macalester College paid for research on the manuscripts of the memoirs in the Russian State Archive of Ancient Documents (RGADA) in Moscow. The extensive Russian holdings at the Columbia University libraries and the NHC librarian, Eliza Robertson, made all other research possible. Edward Kasinec, curator of the Slavic and Baltic Division of the New York Public Library, and Hee-Gwone Yoo shared their knowledge and the resources of a large collection of Russian visual material. Archivist Marina Dobronovskaya performed invaluable services in Moscow.

Sarah M. White intently perused the entire translation. Sharon Bowman greatly improved the opening. Master *dix-huitièmiste* Philippe Roger shared his intimate knowledge of the period. Julie Candler Hayes and Thomas Bonfiglio explained the nature of Catherine's eighteenth-century French and German. Students from New York University and Macalester College in our seminars on French translation and on Tolstoy's *War and Peace* spurred us with their questions about the translation and Catherine.

Simon Dixon reviewed the project at an early stage and suggested several crucial articles and improvements for the preface. Douglas Smith patiently answered the questions of a non-historian privileged to climb the mountain of Catherine scholarship. Other scholars of Russian, French, and German literature and history made invaluable general suggestions that were gratefully accepted: Robert L. Belknap, Ruth Dawson, Gina Kovarsky, Michelle Lamarche Marrese, Peter Pozefsky, Irina Reyfman, and Cynthia Hyla Whittaker. An economist in game theory, Dorothea Herreiner graciously took on the role of the general reader. With a student's insight, Susannah Johnson asked the right questions. Best friend Nancy Workman took time off from having cancer to edit the preface. Monique Hoogenboom kept Catherine in perspective.

Contents

THE MEMOIRS OF CATHERINE THE GREAT

PART ONE   1

NOTE ON THE TRANSLATION

This translation and the annotations follow the edition established by A. N. Pypin in volume 12 of *Sochineniia Imperatritsy Ekateriny II na osnovanii podlinnykh rukopisei i s ob"iasnitel'nymi primechaniiami* (St. Petersburg: Imperial Academy of Sciences, 1907). In the extremely helpful apparatus, the editors nevertheless did not include an explanation of how they modernized her French.[1]

Such a note would have dispelled the myths disparaging Catherine's linguistic abilities not only in French but also in Russian and German. In the eighteenth century, French was not yet standardized; traditionally, typographers served as editors.[2] Punctuation was even less fixed than spelling. Rousseau was among the first to take an interest in the correction of his manuscripts, and he was most concerned about punctuation. Only in the nineteenth century did spelling become an issue of social status and means for social exclusion. The complaints by early French biographers and scholars about Catherine's French reflect this later prejudice. Similarly, eighteenth-century German was not yet standardized; here Catherine's interesting deviations include regionalisms. Eighteenth-century Russian was in great flux, and it was not until the nineteenth century that the status-conscious elite became concerned about correct Russian.[3]

Catherine's critics further posited that her secretaries, writers, and ministers did her writing for her in Russian as well as French. Yet,

Pekarsky first rebutted these arguments as long ago as 1863. In the manuscripts by Catherine that he saw, the corrections by others in French and Russian were limited to orthography and were never substantive. While he found that her Russian contained "incorrect expressions, Germanisms, and grammatical mistakes," he also quotes Catherine as saying that Elizabeth put a stop to Catherine's study of Russian by saying, "That's enough studying for her; she's smart enough without it." According to his source, Catherine "'spoke Russian quite correctly and loved to use simple, native Russian words, of which she knew many.'"[4] As her most recent translator explains, "Catherine's Russian [is] a rare, if not to say unique, mixture of then antiquated expressions, folk or peasant words and phrases, and the esoteric linguistic mannerisms of the Russian Francophile elite."[5] In 1869, Shchebalsky noted that Catherine's French was as good (or bad) as that of Frederick the Great, and although Voltaire was known to have corrected Frederick's French, no one suggested that Frederick did not know French well or write his own works.[6] Clearly, there has long been a double standard applied to Catherine's linguistic ability. Readers can judge for themselves in Catherine's published letters to Mme. Geoffrin, which retain her original French orthography.[7]

In the manuscript of the memoirs, we found the following orthographic habits, of which the first six are common in the eighteenth century:

1. –oi instead of –ai, and –t instead of –s for the first-person singular, which was typical for Catherine ("Je vient de dire que je plaisoit" instead of "Je viens de dire que je plaisais")
2. minimal and inconsistent use of accents
3. "tems" instead of "temps," and the absence of –t in words ending in –ant and –ent
4. double consonants that were officially simplified in 1740 ("jettés" instead of "jetés")
5. uncertainty about whether to hyphenate compound words ("la dessus" instead of "là-dessus")
6. "scavoir" (instead of "savoir"), which was specific to the humanist tradition
7. missing –s on plural nouns and adjectives ("les plus belles maxime" instead of "maximes")
8. rare lapses into phonetic spelling ("vous repartirai" instead of "vous repartirez," or "m'est" and "mais" instead of "mes"), sometimes caused by the awkward insertion of an apostrophe ("s'avoit" instead of "savoit")

9. inconsistent agreement of adjectives with nouns in number and gender ("leurs pretendu vues" instead of "leurs prétendues vues")
10. inconsistent spelling of names

Her vocabulary, on the other hand, is extensive, precise, and almost always correct, and she has idiomatic fluency.

As was typical for the eighteenth century, Catherine used punctuation lightly and inconsistently. Pypin solved this problem with extensive punctuation—especially semicolons—to make sense of the text. In the manuscript, each punctuation mark may have different functions depending on the context. However, periods, which are used sparsely, always indicate the end of a sentence. Catherine inserted commas to emphasize, to end sentences, and to indicate direct discourse. Occasionally, she used periods, semicolons, colons, and quotation marks; there is one exclamation point. She capitalized nouns, as was typical in the eighteenth century, though sometimes this indicates a new sentence. She also capitalized pronouns for royal persons.

There are about forty paragraphs in the whole manuscript of the memoir. Catherine wrote in long paragraphs that are not composed of sentences as we think of them. Rather, her thought unfolds in longer and shorter phrases, some of which stand alone as sentences, but which often function as relative clauses. These clauses may be joined by the word *que* ("that"), or simply strung together by commas.

We paid careful attention to Catherine's punctuation and use of paragraphs. We tried to preserve her cadence in the long sentences and paragraphs as an indication of her style of thinking and her representations of how others think. While much indebted to the three translators who preceded us for solutions to many tricky passages, we wanted to avoid novelizing the memoirs by breaking up the text into paragraphs that followed the plot. Instead, we followed her chronological margin summaries to make paragraphs; as the margin summaries disappeared, we continued to make chronological paragraph breaks using references to seasons, religious holidays, anniversaries, name days, birthdays, and moves between palaces. We also decided to provide summaries at the start of each year, instead of in the margins. When possible, we kept Catherine's punctuation for emphasis, adding it where Pypin had eliminated it.

In our attempt to be faithful to the content, style, and spirit of the original manuscript, we did not change the order of the text, omit anything, or try to improve the text. Pypin omitted several passages relating to Catherine's sex life, and while the contents of those passages have been known from copies and translations, we are the first English translators to restore these passages by consulting the original. Those passages are transcribed below in French, along with a small list of mistakes in Pypin's edition. We aimed for a lexical middle register in order to reflect Catherine's plain, direct prose. We translated such important eighteenth-century Enlightenment words as *esprit* and *caractère* as consistently as possible and retained repetitions. Words not in French are in the original languages, with translations in footnotes where necessary, though Catherine sometimes provides them herself in her text.

We made these decisions in response to the work of the three previous English translators of the final memoirs. The first English translation in 1859 was done quickly from a copy of the manuscript; Pypin catalogs the errors in this copy (710–16). However, the virtue of this translation is that it alone leaves the final memoir intact. In contrast, Moura Budberg's translation (1953, 1954, 1955, 1961), based on Dominique Maroger's French edition of the memoirs (1953, 1959), is an invented compilation of the middle and final memoirs, and is generally unreliable. Lowell Bair (1957) made by far the best translation, reliable and intelligent, with good contemporary English. There are only some omissions and changes, most notably to the opening; it begins with Catherine's arrival in Moscow and then moves back to Peter's biography, without the opening maxim (as does Budberg's translation).

Our translation uses a modified Library of Congress system of transliteration for Russian, without diacritics. Though well-known names of people and places are left as customary (Catherine instead of Ekaterina, Peter instead of Petr, Moscow instead of Moskva), most names are given in their Russian form, with feminine endings for women's family names. Names ending in –skii are rendered –sky in the text but –skii in the notes. For names, Catherine used French spellings and variations, with many inconsistencies, which we have standardized.

Catherine tended to date things using Russia's Julian, or Old Style (O.S.), calendar, which in the eighteenth century was eleven days behind Europe's Gregorian, or New Style (N.S.), calendar. Until 1700, Russia used the Byzantine practice of dating from the beginning of the world (5509 B.C.). In 1700, Peter the Great introduced the Julian calendar, although much of Catholic Europe had long used the calendar introduced by Pope Gregory in 1582. The Protestant parts of the Netherlands, Germany, Denmark, and Switzerland only did so between 1699 and 1701, while Britain waited until 1752. Thus Peter's curious decision to update to an already outmoded calendar in 1700 may have been as much political as religious. In 1918, the Bolsheviks adopted the Gregorian calendar, while the Russian Orthodox Church continued to use the Julian calendar. Dates are given as they appear in Catherine's memoirs and in the Russian newspapers of the time; they are Old Style. Russian practice until 1918 was to give dates as Old Style/New Style, especially as they relate to events outside Russia. Dates in New Style alone are indicated by N.S.

OMITTED PASSAGES

Pypin's edition lists variants in the manuscript (750–56). Below, we list errors in Pypin and provide the three omitted passages concerning Catherine's sex life.

197	strike second "Pierre III"; first margin note should read: "Pierre III, son père, et sa mère," not "son père et as mère"
199, 1.26	"inculquer," not "incalquer"
247, 1.22	"Vers la mi carème," not "Vers le carème"
251, 1.32	"renvoyées," not "renvoyés"
253, 1.12	"manqué," not "mauqué"
297, 1.22	"meilleures," not "mailleures"
328, 1.21	"rats," not "srats"
373, 1.32	close quote where there is no quoted material
377, 1.16	"de oui et de non," not "de oui et non"
383, 1.28	"jeux," not "jeu"
389, 1.24	add "1758" to the margin
393, 1.17	"illuminé," not "illuminéc"
429, 1.1	"secondes," not "secdones"
317	omitted passage: RGADA, Secret packet, fond 1, delo 20, fol. 136v Mad. Tchoglokof lui repondit que pour d'avoir des enfans il n'en

étoit pas question, que ceux ci ne pouvoit venir sans cause et que quoique leurs A.I. étoit mariés depuis 1745. Cependant la cause n'en existoit pas. Alors…

322   omitted passage: RGADA Secret packet, fond 1, delo 20, fol. 141v-142r

Sur ses entrefaites Madame Tchoglokof qui avoit toujour son projet favorit en tete de veiller a la succession, me prit un jour a part et me dit, écoutés, il faut que je vous parle bien sérieusement. J'ouvrit yeux et oreille comme de raison, elle débuta par un long raisonnement de choses à sa maniere, sur son attachement a son mary sur sa sagess, sur ce qu'il fallait et ne fallait pas pour s'aimer, et pour faciliter ou apesantir les liens conjugal ou conjugaux, et puis elle se rabatit a dire qu'il y avoit quelques fois des situations d'un interet majeur quit devoit fair exception a la regles, je la laissoit dire tout ce qu'elle voulut sans l'interompre ne sachant point ou elle en vouloit venir, un peu étonée, et ignorant si c'etait une embuche qu'elle me dressait ou si elle parlait sincerement; au moment que je faisait interieurement ces reflexions elle me dit Vous allez voir comment j'aime ma patrie et combien je suis sincere: je ne doute pas que vous n'ayé jettés un oeuil de preference sur quelqu'un, je Vous laisse a choisir entre S.S. et L.N. Si je ne me trompe c'est le dernier; a ceci je m'ecriais non non pas du tout; la dessus elle me dit: he bien si ce n'est pas lui c'est l'autre sans faute, a cela je ne dis pas un mot et elle continua en me disant Vous verrés que ce ne sera pas moi qui Vous ferés naitre des difficulté, je fit la niaise jusqu'au point qu'elle m'en gronda bien des fois tant a la ville qu'enfin a la campagne ou nous allames après Paques; ce fut alors.…

419   omitted passage: RGADA, Secret packet, fond 1, delo 20, fol. 250r-v

Je vient de dire que je plaisoit, par consequend la moitié du chemin de la tentation étoit faite et il est en pareil cas de l'essence de l'humaine nature que l'autre ne sauroit manquer; car tenter et etre tentée sont fort proche l'un de l'autre, et malgré les plus belles maxime de morales imprimée dans la tete quand la sensibilité s'en mele, dès que celle ci aparoit on en est deja infiniment plus loin qu'on ne le croit, et j'ignore encore jusqu'ici comment on peut l'empecher de venir. Peut etre la fuite seule pourroit y remedier, mais il y a des cas, des situation, des circonstances ou la fuite est impossible, car comment fuir éviter, tourner le dos, au milieu d'une cour, la chose meme feroit jaser, or si vous ne fuyés pas il ni a rien de si dificile selon moi que d'echaper a ce qui vous plait foncierement. Tout ce qu'on vous dira a la place de ceci ne sera que propos de pruderie non calqués sur le coeur humain, et personne ne tient son coeur dans sa main et le ressere ou le relache a poingt fermé ou ouvert a sa volonté.

NOTES

1. See for example the modernization note in each volume of Diderot's collected works, on which we have based our comments. *Diderot: Édition critique et annotée*, 25 vols. (Paris: Hermann, 1975–).

2. The editorial role of typographers allowed Pypin to conclude that the first edition of Catherine's *Antidote*, which was published in 1770 without indicating where, was published in St. Petersburg by inexperienced typographers who failed to make the usual corrections. Moreover, because the many mistakes include those typical for Catherine, Pypin concluded that she had certainly participated in writing what was probably a collaborative work. Her authorship of *Antidote* has long been disputed, in part because there is no copy in her hand. The next edition was published in Amsterdam without those mistakes, presumably by knowledgeable typographers. *Sochineniia*, 7 (1901): xlvi–xlviii.

3. W. Gareth Jones, "The Russian Language as a Definer of Nobility," in *A Window on Russia: Papers from the V International Conference of the Study Group on Eighteenth-Century Russia, Garguano, 1994*, eds. Maria Di Salvo and Lindsey Hughes (Rome: La Fenice Edizioni, 1996), 293–98.

4. A. M. Gribovskii, *Zapiski o imperatritse Ekaterine Velikoi polkovnika, sostoivshago pri ee osobie stats-sekretarem, Adriana Moiseevicha Gribovskogo* (Moscow, 1847), 41, quoted in Pekarskii, *Materialy dlia istorii*, 36.

5. Smith, *Love and Conquest*, lii.

6. P. K. Shchebal'skii, "Ekaterina II kak pisatel'nitsa," *Zaria* 2 (1869): 101–2. "One can name many French statesmen (even at the end of the previous century) who knew nothing, and apparently did not want to know anything, about French grammar" (102). "Until her death, [Catherine] did not know Russian grammar (like nearly all her contemporaries, incidentally), but she knew Russian well, especially in the second half of her reign, though incorrectly, yet completely fluently. Catherine's most common mistakes are incorrect use of cases and of perfective and imperfective verb aspects" (119).

7. *SIRIO*, 1:253–91. Pekarskii retains the original orthography for her epitaph. *Materialy dlia istorii*, 70–72.

Note on Noble Families

In the memoirs, Catherine often mentions a person's relatives to draw a quick portrait, to indicate his or her significance, and to explain a situation. These connections constitute the warp and woof of the Russian court, the government, and the military in the eighteenth century, and they are often unspoken because everyone knew them and took their importance for granted. While the index presents individuals, this note provides some background on the history of the complex interrelationships of noble families, which provides an essential window into the world of Catherine's memoirs.

In this memoir Catherine makes particular mention of the importance of Mme. Vladislavova, appointed by Empress Elizabeth in 1748 as head of Catherine's personal court.

> Her name was Praskovia Nikitichna. She got off to a very good start; she was sociable, loved to talk, spoke and told stories with intelligence, knew all the anecdotes of past and present times by heart, knew four or five generations of all the families, had the genealogies of everyone's fathers, mothers, grandfathers, grandmothers, and paternal and maternal great-grandparents fixed in her memory, and no one informed me more about what had happened in Russia over the past hundred years than she.

The essential lore of the history of kinship relations of noble families at the Russian court proved invaluable to Catherine, who was an outsider.

Armed with this information, she could better understand and use the women and men around her.

Individual families formed noble patronage networks through marriage, especially with the czars. Through their marriages and official and unofficial positions, families fought for prestige and power, or access to the ruler and to the distribution of patronage. Most important for Catherine's purposes, they intrigued in succession struggles to promote their candidates and bring down their opponents. Thus in this memoir, Catherine takes a great personal interest in Mme. Vladislavova's knowledge.

The wives of the seventeenth-century czars created two major extended families, the Naryshkins and the Saltykovs. Peter the Great's mother was Natalia Kirillovna Naryshkina (1651–94), and the extended Naryshkin clan included the Streshnevs (Peter's grandmother) and the Lopukhins (Peter's first wife), and came to include the Golitsyns and the Trubetskois. Peter the Great's half brother and co-ruler, Ivan V, married Praskovia Fedorovna Saltykova (1664–1723); their daughter Anna, Duchess of Courland, became Empress. The Saltykov clan included the Dolgorukovs and Apraksins.[1] As Catherine writes in this memoir, "the Saltykov family was one of the oldest and most noble of this empire. It was related to the Imperial house itself by the mother of Empress Anna, who was a Saltykov." When Peter the Great's daughter Elizabeth succeeded Anna in a coup in 1741, the Naryshkins defeated the Saltykovs by adding several members to Elizabeth's senate, in particular Vice Chancellor (later Chancellor) Count Bestuzhev-Riumin and Prince Alexander Kurakin (1697–1749).[2] The prestige, power, and collective fortunes of these two clans changed, but they remained the two most powerful groups throughout Catherine's reign and into the nineteenth century.[3]

The ruthless competition between these two families during the succession struggles after Peter the Great's death abated under Elizabeth.[4] The Saltykovs expanded to include the Trubetskois (through three marriages), and the Naryshkins added the Kurakins and the Golitsyns.[5] In addition, Elizabeth's mother's family, the Skavronskys, provided a way to advance politically and themselves needed to solidify their power with status. Elizabeth married her niece Anna Skavronskaia to Mikhail Vorontsov (from an old noble family). Vorontsov continued his ascent by plotting with the family of Elizabeth's favorite, the Shuvalovs, against Chancellor Count Bestuzhev-Riumin, and succeeded him after his arrest in 1758, where Catherine's memoir ends. Two husbands of two other Skavronsky nieces likewise succeeded to important posts at this time, as did relatives of the Naryshkins, thus leaving the Saltykovs in the background.[6] Under Peter III, the Vorontsovs placed Elizabeth Vorontsova as his mistress, but Catherine cut short their hopes in 1762 with her coup. However, Vorontsova's sister, Princess Ekaterina Dashkova, was at Catherine's side during the coup, and the family continued to prosper under Catherine.

To maintain the balance of power between rival clans, Elizabeth went outside Russia to choose her own candidate as a wife for her nephew Grand Duke Peter. However, she turned to the two main families ten years later. Elizabeth responded to Peter and Catherine's failure to consummate their marriage and have children with a plan so sensitive that it was left out of the Russian Academy edition of Catherine's final memoir. In 1753, Elizabeth's niece Mme. Choglokova proposed that Catherine take a lover and offered her "L.N." or "S.S." Given the central importance of the Naryshkins and the Saltykovs to the ruling Romanov family, Elizabeth had found a respectable and reasonable, albeit unorthodox, solution to dynastic instability by proposing an affair with either Lev Naryshkin or Sergei Saltykov. Thus Elizabeth could accept Paul as a possibly illegitimate future heir. (Elizabeth herself was illegitimate, which had been an impediment to a royal marriage.) Catherine recalls the affair with Saltykov as a matter of necessity in the account of her lovers that she wrote for Potemkin.[7]

In this memoir, Catherine demonstrates how she understood and used this system of relationships in which women as well as men played potentially important roles. Thus in 1757 Catherine arranged a marriage that improved her relations with the Razumovskys, the family of Elizabeth's favorite and secret husband, at the expense of the family of Elizabeth's other favorite, the Shuvalovs. These two families opposed each other in the succession struggle.

> The marriage of Lev Naryshkin linked me more strongly than ever in friendship with the Counts Razumovsky, who were truly grateful to me for having procured such a good and advantageous match for their niece, nor were they

at all upset to have gotten the upper hand over the Shuvalovs, who were not even able to complain about it and were obliged to conceal their mortification. This was yet one more advantage that I had obtained for them.

Catherine leaves the obvious unsaid: both the Razumovskys and the Shuvalovs needed to solidify their relatively recent ascents as favorites' families, and the Razumovskys gained more prestige and power from a connection with the Naryshkins than with almost any other family, thus significantly outdoing their rivals. The Shuvalovs later married into the Saltykovs. Catherine too does not explain that in return for her support, Kirill Razumovsky was instrumental in organizing her coup. Thus, noble family relations provide an essential key to understanding the dramas at court and continuous rise and fall of Catherine's position in the evolving succession struggle that forms the background for the final memoir.

NOTES

1. John P. LeDonne, "Ruling Families in the Russian Political Order, 1689–1825," *Cahiers du Monde russe et soviétique* 28.3–4:233–322 (July–December 1987). He includes charts of the major families.
2. Bestuzhev-Riumin's brother Mikhail was married to Anna Gavrilovna Golovkina (died 1751), whose father, Gavriil Golovkin, was the second cousin of Natalia Kirillovna Naryshkina. Kurakin's mother, Kseniia Fedorovna Lopukhina (1677–98), was the younger sister of Peter the Great's first wife, Evdokiia. LeDonne, "Ruling Families," 298–99; V. Fedorchenko, *Imperatorskii dom: Vydaiushchiesia sanovniki,* 2 vols. (Moscow: Olma-Press, 2000).
3. Neither Elizabeth nor Catherine, once widowed, officially married, but their favorites performed a similar function for the ruling class. John LeDonne, *Ruling Russia: Politics and Administration in the Age of Absolutism, 1762–1796* (Princeton, N.J.: Princeton University Press, 1984), 4.
4. LeDonne, "Ruling Families," 301.
5. Ibid.
6. Ivan Glebov and Nikolai Korf. LeDonne, "Ruling Families," 300.
7. Catherine to Potemkin, February 21, 1774. Smith, *Love and Conquest,* 9–11.

ILLUSTRATIONS

Page xciv: *First page of manuscript of Catherine the Great's final memoir, 1794, RGADA, Moscow, Secret Packet, f. 1, d. 1. 1. 1.*

The Summer Palace (Catherine Palace), Tsarskoe Selo (Czar's Village), View of Her Imperial Highness's summer home from the north side, 1753 (engraving), Mikhail Ivanovich Makhaev. *From* Vidy S.-Peterburgskikh okrestnostei *(St. Petersburg, 1761). Slavic and Baltic Division, The New York Public Library, Astor, Lenox and Tilden Foundations.*

Lake Ladoga

Gulf of
Finland

*Kronstadt
Island*

Kronstadt • • St. Petersburg
• Shlisselburg
Lomonosov •
Peterhof •
• Tsarskoe Selo
Tikhvin •
Gatchina •

0   50 MILES

• Zagorsk
• Moscow

Orenburg •

R U S S I A N
E M P I R E

Volga R.

Ural R.

URALSK

POLISH PARTITIONS DURING
CATHERINE THE GREAT'S REIGN

First Partition, 1772

Second Partition, 1793

Third Partition, 1795

Polish territory annexed by Prussia

Polish territory annexed by Austria

OTHER LANDS ANNEXED BY RUSSIA

Treaty of Kuchuk Kainardji, 1774

Annexation of the Crimea, 1783

Treaty of Jassy, 1792

1795   Dates indicate year of annexation

0   150   300 MILES

Don R.

1774   1774

1783   1783

*Sea of
Azov*

1783

1774

mea
783

Black Sea

C A U C A S U S

PERSIA

La fortune n'est pas aussi
aveugle qu'on se l'imagine,
elle est souvent le resultat
d'une longue suite de mesures
juste et precise qui ont prece-
dé l'evenement, elle est en cas
dans les personnes plus particuliere-
ment un resultat des qualités
du caractere et de la conduite personelle.

Pour rendre ceci plus palpable
j'en ferai le sillicisme suivant
Les qualités et le caractere
Seront la majeure
La conduite la mineure
La fortune ou l'infortune la
conclusion.
En voici deux exemples frapans

Pierre III
empoisonné à Pierna
à Mera meurt deux mois
environs apres l'avoir mis
au monde de Philisie dans la
petite Ville de Kile en Holstein,
du chagrin de l'i voir établi
d'etre aussi mal marié;
Charles Frederick Duc d'Holstein
Neveu de Charles XII Roy de
Suede, etoit un Prince foible,
laid, petit et pauvre, valingud, voyés le
journal de Berkholtz dans le
Magasin de Buching; Il meu-
rut l'année 1739, et laissa son fils

Catherine II

Pierre III, Son Pere, à la mere.

PART ONE

Fortune is not as blind as people imagine. It is often the result of a long series of precise and well-chosen steps that precede events and are not perceived by the common herd. In people it is also more specifically the result of qualities, of character, and of personal conduct. To make this more concrete, I will make the following syllogism of it:[*]

> *Qualities and character will be the major premise.*
> *Conduct, the minor.*
> *Fortune or misfortune, the conclusion.*

> *Here are two striking examples.*
> *Catherine II.*
> *Peter III.*

[*] Catherine wrote "sollicisme" (correctly, solécisme) instead of "syllogisme." A solecism is, ironically, an incorrect form or usage. A syllogism is a logical statement with a major and minor premise and a conclusion.

1728-43

*Peter III's childhood and education in Holstein;
heir to the Russian throne*

The mother of Peter III, daughter of Peter I, died of consumption about
two months after bringing him into the world in the little town of Kiel in
Holstein, from the despair of being consigned to live there and from
being so unhappily married.* Karl Friedrich, Duke of Holstein, nephew
of Charles XII, King of Sweden, and father of Peter III, was a weak, ugly,
short, sickly and poor prince (see Bergholz's journal in Büsching's *Magazin*).† He died in the year 1739 and left his son, who was around eleven
years old, under the guardianship of his cousin Adolf Friedrich, the
Bishop of Lübeck and Duke of Holstein, since chosen King of Sweden as
a result of the preliminary talks of the Treaty of Åbo on the recommendation of Empress Elizabeth.‡

Peter III's education was directed by Brümmer, the Grand Marshal
of the Court and a Swede by birth, and under him were Grand Chamberlain Bergholz, author of the aforementioned journal, and four chamberlains, two of whom—Adlerfelt, the author of a history of Charles XII,

---

* In 1725, Anna (1708–28), by his second wife, Catherine I (1684–1727), the daughter of
Peter I, "the Great" (1672–1725), married Karl Friedrich (1700–39), Duke of Holstein-Gottorp,
heir to the Swedish throne. Peter III was born on February 21 (N.S.), and his mother died on May
15, 1728 (N.S.).

† F. W. von Bergholz's *Journal of Kamerjunker Bergholz, written by him in Russia during the reign of
Peter the Great from 1721 to 1725* was first published in Anton Friedrich Büsching's *Magazin für die
neue Historie und Geographie*, v. XIX–XXII (Halle, 1785–87).

‡ In August 1743, the Treaty of Åbo ended a war begun by Sweden in July 1741 during the
succession struggle after Empress Anna's death in 1740. Under the guise of supporting Empress
Elizabeth during her coup, Sweden hoped to regain Baltic territory lost to Russia in the Treaty
of Nystadt (1721). However, Elizabeth attacked, taking part of Finland, which she ceded in the
Treaty of Åbo in exchange for naming her candidate to the Swedish throne. Adolf Friedrich
(born 1710), prince-bishop of Lübeck (1727–50) and king of Sweden (1751–71), was Catherine's
maternal uncle. In 1750 in a letter, Catherine secretly reassured her mother that "the interests of
my dear uncle are mine." *SIRIO* 1 (1871): 72.

and Wachtmeister —were Swedish, and the other two, Wolff and Marde-feld, were from Holstein.* They raised the Prince for the throne of Swe-den in a court that was too large for the country in which it was located and that was divided into several factions, which hated each other and vied to control the Prince's mind, which each faction wanted to shape. As a result, these factions inspired in him the reciprocal hatred they felt against the individuals they opposed. The young prince politely detested Brümmer and his overbearing way and accused the Grand Marshal of ex-cessive severity; he despised Bergholz, who was Brümmer's friend and toady, and liked none of his attendants, because they hampered him.

From the age of ten, Peter III was partial to drink.† He had to make many public appearances and was never out of sight day or night. Those he liked best during his childhood and the first years of his stay in Russia were his two old valets: Kramer, a Livonian, and Romberg, a Swede. The latter was his favorite; he was a rather vulgar and rough man who had been a dragoon officer under Charles XII.‡ Brümmer and as a result Bergholz, who trusted blindly in Brümmer, were attached to Adolf Friedrich, Prince Bishop of Lübeck and Prince Guardian and Adminis-trator; all the others were unhappy with this Prince and even more with his entourage.

Once Empress Elizabeth had ascended to the throne of Russia, she sent Chamberlain Korf to Holstein to summon her nephew, whom the Prince Administrator sent off immediately, accompanied by Grand Mar-shal Brümmer, Grand Chamberlain Bergholz, and Chamberlain Ducker, Brümmer's nephew. The Empress's joy was great when he arrived. She left shortly thereafter for her coronation in Moscow.§ She was resolved to declare the Prince her heir. But first he had to profess the Greek Ortho-

---

* Karl Adlerfelt translated into French and published a journal by his father, Gustavus Adler-felt (1671–1709), chamberlain to Charles XII (1682–1718). *Histoire militaire de Charles XII, roi de Suède: depuis l'an 1700, jusqu'à la bataille de Pultowa en 1709*, 4 vol. (Amsterdam, 1740).

† Catherine crossed out the following: "He did not have an entirely bad heart, but a weak man usually does not" (750). In her early memoir, Catherine wrote that in 1739, "there for the first time I saw the Grand Duke, who truly was handsome, amiable, and well mannered; indeed, they hailed this eleven-year-old child, whose father had just died, as a miracle" (443). Catherine first mentions wine in part 1 of the middle memoir, in a later addition possibly made in 1790–91 (see introduction) (20).

‡ Dragoon guards were mounted infantry.

§ Elizabeth I (Dec. 18, 1709 to Dec. 25, 1761) succeeded Ivan VI on November 25, 1741; her coronation was on April 25, 1742.

dox faith.* The enemies of Grand Marshal Brümmer, notably Grand Chancellor Count Bestuzhev and the late Count N. Panin, who had long been Russian minister in Sweden, claimed to have in hand convincing proof that as soon as Brümmer saw the Empress determined to declare her nephew heir apparent to the throne, he took as much care to spoil the mind and heart of his pupil as he had taken to make him worthy of the Swedish crown.†

But I have always doubted this atrocious allegation and have believed that the education of Peter III was undermined by a clash of unfortunate circumstances. I will relate what I have seen and heard, and that in itself will clarify many things. I saw Peter III for the first time when he was eleven years old, in Eutin at the home of his guardian, the Prince Bishop of Lübeck. Some months after the death of Duke Karl Friedrich, Peter III's father, the Prince Bishop had in 1739 assembled all of his family at his home in Eutin to have his ward brought there. My grandmother, mother of the Prince Bishop, and my mother, sister of this same Prince, had come there from Hamburg with me. I was ten years old at the time. Prince August and Princess Anna, brother and sister of the Prince Guardian and Administrator of Holstein, were also there.

It was then that I heard it said among this assembled family that the young duke was inclined to drink, that his attendants found it difficult to prevent him from getting drunk at meals, that he was restive and hot-headed, did not like his attendants and especially Brümmer, and that otherwise he showed vivacity, but had a delicate and sickly appearance. In truth, his face was pale in color and he seemed to be thin and of a delicate constitution. His attendants wanted to give this child the appearance of a mature man, and to this end they hampered and restrained him, which could only inculcate falseness in his conduct as well as his character.

Soon after this Holstein court arrived in Russia, it was followed by a Swedish embassy that requested the Empress allow her nephew to suc-

---

* The Greek or Russian Orthodox faith became the official religion in Russia in 982. Although Peter the Great had put the Church under the administrative control of the government in a process of secularization that continued throughout the eighteenth century, the royal family carefully observed church fasts, rituals, and holidays.

† Count Nikita Ivanovich Panin (1718–83) became ambassador to Denmark in 1747 before moving to Sweden for twelve years; in 1760 he became governor to Catherine's son, Grand Duke Paul, and in 1762, a senior member of the College of Foreign Affairs. He opposed Catherine's coup, supporting instead her son Paul for the throne. In a humorous piece, Catherine wrote that Panin would die "if he ever hurries" (653).

ceed to the Swedish throne. But Elizabeth, who had already declared her intentions In the preliminary talks of the Treaty of Åbo, mentioned above, replied to the Swedish Diet that she had already declared her nephew heir to the throne of Russia and that she adhered to the preliminary talks of the Treaty of Åbo, which made the Prince Administrator of Holstein heir apparent to the Swedish crown. (This Prince had had an older brother to whom Empress Elizabeth had been engaged after the death of Peter I. The marriage had not taken place, because the prince died of smallpox several weeks after the engagement. Empress Elizabeth retained tender feelings for his memory, and she gave tokens of her affection to the prince's entire family.)*

Peter III was thus declared Elizabeth's heir and Grand Duke of Russia after he professed his faith according to the Greek Orthodox rite; Simeon Theodorsky, since named Archbishop of Pskov, was made his spiritual instructor.† The Prince had been baptized and raised in the Lutheran faith, the most rigid and least tolerant, and since his childhood he had always been resistant to all instruction. I heard it said by his attendants that at Kiel it had required great effort to make him go to church on Sundays and feast days, and to make him perform devotional acts, which were forced upon him, and that most of the time he acted irreligiously.

His Imperial Highness took it into his head to dispute every point with Simeon Theodorsky. Often his attendants were called in to cut short these bitter exchanges and to calm the Prince's heated emotions. Finally, after much frustration, the Prince submitted to the wishes of the Empress, his aunt, although, whether from prejudice, habit, or a contradictory spirit, he often made it known that he would have preferred to leave for Sweden rather than stay in Russia.

He kept Brümmer, Bergholz, and his Holstein entourage around him until his marriage. Some other tutors were added to these as a formality: one was Monsieur Isaak Veselovsky for the Russian language, who came at first rarely and eventually not at all; the other, Professor Stählin, was supposed to teach him math and history, but in truth played with him and practically served as his buffoon. The most conscientious teacher was the ballet master Landé, who taught him to dance.

---

* Elizabeth's fiancé was Karl August, Prince of Holstein-Gottorp (1706–27), Catherine's maternal uncle.

† He converted on November 7, 1742.

During this period, the Grand Duke spent all his time making two servants, who had been assigned for his personal service, perform military exercises in his private chambers. He gave them titles and ranks and demoted them according to his whim. These were truly the games of a child and of perpetual childishness. In general he was still very much a child, although he turned sixteen in 1744 when the Russian court was in Moscow.

1744

Catherine's arrival in Russia; Bestuzhev-Riumin and court factions; her illness; her mother's politics at court; her profession of the Orthodox faith and betrothal to Peter; trip to Kiev; Catherine's debts; Peter has measles, then smallpox

That year, Catherine II arrived with her mother in Moscow on February 9. At that time, the Russian court was divided into two large factions or parties. The leader of the first group, who had begun to recover from his weakened position, was Vice Chancellor Bestuzhev-Riumin. He was infinitely more feared than loved, exceedingly scheming, suspicious, willful, and daring, rather tyrannical in his principles, an implacable enemy, but a friend to his friends, whom he abandoned only when they turned their backs on him, and otherwise hard to get along with and often overly exacting. He was in charge of the department of foreign affairs. Having battled with the Empress's entourage, he had lost ground before the journey to Moscow, but had begun to recover. He supported the courts of Vienna, Saxony, and England. The arrival of Catherine II and her mother gave him no pleasure. It was the secret work of the faction opposed to him. The enemies of Count Bestuzhev were numerous, but he made them all tremble. He had the advantage over them in his position and his character, which gave him immense influence in the politics of the antechamber.

The party opposed to Bestuzhev supported France, its ally Sweden, and the King of Prussia. The Marquis de La Chétardie was its soul and the Holstein court its ringleaders; they had won over Lestocq, one of the principal actors of the revolution that had placed the late Empress Elizabeth on the throne of Russia. Lestocq was greatly trusted by Elizabeth. He had been her personal surgeon since the death of Empress Catherine I, to whom he had also been devoted, and had rendered essential services to both mother and daughter. He lacked neither intelligence, shrewdness, nor capacity for intrigue, but he was malicious and had a black and evil heart. All these foreigners aided one another and promoted Count Mikhail

Vorontsov, who had also taken part in the coup d'état and had accompanied Elizabeth the night she took the throne. She had made him marry the niece of Empress Catherine I, Countess Anna Karlovna Skavronskaia, who had been brought up in Empress Elizabeth's household and was very devoted to the Empress. This faction also included Count Alexander Rumiantsev, father of the Marshal who had signed the Treaty of Åbo with Sweden, about which Bestuzhev had been little consulted. The faction also counted upon the Procurator General Prince Trubetskoi, upon the whole Trubetskoi family and, consequently, upon the Prince of Hessen-Hamburg, who had married a princess of this family. The Prince of Hessen-Hamburg, who at the time was highly regarded, was nothing by himself, and his influence came from the large family of his wife, whose father and mother were still alive; the latter was highly respected.* The rest of the Empress's entourage then consisted of the Shuvalov family, who opposed in all matters the Grand Master of the Hunt Razumovsky and a bishop, who for the moment was the leading favorite. Count Bestuzhev knew how to exploit the Shuvalovs, but his principal supporter was Baron Cherkasov, Secretary of the Cabinet to the Empress, who had already served in Peter I's cabinet.† He was a rough and headstrong man who wanted order and justice, and to run everything by the rules. The rest of the court chose one faction or the other according to their interests or daily opinions.

The Grand Duke appeared to rejoice at the arrival of my mother and myself. I was in my fifteenth year. During the first ten days he paid me much attention. Even then and in that short time, I saw and understood that he did not care much for the nation that he was destined to rule, and that he clung to Lutheranism, did not like his entourage, and was very childish. I remained silent and listened, and this gained me his trust. I remember him telling me that among other things, what pleased him most about me was that I was his second cousin,‡ and that because I was related to him, he could speak to me with an open heart. Then he told me that he

---

* The wife of Prince Ludwig-Wilhelm of Hessen-Hamburg was Anastasia Ivanovna Trubetskaia (1700–55), whose mother was Irina Grigorevna Naryshkina (1669–1749), second cousin of Natalia Kirillovna Naryshkina, Peter the Great's mother.

† Baron Ivan Antonovich Cherkasov (1692–1758), father of Baron Alexander Ivanovich Cherkasov, to whom Catherine dedicated part 2 of her middle memoir.

‡ Catherine's maternal and Peter's paternal grandfathers, Christian August (1673–1726), Prince Bishop of Lübeck, and Friedrich IV (1671–1702), Duke of Holstein, respectively, were brothers.

was in love with one of the Empress's maids of honor, who had been dismissed from court because of the misfortune of her mother, one Madame Lopukhina, who had been exiled to Siberia, that he would have liked to marry her, but that he was resigned to marry me because his aunt desired it.* I listened with a blush to these family confidences, thanking him for his ready trust, but deep in my heart I was astonished by his imprudence and lack of judgment in many matters.

The tenth day after my arrival in Moscow, a Saturday, the Empress went to the Trinity Monastery of St. Sergei.† The Grand Duke stayed with us in Moscow. I had already been assigned three tutors: Simeon Theodorsky to instruct me in the Greek Orthodox faith, Basil Adadurov for the Russian language, and Landé, the ballet master, for dancing. To make more rapid progress in Russian, I rose from my bed at night and, while everyone slept, memorized the lessons that Adadurov gave me. Because my room was warm and I had no experience of the climate, I neglected to put on my shoes and studied in my bedclothes. On the thirteenth day after my arrival, I came down with pleurisy, which was nearly fatal. It began with chills the Tuesday after the Empress's departure for Trinity Monastery. I had just gotten dressed to go to dinner with my mother at the Grand Duke's, when I obtained with difficulty her permission to go to bed. When she returned from dinner, she found me almost unconscious with a high fever and an excruciating pain in my side. She thought I was coming down with smallpox, sent for doctors, and wanted them to treat me accordingly. They recommended that I be bled; she was completely against this, saying that it was from being bled that her brother had died of smallpox in Russia and that she did not want the same thing to happen to me.‡ The doctors and the attendants of the Grand Duke, who had not had smallpox, made a detailed report of the state of affairs to the Empress, and while my mother and the doctors were

---

* On August 31, 1743, the Lopukhin family was flogged with the knout and sent to Siberia for an alleged plot against Elizabeth; four, including Natalia Fedorovna Lopukhina (née Balk-Polev), had their tongues cut out. The Lopukhins were the family of Peter I's first wife, Evdokia Lopukhina.

† Troitsa (Trinity) Monastery of St. Sergei (1422), 25 miles NE of Moscow, in Zagorsk.

‡ Bloodletting, or phlebotomy, is an ancient medical art that became hugely popular in the eighteenth and nineteenth century. The Greeks thought that the elements of the body were analogous to those of the earth, made up of air, water, earth, and fire, and for centuries it was believed that good health depended on the balance of the four bodily humors: phlegm, yellow bile, black bile, and blood. Purging, starving, vomiting, and bloodletting were used to restore a proper balance.

arguing, I lay unconscious in my bed, with a burning fever and a pain in my side that made me suffer horribly and moan, for which my mother scolded me, wanting me to endure my suffering patiently.

Finally, at seven on Saturday evening, which was the fifth day of my illness, the Empress returned from Trinity Monastery and, coming to my room as soon as she stepped from her coach, she found me unconscious. Following her were Count Lestocq and a surgeon and, after hearing the doctors' opinion, she herself sat at the head of my bed and had me bled. Just as the blood began to flow, I came to, opened my eyes, and found myself in the arms of the Empress, who had lifted me up. I hung between life and death for twenty-seven days, during which I was bled sixteen times and sometimes four times a day. My mother was almost no longer allowed in my room. She remained opposed to these frequent bleedings and said aloud that they would kill me; nevertheless she began to believe that I would not come down with smallpox. The Empress had placed Countess Rumiantseva and several other women with me, and it seemed that my mother's judgment was distrusted. Finally the abscess that I had on my right side burst under the care of the Portuguese doctor Sanchez; I vomited it up and thereafter recovered.*

I perceived immediately that my mother's conduct during my illness had done her a disservice in the opinion of all. When she saw me gravely ill, she wanted a Lutheran pastor brought to me. I was told that I was awakened and this was proposed to me, and that I replied: "What is the use, send instead for Simeon Theodorsky; I will be happy to talk with him." He was brought to me and he spoke to me in the presence of the attendants in a way that pleased everyone. This act gained me great favor in the opinion of the Empress and of the entire court. Another small affair further undermined my mother. Around Easter, one morning my mother decided to send a chambermaid to tell me to give her a blue-and-silver cloth that my father's brother had given me when I left for Russia, because I liked the cloth very much. I sent word to her that she was free to take it, that it was true that I liked it very much because my uncle had given it to me knowing that it pleased me. My entourage, seeing that I gave the cloth against my will and that I had been between life and death for so long and

---

* The *St. Petersburg Gazette* reported that Elizabeth gave her a diamond brooch and earrings worth 50,000–60,000 rubles when Catherine was first bled, and Peter gave her a watch set in diamonds (March 15, 1744) (719).

only recently had begun to improve, said to one another that it was quite imprudent of my mother to cause a dying child the least displeasure, and that far from wanting to acquire this cloth, she would have done better not to mention it. This incident was recounted to the Empress, who immediately sent me several superb pieces of rich cloth, including a blue-and-silver one. But the incident hurt my mother in her esteem. My mother was accused of having neither tenderness nor concern for me.

During my illness, I grew accustomed to keeping my eyes closed and was thought to be asleep by Countess Rumiantseva and my ladies-in-waiting, who talked among themselves of personal concerns, and in this way I learned many things. When I began to feel better, the Grand Duke would come to spend the evening in the apartment I shared with my mother. He and everyone else had seemed to take the greatest interest in my health. The Empress had shed many a tear over it. Finally, on April 21, 1744, my birthday and the beginning of my fifteenth year, I was well enough to appear in public for the first time since that grave illness. I do not think that people had a very positive impression of me. I had become thin as a skeleton. I had grown, but my face and features had become elongated. My hair was falling out and I was deathly pale. I found myself frighteningly ugly and I could not recognize my physiognomy. That day, the Empress sent me a jar of rouge and ordered me to put some on.

With the advent of spring and fair weather, the Grand Duke's daily visits to us ceased. He preferred to go for walks and to hunt outside Moscow. At times, however, he came to have lunch or dinner with us, and then he would continue his infantile confessions to me, while his entourage talked with my mother, to whose apartment many people came and where there were many many discussions. These could only be displeasing to those who were not included, among them Count Bestuzhev, all of whose enemies met at our home, and among others the Marquis de La Chétardie, who had not yet revealed himself as an official envoy from the French court, but who had his diplomatic credentials with him. In May the Empress again went to Trinity Monastery, where the Grand Duke, my mother, and I followed her.

Some time ago the Empress had begun to treat my mother with great coldness; at Trinity Monastery the cause for this became clear. One afternoon, when the Grand Duke had come to our apartment, the Empress entered unannounced and told my mother to follow her into the other apartment. Count Lestocq went too; the Grand Duke and I remained seated by a window and waited. This conversation lasted for quite a while, and as we saw Count Lestocq leave, he approached the Grand Duke and me, who were laughing, and said: "This great happiness is going to end immediately," and then turning to me, he said: "You have only to pack your bags. You will leave immediately and return to your home." The Grand Duke wanted to know why. He responded, "This you will know later," and then went to deliver the message, still unknown to me, with which he was charged. He left the Grand Duke and me to ruminate on what he had just told us; the Grand Duke's comments were in words, mine in thought. He said, "Even if your mother is at fault, you are not." I replied, "My duty is to follow my mother and to do what she commands." I saw clearly that he would have left me without regret; as for me, seeing his feelings, I was more or less indifferent to him, but not to the crown of Russia. Finally the door to the bedroom opened and the Empress appeared with a very flushed face and an irritated look, and my mother followed her with eyes red and wet from crying. As we hastened to get down from the rather high window where we had perched ourselves, the Empress smiled, kissed us both, and left.

After she had left, we learned more or less what was the matter. The Marquis de La Chétardie, who in the past or more precisely on his first trip or mission to Russia had been strongly in the Empress's favor and confidence, found on this second trip or mission all his ambitions thwarted. His speech was more restrained than his letters, which were full of the most bitter gall. Opened and decoded, his letters revealed details of his conversations with my mother and many other people about current affairs; those details concerning the Empress were rather imprudent. Count Bestuzhev had not failed to place them in the Empress's hands, and as the Marquis de La Chétardie had not presented any credentials, the order was given to expel him from the empire.* The Order of St. Andrei and the portrait of the Empress were taken from him, and he was left with the other gifts of jewelry that this Princess had given him. I do not know if my mother succeeded in excusing herself in the Empress's mind, but it happened that we did not leave; but my mother continued to be treated very coldly and with great reserve. I do not know what had been said be-

---

* France restored relations with Russia in 1739, and de La Chétardie was the French envoy from 1739 to 1742, when he supported Elizabeth's coup for the purpose of furthering France's interests in Russia, which centered on weakening Russia's alliance with Austria, France's enemy. De La Chétardie left on June 6, 1744.

tween her and de La Chétardie, but I know that one day he spoke to me and praised me for being coiffed *à la Moyse*. I told him that to please the Empress I would wear whatever hairstyle pleased her; when he heard my response, he turned and went off in the other direction, and spoke to me no more.

Having returned to Moscow with the Grand Duke, my mother and I were more isolated. Fewer people came to our apartment and I was being prepared to make my profession of faith. June 28 had been fixed as the day of this ceremony, and the following day, the feast of St. Peter, for my betrothal to the Grand Duke. I remember that during this time Marshal Brümmer spoke to me on several occasions to complain about his pupil, and he wanted to use me to correct or improve his Grand Duke, but I told him that this was impossible and that by doing this I would become as odious to him as his entourage already was. Meanwhile, my mother formed an intimate attachment with the Prince and Princess of Hessen and even more so with the Princess's brother, Chamberlain Betskoi. This liaison displeased Countess Rumiantseva, Marshal Brümmer, and everyone else, and while she was in her room with them, the Grand Duke and I would make a racket in the antechamber, which was now completely ours; neither of us lacked childish vivacity.

In July the Empress celebrated peace with Sweden in Moscow, and on this occasion a court was formed for me as the betrothed Grand Duchess of Russia, and immediately after this celebration, the Empress made us leave for Kiev.* She herself left a few days after us. We proceeded by small stages, my mother and I, Countess Rumiantseva and one of my mother's ladies in one carriage, the Grand Duke, Brümmer, Bergholz, and Ducker in another. One afternoon, the Grand Duke, bored with his teachers, wanted to ride with my mother and me; once there, he refused to budge from our carriage. Then my mother, tired of traveling with him and me every day, decided to enlarge the company. She shared her idea with the young members of our group, among whom were Prince Golitsyn, since named Marshal, and Count Zakhar Chernyshev. They took one of the carts carrying our beds, arranged benches all around it, and the next day, my mother, the Grand Duke, and I, Prince Golitsyn, Count Chernyshev, and one or two of the youngest of our suite sat there, and in this way we completed the rest of the journey quite gaily as far as we were

* The celebrations were on July 15, and they departed on July 26, 1744.

concerned; but those who were not in our carriage rebelled against this arrangement, which greatly displeased Grand Marshal Brümmer, Grand Chamberlain Bergholz, Countess Rumiantseva, my mother's lady-in-waiting, and the rest of the company, because they could not sit with us, and while we laughed during the trip, they cursed and were bored. Thus things stood when we arrived after three weeks in Kozelets, where for three more weeks we awaited the Empress, whose journey had been delayed en route by several incidents.* We heard in Kozelets that during the trip there had been several people dismissed from the Empress's entourage and that she was in a very bad mood.

Finally in the middle of August she arrived in Kozelets; we stayed there with her until the end of August. We played faro for high stakes from morning to night in a large hall in the middle of the house, and the rest of the time everyone was packed in tightly; my mother and I slept in the same room, Countess Rumiantseva and my mother's lady in the antechamber, and so forth. One day the Grand Duke entered our room while my mother was writing and had her writing case open next to her, and he wanted to rummage in it out of curiosity. My mother told him not to touch it, and he actually went jumping across the room away from her, but in jumping here and there to make me laugh, he caught the lid of the open case and knocked it over. At this my mother grew angry and there were heated words between them. My mother reproached him for having upset the case deliberately, while he decried her injustice, and both appealed to me, demanding my corroboration. Knowing my mother's temper, I was afraid of being slapped if I did not agree with her, and wanting neither to lie nor offend the Grand Duke, I found myself caught in the cross fire. Nevertheless, I told my mother that I did not think that the Grand Duke had done it intentionally, but that his robe had caught the cover of the case, which had been placed on a very small stool. Then my mother took me to task because when she was upset, she needed someone to quarrel with. I fell silent and began to cry. The Grand Duke, seeing that all my mother's anger fell on me because I had spoken in his favor and because I cried, accused my mother of injustice and excessive fury, while she told him that he was an ill-bred little boy. In a word, it would have

---

* Catherine writes "Koselsk," or "Kozelsk" in the Kaluga Gubernia, but means Kozelets, in the Chernogov Gubernia by Kiev, where Elizabeth's favorite and secret husband, Alexei Razumovsky, had grown up.

been impossible to take the quarrel further without coming to blows, which neither of them did, however. From this moment, the Grand Duke took a great dislike to my mother and never forgot this quarrel; for her part, my mother also held a grudge against him, and their interactions with each other became awkward and distrustful with a tendency toward bitterness. Both of them could barely hide this from me. As hard as I worked to mollify them both, I succeeded only for brief moments. Each always had some sarcastic barb ready to sting the other. My situation grew thornier each day as a result. I strove to obey the one and to please the other, and in truth, at that time the Grand Duke bared his heart to me more than to anyone else, and he saw that my mother often scolded me when she could not quarrel with him. This did not hurt me in his esteem, because he felt he could trust me. Finally, on August 29, we entered Kiev. We stayed there for ten days, after which we returned to Moscow in exactly the same manner that we had come.

Back in Moscow, autumn passed by with plays, balls, and masquerades at court.* Despite this, we saw that the Empress was often in bad humor. One day when my mother and I were at the theater with the Grand Duke in a loge across from that of Her Imperial Majesty, I noticed that the Empress was speaking quite heatedly and angrily with Count Lestocq. When she had finished, Monsieur Lestocq left her and came to our loge. He approached me and said, "Did you see how the Empress was speaking to me?" I said yes. "Well," he said, "she is quite angry with you." "With me? Why?" was my response. "Because," he said, "you have many debts. She says that one can empty wells and that when she was a Princess, she had no more support than you have and an entire household to maintain and that she was careful not to indebt herself because she knew that no one would pay for her."† He said all this dryly and with irritation, apparently so that she could see from her loge how he acquitted himself of his errand. Tears came to my eyes and I fell silent. After he had said his piece, he left. The Grand Duke, who was next to me and who had heard almost the entire conversation, after asking me about what he had not heard, by his expression rather than by his words gave me to understand that he agreed with his aunt and that he was not upset that I had been scolded.

---

* They arrived in Moscow on September 20, 1744.

† Under Empress Anna, Elizabeth had her unlimited yearly support cut to 30,000 rubles annually.

This was indeed his method, and by this he hoped to please the Empress by imitating her opinion when she was angry with someone. As for my mother, when she learned of the situation she said that this was only one more attempt to loosen her hold on me, and since I had been encouraged to act without consulting her, she washed her hands of the affair; thus both lined up against me. As for me, I wanted to put my affairs in order immediately, and the next day I requested my accounts. They showed that I owed seventeen thousand rubles; before leaving Moscow for Kiev, the Empress had sent me fifteen thousand rubles and a large coffer of simple cloths, but I had to be richly dressed. In sum, then, I owed two thousand rubles; this did not seem to me an excessive amount. A variety of causes had forced these expenditures upon me. *Primo,* I had arrived in Russia very poorly outfitted; though I had three or four outfits, I was at the end of the world, and at a court where one changed outfits three times a day. A dozen chemises made up all my lingerie; I used my mother's bed linens. *Secondo,* I had been told that they liked presents in Russia and that with generosity one made friends and became likable. *Tertio,* the most spendthrift woman in Russia, Countess Rumiantseva, had been placed in my company. Always surrounded by merchants, she presented me daily with piles of things that she encouraged me to purchase from these vendors, things I often only bought to give to her because she craved them. The Grand Duke as well cost me a great deal because he was greedy for presents. My mother's ill humor was also easily pacified by things that pleased her, and as she was then often angry and especially with me, I did not fail to use this method once I had discovered it.

My mother's ill humor derived in part from the fact that she was thoroughly in the bad graces of the Empress, who often mortified and humiliated her. Moreover, my mother, whom I had always obeyed, did not see without displeasure that I preceded her, which I avoided everywhere that I could, but which was impossible in public.* In general I had made it a rule to show her the greatest respect and deference possible, but all this did not help me much, and on every occasion some bitter remark escaped her, which neither did her much good nor disposed people in her favor. With her repeated comments and much gossiping, Countess Rumiantseva along with many others contributed enormously to putting my mother in

---

* As Grand Duchess, Catherine outranked Princess Johanna at public ceremonies.

the Empress's bad graces. The eight-seat carriage on the journey to Kiev played an important role in all this. All the older people had been excluded from it, all the young ones invited. God knows what meaning had been ascribed to this arrangement, which was at heart innocent. What was apparent was that it had upset all those who should have been invited because of their rank and had seen preference shown to the most amusing. The basic reason for all these complaints against my mother derived from the fact that Betskoi, whom she had decided to trust, and the Trubetskois had not been invited on the journey to Kiev, and Brümmer and Countess Rumiantseva surely had a hand in this. The carriage for eight, into which they had not been invited by my mother, was a kind of revenge.

In November the Grand Duke came down with measles; as I had not had them, precautions were taken to prevent my infection. The prince's entourage did not come to our rooms, and all entertainment ceased. As soon as the illness had passed and winter set in, we left Moscow for Petersburg in sleds, my mother and I in one, the Grand Duke and Count Brümmer in another.* On December 18, we celebrated the Empress's birthday at Tver, from which we departed the following day. Halfway through our journey, in the town of Shotilova, the Grand Duke fell ill one evening while in my room. They took him to his own room and put him to bed; he had a high fever during the night. The following day at noon my mother and I went to his room to see him, but hardly had I passed the threshold, when Count Brümmer came toward me and told me to go no farther. I wanted to know the reason and he told me that smallpox sores had just appeared on the Grand Duke. As I had not had it, my mother led me quickly from the room, and it was decided that my mother and I would leave the same day for Petersburg, leaving the Grand Duke and his entourage at Shotilova. Countess Rumiantseva and my mother's lady-in-waiting would stay there as well to care for the patient. A message had been sent to the Empress, who had gone ahead of us and was already in Petersburg. At some distance from Novgorod we met the Empress, who, having learned that the Grand Duke had come down with smallpox, was returning from Petersburg to go meet him in Shotilova, where she lodged for the duration of his illness. As soon as the Empress saw us, although it was the middle of the night, she had her sled and ours stopped and asked us for news about the Grand Duke's state.

* December 15, 1744.

My mother told her everything that she knew about it, after which the Empress ordered her driver to go, and we too continued our journey and arrived in Novgorod around morning. It was a Sunday. I went to mass, after which we had lunch, and when we were going to leave, Chamberlain Prince Golitsyn and gentleman of the bedchamber Count Zakhar Chernyshev, who were coming from Moscow and going to Petersburg, arrived; my mother became angry with Prince Golitsyn, as he was traveling with Count Chernyshev, who had committed I know not what treachery. She claimed he was a dangerous man whom we should avoid and who fabricated stories at will. She gave both the cold shoulder, but since this rejection caused us deadly boredom, and since we had no choice as they were more educated and better conversationalists than the others, I did not participate in this sulking, which brought me several angry reproaches from my mother.

Finally we arrived in Petersburg, where we were lodged in one of the houses adjoining the court.* The palace at that time not being large enough for even the Grand Duke to stay there, he occupied a house located between the palace and ours. My apartment was to the left of the stairs, my mother's to the right. As soon as my mother saw this arrangement, she became angry, *primo,* because it seemed to her that my apartment was better furnished than hers; *secondo,* because hers was separated from mine by an adjoining room. In fact each of us had four rooms, two in front and two on the courtyard. Thus the rooms were equal, identically furnished in blue and red cloth, but here is what upset her the most. In Moscow, Countess Rumiantseva had brought me the plan of this house on the part of the Empress, forbidding me to speak of it and counseling me on where we should reside. There was no choice to make, as the two apartments were the same. I said this to the Countess, who made me understand that the Empress would prefer that I have my own apartment rather than lodging, as in Moscow, in the same one as my mother. This arrangement pleased me as well because I was quite uncomfortable in my mother's apartment and in truth, the intimate company that she had assembled pleased me all the less when I saw as clear as day that no one liked these people. My mother caught wind of the plan that I had been shown; she spoke to me about it and I told her the whole truth about how it had happened. She scolded me for having kept it secret

* December 27, 1744.

from her. I told her that I had been forbidden to speak about it, but she did not find this reason satisfactory, and in general I saw that day by day she grew more irritated with me and that she had fallen out with just about everyone, so that she hardly ever came to lunch or dinner, but was served in her apartment. For my part, I visited her three or four times a day.

1745

Catherine's education; her mother's continued political difficulties;
Catherine's personal entourage; her wedding; her mother's
departure; dismissal of Mlle. Zhukova from her court

I used the rest of the time to learn Russian and play the harpsichord, and I bought myself books, so that at fifteen years of age I was isolated in my room and rather studious for my age. At the end of our stay in Moscow, a Swedish embassy arrived, led by Senator Cederkreutz.* A short time later, Count Gyllenborg arrived as well, to announce to the Empress the marriage of the Royal Prince of Sweden, my mother's brother, with a Prussian princess.† We knew Count Gyllenborg. We had seen him in Hamburg, where he had come with many other Swedes upon the departure of the Royal Prince for Sweden. He was a man of great intelligence who was no longer young and whom my mother esteemed greatly. For my part, I was somewhat in his debt because in Hamburg, seeing that my mother paid little or no attention to me, he had told her that she was wrong and that I was certainly a child far beyond my years. Once in Petersburg, he came to visit us, and as in Hamburg, where he had always told me that I had a very philosophical turn of mind, he asked me how my philosophy was faring in the whirlwind in which I had landed. I told him what I was doing in my room. He told me that a philosopher of fifteen could not yet know herself and that I was surrounded by so many pitfalls that it was greatly to be feared that I would stumble unless my soul was of an utterly superior mettle, that I had to nourish it with the best readings possible, and to this end he recommended to me: Plutarch's lives of illustrious men, the life of Cicero (by Middleton) and *The Cause of the*

---

* October 8, 1744.

† The Royal Prince of Sweden Adolf Friedrich married Princess Luise Ulrike (1720–82), sister of Frederick the Great. Count Henning Adolf Gyllenborg (1713–75) was the nephew of the Swedish foreign minister, Karl Gyllenborg.

Grandeur and Decline of the Roman Republic by Montesquieu.* I immediately sent for these books, which were difficult to find in Petersburg at that time, and I told him that I was going to compose my portrait such as I knew myself so that he could see whether or not I knew myself.† I actually did put in writing my portrait, which I entitled "Portrait of the Philosopher at Age Fifteen," and I gave it to him. Many years later, namely in the year 1758, I found this work and was astonished by the depth of self-knowledge that it contained. Unfortunately I burned it that same year along with all my other papers, fearing to keep a single one in my apartment during the unfortunate affair of Count Bestuzhev. Count Gyllenborg returned my work to me a few days later; I do not know if he had a copy made. He joined to it a dozen pages of reflections concerning me, in which he attempted to fortify in me spiritual strength and firm will as well as other qualities of heart and mind. I read and reread his words a number of times, I absorbed them and resolved quite seriously to follow his advice. I promised this to myself, and when I have promised myself something I cannot recall ever having failed to do it. Later I returned Count Gyllenborg's pages to him as he had asked me, and I swear that they greatly aided in forming and fortifying the mettle of my mind and my soul.

At the beginning of February the Empress returned with the Grand Duke from Shotilova. As soon as we were told that she had arrived, we went to greet her and met her in the great hall between four and five in the evening, more or less in darkness. Despite this I was almost frightened to see the Grand Duke, who had grown a great deal but whose physiognomy was unrecognizable. All of his features were enlarged, his face was still completely swollen, and one saw that he would doubtless be quite

---

* Plutarch's *Parallel Lives of the Noble Grecians and Romans* (100 A.D., probably in the 1559 French translation by Jasques Amyot, *Les vies des hommes illustres comparées l'une avec l'autre par Plutarque*), *The Character and Conduct of Cicero, considered, from the history of his life, by the Reverend Dr. Middleton* (1741, probably in the 1743 French translation by Abbé Prévost, because the German translation by T. J. Dusch appeared only in 1757–59), and Baron de Montesquieu's (1689–1755) *Considerations on the Causes of the Greatness of the Romans and their Decline* (1734) (*Considérations sur les causes de la grandeur des Romains et de leur décadence*).

† In part 1 of the middle memoir, Catherine writes: "I promised him to read them and actually did look for them; I found the life of Cicero in German and read a couple of pages; then I was brought *The Cause of the Grandeur and Decline of the Roman Republic* [sic]. When I began to read, it led me to reflect, but I could not read it straight through because it made me yawn, but I said: what a fine book, and tossed it aside to continue getting dressed. I was not able to find Plutarch's life of illustrious men; I read it only two years later" (61).

scarred. As his hair had been cut, he wore an immense wig that disfigured him all the more. He approached me and asked if I found it hard to recognize him. I stammered my congratulations on his recovery, but in truth he had become hideous.

The ninth of February marked a year since my arrival at the Russian court. On February 10, 1745, the Empress celebrated the Grand Duke's birthday; he began his seventeenth year. She dined with me alone on the throne; the Grand Duke did not appear in public that day nor for a long time thereafter. There was no hurry to exhibit him in the state in which smallpox had left him. The Empress complimented me a great deal during this dinner.* She told me that the letters that I had written in Russian to her in Shotilova had brought her great pleasure (in truth, they were composed by Monsieur Adadurov, but I had copied them in my hand) and that she knew I was studying hard to learn the language of the country. She spoke to me in Russian and wanted me to respond in this language, which I did, and then she was happy to praise my good pronunciation. She let me know that I had become prettier since my illness in Moscow. In a word, during the entire meal she only sought to show me signs of her generosity and affection. I returned to my apartment from my dinner very gay and very happy, and everyone congratulated me on this meal. The Empress had brought to her apartment the portrait of me that the painter Caravaque had begun, and she kept it in her room. It is the same one that the sculptor Falconet brought with him to France; it was a vivid likeness of me at that time.† To go to mass or the Empress's apartment, my mother and I had to pass through the Grand Duke's apartment, which was near my own; consequently, we saw him often. He would also come to my apartment in the evening to pass the time, but without any eagerness. On the contrary, he was quite happy to find some pretext to avoid this and stay in his apartment, left to his usual childishness, of which I have already spoken.

Shortly after the arrival of the Empress and the Grand Duke in Petersburg, my mother suffered a violent disappointment that she could not

* Dinner is in the afternoon and supper in the evening.
† Louis Caravaque (1684–1754) lived in Russia (1716–54) and painted numerous portraits of Elizabeth and her family. On Diderot's recommendation, the sculptor Etienne-Maurice Falconet (1716–91) came to St. Petersburg (1766–78), where he made the equestrian statue of Peter the Great (named the *Bronze Horseman,* after Alexander Pushkin's poem), unveiled in 1782 with the Latin inscription, "To Peter I from Catherine II."

hide. Here is what happened. Prince August, my mother's brother, had written to her in Kiev to communicate his desire to come to Russia. My mother had been informed that the only objective of this journey was to have Prince August receive the administration of Holstein when the Grand Duke attained his majority, the date of which some sought to move up. In other words, in the name of the Grand Duke, now of age, they wished to remove guardianship from the elder brother, who had become Royal Prince of Sweden, in order to transfer the administration of Holstein to Prince August, the younger brother of my mother and of the Royal Prince of Sweden. This plot had been hatched by the Holstein party, allied with the Danes, in opposition to the Royal Prince of Sweden, because the Danes could not pardon this Prince for having gained Sweden at the expense of the Royal Prince of Denmark, whom the Dalecarlians had wanted to elect as the successor to the Swedish throne. My mother responded to her brother Prince August from Kozelets that instead of joining in these plots, which pushed him to act against his brother, he would do better to act in the service of Holland, where he was, and to be killed with honor, than to conspire against his brother and join his sister's enemies in Russia. My mother meant by enemies Count Bestuzhev, who supported this plot in order to undermine Brümmer and all the other friends of the Royal Prince of Sweden, guardian of Holstein for the Grand Duke.[*] This letter was opened and read by Count Bestuzhev and by the Empress, who were not at all happy with my mother and already very upset with the Royal Prince of Sweden who, led by his wife, the King of Prussia's sister, had let himself be ruled by all the interests of the French party, which were completely contrary to those of Russia. They condemned his ingratitude and accused my mother of lacking love for her younger brother for having written that he should get himself killed, an expression they found harsh and inhumane, while with her friends, my mother boasted of having used a firm and well-turned expression. The result of all this was that with no regard for my mother's wishes, or rather, to hurt her and spite the entire Holstein-Swedish party, Count Bestuzhev obtained permission for Prince August of Holstein to come to Petersburg unbeknownst to my mother.[†] When she learned that

---

[*] On the heels of the recent war with Sweden, which had concluded with the Treaty of Åbo in 1743, Bestuzhev worked to limit Sweden's power.

[†] Prince August Friedrich (1711–85) arrived in February 1745.

he was on his way, my mother was extremely angry and distressed, and received him coldly, but he, pushed by Bestuzhev, went his own way. The Empress was persuaded to receive him well, which she did in public; however, this did not last and could not last, as Prince August was by himself not a distinguished person. His appearance alone did not speak well for him. He was very small and badly proportioned, with little intelligence, hot tempered, and in addition, was ruled by his entourage, who were themselves nothing at all. Her brother's stupidity, to put it frankly, greatly upset my mother; in a word, she was almost desperate over his arrival. Count Bestuzhev killed many birds with one stone when he took hold of this Prince's mind with the help of his entourage. He could not fail to see that the Grand Duke hated Brümmer as much as he did; Prince August did not like him either, because he was devoted to the Prince of Sweden. Under the pretext of a family relationship and as a Holsteinian, the Prince ingratiated himself with the Grand Duke by continually talking to him about Holstein and discussing his approaching majority with him, so that the Prince brought him to the point where he pressed his aunt and Count Bestuzhev to move forward the declaration of his majority. To do this required the consent of the Roman Emperor, who was at that time Charles VII of the House of Bavaria, but he died while all this was going on, and the affair dragged on until the election of Francis I.* Having received Prince August rather badly and having shown little consideration for him, my mother thereby diminished the little respect that the Grand Duke had retained for her.

At the same time, Prince August as well as the old chamber valets, favorites of the Grand Duke, apparently so feared my future influence that they often discussed with this Prince the manner in which he should treat his wife. Romberg, a former Swedish dragoon, told him that his wife didn't dare breathe in front of him or meddle in his affairs, and that if she simply wanted to open her mouth he ordered her to be quiet, that it was he who was the master of the house, and that it was shameful for a husband to let himself be dominated by his wife like a ninny. The Grand Duke was naturally as discreet as a cannon blast, and when he had a heavy heart and something on his mind, he could not wait to recount it to those

---

* Peter attained his majority on June 17, 1745. Charles VII (1697–1745) was the elector of Bavaria (1726–45) and Holy Roman Emperor (1742–45). Francis I (1708–65) was Holy Roman Emperor from 1745 to 1765.

with whom he was accustomed to speak, without considering to whom he spoke. Indeed, His Imperial Highness himself recounted all these remarks to me with complete openness the first moment he saw me. He always innocently believed that everyone was of his opinion and that there was nothing more natural. I took good care not to share his remarks with anyone, but I did not fail to reflect seriously on the destiny that awaited me. I resolved to show great consideration for the Grand Duke's confidence so that he would at least view me as someone he could trust, to whom he could say everything without any consequences. I succeeded in this for a long time.

Otherwise, I treated everyone as best I could and made it my task to earn the friendship or at least to lessen the enmity of those whom I suspected of being evilly disposed toward me. I showed no preference for any side, did not meddle in anything, always had a serene air, much kindness, attentiveness, and politeness for everyone, and because I was naturally quite cheerful, I saw with pleasure that from day to day I gained the affections of the public, who regarded me as an interesting child who was not without intelligence. I showed great respect to my mother and unlimited obedience to the Empress, the greatest consideration for the Grand Duke, and I sought with the greatest earnestness the public's affection.*

Upon my arrival in Moscow, the Empress had given me ladies- and men-in-waiting, who made up my court. Shortly after her arrival in Petersburg, she gave me Russian ladies-in-waiting so as to facilitate, she said, my active use of the Russian language. This suited me greatly. They were all young, the oldest being around twenty. These girls were all lively, so that from that moment on, I did nothing but sing, dance, and frolick in my room from the moment I awoke until I fell asleep. In the evening after dinner, I would call my three ladies, the two Princesses Gagarina and Mademoiselle Kosheleva, into my room, where we would play blindman's bluff and all sorts of other games suitable to our age. All these girls were mortally afraid of Countess Rumiantseva, but since she played cards either in the antechamber or her residence from morning until night, leaving her chair only to relieve herself, she hardly ever came to my apartment. Amid all these pleasures, I had a whim to assign the care of my

---

* Catherine first made this resolution in part 1 of her middle memoir and later in her epitaph (57).

effects to my ladies. I put my money, my expenses, and my laundry in the hands of Mademoiselle Schenk, the chambermaid whom I had brought from Germany. She was a grumpy and silly spinster who was greatly displeased by our gaiety. Moreover, she was jealous of all her young companions, who were going to share her functions and my affection. I gave the keys to my jewels to Maria Petrovna Zhukova. Having more intelligence and being more joyous and frank than the others, she began to enter into my favor. I entrusted my clothing to my chamber valet, Timofei Evreinov, and my lace to Mademoiselle Balk, who later married the poet Sumarokov. My ribbons were put in the care of Mademoiselle Skorokhodova the elder, since married to Aristarque Kashkin. Her younger sister Anna was given nothing because she was only thirteen or fourteen. The day after I made this nice arrangement, in which I had exerted my rightful authority in my chambers without consulting a single person, there was a play in the evening. To get there it was necessary to pass through my mother's apartment. The Empress, the Grand Duke, and the entire court came. A small theater had been built in a manège that had been used during the time of the Empress Anna by the Duke of Courland, whose apartment I occupied.* After the play, when the Empress had returned to her residence, Countess Rumiantseva came into my room and told me that the Empress disapproved of the arrangement I had made in distributing the care of my effects between my ladies, and that she was ordered to take the keys from Mademoiselle Zhukova and give them to Mademoiselle Schenk, which she did in my presence, after which she departed and left Mademoiselle Zhukova and me with long faces, and Mademoiselle Schenk gloating over the confidence that the Empress had shown her. She began to comport herself arrogantly with me, which made her more foolish than ever and less likeable than she already was.

The first week of Lent, I had a very strange encounter with the Grand Duke. One morning while I was in my room with my ladies, who were all very devout, listening to matins being sung in the antechamber, I received a messenger from the Grand Duke. He had sent his dwarf to ask me how I was feeling and to tell me that because it was Lent he would not come to my apartment that day. The dwarf found us all listening to the prayers and strictly observing Lent according to our rite. I communicated to the Grand Duke through his dwarf the usual compliments and he departed.

---

* Empress Anna's favorite, Ernst Johann Bühren (Biron), Duke of Courland.

Back in his master's chamber, the dwarf—either because he was truly impressed by what he had seen or because he wished to encourage his dear lord and master, who was less than devout, to do the same, or out of thoughtlessness—began to praise highly the devout life that reigned in my apartment and with this, he made the Grand Duke very upset with me. The next time I saw the Grand Duke, he began by ignoring me. After I asked him the reason for this, he scolded me severely for what seemed to him the extreme devotion to which I was given. I asked him who had told him about this, whereupon he said that his dwarf was an eyewitness. I told him that I did no more than was proper and that everyone submitted to it, and that one could not disregard it without scandal, but he was of the opposite opinion. This dispute ended as most do, which is to say that each retained his point of view, and His Imperial Highness, having no one else but me with whom to talk during mass, little by little stopped snubbing me.

Two days later I was again distressed. In the morning, while matins were sung in my apartment, Mademoiselle Schenk entered my room utterly distressed and told me that my mother was ill and had fainted. I ran to her immediately and found her lying on a mattress on the floor, but not unconscious. I took the liberty of asking her what was wrong. She told me that she had wished to be bled, that the surgeon had clumsily cut four times—twice on her hands and twice on her feet—and that she had fainted. I knew that she was afraid of bloodletting. I had not known that she wanted to be bled nor why she needed to be; nevertheless, she reproached me for taking little interest in her health and said a number of disagreeable things to me on the subject. I apologized to her as best I could, swearing my ignorance, but seeing that she was in a very bad mood, I was silent and tried to hold back my tears and I left only when she had ordered me to with considerable bitterness. I returned to my room in tears and my ladies wanted to know the cause, which I very simply told them. I visited my mother's apartment several times during the day, staying briefly so as not to be a burden, which was a major concern of hers, and to which I was so well accustomed that there was nothing I so avoided in my life as being a burden, and I always withdrew as soon as there arose in me the suspicion that I might be a burden and as a result cause boredom. But I know from experience that not everyone has the same principle, because my patience has often been tried by those who do not know when to leave before they have become a burden or induced boredom.

During Lent my mother suffered a real sorrow. Quite unexpectedly, she received the news that her daughter Elisabeth, my younger sister, had died suddenly at the age of three or four years.* She was deeply afflicted by this and I mourned as well. One fine morning a few days later, I saw the Empress enter my room. She sent for my mother and went with her into my dressing room, where the two had a long conversation alone, after which they came back into my bedroom, and I saw that my mother's eyes were very red and tearful as a result of the conversation. I understood that they had discussed the death of Charles VII, Emperor from the House of Bavaria, of which the Empress had just received news. At that time, the Empress was still unallied, and she hesitated between the King of Prussia and the House of Austria, each of which had its partisans. The Empress had had the same grievances against the House of Austria as against France, with whom the King of Prussia was allied, and while the Marquis de Botta, the Minister from the court of Vienna, had been expelled from Russia for unpleasant remarks about the Empress, which at the time had been presented as part of a plot, the Marquis de La Chétardie had also been expelled for the same reasons. I do not know the reason for this conversation, but my mother seemed to take great hope from it and left quite content. At the time, she did not at all lean toward the House of Austria; for my part, I was a very passive spectator in all this, very discreet and almost indifferent.

After Easter, well into spring, I declared to Countess Rumiantseva that I desired to learn to ride a horse; she obtained the Empress's permission for me. I began to have chest pains on the anniversary of my pleurisy, which I had had upon arriving in Moscow, and I remained extremely thin; the doctors advised me to drink milk and seltzer water every morning. I had my first horseback-riding lesson at Countess Rumiantseva's country house in the barracks of the Izmailov Regiment. I had already ridden several times in Moscow, but very badly.

In May the Empress went to live in the Summer Palace with the Grand Duke; my mother and I were assigned a stone building as our residence, which was along the Fontanka Canal next to the house of Peter I. My mother occupied one wing of this building and I the other. At this time all the Grand Duke's visits to me ceased. He had me told by a servant that he was staying too far from my residence to come see me often.

---

* Princess Elisabeth (December 17, 1742, to March 3, 1745).

I was fully aware of his lack of interest and how little I was loved. My self-esteem and my vanity were deeply shaken, but I was too proud to complain. I would have felt demeaned if anyone had demonstrated what I could have taken to be pity. Nevertheless, when I was alone I shed many tears, wiped them gently, and then went to amuse myself with my ladies. My mother too treated me with great coldness and formality. I never failed to visit her apartment several times a day. Deep down I felt a great boredom, but I kept myself from talking about it. However, one day Mademoiselle Zhukova noticed my tears and asked me about them; I gave her the best reasons I could, without telling her the true ones. I wanted more than ever to gain the affection of everyone in general, great and small. No one was neglected by me, and I made it a rule to believe that I needed everyone and as a result to act in such a way as to win their goodwill, in which I succeeded.

After a few weeks at the Summer Palace, they began to discuss the preparations for my wedding. The court left to reside at Peterhof, where people were at closer quarters than in the city. The Empress and the Grand Duke resided in the upper story of the house that Peter I had built, my mother and I below, under the Grand Duke's apartment. We dined with him every day under a tent on the open gallery attached to his apartment; he had supper in our apartments. The Empress was often absent, going to the different country houses that she had here and there. We had a great many outings on foot, on horseback, and in carriages. I saw then clear as day that the Grand Duke's entourage, and notably his governors, had lost all credibility with and authority over him; his military games, which up until then he had concealed, he now basically enacted in their presence. Count Brümmer and his head tutor saw him almost only in public, to follow in his train. He literally spent the rest of the time in the company of valets in infantile pursuits unbelievable for one his age, such as playing with dolls.

My mother took advantage of the Empress's absences to take supper in the surrounding countryside and notably at the residence of the Prince and Princess of Hessen-Hamburg. One evening she had gone there on horseback. After supper I was in my room, which was on the same level as the garden with one door leading to it, when the fine weather tempted me, and I proposed to my ladies-in-waiting and my three maids of honor that we take a stroll in the garden. I had no difficulty in persuading them; there were eight of us, my chamber valet making a ninth, and two valets followed us. We walked around until midnight, as innocently as anything. My mother having returned, Mademoiselle Schenk, who had refused to walk with us and scolded our intended outing, could not wait to tell my mother that I had gone out despite her protests. My mother went to bed, and when I returned with my troupe, Mademoiselle Schenk said to me with a gloating air that my mother twice had sent to know if I had come back in, because she wanted to speak to me, and seeing that it was extremely late and tired of waiting, she had gone to bed. I wanted to run immediately to her apartment, but I found her door locked. I told Schenk that she could have sent for me; she claimed that she would not have been able to find us, but all of this was just a ploy to pick a quarrel in order to scold me. I sensed this clearly and went to bed with much uneasiness about what would come the following day. As soon as I was awake, I went to my mother's apartment and found her in bed. I wanted to approach her to kiss her hand, but she pulled it back with great anger, and scolded me terribly for having dared to go for a walk at night without her permission. I told her that she had not been home. She said the hour had been ungodly, and said everything she could think of to hurt me, apparently to quell my desire for nocturnal outings, but what was certain is that while this walk may have been imprudent, it was the most innocent thing in the world. What hurt me most was that she accused us of having gone up to the Grand Duke's apartment. I told her that this was an abominable calumny, which made her so angry that she seemed beside herself. In vain I got down on my knees to placate her anger; she called my submission playacting and sent me from the room. I returned to my apartment in tears. At dinnertime I went upstairs with my mother, still very upset, to the Grand Duke, who, seeing my red eyes, asked me what was wrong. I told him truthfully what had happened. This time he took my side and accused my mother of capriciousness and excessive anger. I begged him not to talk to her about it, which he did, and little by little her anger passed, but I was still treated very coldly.

Toward the end of July we returned from Peterhof to the city, where all the preparations were being made for my wedding ceremony.* Finally August 21 was fixed by the Empress as the date for the ceremony. As this day approached, I grew more deeply melancholic. My heart did not foresee great happiness; ambition alone sustained me. At the bottom of my

* July 17, 1745.

soul I had something, I know not what, that never for a single moment let me doubt that sooner or later I would succeed in becoming the sovereign Empress of Russia in my own right. The wedding was celebrated with great pomp and magnificence.

That evening in my apartment I found Madame Kruse, sister of the Empress's first lady-in-waiting, whom she had just placed with me as first lady-in-waiting. The following day, I noticed that this woman had already struck fear in all my other ladies, because when I went to talk to one of them in my usual manner, she said to me, "In the name of God, do not come near me. We have been forbidden to talk to you in private." At the same time, my dear spouse paid absolutely no attention to me, but was constantly playing soldier with his valets, drilling them in his room or changing uniforms twenty times a day. I yawned and I was bored, having no one to speak to, or else I appeared in public. The third day after my wedding, which was supposed to be a day of rest, Countess Rumiantseva had me informed that the Empress had excused her from staying with me and that she was going to return to her house with her husband and her children. Neither I nor anyone else greatly regretted this, because she had been the source of much gossip.

The marriage festivities lasted ten days, at the end of which the Grand Duke and I went to reside at the Summer Palace, where the Empress was living, and discussion began about my mother's departure. I had not seen my mother since my wedding, but she had softened greatly toward me. Toward the end of September she departed and the Grand Duke and I accompanied her as far as Krasnoe Selo. Her departure sincerely pained me; I cried a great deal.* When she had left we returned to the city.

Having returned to the Summer Palace, I asked for my lady Mademoiselle Zhukova. I was told that she had gone to see her mother, who had fallen ill; the following morning the same request from me, same response from my ladies. Toward noon, the Empress moved with great pomp from the summer residence into the winter one; we followed her into her

---

* On her relations with the Empress, Princess Johanna wrote to her husband: "Our farewell was very touching; it was almost impossible to take leave of Her Imperial Majesty, and this great monarch for her part did me the honor of being deeply moved." But the English Ambassador Hyndford's dispatch reads: "When she said farewell, she fell at the Empress's feet and begged her with a burst of tears to forgive her if she had in any way offended Her Majesty. The Empress told her that it was too late to think of that now, and that if she had always been so humble it would have been better for her" (Anthony, 158–59).

apartment. Arriving in her ceremonial bedchamber, she stopped, and after several innocuous remarks, she began to talk about my mother's departure and told me with seeming kindness not to be so pained about this, but I thought I would faint when she told me aloud in the presence of about thirty people that at my mother's insistence she had dismissed Mademoiselle Zhukova from my entourage because my mother feared that I had too much affection for this girl who deserved so little, and then with a marked animosity she began to speak extremely ill of the poor Zhukova. In truth I was hardly impressed by this scene nor was I convinced by what Her Imperial Majesty claimed, but I was profoundly pained by the misfortune of Mademoiselle Zhukova, dismissed from the court only because she, by her sociable disposition, pleased me more than my other ladies, for I said to myself, why was she placed with me if she was not worthy? My mother could not have known her as she, not knowing Russian, could not have spoken to her, and Zhukova knew no other language. My mother could rely only on the idiotic reports of Mademoiselle Schenk, who had almost no common sense. I thought, this poor girl suffers for me, therefore I must not abandon her in her misfortune, which is caused solely by my affection. I was never able to find out if my mother truly had asked the Empress to dismiss this woman from my entourage. If it is so, then my mother preferred violent means to mild ones, because she never spoke to me about this girl. Nevertheless, a single word from her would have sufficed to at least put me on guard against an attachment that was basically very innocent. At the same time, the Empress too could have intervened less severely. The girl was young, they had only to find her a suitable match, which would have been very easy to do, but instead, they acted as I have just recounted. Having been dismissed by the Empress, the Grand Duke and I returned to our apartments. On the way, I saw that what the Empress had said had put him in favor of what had just been done. I told him my objections and made him see that this girl was suffering only because they had supposed I was partial to her, and I said that since she suffered out of love for me, I felt within my rights not to abandon her as long as I could do something. Indeed, I immediately sent her money with my chamber valet, but he told me that she had already left with her mother and sister for Moscow. I ordered that the money meant for her be sent to her via her brother, who was a sergeant in the guards. I was told that he and his wife had also been ordered to leave and that he had been placed in a rural regiment as an officer. Even now, I have difficulty finding the slightest plausible reason for all this, and it seems to me that this was gratuitous harm done on a whim without a shadow of a reason, not even a pretext. But things did not stop there, either. Through my chamber valet and my other servants, I sought to find some suitable match for Mademoiselle Zhukova. One was proposed to me, a sergeant of the guards and gentleman of means named Travin. He went to Moscow to marry her if she found him pleasing; she accepted and he was made a lieutenant in a rural regiment. As soon as the Empress learned of this, she exiled them to Astrakhan. It is even more difficult to discern the reasons for this persecution.

In the Winter Palace the Grand Duke and I were lodged in the apartments that had been used for my wedding celebration. The Grand Duke's was separated from mine by an immense staircase, which also served the Empress's apartment. For me to go to his apartment or for him to come to mine, we had to cross the landing, which especially in winter was not the most convenient thing in the world. Nevertheless, he and I would make this journey several times a day. In the evening I would go to play billiards in his antechamber with the Grand Chamberlain Bergholz while the Grand Duke frolicked in the other room with his horsemen.

1746

*Peter a poor husband; Peter spies on Elizabeth; her reprimand;
changes in Peter's and Catherine's entourages; the Chernyshev
"affair"; Catherine's melancholy; trip to Riga*

My billiard matches were interrupted by the departure of Messieurs Brümmer and Bergholz, whom the Empress dismissed from the Grand Duke's entourage at the end of winter, which was spent in masquerades in the principal houses of the city, which were at that time very small. The court and the entire city attended these regularly. The last one was given by the Master General of Police Tatishchev in a house that belonged to the Empress and that was called Smolny Dvorets. The middle of this wooden house had been consumed by a fire, and there remained only the three-story wings. There was dancing in one, but to dine, we had to pass through the courtyard and snow in the month of January; after dinner we had to make the same trip. Back at the house, the Grand Duke went to bed, but the next day he awoke with a severe headache, which kept him from getting up. I sent for the doctors, who stated that he had an extremely high fever. Toward evening he was taken from my bed into my audience chamber, where after being bled, he was placed in a bed that had been prepared for him. He was seriously ill and was bled more than once. The Empress came to see him several times a day and was grateful for my tears.

One evening while I was reading my evening prayers in a little oratory near my dressing room, I saw Madame Izmailova, whom the Empress held dear, enter.* She told me that the Empress, knowing that I was deeply pained by the Grand Duke's illness, had sent her to tell me to have faith in God, to worry myself no more and that she would not abandon me under any circumstances. She asked me what I was reading; I told her that it was the evening prayers. She took my book and told me that I

---

*Anastasia Mikhailovna Izmailova (née Naryshkina) was lady-in-waiting to Elizabeth.

would ruin my eyes reading such small characters by candlelight. I asked her to thank Her Imperial Majesty for her kindness toward me and we parted very affectionately, she to report on her commission, I to go to bed. The following day, the Empress sent me a prayer book with big letters, to preserve my eyes, she said.

Although it adjoined mine, I went to the room in which the Grand Duke had been placed only when I thought I would not be a burden, because I noticed that he did not much care whether or not I was there and that he preferred to be with members of his entourage, whom in truth I did not much care for. Besides, I was not accustomed to passing my time all alone with men. At this point, Lent arrived and I made my devotions the first week. In general at that time I was in a devout frame of mind. I saw clearly that the Grand Duke loved me little; fifteen days after the wedding he had again confided to me that he was in love with 'demoiselle Karr, the Empress's maid of honor, since married to a Prince Golitsyn, Equerry to the Empress.* He had said to Count Devier, his chamberlain, that there was no comparison between this girl and myself. Devier had maintained the opposite, and the Grand Duke had gotten angry with him. This scene practically occurred in my presence, and I noticed his sulkiness. In truth, I told myself that life with this man would certainly be very unhappy if I allowed myself tender feelings that were so ill repaid, and that to die of jealousy was of no benefit to anyone. I endeavored to conquer my pride, to not be jealous at all of a man who did not love me, but the only way to not be jealous was to not love him. If he had wanted to be loved, it would not have been difficult for me. I was naturally inclined toward and accustomed to fulfilling my duties, but for this I would have needed a husband endowed with common sense, and this man did not have any.†

I had fasted the first week of Lent. The Empress informed me on Saturday that I would please her if I fasted again the second week; I responded to Her Majesty, begging her to let me fast all of Lent.‡ The

---

* Ekaterina Alexeevna Karr married Prince Peter Mikhailovich Golitsyn.

† Catherine began part 2 of her middle memoir with a similar discussion.

‡ The Great Fast lasts seven weeks before Easter, the holiest holiday, and is regularly observed by most people. The other major fasts are the six-week Christmas fast, the Apostles' or St. Peter's fast (from the Sunday of All Saints until June 29), and the Assumption fast (from August 1 to 15). Meat and dairy were forbidden, while fish, vegetables, and bread were allowed. No marriages were performed during fasts. Elizabeth was religious, while Catherine observed Church rituals but was not religious.

Marshal of the Empress's court, Sievers, son-in-law of Madame Kruse, who had brought this message, told me that the Empress had been truly pleased by this request and that she granted it. When the Grand Duke learned that I was continuing to fast, he scolded me harshly. I told him that I could not do otherwise; when he was better, he pretended to be sick for a long time thereafter so as not to leave his room, where he was happier than in public court ceremonies. He appeared only the last week of Lent, when he made his devotions.

After Easter he had a marionette theater set up in his room and he invited many people, even ladies. This made for the most insipid spectacle in the world. The room in which this theater was located had a door that had been walled up because it led to another which opened onto the Empress's apartment, where there was a mechanical table that one could raise and lower in order to eat there without servants.* One day the Grand Duke, in his room preparing his so-called spectacle, heard conversation in the other, and in his rash eagerness, he took from the theater a carpenter's tool that was used to make holes in boards and began to drill the boarded door full of holes so that he could see everything that was happening, namely the dinner that the Empress was having there. The Grand Master of the Hunt Count Razumovsky, in a brocaded house robe (he had taken medicine that day), and a dozen other of the Empress's closest confidants were dining there with her. His Royal Highness, not content to enjoy the fruits of his clever labor alone, called his entire entourage so they could amuse themselves by looking through the holes that he had just made with such industry. He did more: when he and those around him had had their fill of this indiscreet pleasure, he invited Madame Kruse and me and my ladies to come to his apartment to see something that we had never seen. He did not tell us what it was, apparently so as to arrange for us a pleasant surprise. Because I did not come quickly enough to satisfy him, he took Madame Kruse and my ladies; I arrived last and found them sitting before the door, where he had set up benches, chairs, and stools for the comfort of the spectators, so he said. As I entered, I asked what this was; he ran to me and told me what was happening. I was horrified and indignant at his temerity, and I told him that I wanted neither to look nor to take part in this scene, which would surely bring him grief if his aunt learned of it, and I told

* Called a hermitage table in part 2 of the middle memoir (83).

him that it would be hard for her not to find out because he had shared his secret with at least twenty people; all those who had been willing to look through the door, seeing that I did not wish to do the same, began to walk away, one by one.* The Grand Duke himself became a little sheepish about what he had done and went back to working with his marionette theater, and I returned to my room. We heard no mention of anything until Sunday, but that day for some reason I arrived a little later than usual at mass. Back in my room, I was going to remove my court dress when the Empress entered looking slightly flushed and very irritated. Since she had not been at mass in the chapel but had attended the divine service in her little private chapel, as soon as I saw her, I approached her as was my custom to kiss her hand, since I had not yet seen her that day. She kissed me, sent for the Grand Duke, and while waiting scolded me for having come late to mass and for preferring finery to the good Lord. She added that during the reign of Empress Anna, although she had not resided at the court but in a house a good distance from it, she had never failed to perform her duties and had often risen before dawn to fulfill them.† Then she sent for my chamber valet in charge of wigs and told him that if in the future he coiffed me so slowly, she would have him dismissed. When she had finished with all this, the Grand Duke, who had undressed in his room, entered in a dressing robe, nightcap in hand, looking quite joyful and carefree, and ran to kiss the hand of the Empress, who kissed him and began to ask him where he had found the temerity to do what he had done, that she had gone into the room with the mechanical table, that she had found the door full of holes, and that all these holes opened toward the place where she normally sat, that apparently in doing this he had forgotten everything that he owed her, that she could only consider him ungrateful, that her own father Peter I had also had an ingrate for a son, whom he had punished and disinherited,‡ that at the time of the Empress Anna, she had always shown her the respect owed to one who wore a crown and who was anointed by God, that that Empress did not tolerate pranks and had those who failed to show her respect locked in the fortress, that he was nothing but a little boy and that she would show him how to behave. At

---

* According to part 2 of the middle memoir, Catherine looked once to please Peter (83).

† At this time, Elizabeth lived under the threat of being sent to a convent.

‡ Alexei escaped to Austria, from where Peter the Great had him lured back to Russia and imprisoned, where he was tortured, and died.

this he began to get angry and wanted to reply to her, and to that end he stammered a few words, but she ordered him to be silent, and got so angry that she no longer controlled her fury, which often happened when she got upset, and she insulted him and said all kinds of shocking things, showing him as much disdain as anger. We were both stupefied and speechless, and although this scene was not aimed directly at me, I had tears in my eyes. She noticed this and said to me, "What I say is not meant for you. I know that you did not take part in what he did and that you neither looked nor wanted to look through the door." This just observation calmed her a little and she fell silent, and indeed it was difficult to add anything to what she had just said. After this she said good-bye and left for her apartment extremely red in the face and with her eyes flashing. The Grand Duke returned to his apartment, and I removed my dress in silence, ruminating on all that I had just heard. When I was undressed, the Grand Duke came to find me, and he said to me in a tone that was half contrite and half sarcastic, "She was like a fury and did not know what she was saying." I replied, "She was in an extreme fit of anger." We discussed what we had just heard, after which we dined together alone in my room.

When the Grand Duke had returned to his apartment, Madame Kruse entered my room and said to me, "One must admit that today the Empress acted like a real mother." I saw that she wanted to make me talk, and because of that I was silent. She continued, "A mother gets angry and scolds her children and then it passes. Both of you should have said to her, 'Виноваты, матушка, we beg your pardon, mother,' and you would have disarmed her." I told her that I was overwhelmed and astounded by Her Majesty's fury and that all I was able to do at that moment was listen and be silent. She left my room, apparently to go make her report. For my part, the *"I beg your pardon, mother"* that would disarm the Empress's anger stayed in my head, and thereafter I had occasion to use it with success, as will be seen later.

Sometime before the Empress dismissed Count Brümmer and the Grand Chamberlain Bergholz from their functions in the Grand Duke's service, when I left my rooms earlier than usual one morning and went into the antechamber, Brümmer, who was nearly alone, used the occasion to talk to me. He begged and urged me to go into the Empress's dressing room every morning, since upon her departure, my mother had obtained permission for me to do this, a privilege that I had taken little advantage of up until then because this prerogative greatly bored me.* I had gone there one or two times and had found the Empress's ladies, who little by little had withdrawn so that I remained alone. I told him this; he told me that this meant nothing and that I had to continue. To tell the truth, I understood nothing of this courtier's perseverance; it might be useful for his purposes, but it did nothing for me to stand about in the Empress's dressing room and still less to be a burden to her. I shared my disgust with Count Brümmer, but he did everything he could to persuade me, without success. I was happier in my own apartment, especially when Madame Kruse was not there. That winter I discovered that she was quite partial to drink, and as she was soon marrying off her daughter to Marshal of the Court Sievers, either she would go out or else my servants would find the means to get her drunk and then she would go to sleep. This would rid my room of this cantankerous Argus.†

Count Brümmer and Grand Chamberlain Bergholz having been dismissed from the Grand Duke's service, the Empress named General Prince Vasily Repnin to attend the Grand Duke. This nomination was surely the best thing the Empress could do, because Prince Repnin was not only a man of honor and of probity, but he was also an intelligent and very gallant man, full of sincerity and loyalty. For my own part, I could only praise Prince Repnin's conduct; as for Count Brümmer, I did not have great regrets. He bored me with his endless political discussions, which smacked of intrigue, while the honest and military character of Prince Repnin inspired trust in me. As for the Grand Duke, he was enchanted to be free of his tutors, whom he hated. Upon parting from him, however, they instilled in him a great fear that they were leaving him at the mercy of Count Bestuzhev's plots, the mainspring of all these changes, which were made under the plausible pretext of His Imperial Highness attaining his majority in his Duchy of Holstein. Prince August, my uncle, was still in Petersburg and overseeing the administration of the Grand Duke's hereditary lands.

In May we went to the Summer Palace. At the end of May the Empress placed with me as chief governess Madame Choglokova, one of her

---

* In part 2 of the middle memoir, Catherine explains that Brümmer wants her to speak to Elizabeth on his behalf (80–81).

† In classical mythology, Juno charges Argus, a giant with one hundred eyes, to guard Io.

maids of honor and a relative.* This was a serious blow for me, since this woman was entirely on the side of Count Bestuzhev, extremely simpleminded, cruel, capricious, and very self-serving. Her husband, the Empress's chamberlain, had at that time gone to Vienna with I know not what commission. I cried a great deal when she arrived and for the rest of the day; I had to be bled the following day. The morning before my bloodletting, the Empress came into my room, and seeing my red eyes, said to me that young women who did not love their husbands always cried, but that my mother had assured her that I had no aversion to marrying the Grand Duke, and that besides, she would not have forced me to do it, but that since I was married, I should not cry anymore. I remembered Madame Kruse's instructions, and I said to her, "Виноваты, матушка, I beg your pardon, mother," and she was appeased. Meanwhile the Grand Duke arrived, whom the Empress greeted graciously this time, and then she left. I was bled, and in this instance I needed it greatly; then I went to bed and cried all day long. The following day the Grand Duke took me aside after dinner, and I saw clearly that he had been informed that Madame Choglokova had been placed with me because I did not love him. But as I told him, I did not understand how they believed they would increase my tenderness for him by giving me this woman. To serve as my Argus was another matter, but for this, it would have been necessary to choose someone less stupid, and certainly this position required more than being cruel and malevolent. Madame Choglokova was believed to be extremely virtuous because at that time she loved her husband adoringly; she had married him out of love. Such a fine example, placed before me, was perhaps meant to persuade me to do the same. We will see whether this succeeded.

Here is what precipitated this arrangement, or so it seems. I say "precipitated" because I think that since the beginning, Count Bestuzhev had always had the intention of surrounding us with his creatures. He would very much have liked to do the same with Her Imperial Majesty's entourage, but there the matter was more complicated. Upon my arrival in Moscow, the Grand Duke had in his chambers three servants named Chernyshev, all three sons of grenadiers in the Empress's bodyguard; they held the rank of lieutenant, a distinction that she had given them as

---

* Madame Choglokova (née Countess Hendrikova) was the daughter of Elizabeth's maternal aunt Kristina Skavronskaia.

recompense because they had put her on the throne. The eldest Chernyshev was a cousin of the other two, who were brothers. The Grand Duke
had great affection for all three of them; they were his closest intimates
and truly served him well, all three being big and well built, especially the
eldest. The Grand Duke used him for all his commissions and sent him to
my apartment several times a day. It was in him moreover that the Grand
Duke confided when he did not wish to come see me. This man was a
friend of and very close to my chamber valet Evreinov, and I often
learned things by this channel that I would not have known otherwise.
Both were greatly devoted to me in heart and soul, and I often gained insight from them into a great many matters that I would have acquired
otherwise only with difficulty. I know not in what context, but one day the
eldest of the Chernyshevs had said while speaking of me to the Grand
Duke, "Вить она не моя невеста ваша, she is not my fiancée, but
yours." This remark had made the Grand Duke laugh; he related it to me,
and from that moment it had pleased His Imperial Highness to call me
his fiancée, "ево невеста," and when Andrei Chernyshev spoke with
me, he called the Grand Duke your fiancé, "ваш жених." To finish this
joke, after our marriage, Chernyshev proposed to His Imperial Highness
that he, Chernyshev, call me mother, "matushka," and that I call him son,
"сынок." But since this son was a constant subject of conversation both
for the Grand Duke, who loved this man dearly, and for me, who had
great affection for him as well, my servants grew agitated, some out of
jealousy, others out of fear for the consequences that could result both for
them and for us.

One day when there was a masked ball at the court and I had returned
to my room to change my dress, my chamber valet Timofei Evreinov
took me aside and told me that he and all of my house servants were
frightened by the danger into which they saw me rushing. I asked him
what this could be; he said to me, "You are only making people talk and
you are always thinking about Andrei Chernyshev." "Well," I said with
my innocent heart, "what harm is there in that? He is my son. The Grand
Duke loves him as much as and even more than I, and he is devoted and
faithful to us." "Yes," he replied to me, "this is true. The Grand Duke can
do as he pleases, but you do not have the same right. What you call kindness and affection because this man is faithful to you and serves you, your
servants call love." When he had pronounced this word, which I had not
even suspected, I was struck as if by lightning, both by the judgment of

my servants, which I found rash, and by the situation in which I found myself without even suspecting it. He told me that he had advised his friend Andrei Chernyshev to say that he was ill in order to put an end to this talk. He had taken Evreinov's advice, and his supposed illness lasted until around the month of April. The Grand Duke was greatly concerned by this man's illness and spoke to me constantly about it, knowing nothing of the truth. Andrei Chernyshev reappeared in the Summer Palace; I could no longer see him without embarrassment.

Meanwhile the Empress had seen fit to make a new arrangement for the court servants. They took turns serving in all the rooms, and consequently, Andrei Chernyshev did as the others. At that time the Grand Duke often held concerts in the afternoon; he played the violin himself. During one of these concerts, I grew bored as usual and went to my room, which led out to the great hall of the Summer Palace, whose ceiling was being painted and which was entirely filled with scaffolding. The Empress was absent, and Madame Kruse had gone to the house of her daughter, Madame Sievers; I did not find a single living soul in my room. Out of boredom I opened the door to the hall and saw at the other end Andrei Chernyshev. I made a sign for him to approach; he came to the door with, to be honest, a great deal of apprehension. I asked him if the Empress would return soon. He said to me, "I cannot speak to you, there is too much noise in the hall. Invite me into your room." I replied to him, "That is something I will not do." He was on one side of the door and I on the other, holding the door half open and speaking to him. A sudden movement made me turn my head away from the door next to which I was standing. Behind me at the other door of my dressing room I saw Chamberlain Count Devier, who said to me, "The Grand Duke is asking for you, Madame." I closed the door to the hall and went with Count Devier into the apartment where the Grand Duke was having his concert. I learned afterward that Count Devier was a kind of spy charged with this mission, like several others close to us.

The following day, a Sunday, after mass the Grand Duke and I learned that the three Chernyshevs had been placed as lieutenants in the regiments near Orenburg, and that afternoon Madame Choglokova was placed in my entourage. A few days later, we were ordered to prepare to accompany the Empress to Revel.* At the same time, Madame Choglo-

---

* The Russian name for Tallinn, Estonia; Reval in German.

kova came to tell me on behalf of Her Imperial Majesty that I had been excused from coming in the future into her dressing room and that if I had something to tell her, it should only be through her, Madame Choglokova. Deep down I was extremely happy with this order, which freed me from having to stand about waiting among the Empress's women, and besides, I did not go there often and only saw Her Majesty very rarely. Since I had started going there, she had shown herself to me only three or four times, and little by little, one by one, the Empress's ladies usually left the room when I entered; so as not to be alone, I did not stay there very long either.

In the month of June the Empress left for Revel and we accompanied her. The Grand Duke and I traveled in a four-seated carriage; Prince August and Madame Choglokova were our companions. Our manner of traveling was neither pleasant nor comfortable. The houses and way stations were occupied by the Empress; we were either given tents or else placed in the servants' quarters. I remember that one day during this trip I got dressed next to an oven in which they had just baked bread, and that another time when I walked in, there was water ankle-deep in the tent in which my bed had been set up. Moreover, as the Empress had no fixed hour either for departing or for arriving, nor for meals or rests, we were all, both masters and servants, exhausted to an extraordinary degree. Finally, after ten or twelve days of travel, we arrived at a property of Count de Stenbock at forty versts* from Revel, from where the Empress departed with great ceremony, wishing to arrive at Catherinenthal during the day. But I know not how it happened that the journey lasted until one-thirty in the morning. During the whole journey from Petersburg to Revel, Madame Choglokova plunged our carriage into boredom and grief. She responded to the least remark that anyone made with, "Such talk would displease Her Majesty," or "Such things would not be approved by the Empress." She sometimes attached such judgments to the most innocent and the most unimportant things. I for one remained aloof. I did nothing but sleep during the journey in the carriage.

On the day following our arrival in Catherinenthal, the usual rhythm of the court recommenced; that is to say that from morning to evening and very late into the night, we played for rather high stakes in the Empress's antechamber, which was a hall that divided the house and the

* A verst is .66 miles, about one kilometer.

three stories of this building in two. Madame Choglokova was a gambler. She urged me to play faro like all the others. All of the Empress's favorites usually participated when they were not in Her Imperial Majesty's apartment, or rather in her tent, because she had had a very large and magnificent one set up next to her chambers, which were on the ground floor and very small, in the manner that Peter I had normally had them constructed. He had built this country house and planted the garden. The Prince and Princess Repnin, who were on this trip and who knew that Madame Choglokova had conducted herself with arrogance and without common sense during the journey, urged me to speak about her with Countess Shuvalova and Madame Izmailova, the ladies highest in the Empress's affections.* These women did not like Madame Choglokova and they were already informed of what had happened; the little Countess Shuvalova, who was indiscretion itself, did not wait for me to talk with her about it, but sitting next to me during a card game, she herself began to speak of it, and since she had a very mocking tone, she so ridiculed Madame Choglokova's conduct that the latter soon became everyone's laughingstock. She went further. She recounted to the Empress all that had happened. Apparently Madame Choglokova was scolded, because she softened her tone toward me a great deal.

To tell the truth, I was in great need of this change because I began to feel a strong inclination toward melancholy. I felt completely isolated. At Revel, the Grand Duke took a passing fancy to a Madame Cedersparre; as was his usual custom, he did not fail to tell me about it immediately. I had frequent chest pains and began to spit up blood at Catherinenthal, for which I was bled. In the afternoon of that same day, Madame Choglokova entered my room and found me with tears in my eyes, and with an extremely gentle look on her face, she asked me what was wrong, and proposed to me on behalf of the Empress that to dispel my depression, so she said, I should take a walk in the garden. That same day the Grand Duke had gone hunting with the Grand Master of the Hunt Count Razumovsky. Besides this, also on behalf of Her Imperial Majesty, she gave me three thousand rubles to play faro. The ladies had noticed that I was short of money and had told the Empress. I asked her to thank Her Imperial

* Countess Mavra Egorovna Shuvalova (née Shepeleva) was the first wife of Count Peter Ivanovich Shuvalov.

Majesty for her generosity, and I went with Madame Choglokova to walk in the garden and take some air.

A few days after our arrival at Catherinenthal, we saw Grand Chancellor Count Bestuzhev arrive, accompanied by the Imperial Ambassador Baron von Bretlach, and we learned from the greetings he gave us that the two imperial courts had just been united by a treaty of alliance.* Following this, the Empress went to see the fleet exercises, but except for the cannon smoke, we saw nothing; the day was excessively hot and the air perfectly calm. Upon our return from these maneuvers there was a ball in the Empress's tents, which were set up on a terrace; dinner was served outside around the pool, in which there was supposed to be a fountain. But hardly had the Empress sat down at the table when a downpour came, drenching the whole company, which withdrew as best it could into the house and the tents; thus ended this banquet.

A few days later the Empress left for Rogervik. The fleet again performed maneuvers there, and again we saw only smoke. This trip bruised everyone's feet in a singular way. The ground there is rock, covered with such a thick layer of pebbles that when one stands for some time in the same place, one's feet sink and the pebbles cover them. We camped on that terrain in our tents for several days and were obliged to go from one tent to the other; afterward my feet hurt for more than four months. The galley slaves who worked on the breakwater wore wooden shoes, and these shoes hardly lasted more than eight to ten days. The Imperial Ambassador had followed Her Imperial Majesty to this port, where he dined and supped with her. Halfway between Rogervik and Revel, an old woman who looked like a walking skeleton, aged 130 years, was brought to the Empress during dinner. She gave the woman plates from her table and silverware and we continued on our way. Back in Catherinenthal, Madame Choglokova had the pleasure of finding her husband back from his mission to Vienna.

Many carriages from the court were already on the road to Riga, where the Empress wanted to visit, but back from Rogervik, she suddenly changed her mind. Many people racked their brains trying to divine the reason for this change in plan; several years later the reason for it was discovered. When Monsieur Choglokov had passed through Riga, a Lutheran pastor who was either crazy or fanatical gave him a letter and

---

* The secret articles of the Treaty of May 1746 between Russia and Austria committed them to fight together against Prussia and Turkey.

a memorandum for the Empress in which he exhorted her not to undertake this journey, telling her that she ran the greatest risks and that there were people placed by the Empire's neighboring enemies to kill her, and other nonsense of that sort. These documents, handed to Her Imperial Majesty, quenched her desire to go any farther; as for the pastor, he was discovered to be crazy, but the journey did not take place. We returned in small stages from Revel to Petersburg; during this trip I came down with a very sore throat and had to stay in bed for several days.* Afterward we went to Peterhof, and from there we made weekly excursions to Oranienbaum.

At the beginning of August the Empress had the Grand Duke and me informed that we should make our devotions; we both obeyed her wishes, and we immediately began to have matins and vespers sung in our residence, and we went to mass every day. One Friday, when it was time to go to confession, the reason for this order to make our devotions became very clear. Simeon Theodorsky, the Bishop of Pskov, questioned us both a great deal, each one separately, about what had happened between the Chernyshevs and us. But as nothing at all had happened, he was a bit contrite when he saw that with the candor of innocence we told him that there was not even the shadow of what they had dared to suppose. To me he let slip this question: "But then whence is the Empress informed to the contrary?" At this, I told him that I did not know. I suppose that our confessor transmitted our confession to the Empress's confessor, and that he informed Her Imperial Majesty of what had happened, which certainly could not damn us. We received communion on Saturday, and on Monday we went to Oranienbaum for a week, while the Empress made an excursion to Tsarskoe Selo.

Upon arriving at Oranienbaum, the Grand Duke enlisted his entire entourage, the chamberlains, the gentlemen of the bedchamber, the courtiers, Prince Repnin's adjutants and even his son, the court servants, the huntsmen, the gardeners. All had muskets on their shoulders. His Imperial Highness drilled them daily, and put them on guard duty. The hallway of the house served as their guardroom, where they spent the day. For meals the gentlemen went upstairs, and in the evening they came into the hall to dance in gaiters. The only women were myself, Madame Choglokova, Princess Repnina, my three maids of honor, and my three

---

* They returned to St. Petersburg on July 30, 1746.

ladies-in-waiting. As a result, the ball was meager and poorly arranged, the men exhausted and in bad humor from their continuous military exercise, which was hardly to the taste of courtiers. After the ball they were allowed to go sleep in their apartments. In general I and everyone else were overcome by the boring life that we led at Oranienbaum, where we were five or six women isolated and in each other's company from morning until night, while for their part, the men drilled against their will.

I found solace in the books that I had brought. Since my marriage, all I did was read. The first book that I read as a newlywed was a novel entitled *Tiran the Fair,* and for an entire year I read only novels.* But as these began to bore me, I came by chance upon the letters of Madame de Sévigné; this reading greatly entertained me.† When I had devoured them, the works of Voltaire fell into my hands; after reading them, I sought books with more discrimination.‡ We returned to Peterhof, and after two or three round trips between Peterhof and Oranienbaum, always with the same pastimes, we returned to Petersburg and the Summer Palace.

At the end of autumn, the Empress moved to the Winter Palace, where she resided in the apartments that we had lived in the preceding winter, and we were lodged in those that the Grand Duke had occupied before our marriage. We liked these apartments very much and they were truly very comfortable; they had been Empress Anna's. Every evening our entire court would assemble in our apartments. We played all kinds of little games or had concerts. Twice a week there was a production in the large theater, which was at that time across from the Kazan cathedral. In a word, that winter was one of the most joyous and best planned that I have spent in my life. We literally did nothing but laugh and play all day long.

---

* Tiran the Fair was a knight-errant of the kind mocked by Cervantes in *Don Quixote,* originally *Tirant lo Blach* by Mossen Johanot Matorell (Valencia, 1490). Catherine may have read a French imitation by Count A. Cl. de Caylus, *Histoire du vaillant chevalier Tiran le Blanc* (London, Paris, 1737).

† The letters of Madame de Sévigné (1629–96), especially to her daughter, were prized for their simple and natural tone, and for the vividness with which they evoked the glory of the seventeenth-century court of Louis XIV.

‡ In September 1763, Catherine wrote Voltaire: "From the time that I could do what I liked until 1746, I read only novels. By chance, [your] works fell into my hands. I could not stop reading them.... I always returned to the first mainspring of my taste and of my most valued enjoyment, and assuredly, if I have any knowledge, it is to [you] alone that I owe it" (Besterman no. 10597).

1747

Chernyshevs imprisoned; father's death; boredom; various pastimes

Around the middle of winter the Empress told us to follow her to Tikhvin, where she meant to go. This was a pilgrimage, but at the moment that we were climbing into the sleighs, we learned that the trip had been delayed. We were quietly informed that Grand Master of the Hunt Count Razumovsky had come down with gout and that the Empress did not want to leave without him.

During this time, while he was arranging my hair one morning, my chamber valet, Evreinov, said to me that by a great stroke of luck he had discovered that Andrei Chernyshev and his brothers were in Ribacha Sloboda under arrest in a country house that belonged to the Empress herself and that she had inherited from her mother. Here is how this was discovered. During carnival, my servant with his wife, her sister, and the sister's husband had made a little excursion in a sleigh. The sister's husband was a secretary to the magistrate of St. Petersburg. This man had a sister married to an undersecretary of the Secret Chancery. One day they went around Ribacha Sloboda and visited the home of the man charged with the administration of this domain belonging to the Empress. They had an argument about what day Easter fell on; their host said to them that he would quickly put an end to this dispute, that they had only to ask one of the prisoners for a book entitled *Святцы* in Russian, in which one finds all the feast days and the calendar for several years. A few moments later the book was brought; Evreinov's brother-in-law took the book, and upon opening it, the first thing he saw was that Andrei Chernyshev had written his name in it and the date on which the Grand Duke had given him this book, after which he looked up the date for Easter. This dispute over, the book was sent back, and they returned to Petersburg, where a few days later Evreinov's brother-in-law shared this discovery with him. He immediately begged me not to speak of this with the Grand Duke, because he did not at all trust his discretion; I promised and I kept my word to him.

Two or three weeks later, we left for Tikhvin. This journey lasted only five days and then we returned, passing on the way there and back through Ribacha Sloboda, and in front of the house in which I knew the Chernyshevs were being held, I tried to see them through the windows, but I saw nothing. Prince Repnin was not with us on this journey; we were told that he had kidney stones. Madame Choglokova's husband fulfilled Prince Repnin's functions during this journey, which did not much please everyone: he was an arrogant and brutal fool. Everyone feared both this man and his wife dreadfully, and to tell the truth, they were truly wicked. However, there were ways, as became clear later, not only to put these Arguses to sleep but even to win them over; at that time we were just discovering these ways. One of the surest was to play faro with them; they were both gamblers and very intense ones at that. This weakness was the first discovery; others came later.

That winter Princess Gagarina, my maid of honor, died from a severe fever at the moment she was going to marry Chamberlain Prince Golitsyn, who later married her younger sister. I missed her greatly, and during her illness I went to see her several times despite Madame Choglokova's protests. The Empress had her older sister, since married to Count Matiushkin, come from Moscow and take her place.

Toward the middle of Lent, we went with the Empress to Gostilitsa for the birthday of Grand Master of the Hunt Count Razumovsky. There we danced and amused ourselves quite well, after which we returned to the city. A few days later I was informed of the death of my father, which deeply grieved me.* For a week I was allowed to cry as much as I wanted, but at the end of the week Madame Choglokova came to tell me that I had cried enough, that the Empress ordered me to stop crying, that my father had not been a King. I replied to her that it was true that he had not been a King, but that he was my father. At this she retorted that it was not fitting for a Grand Duchess to mourn any longer for a father who was not a King. Finally it was decided that I would appear in public the following Sunday and wear mourning clothes for six weeks. The first time I left my room, I found Count Santi, the Empress's Grand Master of Ceremonies, in Her Imperial Majesty's antechamber. I addressed a few quite ordinary remarks to him and continued on my way. A few days later, Madame Choglokova came to tell me that the Empress had learned from Count Bestuzhev, to

* He died March 16, 1747.

whom Santi had given it in writing, that I had said to him, Santi, that I found it very strange that the ambassadors had not expressed their condolences to me on the death of my father, that the Empress had found my remark to Count Santi ill-advised, that I was too proud and that I should remember that my father was not a King, and that for this reason, I should not and could not expect condolences from foreign ministers. I almost fell off my chair listening to Madame Choglokova. I told her that if Count Santi had said or written that I had said to him a single word even barely touching on that subject, he was a remarkable liar, that nothing of the sort had ever entered my mind and that I therefore had neither made to him nor to anyone else any remarks on the subject. This was the strictest truth because I had made it an immutable rule to expect nothing, no matter what, and to conform to the Empress's will in all things and do what I was told to do. Apparently the candor with which I responded to Madame Choglokova convinced her; she told me that she would not fail to tell the Empress that I made a formal denial of Count Santi's story. And indeed, she went to Her Imperial Majesty's apartment and came back to tell me that the Empress was very angry with Count Santi for having told such a lie and that she had ordered that he be reprimanded. A few days later, Count Santi sent forth several people, among them Chamberlain Nikita Panin and the Vice Chancellor Vorontsov, to tell me that Count Bestuzhev had forced him to tell this lie and that he was very upset that because of it, he found himself in disgrace with me. I said to these gentlemen that a liar is a liar, whatever his reasons for lying, and that fearing that this gentleman would involve me in his lies, I would speak to him no more. I kept my word; I spoke to him no more.

Here is what I believe about this story. Santi was an Italian; he loved to negotiate and was very preoccupied with his position as Grand Master of Ceremonies. I had always spoken to him as I spoke to everyone; perhaps he believed that condolences from the diplomatic corps on the subject of my father's death might be in order and given this, hoped to do me a service. He therefore went to see Count Bestuzhev, the Grand Chancellor, his superior, and told him that I had appeared in public for the first time and that I had seemed deeply affected by my father's death, and perhaps on this occasion he added that the lack of condolences had contributed to my suffering. Count Bestuzhev, ever vicious and happy to humiliate me, immediately had put in writing what Santi had just said or insinuated to him and had attributed to me, and made him sign this document. The other, fearing his superior's wrath and above all the possibility of losing his position, did not hesitate to sign this lie rather than sacrifice his existence. The Grand Chancellor sent the note to the Empress; she was angered to see my pretentiousness and sent Madame Choglokova as I have just recounted. But after she heard my response, which was based on the perfect truth, the only result was the embarrassment of the Grand Master of Ceremonies.

In the spring we went to live in the Summer Palace, and from there we went to the country. Under the pretext of his ill health, Prince Repnin obtained permission to withdraw to his house, and Monsieur Choglokov continued to be charged with Prince Repnin's duties in our service in the interim. Choglokov's influence first became apparent with the dismissal from our court of Chamberlain Count Devier, who was placed in the army as a brigadier, and with that of Gentleman of the Bedchamber Villebois, who was sent to be a colonel because of the protests of Monsieur Choglokov, who disliked them both because the Grand Duke and I both esteemed them. Similar dismissals had already occurred, for example, that of Count Zakhar Chernyshev in 1745 at the behest of his mother, but nevertheless these dismissals were seen as disgraces by the court and were very deeply felt by the individuals who suffered them. The Grand Duke and I were very sensitive to all this. Prince August, having obtained all that he had sought, was told on behalf of the Empress to depart. This too was a plot of the Choglokovs, who wished to utterly isolate the Grand Duke and me; in this they were following the instructions of Count Bestuzhev, who was suspicious of everyone and loved to cause and sustain divisions everywhere, fearing conspiracies against him. Despite this, all minds joined together in hatred of him, but he hardly worried about this as long as he was feared.

That summer, with nothing better to do and the boredom increasing at our residence and court, my dominant passion became horseback riding; the rest of the time I read in my room everything that fell into my hands. As for the Grand Duke, since the servants he loved best had been taken from him, he chose new ones from the court servants. In the country, he acquired a pack of hunting dogs and began to train them himself; when he was tired of tormenting them, he began to saw away on his violin. He knew not a note, but he had a good ear and made the beauty of the music consist of the force and violence with which he drew sounds from his instrument. Those who heard him, however, often would have willingly plugged their ears if they had dared because he grated on them terribly. This life continued both in the country and in the city.

Back in the Summer Palace, Madame Kruse, who had not ceased to be an Argus and recognized as such, became sweeter to such an extent that very often she was willing to deceive the Choglokovs, who had become everyone's bête noires. She did more. She procured for the Grand Duke toys, dolls, and other childish things that he loved madly; during the day they were hidden in and under my bed. The Grand Duke went to bed first after supper, and as soon as we were in bed, Madame Kruse locked the door with a key and then the Grand Duke played until one or two in the morning. Like it or not, I was obliged to take part in this fine pastime, as was Madame Kruse. Often I laughed about it, but even more often I was irritated and inconvenienced, as the bed was covered with and full of dolls and toys, which were sometimes quite heavy. I do not know if Madame Choglokova caught wind of these nocturnal amusements, but one evening toward midnight, she knocked at the bedroom door. We did not open it for her immediately, because the Grand Duke, Madame Kruse, and I were in such a hurry to hide and clear the bed of these toys, and to this end the bedcover served us well because we stuffed them underneath it. This done, we opened the door, but she took this occasion to speak angrily of the fact that we had made her wait and told us that the Empress would be very upset when she learned that we were not yet asleep at such an hour. Then she went away growling, having made no other discovery. After she had departed, the Grand Duke continued as before until he grew sleepy.

At the beginning of autumn, we moved once again into the apartments that we had first occupied in the Winter Palace after our wedding. Here the Empress declared a very strict prohibition, communicated by Madame Choglokova, that no one was to enter my or the Grand Duke's apartment without the express permission of Monsieur or Madame Choglokova, with an order to the ladies and gentlemen of our court to remain in the antechamber, not to go beyond the threshold and only to speak to us aloud; the same order was given to servants upon pain of dismissal. The Grand Duke and I thus reduced to being face-to-face, we complained and shared with each other our thoughts about this seeming prison, which neither of us deserved.

To have more amusement during the winter, the Grand Duke ordered eight or ten hunting dogs from the country and placed them behind a wooden partition, which separated the alcove of my bedroom from an immense vestibule located behind our apartments. As the alcove was made only of wood boards, the odor from the kennel penetrated into the alcove, and it was in this stench that we both slept. When I complained about it, he replied that there was no other way; because the kennel was a huge secret, I endured this inconvenience without betraying His Imperial Highness's secret.

1748

Catherine's debts; measles; collapse of house at Gostilitsa; letters from her mother; Choglokov's affair; summer at Oranienbaum; Mme. Vladislavova put in charge of her entourage; Count Lestocq's arrest; move to Moscow for winter

On January 6, 1748, I came down with a high fever accompanied by a rash. When it passed, since there was no entertainment at court during carnival that year, the Grand Duke decided to hold masquerades in my room. He had his and my servants and my ladies wear masks and had them dance in my bedroom; he himself played the violin and danced along. This would last rather late into the night. For my part, under different pretexts of a headache or fatigue, I would lie down on a couch, but always dressed in a mask and bored to death by the insipidness of these masked balls that amused him to no end. With the arrival of Lent, four more people were removed from his service, including three pages that he liked more than the others. These frequent dismissals disturbed him, but he did not take a single step to stop them or else took steps that were so awkward that they could only make things worse.

During that winter we learned that Prince Repnin, ill as he was, would command the troops that were being sent to Bohemia to aid Queen Empress Maria Theresa.* This was a formal disgrace for Prince Repnin; he went there and never returned, because he died of despondency in Bohemia. It was Princess Gagarina, my maid of honor, who gave me the first inkling of this, despite all the prohibitions against allowing the least word of what was happening in the city or at court to reach us. One can see by this the real worth of such prohibitions, which are never executed rigorously, because there are too many people interested in contravening them. All those in our service and even the Choglokovs' closest relatives

---

* The 30,000 troops under Repnin ensured the successful peace negotiations at Aachen to end the War of the Austrian Succession (1740–48), which involved all the major powers.

sought to reduce the harshness of what was in effect a political prison, in which we were kept with great effort. Even Madame Choglokova's own brother, Count Hendrikov, often slipped me useful and necessary information, and others too used him to get news to me, a task that he always undertook with the sincerity of a fine and upstanding man, deriding the stupid and brutal actions of his sister and brother-in-law, so that with him everyone was at ease and without any sort of suspicion, since he had never compromised or failed a living soul. He was a man of fairness, but narrow-minded, ill-mannered, and very ignorant, though solid and without malice.

One day toward noon during this same Lent, I entered the room where the ladies and gentlemen waited; the Choglokovs had not yet arrived, and while speaking to various people, I approached the door next to which stood Chamberlain Ovtsyn. He gave forth in a low voice on the boring life we were leading and, moreover, on how others had put us in the Empress's bad graces. A few days earlier, while dining, Her Imperial Majesty had said that I was overloaded with debts, that everything I did was marked by stupidity, that I imagined myself to have great intelligence, but that I was the only one who thought this of myself, and that I deceived no one, that my complete stupidity was known to everyone, and that because of this, it was less necessary to watch out for what the Grand Duke did than what I did, and he added with tears in his eyes that he had received an order from the Empress to tell me this, but he begged me to act as if I did not know that he had told me that he had been ordered to transmit this message. I replied to him that concerning my stupidity, the fault could not be attributed to me, each person being as the good Lord created him, that with respect to my debts, it was not too astonishing that I had some, because though I had thirty thousand rubles of support, my mother had left me sixty thousand rubles of her debt to pay off; that moreover, Countess Rumiantseva had urged me to make a thousand expenditures that she regarded as indispensable, that Madame Choglokova alone was costing me seventeen thousand rubles that year, and that he himself knew the hellish amount I had to gamble with them at cards every day, that he could give this response to those from whom he had received his commission, and that otherwise, I was very angered to know that I had been put in the bad graces of Her Imperial Majesty, to whom however I had never failed to show respect, obedience, or deference, and that the more they spied upon me, the more they would be convinced of this. I promised to keep his secret as he asked and did so. I do not know if he reported what I asked him to, but believe that he did, though I did not hear any more talk on this matter, and did not seek to continue such a disagreeable conversation.

The last week of Lent, I came down with measles; I could not appear for Easter mass, and on Saturday I took communion in my room. During this illness, Madame Choglokova, although hugely pregnant, hardly ever left me and did what she could to amuse me. I had at that time a little Kalmuck girl whom I loved greatly; this child caught measles from me.

After Easter we went to the Summer Palace, and from there at the end of May for Ascension to Count Razumovsky's at Gostilitsa; on the twenty-third of the same month, the Empress had brought there Ambassador of the Imperial Court Baron von Bretlach, who was leaving for Vienna. He spent the evening there and had supper with the Empress. This evening meal ended quite late at night, and we returned to the little house in which we were lodged after sunrise. This little wooden house was situated on a small rise and next to the sleigh runs. The location of this little house had pleased us the winter that we had gone to Gostilitsa for the Grand Master of the Hunt's birthday, and to please us he had lodged us there this time as well. It had three stories; the upper one had a staircase, a salon, and three small rooms. We slept in one, the Grand Duke dressed in another, and Madame Kruse occupied the third; below were lodged the Choglokovs, my maids of honor, and my ladies-in-waiting. Upon returning from supper, everyone went to bed. Around six in the morning, a sergeant of the guards named Levashov arrived from Oranienbaum to speak with Choglokov about the buildings that were being constructed there. Finding everyone asleep in the house, he sat down next to the sentry, and heard creaking noises that aroused his suspicions. The sentry told him that these creaking sounds had occurred several times since he had been on duty. Levashov got up and ran outside the house. He saw that large blocks of stone underneath the house were breaking off. He ran to awaken Choglokov and told him that the house's foundation was giving way and that he had to try to evacuate everyone who was inside. Choglokov put on a bathrobe and ran upstairs, where finding the doors—which had glass panes—locked, he broke the locks. Thus he arrived in the little room where we slept, and drawing the curtain, he awoke us and told us to get up as quickly as possible and to get out because the house's foundation was giving way. The Grand Duke leaped from the bed, took his bathrobe, and fled. I told Choglokov that I was going to follow him, and he left. I dressed in haste; while dressing myself I remembered that Madame Kruse was sleeping in the other room and went to wake her up. As she slept deeply, I succeeded with difficulty in waking her up and then making her understand that we had to leave the house. I helped her get dressed, and when she was ready, we moved beyond the threshold and entered the salon, but at the moment that we set foot there, there was a tremendous tremor, accompanied by a sound like that of a ship being launched from the shipyard. Madame Kruse and I fell to the floor; as we fell, Levashov entered through the door of the staircase facing us. He lifted me off the floor and carried me out of the room. I happened to glance at the sleigh run. It had been level with the third floor; it was no longer there but at least an arshin higher.* Arriving with me at the main staircase by which he had ascended, Levashov could no longer find it. It had collapsed, but several people had climbed onto the rubble. Levashov handed me to the nearest person, who handed me to the next, and so from one set of hands to another, I arrived at the foot of the staircase in the vestibule, and from there I was carried out of the house and into a field. There I found the Grand Duke in his bathrobe. Once out of the house, I began to look at what was happening around it, and I saw that several people were walking out covered in blood and that others were being carried. Among the most seriously wounded was Princess Gagarina, my maid of honor. She had wanted to escape from the house like the others, and while she passed through a room attached to hers, a collapsing stove fell on a screen, which knocked her onto a bed that was in the room. Several bricks fell on her head and seriously wounded her and a girl who was escaping with her. On this lower floor there was also a little kitchen where several servants slept, three of whom were killed by the fireplace's collapse. This was nothing in comparison to what had happened between the house's foundation and the ground floor. Sixteen workers assigned to the sleigh run slept there, and all had been crushed by the building's collapse.

The cause for all this was that the house had been built hastily in the autumn. It had four courses of limestone blocks for the foundation; on the ground floor the architect had placed twelve beams to serve as pillars in the vestibule. He had had to leave for Ukraine, and when he left, he told the steward of Gostilitsa to allow no one to touch these twelve beams

---

* An arshin is twenty-eight inches.

until his return. Despite the architect's prohibition, when the steward learned that we were to stay in this little house, he could not wait to have these twelve beams knocked down, since they disfigured the vestibule. With the coming of the spring thaw, everything settled on the four limestone courses, which slid in different directions, and the building itself slid against a rise that held it up. I escaped with a few bruises and a great scare, for which I was bled. The scare had been so great for everyone that during the next four months, every door that was closed with even a little force caused us to tremble. When the initial fright had passed that day, the Empress, who was staying in another house, called us to her residence, and as she wanted to make light of the accident, everyone tried to discount the danger and some even saw none. My own shock displeased her greatly and she hardly spoke to me. The Grand Master of the Hunt wept and despaired, he spoke of killing himself with a pistol; apparently he was prevented from this, because he did not do it, and on the following day we returned to Petersburg and after several weeks returned to the Summer Palace.

I do not recall exactly, but it seems to me that it was around this time that Chevalier Sacromoso arrived in Russia. It had been a long time since a Knight of Malta had come to Russia, and generally we saw very few foreigners come to Petersburg. His arrival was therefore a kind of event. He was treated in the best possible manner and taken to see all of the most remarkable things in Petersburg, and in Kronstadt a distinguished naval officer was named to accompany him; this was Monsieur Poliansky, then a captain of a warship and since named admiral. He was presented to us; while he kissed my hand, Sacromoso slipped a very tiny note into my hand and said to me in a very low voice, "This is from Madame your mother." I was almost overcome with fright at what he had just done. I was dying from fear that someone might have seen him and above all the Choglokovs, who were very near. Nevertheless I took the note and slipped it into my glove; no one noticed. Back in my room, I found in this rolled-up note, which informed me that a response was expected through an Italian musician who was coming to the Grand Duke's concert, another note that was in fact from my mother, who, anxious about my involuntary silence, asked me the reason for it and wanted to know my situation. I responded to my mother and informed her of what she wanted to know. I told her that I had been forbidden to write to her or anyone else, under the pretext that it was not fitting for a Grand Duchess of Rus-

sia to write any letters other than those composed by the Ministry of Foreign Affairs, to which I only had to affix my signature, that I should never
say what should be written, because the Ministry knew better than I what
was proper to include, and that Monsieur Olsufiev had almost been
charged with a crime because I had sent him a few lines that I had asked
him to insert in a letter to my mother. I informed her about several other
things that she asked me about. I rolled up my note in the same manner
as that which I had received and waited impatiently for the moment when
I could dispose of it. At the first concert held at the Grand Duke's residence, I made a tour of the orchestra and stopped behind the chair of the
cellist d'Ologlio, who was the man who had been indicated to me. When
he saw me stop behind his chair, he pretended to take his handkerchief
from his coat pocket and in this manner opened the pocket wide, into
which I slipped my note without seeming to and then went off in the
other direction and no one suspected anything. During his stay in Petersburg, Sacromoso slipped me two or three other notes on the same subjects, and my responses were given in the same way, and no one ever
found out. From the Summer Palace we went to Peterhof, which was then
being rebuilt.

We were housed on the upper floor of Peter I's old building, which was
still standing. Here, out of boredom, the Grand Duke began to play two-
handed ombre with me every afternoon; when I won he would get angry,
and when I lost he would demand payment immediately. I did not have a
cent, so he began to play hazard with me. I remember that one day his
night bonnet served as our marker for ten thousand rubles. But when he
would lose, at the end of the game he would become furious and was capable of sulking for several days; I was in no way comfortable with this
game.

During the stay at Peterhof, from our windows that looked out on the
garden toward the sea, we saw that Monsieur and Madame Choglokov
were constantly coming and going from the palace on the hill toward
that of Monplaisir by the water, in which the Empress was then living.
This intrigued us and Madame Kruse. In order to learn the reason for
these frequent comings and goings, Madame Kruse went to the residence of her sister, who was the Empress's first lady-in-waiting. She returned beaming, having learned that all these trips were occurring
because the Empress had learned that Monsieur Choglokov was having
an affair with one of my maids of honor, Mademoiselle Kosheleva, and

that she was pregnant. The Empress had sent for Madame Choglokova and had told her that her husband was deceiving her, whereas she loved this husband madly, that she had been blind to the point that she had had this girl, the good friend of her husband, live with her and that if she wanted to separate from her husband immediately, she would do something that did not displease the Empress, who had not looked with pleasure in the first place upon Madame Choglokova's marriage with her husband. The Empress flatly declared to her that she did not want her husband to remain with us, that she would dismiss him and leave the position to his wife. At first the wife denied her husband's passion to the Empress and claimed that this was a slander, but Her Imperial Majesty, while speaking to the wife, had also had the young woman questioned. She had divulged everything completely, which made the wife furious with her husband. She returned to her house and blasted her husband with insults; he fell to his knees and begged her pardon and used all of his power over her to calm her down. Their brood of children helped them to patch up their relationship, which however was hardly any more honest thereafter. Apart in love, they were united by interest. The wife pardoned her husband, went to the Empress's residence, and told her that she had forgiven her husband everything, and she wished to stay with him out of love for her children. On her knees she begged the Empress not to dismiss her husband from the court in shame, that this would dishonor her, and would overwhelm her with sorrow. In the end, she behaved on this occasion with as much firmness as generosity, and her sorrow moreover was so real that she disarmed the Empress's anger. She did more. She brought her husband before Her Imperial Majesty, scolded him severely, and then kneeled with him at the Empress's feet and begged her to pardon her husband out of regard for her and her six children, whose father he was. All these different scenes lasted five or six days, and we learned almost hour by hour what had occurred, because we were less watched during this period and because everyone hoped to see these people dismissed. But the conclusion did not at all meet the expectations that we had formed, because only the maiden was dismissed, and returned to her uncle, Grand Marshal of the Court Shepelev, and the Choglokovs remained, less proud, however, than they had been before. The day was chosen when we would go to Oranienbaum, and while we departed in one direction, the maiden was sent off in the other.

At Oranienbaum that year we lodged in the wings to the right and left of the small main building. The adventure at Gostilitsa had been so frightening that the ceilings and floors were examined in all the houses of the court, after which those in need of it were repaired. Here is the life that I led at that time at Oranienbaum. I arose at three in the morning and dressed myself from head to foot in a man's outfit. An old huntsman in my service was already waiting for me with some rifles; there was a fishing skiff close by on the shore. We crossed the garden on foot, rifles on our shoulders, and he, I, a pointer, and the fisherman who guided us got in the skiff, and I went to shoot ducks in the reeds that bordered the sea on either side of the Oranienbaum canal, which stretches two versts into the sea. We often went out beyond the canal and consequently were sometimes caught in rough weather on the open sea in the skiff. The Grand Duke would come there an hour or two after us because he always needed breakfast, and God knows what else he dragged along with him. If he met us, we went along together, if not, then each went shooting and hunting on his own. At ten o'clock and sometimes later I returned and dressed for dinner; after dinner we rested and in the evening the Grand Duke had a concert or else we went horseback riding. After about a week of leading this life, I felt quite overheated and drowsy; I understood that I needed rest and fasting. For twenty-four hours I ate nothing and drank only cold water, and for two nights slept as much as I could, after which I again led the same life and felt quite well. I remember that at that time I read Brantôme's memoirs, which I greatly enjoyed; before this I had read the life of Henry IV by Péréfixe.*

Toward autumn, we returned to the city and were told that we would go to Moscow during the winter. Madame Kruse came to tell me that I had to increase my stock of linen for this journey. I attended to the details of my linens, and Madame Kruse pretended to amuse me by having the linen cut in my room, to instruct me, she said, in how many chemises could be produced from one piece of cloth. This lesson or entertainment apparently displeased Madame Choglokova, who was in a worse mood than ever since the discovery of her husband's infidelity. I do not know what she went to tell the Empress, but it happened that one afternoon she

---

* Brantôme, Pierre de Bourdeille, seigneur de (d. 1614), *Mémoires des messire Pierre de Bourdeille, seigneur de Brantôme, contenans les anecdotes de la cour de France, sous les rois Henry II, François II, Henry III & IV, touchant les duels* (1665); Hardouin de Beaumont de Péréfixe (1605–71), *Histoire du roi Henri le Grand* (1661).

came to tell me that the Empress was dismissing Madame Kruse from my service, that she was going to retire to the house of Chamberlain Sievers, her son-in-law, and the next day she brought me Madame Vladislavova to take her place.

She was a big woman who appeared to have a nice figure and whose lively physiognomy pleased me at first sight. I consulted my oracle, Timofei Evreinov, on this choice, and he told me that this woman, whom I had never seen before, was the mother-in-law of Count Bestuzhev's head clerk, the Counselor Pugovishnikov, that she lacked neither intelligence nor gaiety, but that she was said to be very crafty and that I should watch how she conducted herself and above all not show her too much trust. Her name was Praskovia Nikitichna. She got off to a very good start; she was sociable, loved to talk, spoke and told stories with intelligence, knew all the anecdotes of past and present times by heart, knew four or five generations of all the families, had the genealogies of everyone's fathers, mothers, grandfathers, grandmothers, and paternal and maternal great-grandparents fixed in her memory, and no one informed me more about what had happened in Russia over the past hundred years than she. This woman's intelligence and appearance rather pleased me, and when I was bored, I got her talking, which she was always willing to do. I discovered without difficulty that she very often disapproved of the words and deeds of the Choglokovs, but as she also very often went to the Empress's apartment and nobody knew at all why, everyone was suspicious of her to a certain extent, not knowing how the most innocent actions or remarks would be interpreted.

From the Summer Palace we moved to the Winter Palace. Here we were presented with Madame La Tour Launais, who had been in the Empress's service since her early youth and had followed Princess Anna Petrovna, eldest daughter of Peter I, when she had left Russia with her husband, the Duke of Holstein, during the reign of Emperor Peter II.* After the death of this Princess, Madame Launais had returned to France, and soon thereafter she had returned to Russia either to settle there or else to journey back after obtaining several favors from the Empress. Madame Launais hoped that because of her longstanding acquaintance she would return to the Empress's favor and intimacy, but she was sorely mistaken. Everyone conspired together to exclude her. In the first days

* She was the sisters' French governess.

after her arrival, I foresaw what would happen and here is why. One evening there was gambling in the Empress's apartment, with Her Imperial Majesty coming and going from one room to another and not settling anywhere, as was her custom. Madame Launais, apparently believing that she was showing her respect, followed everywhere she went. Seeing this, Madame Choglokova said to me, "Look at how this woman follows the Empress everywhere, but this will not last long. This habit of running after her will soon be broken." I took her at her word, and in fact Madame Launais began to be excluded and then was sent back to France with some presents.

That winter, Count Lestocq and Mademoiselle Mengden, the Empress's maid of honor, were married. Her Imperial Majesty and the entire court attended the wedding, and she did the newlyweds the honor of going to their home. One might have thought that they enjoyed the greatest favor, but one or two months later, their luck changed. One evening, while we were gambling in the Empress's apartment, I saw Count Lestocq there. I approached him. He said to me in a low voice, "Do not come near me. I am a man under suspicion." I thought he was joking; I asked him what he meant to say by this. He replied, "I repeat to you very seriously that you must not come near me, because I am a man under suspicion whom you should flee." I saw that he looked completely different and was extremely flushed. I thought he was drunk, and I went off in the other direction. This happened on a Friday. On Sunday morning, while doing my hair, Timofei Evreinov said to me, "Do you know that last night Count Lestocq and his wife were arrested and taken to the fortress as state criminals?" No one knew why, but it was learned that General Stepan Apraksin and Alexander Shuvalov had been named as commissioners for this affair.[*]

The court's departure for Moscow was fixed for December 16. The Chernyshevs had been transferred from the fortress to one of the Empress's houses, called Smolny Dvorets. The eldest of the three brothers got his guards drunk on several occasions and then went around the city to his friends' houses. One day a Finnish wardrobe girl of mine who was engaged to a court servant, a relative of Evreinov, brought me a letter

---

[*] Count Armand Lestocq's wedding was on November 11, 1747. The order for his arrest was given November 13, 1748; he was taken to the fortress November 17, tortured November 23, had his property confiscated November 24, and was convicted on November 29 to exile, though he remained in the fortress until 1753, when he was sent to Velikii Ustiug.

from Andrei Chernyshev, in which he begged several things of me. This girl had seen him at her fiancé's house, where they had spent the evening together. I did not know where to put this letter when I received it; I did not want to burn it, in order to remember what he asked me. For a long time I had been forbidden from writing even to my mother. Through this girl, I purchased a silver pen and a writing case. During the day, I had the letter in my pocket; when I undressed, I stuffed it under my garter into my stocking, and before going to bed, I pulled it from there and put it in my sleeve. Finally I responded, and I sent him what he had requested by the same channel to which he had entrusted his letter, and I chose a propitious moment to burn the letter that had given me such great worries.

Toward the middle of December, we left for Moscow. The Grand Duke and I were in a large sleigh, the gentlemen in our service riding in front. During the day, the Grand Duke would ride in a town sleigh with Choglokov and I would stay in the large sleigh that we never closed, and I conversed with those who were seated in front. I remember that Chamberlain Prince Alexander Iurievich Trubetskoi recounted to me at this time how Count Lestocq, a prisoner at the fortress, had wanted to let himself die of hunger the first eleven days of his detention, but had been forced to eat. He had been accused of taking ten thousand rubles from the King of Prussia to support his interests and of poisoning a certain Oettinger, who could have testified against him. He was tortured and then exiled to Siberia. On this journey, the Empress passed us at Tver, and since the horses and provisions that had been prepared for us were taken for her entourage, we spent twenty-four hours at Tver without horses and food. We were very hungry; toward evening, Choglokov got us a roasted sterlet, which we found delicious. We left during the night and arrived in Moscow two or three days before Christmas.

The first thing that we learned there was that the chamberlain of our court, Prince Alexander Mikhailovich Golitsyn, had received at the moment of our departure from Petersburg the order to go to Hamburg as Russian minister with a salary of four thousand rubles. This was seen as yet another exile. His sister-in-law Princess Gagarina, who was in our service, cried a great deal about this, and we were all very sorry.

In Moscow, we occupied the apartment that I had had with my mother in 1744. To get to the large church from the court, we had to go around the house by carriage. On Christmas Day it was twenty-eight or twenty-nine degrees below zero; we were going to take the carriage to mass and were already on the staircase landing when we were told on behalf of the Empress that We were excused from going to mass that day because of the excessively cold weather. It is true that it nipped our noses. I was obliged to remain in my room during my first stay in Moscow because of the excessive number of pimples that had broken out on my face; I was scared to death of being scarred. I sent for Doctor Boerhave, who gave me sedatives and all kinds of things to clear up these pimples. Finally when nothing had worked, he said to me one day, "I am going to give you something that will really get rid of them." Out of his pocket he drew a little flask of oil of talc and told me to put a drop in a cup of water and wash my face with this from time to time, every week, for example. The oil of talc did indeed clean my face, and after ten days I was able to appear in public.

1749

Elizabeth's illness; Catherine's reading and Peter's hunting dogs;
summer trips around Moscow with Elizabeth; Catherine's
toothache; Alexander Naryshkin's wedding; Peter compromised in
coup plot by Baturin; Catherine's tooth pulled

A short time after our arrival in Moscow, Madame Vladislavova came to tell me that the Empress had ordered that the marriage of my Finnish wardrobe girl take place as soon as possible. It seemed the only reason that this wedding was hastened was that I had apparently shown some predilection for this girl, who was a very delightful girl, who from time to time made me laugh by imitating everyone, and notably Madame Choglokova, in a very humorous manner. She was married off, and that was the end of the matter.

In the middle of carnival, during which there was no amusement or entertainment of any kind, the Empress suffered from a bad case of colic, which appeared to be getting very serious. Madame Vladislavova and Timofei Evreinov came to whisper this in my ear, immediately begging me not to tell anyone that they had told me. Without naming them I informed the Grand Duke, who was quite agitated. One morning Evreinov came to tell me that Chancellor Bestuzhev and General Apraksin had spent that night in Monsieur and Madame Choglokov's apartment, which gave the impression that the Empress was seriously ill. Choglokov and his wife were more solemn than ever, and they came to our residence, had dinner and supper there, but did not let a word slip about the illness, and we did not speak of it either, nor consequently did we dare to ask how the Empress was doing, because they would have immediately asked how and where and from whom do you know she is ill, and those who would have been either named or suspected would have certainly been dismissed, exiled, or even sent to the Secret Chancery—the state inquisition—which was feared more than anything. Finally after ten days, when the Empress was feeling better, the marriage of one of her maids of honor was held at the court. At the banquet, I found myself sitting next to Countess Shu-valova, the Empress's favorite. She told me that Her Imperial Majesty was still so weak from her terrible illness that she had crowned the bride with her diamonds (an honor she conferred on all her maids of honor) while seated on her bed, and that for this reason she had not appeared at the wedding banquet. As Countess Shuvalova was first to tell me of this illness, I shared with her the pain that Her Majesty's state had caused me and the concern that I felt. She told me that the Empress would learn with satisfaction how I felt. Two days later Madame Choglokova came into my room in the morning and told me in the presence of Madame Vladislavova that the Empress was very annoyed with the Grand Duke and me because of the little concern that we had shown over her illness, because up until then, we had not even sent once to ask how she was feeling. I said to Madame Choglokova that I relied on her, that neither she nor her husband had said a single word to us about the Empress's illness, that knowing nothing of it, we had not been able to show the concern that we felt. She replied to me, "How can you say that you knew nothing of it? Countess Shuvalova told the Empress that you spoke with her at table of her illness." I responded, "It is true that I spoke to her about it, because she told me that Her Majesty was still weak and could not appear in public, and at that point I asked her for details about the illness." Madame Choglokova left grumbling. And Madame Vladislavova said to me that it was quite strange to pick a quarrel with people over something they did not know about, that since the Choglokovs alone had the right to speak of it, if they had not spoken, it was their fault and not ours if out of igno-rance we had failed to act. Sometime afterward, on a day when she held court, the Empress drew near me, and I found a favorable moment to tell her that neither Choglokov nor his wife had informed us of her illness and that because of this we had been unable to show her the concern that we had felt. She received this very well, and it seemed to me that their credibility had diminished.

One day the Empress went to dine at the home of General Stepan Apraksin; we took part in this meal. Afterward an old blind Prince Dol-goruky, who lived across from General Apraksin's house, was brought to the Empress. This was Prince Mikhail Vladimirovich Dolgoruky, who formerly had been a senator, but knew neither how to read nor write anything except his name. Nevertheless he was said to have much more intelligence than his brother, Marshal Prince Vasily Dolgoruky, who had died in 1746. The following day I learned that the third daughter of General Stepan Apraksin, at whose home we had dined the day before, had died of smallpox that same day. I was terrified. All the ladies who had lunched with us at General Apraksin's home had done nothing but go back and forth between the sick child's room and the apartment where we were. However, once again I escaped with only a scare. That day I saw for the first time General Apraksin's two daughters, the elder of which was becoming quite pretty. She may have been thirteen at the time; she has since married Prince Kurakin. The second one was only six years old; she was skinny at the time, spat blood, and was in truth only skin and bones. Certainly no one suspected that she would become as big, as colossal, as monstrously powerful, as all those who knew her found Madame Talyzin, because it was she herself, at that time still only a very small child.

The first week of Lent, Monsieur Choglokov wanted to make his devotions; he went to confession, but the Empress's confessor forbade him from taking communion. The whole court said that this was on Her Imperial Majesty's orders because of his adventure with Mademoiselle Kosheleva. During part of our stay in Moscow, Monsieur Choglokov appeared to be very intimately linked with Chancellor Count Bestuzhev-Riumin and with that man's henchman, General Stepan Apraksin. He was constantly at their homes or with them, and to hear him talk, one would have thought that he was the intimate adviser of Count Bestuzhev, which, however, could not have been the case, because Bestuzhev had far too much intelligence to allow himself to be advised by such an arrogant ass as Choglokov. But toward the middle of our stay in Moscow this extreme intimacy suddenly ceased for reasons that I do not really know, and Choglokov became the mortal enemy of those whose intimacy he had enjoyed shortly before.

A little after my arrival in Moscow, out of boredom I began to read the *History of Germany* by Father Barre, a canon at the cathedral of St. Geneviève, which was eight or nine volumes in quarto.* Every week I fin-

* Father Joseph Barre (1692–1764), *Histoire générale d'Allemagne* (1748), 10 vols. Dacier's *Oeuvres de Platon traduites de grec en français, avec des remarques et la vie de ce philosophe,* 2 vols. (1699, 1744).

ished one, after which I read the works of Plato. My rooms looked out onto the street. The rooms opposite were occupied by the Grand Duke; his windows looked onto a little courtyard. I would read in my room. A chambermaid would usually come in and stand as long as she liked and then leave, and another would take her place when she judged it fitting. I made Madame Vladislavova understand that this only served to annoy me, and besides, I had to suffer a lot from my proximity to the Grand Duke's apartment and to what was going on there, from which she herself suffered as much as I because she occupied a little room that was right at the end of my apartment, and she consented to excuse the chambermaids from this kind of etiquette.

Here is what made us suffer. Morning, afternoon, and far into the night, with a rare perseverance the Grand Duke would train a pack of hunting dogs, making them run from one end to the other of his two rooms (for he did not have more) with strong lashes of the whip and yelling as huntsmen yell. Those dogs that got tired or fell behind were rigorously punished, which made them cry out even more. When he finally got tired of this exercise, which offended the ears and disturbed the sleep of his neighbors, he picked up a violin that he sawed on very badly and with an extraordinary violence while walking around his room, after which he recommenced the training and punishment of the pack, which in truth seemed cruel to me. One day, hearing a poor dog cry terribly for a very long while, I opened the door of my bedroom, where I was sitting and which joined to the room where the scene was occurring. I saw that the Grand Duke had one of his dogs in the air by the collar and that a Kalmuck boy in his service held the same dog up by the tail. It was a poor little English King Charles spaniel, and the Grand Duke struck this dog with all his strength with the thick butt of a whip. I began to intercede on the poor beast's behalf, but this only made him redouble his blows. Unable to endure this cruel spectacle, I returned to my room in tears. In general, tears and cries, instead of arousing the Grand Duke's pity, made him angry; pity was a painful, even unbearable sentiment for his soul.

Around this time, my chamber valet, Timofei Evreinov, gave me a letter from his former comrade Andrei Chernyshev, who had finally been freed and was passing near Moscow to go to the regiment in which he had been placed as a lieutenant. I treated this letter as I had the last one, and I sent him everything that he asked of me, and said not a word about it to the Grand Duke or any living soul.

In the spring the Empress had us come to Perova, where we spent a few days with her at Count Razumovsky's home.* The Grand Duke and Monsieur Choglokov hunted almost daily in the woods with the master of the house. I read in my room, or else Madame Choglokova, when she was not playing cards, would keep me company out of boredom. She complained a great deal about the ennui that reigned in that house and about her husband's continual hunts; he had become a passionate huntsman since he had been given a very beautiful English greyhound in Moscow. I learned from others that her husband was the laughing-stock of all the other huntsmen and that he imagined and was made to believe that his Circe (this was his dog's name) caught all the hares that were taken. In general, Monsieur Choglokov was quite ready to believe that everything that belonged to him was of a rare beauty and goodness. His wife, his children, his servants, his house, his food, his horses, his dogs—everything that he owned, though it was all very mediocre, was part of his self-love, and belonging to him, became incomparable in his eyes.

One day at Perova I was seized by a headache so violent that I do not remember having had a comparable one in my life. The extreme pain gave me violent nausea, I vomited several times, and even footsteps in my room increased my pain. I remained in this state almost twenty-four hours and finally fell asleep. The following day I felt only weakness. Madame Choglokova took all possible care of me during this violent attack; in general my attendants, though placed around me by surely the most marked wickedness, within a very short time felt an involuntary benevolence for me, and when they were neither prompted nor newly incited, they acted against the principles of those who had employed them, and allowed themselves to follow the inclination that drew them toward me, or rather, toward the sympathy that I inspired in them. They never found me either sulky or bad-tempered, but always ready to respond to their smallest overtures. In all this my joyful manner served me very well, for all these Arguses were often amused by the remarks I made to them and gradually cheered up despite themselves.

At Perova the Empress came down with a new attack of colic. She had herself transported to Moscow and we slowly proceeded to the palace that is only four versts from there. This attack did not last, and a short

* May 22, 1749.

while later the Empress made a pilgrimage to Trinity Monastery.* Her Imperial Majesty wanted to do these sixty versts on foot, and to this end she went to her house in Pokrovskoe. We took the road to the monastery and set up in a very small country house called Raiova that belonged to Madame Choglokova on that road, eleven versts from Moscow. The entire lodging consisted of a small salon in the middle of the house and two very small rooms to either side; our whole entourage was placed in tents pitched around the house. The Grand Duke had one tent there. I occupied one little room, Madame Vladislavova the other; the Choglokovs were in the other rooms. We took meals in the salon. The Empress did three or four versts on foot, then rested a few days. This trip lasted almost the entire summer. We went hunting every afternoon.

When the Empress arrived at Taininskoe, which almost faces Raiova on the other side of the main road to Trinity Monastery, the Hetman Count Razumovsky, the younger brother of the favorite, who was living in his country home Petrovskoe, which was on the Petersburg road on the other side of Moscow, decided to come every day to our residence at Raiova. He was quite cheerful and about our age. We liked him very much; since he was the brother of the favorite, the Choglokovs received him readily into their home. His regular visits continued the entire summer, and we always saw him with joy. He dined and supped with us and after supper returned again to his estate; consequently he covered forty or fifty versts every day. About twenty years later, I one day decided to ask him what could have made him come like that to share the boredom and insipidness of our stay at Raiova back then, while his own house teemed daily with the best company then in Moscow. He replied to me without hesitating, "Love." "But my God," I said, "with whom could you have been in love at our place?" "With whom?" he asked. "With you." I burst out laughing because my whole life I had never suspected it. Besides, he had been married for many years to a rich heiress from the Naryshkin family, whom the Empress had made him marry somewhat against his will, but with whom he seemed to get along well. Besides, it was known that all the prettiest ladies of the court and city fought for his attention, and he truly was a handsome man, very pleasant and with an original mind, and he had incomparably more intelligence than his brother, who nevertheless equaled him in beauty, and surpassed him in generosity and

* June 21, 1749.

kindness.* These two brothers were the best-loved favorites that I ever saw.

Toward the feast of Saint Peter, the Empress told us to join her in Bratovshina. We went there immediately. Because I had spent all spring and part of the summer either hunting or else constantly outdoors, the house at Raiova being so small that we would spend most of the day in the surrounding woods, I arrived in Bratovshina overly sunburned and flushed. Upon seeing me, the Empress exclaimed at my redness and told me that she would send me a rinse to get rid of my sunburn. Indeed, she immediately sent me a vial with a liquid composed of lemon, egg white, and *eau de vie* from France. She ordered my ladies to learn the ingredients and proportions needed to make it. After a few days my burn disappeared, and since then I have always used this rinse and have given it to several people for use in similar circumstances. When the skin is overheated, I know of no better remedy. It also works for what is called in Russian *лишей,* in German *flechten,* and I do not recall for the moment the name in French, and which is nothing but an inflammation that makes the skin crack.†

We spent the feast of Saint Peter at Trinity Monastery, and as there was nothing for the Grand Duke to do that afternoon, he decided to hold a ball in his room, where, however, there were only himself and two of his valets, and two ladies that I had with me, one of whom was more than fifty years old. From the monastery, the Empress went to Taininskoe, and we went once again to Raiova, where we led the same life as before.

We stayed there until mid-August, when the Empress made a journey to Sophino, sixty or seventy versts from Moscow. We camped there. The day following our arrival at this place, we went to her tent; there we found her scolding the man who was in charge of this land. She had gone there to hunt and not found any hares. The man was pale and trembling, and there was no insult that she did not hurl at him; she was really furious. Seeing us approach to kiss her hand, she kissed us as usual, then continued to scold her man; in her anger she would attack whomever upset her or was present. She grew angrier by degrees and spoke with great volubility. Among other things, she began to say that she was very familiar with land management, and that the reign of Empress Anna had taught her about it, that having little, she knew how to avoid expendi-

* He married Ekatarina Ivanovna Naryshkina on October 27, 1746.
† Herpes.

tures, that if she had had debts, she would have been afraid of damning herself, that if she had died with debts, no one would have paid them and that her soul would have gone to hell, which she did not want; that for this reason, when she was at home and when duty permitted, she wore very simple clothes, a white taffeta on top and cheap black cloth beneath, by which she saved money, and that she was not interested in wearing rich dresses in the country or while traveling. Now all this was aimed at me; I had on a dress of lilac and silver. I considered myself warned. This disquisition, which is what it was, to which no one replied a single word, seeing her red and burning with fury, lasted a good forty-five minutes. Finally one of her fools named Aksakov silenced her: he entered and brought her a little porcupine, which he presented to her in his hat. She approached him to look at it, and as soon as she had seen it, she let out a piercing cry and said that it looked like a mouse and fled as fast as she could into her tent because she was mortally afraid of mice. We did not see her again; she dined in her tent, went hunting in the afternoon, and took the Grand Duke with her, and as for me, I was ordered to return with Madame Choglokova to Moscow, where the Grand Duke returned a few hours after me, since the hunt had been short because of the very strong wind that day.

One Sunday the Empress had us come to Taininskoe from Raiova, to which we had returned, and we had the honor of dining there at the table with Her Imperial Majesty.* She was alone at the end of the table, the Grand Duke to her right, I to her left, across from him; next to the Grand Duke was Marshal Buturlin, next to me Countess Shuvalova. The table was very long and narrow, the Grand Duke thus seated between the Empress and Marshal Buturlin, and with the help of the Marshal, who did not dislike alcohol, he drank so much that he got blind drunk, no longer knew what he was saying or doing, slurred his words, and made for such an unpleasant sight that tears came to my eyes, for I hid or disguised as much as possible what was reprehensible in him. The Empress was grateful for my sensitivity and left the table sooner than usual. His Imperial Highness was supposed to go hunting that afternoon with Count Razumovsky. He stayed at Taininskoe and I returned to Raiova.

On the way, I came down with a terrible toothache. The weather began to get cold and humid, and there was almost nothing at Raiova except a

* September 17, 1749.

roof. The brother of Madame Choglokova, Count Hendrikov, who was chamberlain in my service, proposed to his sister to heal me on the spot. I agreed to undergo his remedy, which did not seem to be anything at all, or rather perfect quackery. He immediately went into another room and brought out a very small roll of paper, which he told me to chew with the sore tooth. Hardly had I done what he had suggested than the pains in my tooth became so strong that I had to lie down in bed; I came down with a bad fever that was so high I became delirious. Frightened by my state and attributing it to her brother's cure, Madame Choglokova scolded him severely. She did not leave my bed during the night; she sent word to the Empress that her house at Raiova was in no way fitting for someone who was as gravely ill as I seemed to her, and she carried on so much that the following day I was brought back to Moscow very sick. I was in bed ten or twelve days, and the pain in my tooth came back every afternoon at the same time.

At the beginning of September, the Empress went to Ascension Monastery, where we were ordered to go for her name day. On that day, she named Monsieur Ivan Ivanovich Shuvalov gentleman of the bedchamber. This was an event at court; everyone whispered that he was a new favorite. I rejoiced at his promotion because when he was a page, I had noticed him as a person of promising diligence; one always found him with a book in hand. Back from this excursion, I fell ill with a terrible sore throat and high fever; the Empress came to see me during this illness. I had hardly begun to get better and was still very weak, when Her Imperial Majesty through Madame Choglokova ordered me to put the headdress on Countess Rumiantseva's niece and attend her wedding to Monsieur Alexander Naryshkin, who afterward became the Grand Cupbearer. Madame Choglokova, who saw that I was just barely convalescing, was a bit pained when she told me of this compliment; it did not bring me much pleasure, because I saw clearly that my health and perhaps my life concerned others very little. I spoke about it in this way with Madame Vladislavova, who seemed to me as little pleased as I was by this order, given without consideration or attention. I gathered my strength, and on the day of the wedding, the bride was brought into my room; I crowned her with diamonds, and when this was done, she was taken to the court church to be married.* For my part, I was made

* October 8, 1749.

to go in the company of Madame Choglokova and my court to the Naryshkin's house. Now, in Moscow we were staying in the palace at the end of the German Sloboda. To get to the Naryshkin's house, one had to cross all of Moscow and cover at least seven versts. This was in October toward nine in the evening; it was freezing enough to crack stone, and the layer of ice was such that one could only advance with very small steps. It took me at least two and a half hours on the path both going and coming, and there was not a single man, nor a single horse in my entourage, that did not fall at least once. Finally arriving at Kazansky Church, near the gate known as Trinity, we encountered another problem. In this church, the sister of Ivan Ivanovich Shuvalov, who had been crowned by the Empress while I was putting the headdress on Mademoiselle Rumiantseva, was being married at the same time, and a whole tangle of carriages was at this gate.* We would stop with each step, then the falling would begin again, since no horse was shod for the ice. Finally we arrived, not however in the best of moods. We waited a very long time for the newlyweds, who had endured more or less the same accidents as we had. The Grand Duke accompanied the young couple, then we continued to wait for the Empress. Finally we went to the banquet; after dinner we performed a few rounds of ceremonial dance in the room, then were told to lead the newlyweds to their apartment. To do this, we had to traverse several rather cold hallways, climb several staircases, which were no less cold, then pass through long galleries hastily constructed from wet planks, from which water dripped everywhere. Finally reaching the apartment, we sat at a table covered with desserts; we stayed only to toast the health of the newlyweds, then conducted the bride to the bedroom, and we departed to return home. The following evening we had to return there. Who would have believed that rather than harm my health, this ordeal in no way impeded my convalescence? The next day, I was better than I had been the day before.

At the beginning of winter, I saw that the Grand Duke was in a very anxious state. I did not know why this was; he no longer trained his pack of hunting dogs; he came into my room twenty times a day with a very pained air, and was dreamy and distracted. He bought himself some German books, but what books? One set consisted of Lutheran prayer books,

---

* Praskovia Ivanovna Shuvalova married Prince Nikolai Fedorovich Golitsyn.

and the other of the history and trials of several highway robbers, who had been hanged or broken on the wheel. He read all this by turns when he was not playing the violin. Since he usually could not keep what was bothering him to himself for long, and he could tell no one but me, I waited patiently for him to talk about it. One day he finally revealed to me what was tormenting him. I found that the thing was infinitely more serious than I had supposed.

During almost the entire summer, at least during our stay at Raiova and on the way to Trinity Monastery, I had hardly seen the Grand Duke except at meals and in bed. He came to bed after I had fallen asleep and got up before I awoke; he had passed the rest of the time almost entirely with hunting or with preparations for the hunt. Under the pretext of amusing the Grand Duke, Choglokov had obtained two packs of dogs from the Grand Master of the Hunt, the one of Russian dogs, and the other of French and German dogs, attached to which was an old French whipper-in, a boy from Courland, and a German. As Monsieur Choglokov had taken upon himself to run the Russian pack, His Imperial Highness took over management of the foreign pack, for which Choglokov cared not at all. Each of them managed in great detail everything regarding his enterprise. Consequently, His Imperial Highness himself went continuously to his pack's kennel or else the huntsmen came to his residence to inform him of the state of the pack, of its conditions and needs, and to speak frankly, he worked his way into the company of these people, eating and drinking with them; on the hunt he was always in their midst.

At that time the Butirsky regiment was in Moscow. In this regiment there was a lieutenant named Iakov Baturin, who was deeply in debt, a gambler, and known as a very bad fellow, and at the same time a very resolute man. I do not know by what chance or how this man became acquainted with the huntsmen of the French pack, but I believe that the one and the other had their quarters in or near the village of Mutishcha or Alexeevsky. Eventually it happened that the huntsmen told the Grand Duke that there was a lieutenant of the Butirsky regiment whom they knew who showed a great devotion to His Imperial Highness and who said that the entire regiment felt the same. The Grand Duke listened to this story with self-satisfaction, wanting to know from his huntsmen details about the regiment. He was told many bad things about the leaders and many good things about the subordinates. Finally Baturin, still acting through the huntsmen, asked to be presented to the

Grand Duke during the hunt. At first the Grand Duke was not entirely willing to do this, but eventually he consented. One thing led to another, and one day while the Grand Duke was hunting, Baturin waited in an isolated spot. Upon seeing him, Baturin fell to his knees swearing that he recognized no other master but him and would do all that he ordered. The Grand Duke told me that he, the Grand Duke, hearing this oath pronounced, was frightened by it and that he spurred his horse on and left the other man on his knees in the woods, and that the huntsmen who had introduced him had not heard what Baturin had said. The Grand Duke claimed that he had not had other contacts with this man, and that he had even warned the huntsmen to be careful lest this man bring them harm. His present worries arose from the fact that the huntsmen had come to tell him that Baturin had been arrested and transferred to Preobrazhenskoe, site of the Secret Chancery, which had jurisdiction over crimes against the state. His Imperial Highness trembled for the huntsmen and greatly feared being compromised. As for the huntsmen, his fears were soon realized, for he learned a few days later that they had been arrested and taken to Preobrazhenskoe. I tried to quell his anguish, telling him that if he had truly not entered into any discussion with that man other than what he was telling me, as guilty as the other man might be, I did not believe that one could find much to criticize in what he had done, and it seemed to me at most an imprudence to have fallen in with such bad company. I cannot say if he was telling me the truth; I have reason to believe that he played down what the discussions had been because to me personally he pronounced only a few short remarks on this affair rather reluctantly. However, the excessive fear that he felt could also have produced the same effect on him. Sometime later, he told me that the huntsmen had been released, but ordered across the border, and that they had let him know that they had not mentioned his name, which made him jump with joy; calm returned to his spirit, and there was no more talk of this affair. As for Ioasaf Baturin, he was found utterly guilty. I neither read nor witnessed his case, but I have since learned that he was planning nothing less than to kill the Empress, set fire to the palace, and by this horror and in this chaos, to carry the Grand Duke to the throne. After being tortured, he was condemned to spend the rest of his days at Shlusselburg locked in the fortress and during my reign, having tried to break out of prison, he was sent to Kamchatka, from which he escaped with Beniovsky, and he was killed while pillaging on the Island of Formosa in the Pacific Ocean.[*]

On December 15 we left Moscow for St. Petersburg. We traveled day and night in an open sleigh. Halfway there I again came down with a severe toothache; despite this the Grand Duke would not consent to close the sleigh. Grudgingly he allowed me to pull the curtain of the sleigh a little in order to protect myself from the cold, humid wind that struck me in the face. Finally we arrived at Tsarskoe Selo, where the Empress already was, having passed us along the way, which was her custom. As soon as I got out, I went to the apartment set aside for us and sent for the Empress's chief doctor, Boerhave, nephew of the famous one, and I begged him to pull this tooth, which had been tormenting me for four or five months. He consented only reluctantly, but I absolutely wanted this, and finally he sent for my surgeon, Guyon. I sat on the floor with Boerhave to one side and Choglokov to the other, and Guyon pulled the tooth, but at the moment that he pulled it, my eyes, my nose, and my mouth became a fountain, with blood flowing from my mouth, and water from my nose and eyes. Then Boerhave, who had very sound judgment, cried, "Clumsy fool!" and having been given the tooth, he said, "It is just as I feared and why I did not want this tooth to be pulled." Guyon, while pulling the tooth, had pulled out a piece of my lower jaw, to which the tooth had been attached. The Empress came to the door of my room at the moment all this was happening; I was told later that she was moved to tears. I was put to bed, and suffered a great deal for more than four weeks. Despite all this, we went to the city the following day, again in an open sleigh. I did not leave my room until halfway through January 1750, because on my lower cheek, Monsieur Guyon's five fingers had imprinted blue and yellow marks.

[*] In part 3 of her middle memoir, dated 1791, Catherine writes that she sent Baturin to Kamchatka in 1770, and that Beniovsky and his followers deserved to hang (167). She evidently did not know that Baturin had died in 1772. However, in 1773 she pardoned Beniovsky and his followers, allowing them to return to Russia. In a letter to Procurator General Prince Viazemsky (October 2, 1773), she explains that their request to return "shows how the Russian loves his Russia, and their trust in me and my mercy has touched my heart" (quoted in Böhme 2:102). This internal evidence indicates that parts 2 and 3 of the middle memoir, the so-called 1791 memoir, were written after part 1 (dated 1771), finished before October 1773, and only edited in 1791 (ix).

1750

Peter's confidantes, the Princess of Courland and the Countess
Vorontsova; his refusal to take baths; his accident with a whip;
Holstein oysters; his negotiations over Holstein with Denmark;
Mme. d'Arnim's challenge to Catherine's skill on horseback;
court masquerades; Elizabeth's new favorite; Catherine's English
spaniel; her simple ball dress

The first day of that year, wanting my hair done, I saw my young hairdresser, a Kalmuck whom I had raised, exceedingly flushed and with a heavy look in his eyes. I asked him what was wrong; he told me that he had a severe headache and was very hot. I dismissed him, telling him to go to bed because he truly was exhausted. He went away, and that evening I was told that he had just shown signs of smallpox. I escaped with only the fear that I had of catching smallpox, for I did not come down with it, although he had combed my hair.

The Empress spent much of carnival at Tsarskoe Selo. Petersburg was almost empty; most people who lived there stayed out of duty, not out of liking for it. When the court was in Moscow and about to return to Petersburg, all the courtiers rushed to ask for leaves for a year, six months, or at least a few weeks in order to stay in Moscow. The officials, such as senators and others, would do the same, and when they feared not obtaining a leave, then came the fake or real illnesses of husbands, wives, fathers, mothers, brothers, sisters, or children, or else trials and other indispensable affairs to settle. In a word, six months and sometimes more were necessary before the court and the city returned to what they had been before the court's departure, and while the court was absent, grass grew in the streets of Petersburg because there were almost no carriages in the city. Under these circumstances, for the moment not a lot of company could be expected, especially for us, who were moreover kept quite isolated. Monsieur Choglokov decided during this time to entertain us, or rather, since he and his wife did not know what to do in their boredom, he invited the Grand Duke and me to come every afternoon to play cards at their residence in the apartment that he occupied at the court, which consisted of four or five rather small rooms. He invited the gentlemen and ladies of the court, and the Princess of Courland, daughter of Duke Ernst Johann Biron, the former favorite of Empress Anna. Empress Elizabeth had let this Duke come back from Siberia, where during the regency of Princess Anna he had been exiled. He had been assigned to stay in the city of Yaroslavl, on the Volga; there he had lived with his wife, his two sons, and his daughter.

This girl was neither beautiful, nor pretty, nor shapely—she was hunchbacked and rather small—but she had pretty eyes, intelligence, and a singular capacity for intrigue. Her father and her mother did not love her very much; she claimed that they constantly mistreated her. One fine day, she escaped from the paternal household and fled to the house of Madame Pushkina, the wife of the governor of Yaroslavl. This woman, delighted to make herself important at the court, brought her to Moscow and spoke to Madame Shuvalova, and they passed off the Princess of Courland's flight from her father's house as the result of the persecution that her parents had inflicted upon her because she had manifested a desire to embrace the Greek Orthodox religion. And indeed the first thing she did at the court really was to confess her faith. The Empress was her godmother, and afterward she was given an apartment among the maids of honor. Monsieur Choglokov took pains to cultivate her because the Princess's older brother had provided the foundation for his fortune by taking him from the cadet corps, where he had been raised, into the horse guard, and keeping him in his service as an errand boy.[*]

Having made her way into our company and playing cards several hours every day with the Grand Duke, Choglokov, and me, the Princess of Courland at first conducted herself with great restraint. She was flattering, and her wit made one forget the disagreeable aspect of her figure, especially when she was seated. She spoke to each person in a manner that would please him. Everyone regarded her as an interesting orphan; she was considered a person of practically no consequence. In the eyes of the Grand Duke she had another merit, which was of no small importance. She was a kind of foreign Princess, and what is more, German; consequently they spoke only German together. This made her charming in

[*] Her brothers were Peter and Karl Ernst.

his eyes; he began to pay her as much attention as he was capable of giv-ing. When she dined in her residence, he sent her wine and a few of the fa-vorite dishes from his table, and when he acquired some new grenadier's hat or some bandolier, he sent them to her so she could see them.

The Princess of Courland, who at the time was twenty-four or twenty-five years old, was not the only acquisition that the court had made in Moscow. The Empress had engaged the two Countesses Vorontsova, nieces of the Vice Chancellor and daughters of Count Roman, his younger brother. The elder girl, Maria, may have been fourteen; she was placed among the Empress's maids of honor. The younger, Elizabeth, was only eleven; she was given to me. She was a very ugly child with a sallow com-plexion and she was extremely dirty. They both started out in Petersburg by catching smallpox at the court, and the younger one became even uglier as a result because her facial features were totally deformed and her face was covered not with pockmarks but with scars.

Toward the end of carnival, the Empress returned to the city.* The first week of Lent, we began to make our devotions. Wednesday evening I was supposed to go bathe in Madame Choglokova's house, but the evening before, she came into my room, where the Grand Duke was too, and conveyed to him as well on the Empress's behalf the order to go bathe. Now, not only did he have a great dislike for bathing and all the other Russian customs or national habits, he even mortally detested them. He said quite firmly that he would do no such thing. She was also very stubborn and blunt in her speech, and told him that this would be disobeying Her Imperial Majesty. He declared that he could not be or-dered to do what was repugnant to his nature, that he knew that the baths, to which he had never been, did not agree with him, that he did not want to die and that he held life most dear, and that the Empress would never force him to go. Madame Choglokova shot back that the Empress would know how to punish his disobedience. At this he became incensed and said angrily to her, "I will see what she does to me. I am not a child." Then Madame Choglokova warned him that the Empress would have him put in the fortress. At this he began to cry bitterly and they said to each other the most outrageous things that fury inspired in them, and indeed neither had any common sense. Finally she departed, saying that she was going to report this conversation word for word to

* February 17, 1750.

the Empress. I do not know what she did, but she returned and the subject of argument changed, because she came to say that the Empress said that we did not have any children, that she was very angry, that she wanted to know which of us was at fault, and that she would send me a midwife and him a doctor. To all this she added many other outrageous remarks, of which we could make neither heads nor tails, and ended by saying that the Empress excused us from our devotions that week because the Grand Duke had said that the bath would undermine his health. During these two conversations, it should be known that I did not open my mouth, *primo,* because they both spoke with such vehemence that I could not get a word in; *secondo,* because I saw that they were both talking the most complete nonsense. I do not know how the Empress judged all this, but in the end, there was no more talk of either matter beyond what I have just reported.

Toward the middle of Lent, the Empress departed for Count Razumovsky's house at Gostilitsa to celebrate his birthday and she sent us with her maids of honor and our usual entourage to Tsarskoe Selo. The weather was extraordinarily mild and even so warm that on March 17 there was no more snow but dust on the road. Upon arriving at Tsarskoe Selo, the Grand Duke and Choglokov began to hunt. The ladies and I went out, sometimes on foot, sometimes in carriages as often as we could. In the evenings we played different little games. Here the Grand Duke developed a decided taste for the Princess of Courland, especially when he had drunk in the evening at supper, which he did almost every day. He was never more than a step away from her and spoke only to her. Eventually this affair was in full swing in my presence and that of everyone, which began to shock my vanity and my self-esteem, seeing that this monstrous little figure was preferred over me. One evening, as I rose from the table, Madame Vladislavova said to me that everyone was shocked that this little hunchback was preferred over me. I replied to her, "What can I do?" Tears came to my eyes and I went to bed. I had only just fallen asleep when the Grand Duke came to bed as well. As he was drunk and did not know what he was doing, he tried to strike up a conversation with me about the eminent qualities of his belle. I pretended to be in a deep sleep so as to make him shut up more quickly, but after having spoken even more loudly to wake me up and seeing that I gave no sign of being awakened, he gave me two or three rather hard punches in the side, cursing the depth of my slumber, then turned, and fell asleep. I cried a great deal that night over the affair and the blows he had given me, and over my situation, which was in every way as disagreeable as it was tedious. The following day, he seemed ashamed of what he had done; he did not speak to me about it and I pretended not to have felt anything.

Two days later we returned to town. The last week of Lent we began again to make our devotions; no more mention of bathing was made to the Grand Duke. Another accident happened to him that week that made him think a bit. In his room during the day, he was almost always doing one thing or another. One afternoon he practiced cracking an immense coachman's whip that he had had made. He snapped it right and left with large strokes and continually made his valets run from one corner to the other for fear of getting slashed. I do not know how he did it, but it happened that he gave himself a very big lash on the cheek. The scar went down the entire left side of his face and was bleeding. He was very alarmed, fearing that he would be unable to appear in public on Easter and that since he had a bloody cheek, the Empress would again forbid him from making his devotions, and that when she learned the reason, the whip exercise would bring him some unpleasant reprimand. He could think of nothing better to do in his distress than to come running to me for advice, which he never failed to do in such cases.

I saw him enter with his bloody cheek. I cried out on seeing him, "My God, what has happened to you?" He told me the story. Having considered the situation a bit, I said to him, "Well, perhaps I will get you out of this mess. First of all, go back to your room and make it so that your cheek is seen as little as possible. I will come into your apartment as soon as I have what I need, and I hope that no one will notice." He departed and I remembered that when I had fallen a few years before in the garden at Peterhof and scratched my cheek so badly it bled, my surgeon, Guyon, had given me a salve with white lead* with which I covered my scratch. I went on appearing in public and no one even noticed that I had scratched my cheek. I immediately sent for this salve, and when it was brought to me, I went into the Grand Duke's apartment and I treated his cheek so well that in the mirror he himself could see nothing. Thursday we went to communion with the Empress in the big court church, and when we had taken

---

* A white heavy powder used in medical ointments for burns.

communion we returned to our places. The sunlight shone on the Grand Duke's cheek, and Choglokov approached us to say I know not what. Looking at the Grand Duke, he said, "Wipe your cheek because there is ointment on it." At this I said to the Grand Duke, as if playing, "And I who am your wife forbid you to wipe it." Then the Grand Duke said to Monsieur Choglokov, "You see how these wives treat us. We dare not even wipe ourselves when they do not want it." Monsieur Choglokov began to laugh and said, "What a truly feminine whim." The matter rested there, and the Grand Duke was grateful to me, both for the ointment, which did him a service by sparing him unpleasantness, and for my presence of mind, which did not leave even the least suspicion in the mind of Monsieur Choglokov.

As I had to stay up Easter night, I went to bed on Holy Saturday around five o'clock in the afternoon in order to sleep until the time when I would get dressed. I was hardly in bed when the Grand Duke came running with all his might and told me to get up and come without delay to eat the very freshest oysters that had just been brought to him from Holstein. When they arrived it was for him a grand and double feast; he loved them, and they also came from Holstein, his native land, for which he had a great predilection but which he did not govern any better for that, and in which he did and was made to do terrible things, as will be seen later. I would have offended him and exposed myself to a very violent quarrel if I had not gotten up. Therefore I arose and went to his apartment, although I was exhausted from performing my devotions for Holy Week. Once in his apartment, I found the oysters already served; I ate a dozen of them, after which he allowed me to return to my room to go back to bed, and it was for him to finish his oyster repast. I further pleased him by not eating too many because there remained more for him; he was infinitely greedy when it came to oysters. At midnight I got up and dressed myself to go to matins and to Easter mass, but I was unable to stay until the end of the service because I was seized by violent stomach cramps; I do not remember in all my life having had such pains. I returned to my room with only Princess Gagarina, all my servants being at church. She helped me undress for bed and sent for doctors. I was given medicine; I spent the first two days of the feast in bed.

It was around this time or a little before that Count de Bernis, Ambassador from the court of Vienna; Count Lynar, the Danish envoy; and

General Arnim, the Saxon envoy, came to Russia; the latter brought his wife, née Hoym, with him.* Count de Bernis was Piedmontese. At that time he was just over fifty years old, witty, amiable, merry, and educated, and of such a character that young people preferred him over and enjoyed themselves with him more than with those of their own age. He was generally loved and esteemed, and a thousand times I said and repeated that if this man or one like him had been placed in the Grand Duke's service, it would have resulted in great good for this Prince, who like me had developed an affection and a particular and very distinguished esteem for Count de Bernis. The Grand Duke himself said that with such a man by one's side, one would be ashamed to commit foolishness. This was an excellent thing to say, which I have never forgotten. Count de Bernis had with him Count Hamilton, a Knight of Malta, as gentleman of the embassy. One day at the court, when I asked the latter for news about the health of the ambassador, Count de Bernis, who was indisposed, I decided to tell Knight Hamilton that I had the highest opinion of Count Bathyany, whom the Queen Empress Maria Theresa had just then named the governor of her two eldest sons, the archdukes Joseph and Charles, because in this function he had been preferred over Count de Bernis. In the year 1780, when I had my first meeting with Emperor Joseph II at Magilov, His Imperial Majesty told me that he knew I had made this remark. I replied to him that apparently he had heard it from Count Hamilton, who had been placed in this Prince's service when Hamilton had returned from Russia. He said that I had guessed rightly and that Count de Bernis, whom he had not known, had been reputed to be more apt for this position than his former governor.

Count Lynar, the envoy of the Danish King, had been sent to Russia to negotiate the exchange of Holstein, which belonged to the Grand Duke, for the County of Oldenburg. He was a man who united, so it was said, a great deal of knowledge with equal ability. His outward appearance was that of the most complete fop. He was big and well built, had reddish-blond hair and a woman's white complexion. It was said that he took such great care of his skin that he slept only after covering his face and his hands with cream and wore gloves and a night mask. He boasted that he had eighteen children and claimed that he had always prepared his chil-

* Count Lynar arrived February 7, 1750.

dren's wet nurses by putting them in the family way.* Very white himself, Count Lynar wore the White Order of Denmark and had clothes in only extremely light colors, such as sky blue, apricot, lilac, flesh tones, etc., although at that time one rarely saw such light shades on men. At their home, Grand Chancellor Count Bestuzhev and his wife treated Count Lynar like the child of the house, and he was much feted there, but this did not shield his dim-wittedness from ridicule. He had yet another strike against him, which was that there were still fresh memories of his brother, who had been more than well received by Princess Anna, whose regency had been despised.† As soon as this man arrived, he could not wait to brag about his negotiations over the exchange of Holstein for the County of Oldenburg. Grand Chancellor Count Bestuzhev had Monsieur Pechlin, the Grand Duke's minister for his Duchy of Holstein, come to his home and told him what Count Lynar had come for.

Monsieur Pechlin made a report about this to the Grand Duke, who passionately loved his land of Holstein. Ever since he had been in Moscow, it had been represented to His Imperial Highness as insolvent. He had asked the Empress for money; she had given him a little. This money had never arrived in Holstein and instead had paid His Imperial Highness's immense debts in Russia. Monsieur Pechlin represented the financial affairs of Holstein as desperate. This was easy for Monsieur Pechlin to do because the Grand Duke left the administration to him and gave it only little attention or none at all, to the extent that once an impatient Pechlin told him in a sober voice, "My lord, it is up to a sovereign to involve himself or not with the governing of his country. If he does not get involved, then the country governs itself, but it governs itself badly." This Pechlin was a very short, very fat man, who wore an immense wig, but he lacked neither knowledge nor ability. This thickset, squat figure was inhabited by a sharp, nimble intelligence; he was accused only of being indelicate in his choice of means. Grand Chancellor Count Bestuzhev trusted him a great deal, and Pechlin was one of his most intimate confidants.

Monsieur Pechlin made clear to the Grand Duke that to listen was not to negotiate, that negotiation was far from agreement, and that he would always have the power to break off the discussions when he judged it ap-

---

* By 1751, he had ten children, and eventually he had twelve.

† Count Moritz Karl Lynar was the favorite of Anna Leopoldovna, regent (1740–41) for Ivan VI.

propriate. Eventually one thing led to another and the Grand Duke was persuaded to authorize Monsieur Pechlin to hear the minister of Denmark's proposals, and in this way the negotiations were opened. Deep down these discussions pained the Grand Duke; he spoke to me about it. I had been raised with the house of Holstein's ancient hatred of Denmark and had been told repeatedly that Count Bestuzhev had only harmful designs against the Grand Duke and me. I listened to talk of these negotiations only with a great deal of impatience and anxiety, and I tried to thwart the negotiations as much as I could by influencing the Grand Duke. At any rate, no one said a word about all this to me except for him, and he was advised to keep it very secret, especially, they added, around ladies. I think that this remark was directed at me more than anyone else, but they were deceived, because His Imperial Highness could not wait to tell me about them. The further the negotiations advanced, the more they tried to present them to the Grand Duke in a favorable and pleasant light. I often saw him enchanted with what he would acquire, and then he would have bitter changes of heart and regrets about what he was going to abandon. When he was seen to be drifting, the conferences were slowed down, and they were restarted only after some new enticement had been invented to make things appear in a favorable light.

At the beginning of spring, we were made to move into the summer garden and to live in the little house built by Peter I, where the apartments are on the same level as the garden.* The stone quay and the Fontanka bridge did not yet exist.† In this house, I had one of the most bitter sorrows that I had during the whole reign of Empress Elizabeth. One morning I was told that the Empress had removed my old chamber valet, Timofei Evreinov, from my service. The pretext for this dismissal was a quarrel that he had had in a wardrobe with a man who was serving us coffee, during which the Grand Duke had unexpectedly appeared and had heard some of the insults that the men had said to each other. Evreinov's antagonist had gone to complain to Monsieur Choglokov and had told him that without consideration for the Grand Duke's presence, Evreinov had uttered all manner of abuse to him. Monsieur Choglokov immediately made a report of this to the Empress, who ordered that both men be

---

* April 30, 1750.

† As Catherine points out in part 3 of the middle memoir, "That meant that the Empress did not wish to have us as close to her apartment as we had been before" (181).

dismissed from the court, and Evreinov was banished to Kazan, where he was later made chief of police. The truth of the matter was that Evreinov and the other man were both very devoted to us, especially the former, and this was only a long-sought pretext to take him from me. He was in charge of all my belongings. The Empress ordered that a man named Shkurin, whom Evreinov had taken as an assistant, take his place. At the time I did not trust this man.

After staying in Peter I's house for a while, we were moved to the wooden Summer Palace, where new apartments had been prepared for us that on one side looked out on the Fontanka, which was then nothing but a muddy swamp, and on the other onto an ugly, narrow little courtyard. On Pentecost, the Empress told me to invite the wife of the Saxon envoy, Madame d'Arnim, to accompany me on horseback to Catherinenhof. This woman had claimed that she loved horseback riding and boasted that she did it well, and the Empress wanted to see if this was so. I therefore sent an invitation to Madame d'Arnim to come with me. She was a tall woman, very well built, between twenty-five and twenty-six years old, and a bit thin, and her face was anything but pretty, as it was quite long and rather scarred by smallpox, but since she dressed well, from a distance she had a kind of glamour and appeared to have rather fair skin. Madame d'Arnim arrived at my residence around five o'clock in the afternoon dressed as a man from head to foot, with a coat of red cloth trimmed with gold braid and a green *gros de tours* jacket also trimmed in gold. She did not know where to put her hat and her hands, and she seemed rather gauche to us. As I knew that the Empress did not like me to go riding astride like a man, I had had an English lady's saddle prepared for me, and I wore an English riding habit of very rich azure and silver cloth with crystal buttons, which almost perfectly resembled diamonds, and my black helmet was bordered with a row of diamonds. I went down to mount my horse. At this moment the Empress came to our apartments to watch us depart. Since I was very agile then and very accustomed to this exercise, as soon as I was near my horse I jumped on it. I let my skirt, which was open, fall to either side of the horse. I was told that the Empress, seeing me mount with such agility and deftness, exclaimed in astonishment that it was impossible to mount more skillfully. She asked what saddle I was using and, upon learning that I was on a woman's saddle, said, "One would swear that she is on a man's saddle." When it was Madame d'Arnim's turn, her skill did not overwhelm Her Imperial Majesty. This woman had had her horse brought from her house. It was an ugly black nag, very big and very heavy, which our servants claimed was one of the wheelhorses for her carriage. She needed a ladder to mount it. All this was done with all kinds of fuss, and finally with the aid of several people she was placed on her nag, which broke into a rough trot that bounced the woman a great deal since she was neither firm in her saddle nor in her stirrups, and held on to the saddle with her hand. Seeing her mounted, I set off, and those who could followed me. I caught up to the Grand Duke, who had started before me, and Madame d'Arnim and her nag stayed behind. I was told that the Empress laughed heartily and was little impressed with Madame d'Arnim's manner of riding. I believe that at some distance from the court Madame Choglokova, who followed in a carriage, collected the lady, who had lost first her hat, then her stirrups. Finally she was brought to Catherinenhof, but the adventure was not yet over.

It had rained that day until three in the afternoon, and the stairway landing at Catherinenhof was covered in pools of water. After I had dismounted from my horse and been in the salon for some time, where there were many people, I decided to walk across the exposed landing to go to another room, where my ladies were. Madame d'Arnim wanted to follow me, and because I was walking quickly, she could follow me only by running and ended up in the puddle of water, where she slipped and fell her entire length, which made the numerous spectators on the landing laugh. She got up a bit confused, blaming her fall on new boots that she wore that day. We returned from the jaunt in a carriage, and on the way she spoke to us of the quality of her nag, while we bit our lips so as not to burst out laughing. Thus for several days she gave the court and city something to laugh about. My ladies claimed that she had fallen because she had tried to imitate me without being as agile as I was. Madame Choglokova, who was not a jovial person, laughed until she cried when the story was retold and long thereafter.

From the Summer Palace we went to Peterhof, where that year we resided at Monplaisir.* We would regularly spend part of the afternoon at Madame Choglokova's residence, and since people often went there, we were kept sufficiently amused. From there we went to Oranienbaum,

* June 6, 1750.

where we would hunt every day that God granted, sometimes spending thirteen hours a day on horseback. That summer was rather rainy, however. I remember that one day when I was returning to the house completely wet, I met my tailor as I got off my horse, and he said to me, "Seeing you in this state, I am no longer surprised that I can barely keep you in riding habits and that I am continually asked for new ones." I wore only silk camlet habits, which the rain would crack while the sun would ruin the colors, and consequently I always needed new ones. It was during this time that I invented my own saddles, on which I could sit as I wanted. They had English pommels, and one could pass one's leg over them to sit like a man. Moreover, the pommel unscrewed, and a stirrup could be lowered and raised at will according to what I judged appropriate. If the grooms were asked how I rode, they said, On a woman's saddle, in accordance with the Empress's wishes. They did not lie. I slipped my leg over only when I was sure not to be seen, and since I did not boast about my invention and the grooms were happy to do me the favor, I did not have any trouble. The Grand Duke cared very little about how I rode. As for the grooms, they found less risk in me riding astride, especially as I continually ran with the hunt, than on English saddles, which they detested, always fearing some accident for which they might later be blamed. To tell the truth, I cared not at all for hunting, but I passionately loved horseback riding. The more violent this exercise, the better I liked it, so that if a horse broke loose, I chased after it and brought it back. Also during this time, I always had a book in my pocket; if I had a moment to myself, I used it to read.

I noticed that during these hunts, Monsieur Choglokov softened his demeanor greatly and above all toward me. This made me fear that he had decided to court me, which was in no way acceptable to me. He was blond and foppish, very fat, and equally thick in mind and body. He was hated like a toad by everyone and was not at all pleasant either. His wife's jealousy, nastiness, and malevolence were also to be avoided, especially by me, who had no other support in the world but myself and whatever merit I had. I therefore ducked and dodged very skillfully, as it seemed to me, all of Monsieur Choglokov's pursuits, without him ever being able to complain about my politeness, however. All this was perfectly clear to his wife, who was grateful to me for it and afterward formed a strong friendship with me, in part because of this, as I will recount later.

There were at our court two chamberlains Saltykov, sons of the general adjutant Vasily Fedorovich Saltykov, whose wife, Maria Alekseevna, née Princess Golitsyn, mother of these two youths, was highly considered by the Empress because of the notable services that she had rendered during her accession to the throne, having shown her a rare fidelity and devotion. The younger of these sons, Sergei, had shortly before married one of the Empress's maids of honor, Matrena Pavlovna Balk. His older brother was named Peter. He was a fool in every sense of the word, and he had the most stupid physiognomy that I have seen in my life: big vacant eyes, a pug nose, and a mouth that hung open, with which he was a supreme tattler and as such quite welcome at the Choglokovs' home, where he was otherwise considered a man of no importance. I suspect that it was Madame Vladislavova who, on account of her long-standing acquaintance with this imbecile's mother, suggested to the Choglokovs the idea of marrying him to the Princess of Courland. And so it happened that he got himself ready to court her, proposed marriage, and obtained her consent, while his parents requested the Empress's. The Grand Duke learned of all this only when the matter was already completely arranged. Upon our return to the city, he was very upset by it and treated the Princess of Courland coldly.* I do not know what excuse she gave him, but it happened that although he greatly disapproved of her marriage, she did not fail to keep a place in his affections and for a very long time maintained some influence with him. For my part, I was delighted with this marriage and had a superb wedding gown embroidered for the bride. At that time, weddings at the court, after receiving the Empress's consent, happened only after several years of waiting because Her Imperial Majesty fixed the date herself, very often forgetting it for quite a while, and when she was reminded, she postponed it from one day to another. So it happened in this case. In autumn we returned to the city, and I had the satisfaction of seeing the Princess of Courland and Monsieur Peter Saltykov thank Her Imperial Majesty for the consent that she had deigned to give to their union. In any event, the Saltykov family was one of the oldest and most noble of this empire. It was related to the Imperial house itself by the mother of Empress Anna, who was a Saltykov, but from another branch of the family, whereas Monsieur Biron, made Duke of Courland by the favor of Empress Anna, had only been the son of a

* September 17, 1750.

small farmer for a gentleman of Courland.* This farmer was named Biren, but the favor that the son enjoyed in Russia led the Biron family in France to recognize him as their own, persuaded as they were by Cardinal de Fleury, who, wanting to win over the Russian court, cultivated the views and vanity of Biren, Duke of Courland.

As soon as we returned to the city, we were told that besides the two days per week already devoted to French theater, there would be two other days of masked balls each week. The Grand Duke added another day for concerts in his apartment, and court was usually held on Sunday. We thus prepared for a quite merry and animated winter. One of the masked balls was for the court alone and those whom the Empress deigned to admit; the other was for all the titled people in the city to the rank of colonel and those who served as officers in the guards. Sometimes the entire nobility and the wealthiest merchants were also permitted to come. The court balls did not exceed 150 to 200 people and those that were called public, 800 maskers. In the year 1744, in Moscow, the Empress had enjoyed making all the men appear at the court masquerades in women's clothing, all the women in men's clothing, without masks on their faces. It was a day of perfect metamorphosis at court. The men wore large hoop skirts with women's coats and were coiffed like the ladies were every day at court, and the women were in men's outfits like those worn on court days. The men did not much like these days of metamorphosis. Most were in the worst possible humor because they felt that they were hideous in their costumes. Most of the women resembled stunted little boys, and the eldest had fat, short legs that hardly flattered them. No women looked truly and perfectly good in men's clothing except the Empress herself; since she was very tall and had a somewhat powerful build, men's clothes suited her marvelously. She had more beautiful legs than I have ever seen on any man and admirably proportioned feet. She danced perfectly and had a particular grace in all that she did, whether dressed as a man or a woman. One would have liked to gaze only at her, and one turned away only with regret because no other object could replace her. One day at one of these balls, I watched her dance a minuet. When she finished, she came over to me. I took the liberty of saying to her that it was very fortunate for the ladies that she was not a man and that her portrait

* Praskovia Fedorovna Saltykova was married to Ivan V, Peter I's half brother and co-ruler until Ivan's death. Biron's father, Karl Bühren, was a cornet in the Polish army.

alone, painted in this guise, could turn the head of more than one woman. She received my heartfelt effusion very well and replied to me in the same tone and in the most gracious possible way, saying that if she were a man she would give me the golden apple. I bent over to kiss her hand for such an unexpected compliment; she kissed me, and the entire company sought to discover what had passed between the Empress and me. I did not keep it a secret from Madame Choglokova, who quietly repeated it to two or three people, and within a quarter hour almost everyone knew it by word of mouth.

During the court's most recent stay in Moscow, Prince Iusupov, senator and head of the cadet corps, had been the commander in chief of the city of St. Petersburg, where he had stayed in the court's absence. For his amusement and that of the important persons who were there with him, he had had the cadets alternately perform the best Russian tragedies, by Sumarokov, and the best French ones, by Voltaire. These latter were as poorly spoken as performed by these youths, and the female roles were also taken by cadets, who in general deformed these plays. Upon her return from Moscow, the Empress ordered that Sumarokov's plays be performed at the court by this troupe of young men. The Empress took pleasure in watching these performances, and soon people seemed to notice that she watched them performed with a greater interest than one might have expected. The theater, which was set up in one of the halls of the palace, was transported into her apartment. She took pleasure in dressing the actors. She had superb costumes made for them, and they were completely covered in Her Imperial Majesty's jewels. Above all we noticed that the leading man, who was a rather handsome boy of eighteen or nineteen, was, as one might expect, the most adorned. Outside the theater, he was seen wearing very exquisite diamond buckles, rings, watches, lace, and linen. Eventually he left the cadet corps, and the Grand Master of the Hunt Count Razumovsky, former favorite of the Empress, immediately took him as his adjutant, which gave the former cadet the rank of Captain. At this the courtiers drew conclusions in their usual way and figured that since Count Razumovsky had taken cadet Beketov for his adjutant, this could have no other motive than to counterbalance the favor shown Monsieur Shuvalov, gentleman of the bedchamber, who was known to be neither on good terms nor allied with the Razumovsky family, and finally there was speculation that this young man was beginning to enjoy very great favor with the Empress. Moreover, it was also known that Count Razumovsky had placed in his new adjutant's service another orderly of his, Ivan Perfilievich Elagin. He was married to the Empress's former lady-in-waiting, who had taken care to furnish the young man with the aforementioned linen and lace, and as she was hardly rich, it was easy to imagine that the money for these expenses did not come from this woman's purse.

No one was more intrigued by this young man's growing favor than Princess Gagarina, my maid of honor, who was no longer young and sought to find herself a match to her liking.* She had her own fortune, was not pretty, but had great intelligence and cunning. This was the second time that she had set her heart on the very person who would later enjoy the Empress's favor: the first was Monsieur Shuvalov; the second, this same Beketov, whom I have just discussed. Many young and pretty women were linked to Princess Gagarina; moreover, she had a very large extended family. They accused Monsieur Shuvalov of being the secret reason that the Empress continually had Princess Gagarina reprimanded for her finery, and that she had forbidden her and many other young ladies from wearing now one chiffon and now another. Hating this treatment, Princess Gagarina and all the youngest, prettiest women of the court spoke badly of Monsieur Shuvalov, whom they all began to detest, though they had greatly loved him up until then. He thought to mollify them by paying them his respects and having his most faithful servants make gallant remarks on his behalf, which they regarded as a new offense. He was repulsed and badly received everywhere. All these women fled him like the plague.

While this was going on, the Grand Duke gave me a little English water spaniel that I had wanted. There was a stoker assigned to my room named Ivan Ushakov, who took care of the spaniel. The other servants decided, I know not how, to call my water spaniel Ivan Ivanovich, after this man. Left alone, this spaniel was a nice animal. He walked on his hind legs like a person most of the time and was incredibly frisky—I and my ladies did his hair and dressed him every day in a new way, and the more we dressed him up, the crazier he became. He would sit at the table with us. We would give him a napkin and he would eat very properly from his plate. Then he turned his head and asked to drink by yapping to whoever was behind him. Sometimes he climbed onto the table to take whatever

* Born 1716.

he fancied, like a meat putty or a cookie or something of the sort, which made the company laugh. As he was small, he inconvenienced no one, and we left him alone because he did not abuse the liberty that he enjoyed and he kept himself perfectly clean. This spaniel amused us the whole winter, and the following summer he was taken to Oranienbaum, where Chamberlain Saltykov the younger had come with his wife, who with all the ladies of our court did nothing all day but sew and fashion the hair and the outfits for my spaniel, over which they fought. Eventually Madame Saltykova developed such an affection for the dog that it grew particularly attached to her, and when she left, the dog no longer wanted to leave her nor she the dog, and she begged me so much to let the dog go with her that I gave it to her. She took it under her arm and accompanied by the spaniel, left directly for the estate of her mother-in-law, who was then ill. Seeing her arrive with the dog and perform a thousand silly antics with him, the mother-in-law wanted to know the dog's name, and hearing that it was Ivan Ivanovich, she could not hide her astonishment from the various people who had come to see her from the court at Peterhof. They returned to the court, and after three or four days, the city and the court were buzzing with the tale that all the young women, who were enemies of Monsieur Shuvalov, had a white spaniel named Ivan Ivanovich to deride the Empress's favorite and that they made these spaniels perform all kinds of antics, and wear the bright colors that Shuvalov liked to dress in. The matter went so far that the Empress had the young ladies' parents told that she found it impertinent for them to permit such things. The spaniel's name was immediately changed, but he was fawned over as before and stayed in the Saltykov's house, cherished until his death by his masters, despite the imperial reprimand over him. In fact this was slander, and there was only this one dog, who moreover was black, given this name, and we had not thought of Monsieur Shuvalov in naming him. As for Madame Choglokova, who did not like the Shuvalovs, she had pretended not to notice the dog's name, though she heard it constantly and herself had given many meat patties to the dog, and had laughed at its antics and tricks.

During the last months of that winter and the frequent masquerades and balls at the court, we again saw my two former gentlemen of the bedchamber, Alexander Villebois and Count Zakhar Chernyshev, who had been made colonels in the army. As they were sincerely devoted to me, I was very content to see them again and consequently I received them. For their part, they did not miss a single occasion to give me signs of their affectionate feelings. At that time, I loved to dance. At public balls I usually changed costume three times. My jewelry was always very fine, and if the costume I wore attracted everyone's praise, I was sure never to wear it again, because I had a rule that if it had made a big impression once, it could only make a smaller one the next time. On the other hand, at court balls that the public did not attend, I dressed as simply as I could, and so I paid my respects to the Empress, who did not much like anyone to appear overdressed. However, when the ladies were ordered to come in men's clothes, I came in superb outfits that were meticulously embroidered or gorgeously refined, and this passed without criticism. On the contrary, this pleased the Empress, and I do not really know why. It must be admitted that at that time the cultivation of coquetry was an important part of court life, and there was competition to see whose finery would be the most elegant. I remember that one day at one of these public masquerades, after learning that everyone was having the most beautiful new outfits made, and despairing of surpassing the other women, I decided to put on a bodice of white *gros de tours* and a skirt of the same material over a very small hoop (at the time I had a very thin waist). I had my hair arranged as best I could in front; in back, I had my hair, which was long, very thick, and quite beautiful, curled, and I had it tied with a white ribbon in a ponytail. I had a single rose whose bud and leaves perfectly resembled the real thing placed in my hair. I attached another to my bodice. I put a ruff of very white gauze around my neck, put on cuffs and a little apron of the same gauze, and I went to the ball. As I entered, I clearly saw that all eyes were fixed on me. Without stopping, I crossed the gallery and went into the facing apartment. I met the Empress, who said to me, "Good God, what modesty. What, not even a beauty spot!" I began to laugh and replied that it was for simplicity's sake. She pulled her box of beauty spots from her pocket and chose one of medium size, which she applied to my face. Upon leaving her, I went very quickly into the gallery, where I showed my beauty spot to my intimates. I did the same with the Empress's favorite ladies, and as I was in high spirits, that evening I danced more than usual. In my life, I do not recall having had so much praise from everyone as on that day. They said that I was very beautiful and particularly radiant. To tell the truth, I have never believed myself to be extremely beautiful, but I knew how to please and I think that this was my forte. I returned to the house very happy with my simple invention, whereas all the other outfits were exceptionally fancy. It was with such entertainments that 1750 ended. Madame d'Arnim danced better than she rode. I remember that one day, when she and I wanted to see who would tire sooner, it turned out to be her, and seated on a chair, she confessed that she could no longer go on, whereas I was still dancing.

*Grand Duchess Ekaterina Alekseevna (the future Catherine the Great)
wearing the Order of St. Catherine (1745).*

GEORG CHRISTOPH GROOTH

*Grand Duchess Ekaterina Alekseevna
and Grand Duke Peter Fedorovich
(1744 – 45).*
GEORG CHRISTOPH GROOTH

*Empress Elizabeth in a
black masquerade domino
with a mask in her hand
(1748).*
GEORG CHRISTOPH
GROOTH

Catherine the Great holding her Instruction *(1765–79).*
Although she first wrote it in French (1765–67), the text is in Russian;
on the table are a bust of Peter the Great and books she consulted,
including Montesquieu's Spirit of the Laws *(1748);*
an orb representing her power nestles in
the arm of the chair.

St. Petersburg and Neva River panorama (1753).
MIKHAIL IVANOVICH MAKHAEV

Peterhof and the Grand Cascade (1753), on the Gulf of Finland,
where Peter the Great originally had his summer palace.
MIKHAIL IVANOVICH MAKHAEV

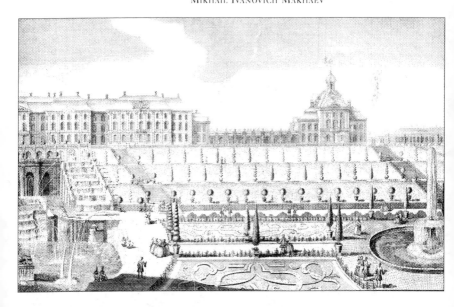

Oranienbaum (1753), home of Peter III and, later, Catherine the Great's summer residence; today called Lomonosov.

MIKHAIL IVANOVICH MAKHAEV

The Summer (or Catherine) Palace, Tsarskoe Selo (Czar's Village):
View of Her Imperial Highness's summer home from the north side (1753).
MIKHAIL IVANOVICH MAKHAEV

PART TWO

1751

At the beginning of 1751 the Grand Duke, who had taken Count de Bernis, Ambassador from the court of Vienna, into his affection as much as I had, decided to talk to him about his Holstein affairs, about the debts with which this land was burdened at the time, and about the negotiations initiated by Denmark, which he had authorized. He told me one day to speak about this with Count de Bernis too. I replied to him that if he ordered me to do it, I would. And indeed, at the next masked ball, I approached Count de Bernis, who stood near the balustrade beyond which there was dancing, and said that the Grand Duke had ordered me to speak to him about the affairs of Holstein. Count de Bernis listened to me with a great deal of interest and attention. I told him quite frankly that being young and devoid of counsel, as well as perhaps poorly understanding affairs of state, and having no experience to cite in my favor, my ideas were my own, that I might lack a great deal of knowledge, but that it seemed to me first of all that the affairs of Holstein were not as desperate as people wanted to make them seem. That moreover, as concerned the exchange itself, which I understood rather well, it might be more advantageous for Russia than for the Grand Duke personally, that assuredly as heir to the throne, the interests of the empire should be dear and precious to him. If for these interests it was absolutely necessary for the Grand Duke to give up Holstein in order to put an end to the interminable disputes with Denmark, then even if Holstein were kept for now, it would only be necessary to choose the right moment and the Grand Duke would consent to give it up. It seemed to me that now was not that moment, neither for the Grand Duke's interests nor his personal glory, that a time or circumstance might come, however, that would render this act both more consequential and more glorious for him and perhaps even more advantageous for the

Russian Empire. But at present, all of this had such a manifest air of intrigue about it that if it succeeded, it would make the Grand Duke appear so weak that he would perhaps never recover from it in public opinion. He had been managing the affairs of his country for only a few days, so to speak. He loved this country passionately, and despite this, they had succeeded in persuading him to exchange it, without him really knowing why, for Oldenburg, which he hardly knew and which was farther from Russia. Besides, in the hands of the Grand Duke, the port of Kiel alone could be important for Russian shipping. Count de Bernis considered all my arguments and in the end said, "As Ambassador, I have no instructions concerning all this, but as Count de Bernis, I think that you are right." The Grand Duke said to me after this that the Imperial Ambassador told him, "All that I can say to you on this subject is that I believe that your wife is right, and that you will do very well to listen to her." As a result, the Grand Duke cooled considerably toward these negotiations, which apparently was noticed and was why the matter was mentioned to him less often.

After Easter, we went as was customary to reside for a while in the Summer Palace, and from there to Peterhof.* The annual stays here began to get shorter. That year an event occurred that gave the courtiers something to gossip about. It was brought about by the intrigues of Messieurs Shuvalov. Things had reached the point that from one day to the next, everyone waited to see which of the two would cede his place to the other, that is, Beketov to Ivan Shuvalov or the latter to the former. Colonel Beketov, who was already mentioned above, out of boredom and not knowing what to do with the favor that he enjoyed, decided to have the Empress's choirboys sing at his residence. He developed a particular affection for several of them because of the beauty of their voices, and as he himself and his friend Elagin were versifiers, he wrote songs for them, which these children sang. This was given an odious interpretation; it was known that the Empress detested nothing more than this particular vice. With an innocent heart, Beketov walked with these children in the garden. This was imputed to him as a crime. The Empress departed for Tsarskoe Selo for a couple of days and then came back to Peterhof, and Monsieur Beketov, under the pretext of an illness, was ordered to stay there. He remained with Elagin, came down with a severe fever that he thought would kill

---

* April 30 to June 8, 1751.

him, and in his delirium he dreamed only of the Empress, with whom he was obsessed. He recovered, but he remained disgraced and withdrew from the court, after which he was placed in the army, where he had no success. He was too effeminate for the military profession.

Meanwhile we went to Oranienbaum, where we went hunting every day, and toward autumn, we returned to the city. In the month of September the Empress placed in our court Monsieur Lev Naryshkin as a gentleman of the bedchamber. He had only just returned from Moscow with his mother, brother, sister-in-law, and three sisters.* He was one of the most singular personages that I have known, and no one ever made me laugh as much as he. He was a born Harlequin, and if he had not been of noble birth, he could have made a living and acquired much with his real comic talent. He had no lack of wit, he had heard all the gossip, and he had a unique ability to keep everything in his head. He was capable of discoursing on any given art or science. He employed the technical terms of the subject and spoke continuously for a quarter hour or more, and at the end, neither he nor anyone could make anything of the stream of words that flowed from his mouth, and everyone just burst out laughing. Speaking of history, he said among other things that he did not at all like history in which there were tall tales, and that for history to be any good, it had to be devoid of such tales, and that anyway, history was becoming gibberish. But it was really on politics that he was inimitable. When he began to speak, even the humorless could not resist. He also said that most well-written comedies were boring. He had hardly arrived at court when the Empress ordered his elder sister to marry a Monsieur Seniavin, who was therefore placed in our court as a gentleman of the bedchamber. This was a serious blow to the young woman, who married this man only with the greatest revulsion. This marriage was very poorly received by the public, which placed all the blame on Monsieur Shuvalov, the Empress's favorite. Before coming into favor, he had been quite fond of this young maiden, who was married off badly so that he would lose sight of her. This was a truly tyrannical form of persecution; eventually she married, became consumptive, and died.[†]

At the end of September we returned to the Winter Palace.[‡] At that

* Lev Alexandrovich Naryshkin's brother was Alexander, whose wife was Anna Nikitichna (née Rumiantseva); his sisters were Natalia, Maria, and Agrafena.

† Natalia died in 1760.

‡ Actually, November 2, 1751.

time, the court had so little furniture that even the mirrors, beds, chairs, tables, and commodes that served us in the Winter Palace went with us to the Summer Palace and from there to Peterhof, and even followed us to Moscow. A good number broke and were damaged in these journeys, and they were given to us in this battered state, so that we had a hard time using them. As it was necessary to have an express order from the Empress to obtain others, and since most of the time access to her was difficult or even impossible, I resolved little by little to buy myself commodes, tables, and the most necessary furniture with my money for both the Winter and Summer Palaces, and when I went from one residence to the other, I found everything that I needed without the difficulty and the inconveniences of transport. This arrangement pleased the Grand Duke; he did the same for his apartment. At Oranienbaum, which belonged to the Grand Duke, we had everything we needed at our own expense. In my apartment there, I spent my own money to avoid all disagreement and difficulty because although His Imperial Highness spent freely on all his fancies, when it came to me, in general he was anything but generous. But since what I spent from my purse on my apartment served to embellish his house, he was very content.

That summer, Madame Choglokova developed a very particular affection for me that was so real that upon her return to the city, she could hardly do without me, and got bored when I was not with her. The basis for this affection was that I had not at all responded to that which it had pleased Monsieur her husband to show me, and this had given me a singular merit in the eyes of the wife. Back in the Winter Palace, Madame Choglokova invited me almost every afternoon to come to her apartment. Few people were there, but always more than in mine, where I would read all alone, except when the Grand Duke would pace my room in great strides and talk to me of things that interested him, but which were of no importance to me. These walks lasted one or two hours and were repeated several times a day. I had to walk with him until his strength gave out, I had to listen to him attentively, I had to respond. Most of the time I could make neither heads nor tails of his remarks, in which he often gave free rein to his imagination. I recall that he spent almost one whole winter occupied with plans to build a country house near Oranienbaum in the form of a Capuchin monastery, where he and I and his whole court would be dressed as Capuchins. He found this costume charming and comfortable. Each person was to have a donkey and take turns leading it to find water and bring provisions to the so-called monastery. He was overcome with laughter and joy over the wonderful and amusing effect that his creation would produce. He made me do a pencil sketch of the ground plan of this beautiful project, and every day I had to add or subtract something. As resolved as I was to be indulgent and patient with him, I frankly admit that I was very often overcome with boredom on these visits, walks, and conversations, which were of an insipidness that I have never seen equaled. When he left, the most boring book seemed a delicious amusement.

At the end of autumn, the court and public balls recommenced at court, as did the finery and the elegant outfits for the masked balls. Count Zakhar Chernyshev returned to Petersburg. As he was an old acquaintance, I always treated him very well. This time I was free to interpret his attentions as I pleased. He began by telling me that he found me much prettier. This was the first time in my life that someone had said such a thing to me. I did not find it displeasing. In fact, I had the goodness of heart to believe he was telling the truth. At each ball there was a new remark of this nature. One day Princess Gagarina brought me a sealed note on his behalf. Opening it, I noticed it had been opened and resealed. The note was printed as usual, but contained two very tender verses full of feeling. In the afternoon I had some notes brought to me, and I looked for one that would respond to his without compromising me. I found one, inserted it in an envelope shaped like an orange, and gave it to Princess Gagarina, who passed it on to Count Chernyshev. The following day, she gave me another one from him, but this time I found in it a note with a few lines in his hand. This time I responded personally. There we were in a regular and very sentimental correspondence. At the next masquerade, while dancing with me, he told me that he had a thousand things to say to me that he could not confide to paper nor place in a note that Princess Gagarina might open in her pocket or lose on the way. He begged me to grant him a brief audience in my room or wherever I judged appropriate. I told him that this was utterly impossible, that my chambers were inaccessible, nor could I leave them. He told me that he would disguise himself as a servant if necessary, but I firmly refused, and things went no further than this correspondence, stuffed in envelopes. Eventually Princess Gagarina realized what might come of this, scolded me for involving her, and no longer wanted to accept them. With these events, 1751 ended and 1752 began.

1752

*Catherine's unfortunate sleigh ride; Mme. Choglokova's
interception of Catherine's gift to Elizabeth; Sergei Saltykov's
courtship of Catherine; Elizabeth's rebuke to Catherine for
not having children yet; trip to Kronstadt; Elizabeth's order
to procure a mistress for Peter*

At the end of carnival, Count Chernyshev left for his regiment. A few
days before his departure, I needed to be bled. It was a Saturday. The following Wednesday, Monsieur Choglokov invited us to his island in the
mouth of the Neva. The house there was composed of a salon in the middle and a few rooms to the side. Near this house he had built a sleigh run.
Upon arriving there, I found Count Roman Vorontsov, who seeing me
said, "I have just the thing for you. I have had an excellent little sleigh
made for the sleigh run." As he had often taken me before, I accepted his
offer willingly, and immediately he had his little sleigh brought, in which
there was a kind of little armchair where I sat down, and he placed himself behind me and we descended. But halfway down the slope, Count
Vorontsov was no longer in control of the little sleigh, which tipped over.
I fell out, and Count Vorontsov, who was very heavy and clumsy, fell on
me, or rather on my left arm, from which I had been bled four or five days
before. I got up and he too, and we went on foot to meet a sleigh from the
court, which awaited those who went down the slope and took them back
to where they had started from, so that those who wanted could descend
again. Seated in this sleigh with Princess Gagarina, who had followed me
with Count Ivan Chernyshev, who stood in the back of the sleigh with
Vorontsov, I felt an inexplicable warmth on my left arm. I put my right
hand in the sleeve of my coat to see what it was, and pulling out my hand
I found it covered in blood. I said to the two Counts and to the Princess
that I thought that my vein had opened and was bleeding. They made the
sleigh go faster and we went to the house instead of the sleigh run; there
we found only a butler. I took off my coat, the butler gave us some vine-

gar, and Count Chernyshev acted as surgeon. We all agreed not to breathe a word about this adventure. As soon as my arm was bandaged, I returned to the sleighing hill. I danced the rest of the evening. I dined and we returned very late to the house without anyone suspecting what had happened to me. However, for nearly a month my thumb was limp, but little by little this passed.

During Lent I had a violent altercation with Madame Choglokova. Here is the reason. Sometime earlier, my mother had gone to Paris. Upon returning from this capital, General Ivan Fedorovich Glebov's eldest son gave me two pieces of quite rich and very beautiful cloth from my mother. While I was looking at them in the presence of Shkurin, who unfolded them for me in my dressing room, I let slip that these fabrics were of such quality that I was tempted to present them to the Empress. And in fact I waited for the moment to speak about them to Her Imperial Majesty, whom I saw only very rarely and then mostly in public. I did not speak of them at all to Madame Choglokova. It was a present that I kept to myself; I forbade Shkurin to tell any living soul what I had let slip in front of him alone. But he ran immediately to repeat what I had just let slip to Madame Choglokova. One fine morning, a few days later, Madame Choglokova came into my room and told me that the Empress thanked me for my fabrics, that she had kept one and was sending the other back to me. I was struck with astonishment upon hearing this! "What?" I said to her. Then Madame Choglokova added that she had brought my fabrics to the Empress, having heard that I had meant them to go to Her Imperial Majesty. At this, I got angrier than I remember ever having been. I stammered; I hardly spoke. Nevertheless I said to Madame Choglokova that I had been looking forward to presenting the Empress with these fabrics and that she had deprived me of this pleasure by taking my fabrics and presenting them unbeknownst to me to Her Imperial Majesty, that she, Madame Choglokova, could not know my intentions, because I had not spoken of them to her, and that if she had known them, it was only by the mouth of a treacherous servant, who betrayed his mistress, though she daily showered him with gifts. Madame Choglokova, who always had her reasons, insisted that I should never speak of anything to the Empress, that she had notified me of Her Imperial Majesty's order to this effect, and that my servants should report to her everything I said. Consequently, my servant had only done his duty and she hers by bringing the fabrics that I had designated for the Empress to Her Imperial Majesty, unbeknownst to me, that this was all according to the rules, I let her speak because fury left me speechless.

Finally she left, and then I went into a little antechamber where Shkurin normally spent the morning and where my old clothes were kept. Finding him there, I gave him a hard, well-aimed slap with all my strength and told him that he was a traitor and the most ungrateful of men to have dared to report to Madame Choglokova what I had forbidden him to say, that I showered him with gifts and that he had nevertheless betrayed me over such innocent remarks, that from that day on I would no longer give him anything, and that I would have him both dismissed and thrashed. I asked him what he hoped to gain from his conduct. I myself would always remain what I was, while the Choglokovs, hated and detested by everyone, would end up getting themselves dismissed by the Empress herself, who sooner or later would surely recognize their profound stupidity and inadequacy for the position in which they had been placed by an evil man's intrigue. If he wanted, he was free to go repeat what I had just said. I was certain nothing would happen to me, but he would see what would become of him. My manservant fell at my knees sobbing, and begged my pardon with a remorse that seemed sincere to me. I was touched and told him that his future conduct would decide my treatment of him, that his conduct would determine mine. He was an intelligent boy who did not lack talent and has never failed me since; on the contrary, during the most difficult times, I have had the clearest proof of his zeal and fidelity.* I complained to everyone I could about the trick that Madame Choglokova had played on me, so that it would reach the Empress's ears. The Empress thanked me for my fabrics when she saw me, and I knew from a third party that she disapproved of the manner in which Madame Choglokova had acted, and the matter ended there.

After Easter we moved to the Summer Palace. For some time already I had noticed that Chamberlain Sergei Saltykov was present more often than usual at court. He always came in the company of Lev Naryshkin, who amused everyone with his originality, several aspects of which I have already mentioned. Sergei Saltykov was the bête noire of Princess Gagarina, whom I liked dearly and even trusted. Lev Naryshkin was tolerated by everyone and regarded as an entirely inconsequential and very origi-

* During and after the coup, she entrusted her son Paul to him.

nal person. Sergei Saltykov insinuated himself as much as he could with the Choglokovs. Since they were neither likable, nor witty, nor amusing, there could only be some hidden design in his attentions. Madame Choglokova was pregnant at the time and often indisposed. She claimed that I amused her, and during the summer as during the winter, she often desired that I come to her residence. Sergei Saltykov, Lev Naryshkin, and Princess Gagarina were usually at her home, when there was not a concert in the Grand Duke's apartment or else a play at court. The concerts bored Madame Choglokova, who would only arrive at them late, if at all. Monsieur Choglokov never missed the concerts. Sergei Saltykov found a unique way to keep him occupied. I do not know how, but in this dense man, who was totally devoid of imagination and intelligence, he detected a passion for versifying nonsense songs. Once this was discovered, every time that we wanted to get rid of Monsieur Choglokov, we begged him to compose a new song. He would go sit in a corner, usually by a stove, and with great enthusiasm begin to write his song, which took all evening. Then his song would be declared charming, and this encouraged him to keep composing new ones. Lev Naryshkin put his songs to music and sang them with him, and meanwhile, the conversation continued without interruption, and one could speak freely. For, once Choglokov was seated, he did not get up again the entire evening. Where he was sitting made him pleasant or unpleasant, unbearable or charming, which he never was except when he was far enough away. I had a large book of his songs; I do not know what became of it.

During one of these concerts, Sergei Saltykov intimated to me the reason for his frequent appearances. At first I did not respond. When he spoke to me about it again, I asked him what he hoped to gain. He began to paint a picture as cheerful as it was passionate of the happiness he expected. I said, "And your wife, whom you married for love two years ago and with whom you are said to be madly in love, and she with you, what would she say?" He told me that all that glittered was not gold, and that he was paying dearly for a moment of blindness. I did everything I could to make him change his mind. I truly believed that I was succeeding. I pitied him. But to my misfortune I listened to him. He was remarkably handsome, and surely no one equaled him in the grand court, much less in ours. He lacked neither intelligence, nor that breadth of knowledge, manners, and tact that high society, but especially the court, provides. He was twenty-six years old. All in all, he was both by his birth and by several other qualities a distinguished gentleman. He knew how to hide his faults, the greatest of which were a mind for intrigue and lack of principles; at the time, these were not yet evident to me. I held out during the spring and part of the summer. I saw him almost every day. I did not change my conduct with him at all. I was as I had always been with him and as I was with everyone else. I saw him only in the presence of the court or a part of it. One day, to get rid of him for good, I decided to tell him that his attentions were in vain. I added, "For all you know, my heart may belong to another." Instead of discouraging him, I saw that his pursuit only became more ardent. The question of my dear husband never arose, because it was known and accepted that he was not very lovable, even to those with whom he was in love, as he continually was, since he courted, so to speak, all women. Only she who was called his own was excluded from his attentions.

Meanwhile, Choglokov invited us to hunt on his island, where we went in a rowboat; our horses had gone ahead of us. As soon as I arrived, I mounted a horse, and we went to find the dogs. Sergei Saltykov waited for the moment when the others were in pursuit of the hares and approached me to speak of his favorite subject. I listened to him more patiently than usual. He described in detail the plan that he had devised to shroud in complete secrecy, so he said, the pleasures that one could enjoy in such a situation. I did not say a word. He took advantage of my silence to persuade me that he loved me passionately, and he begged me to allow him to believe that he could hope, and that at least I was not indifferent to him. I told him that he could give rein to his imagination without me being able to prevent him. Finally he made comparisons between himself and other people in the court and made me admit that he was preferable to them, and from there he concluded that he was preferred. I laughed at what he said, but deep down I confess that he pleased me rather well. After an hour and a half of conversation, I told him to go because such a long conversation could become suspicious. He told me that he would not go unless I told him that he was tolerated. I replied, "Yes, yes, but go away." He said, "I take you at your word," and spurred his horse, and I cried, "No, no," and he repeated, "Yes, yes." We parted in this way. Back at the house on the island, we supped, and during supper, a great wind arose at sea, which made the water rise so considerably that it reached the bottom of the stairs, and the island was covered in several feet of seawater. We were obliged to remain on

Choglokov's island until the storm and the waters had subsided, which took until two or three in the morning. During this time, Sergei Saltykov said to me that heaven itself was favorable to him that day because it let him enjoy seeing me for a while longer, and numerous other such things. He already believed himself very fortunate, but I was not. A thousand worries troubled my thoughts, and I think I was very sullen that day and very unhappy with myself. I had believed myself able to govern and elevate both his thoughts and mine, and I understood that both were difficult, if not impossible.

Two days later, Sergei Saltykov told me that one of the Grand Duke's gentlemen of the bedchamber, Bressan, of French nationality, had told him that His Imperial Highness had said in his room, "Sergei Saltykov and my wife are deceiving Choglokov, making him believe what they want and then mocking him." It has to be said in truth that there was something to this and that the Grand Duke had noticed. I replied by advising him to be more circumspect in the future. A few days later I came down with a terrible sore throat, which lasted more than three weeks, with a severe fever, during which the Empress sent me Princess Kurakina, who was getting married to Prince Lobanov. I was supposed to crown her with the ceremonial headdress; for this purpose we had her sit in her court gown and big hoop on my bed. I did what I could, but Madame Choglokova, seeing that it was impossible for me to finish crowning her, had her get down off the bed and finished the headdress. I have not seen this woman again since then. At the time, the Grand Duke was in love with demoiselle Marfa Isaevna Shafirova, whom the Empress had recently placed in my service along with her elder sister, Anna Isaevna. Sergei Saltykov, who was an intriguing devil, insinuated himself with them to discover what the Grand Duke might be saying to the two sisters about him, so as to turn it to his advantage. These girls were poor, rather stupid, and very ambitious, and in fact in very little time they became his close confidantes.

Meanwhile, we went to Oranienbaum, where I again went riding every day and, except on Sundays, wore a man's habit. Choglokov and his wife had become sweet as lambs. In Madame Choglokova's eyes I acquired a new virtue. I dearly loved and fawned over one of her children. I made outfits for him, and God knows how many toys and togs I gave him. The mother was truly crazy about the child, who afterward became such a good-for-nothing that he was sentenced to fifteen years imprisonment in a fortress for his mischief.* Sergei Saltykov had become the friend, confidant, and adviser of Monsieur and Madame Choglokov. Certainly no man with common sense would have been able to submit to a trial as difficult as listening to these two proud, arrogant, and egotistical fools talk nonsense all day, without having much at stake. People guessed and speculated about his motives. This reached Peterhof and the ears of the Empress. Now, at this time it often happened that when Her Imperial Majesty wanted to scold someone, she scolded not that for which she could have scolded, but used a pretext to scold something that one never would have imagined her scolding. This observation comes from courtiers. I have it from the very mouth of its author, Zakhar Chernyshev.

At Oranienbaum, everyone in our entourage, both men and women, had agreed to have outfits of the same color made for the summer: the tunic gray and the rest blue, with a black velvet collar and no other trimming. This uniformity was convenient in more than one way. There was a clash over this costume, and more particularly, over the fact that I always dressed in a riding habit and that I rode astride like a man. Having come to Peterhof for a day of court, the Empress said to Madame Choglokova that this way of riding kept me from having children and that my costume was not at all proper. When she herself rode in a man's habit, she changed her clothes as soon as she dismounted. Madame Choglokova replied that there was no question of having children, that this could not happen without a cause and that although Their Imperial Highnesses had been married since 1745, the cause for children did not exist. Then† Her Imperial Majesty reprimanded Madame Choglokova and told her that she held her responsible because she neglected to preach to the interested parties on this subject, and overall she displayed much ill humor, and told her that her husband was a simpleton who let himself be deceived by snot-nosed brats. Within twenty-four hours, the Choglokovs repeated all this to their confidants. Hearing the words snot-nosed brats, the brats wiped their noses, and in a special meeting held for this purpose by the brats, resolved and determined that Sergei Saltykov and Lev Naryshkin would perfectly fulfill Her Imperial Majesty's wishes, by feigning to incur Monsieur Choglokov's disfavor, in a ruse that he himself might not suspect. Under the pretext of a relative's illness, they would withdraw to their houses for

* Three of her sons ended up in prison.

† From "Madame Choglokova replied" to "exist. Then" left out of the Russian Academy edition (1907) of Catherine's works.

three weeks or a month to let the rumors die down. This was executed to the letter, and the following day they left to go confine themselves with their families for a month. For my part, I immediately changed costume, and anyway, the other had become unnecessary. The first idea for uniforms had come from what we wore on court days at Peterhof: the tunic was white, the rest green, and everything decorated with silver braid. Sergei Saltykov, who was dark, said that in this white and silver outfit he resembled a fly in milk. Otherwise, I continued to visit the Choglokovs as before, except that now I endured greater boredom. Husband and wife regretted the absence of the two principal champions of their society. I certainly did not contradict them. The illness and death of Sergei Saltykov's mother further prolonged his absence.

Meanwhile the Empress told us to come from Oranienbaum to join her in Kronstadt, where she was going to open the canal that Peter I had begun and that had just been completed. She went ahead of us to Kronstadt. The night after she arrived was very stormy, and Her Imperial Majesty, who since her arrival had sent for us to come join her, believed that we were at sea during this storm. She was very anxious the entire night, and it seemed to her that she saw from her windows a ship struggling on the sea that could well be the yacht in which we were to cross. She turned for succor to relics that she always had beside her bed. She carried them to the window and waved them in a direction opposite that of the ship, which was in distress in the storm. She cried out several times that we were surely going to perish and that it would be her fault because, after her recent reprimand to us, we would have left immediately after the yacht's arrival to show her our devotion. But in fact the yacht arrived only after this storm at Oranienbaum so that we did not board it until the following afternoon. We spent three days in Kronstadt, during which the blessing of the canal took place with much ceremony and water was introduced for the first time into this canal.* In the afternoon there was a large ball. The Empress wanted to stay at Kronstadt to see the water flow out again, but she left on the third day before this could happen. This canal was not drained until my reign, when I had a steam mill built to drain it. In any case, it would have been impossible to let the water out, because the bottom of the canal was below sea level, but this was not known at the time.

* July 30, 1752.

From Kronstadt each returned to his home. The Empress went to Peterhof and we to Oranienbaum. Monsieur Choglokov requested and obtained permission to go to one of his estates for a month. During his absence, his wife took great pains to execute the Empress's orders to the letter. First she had several conferences with the Grand Duke's gentleman of the bedchamber, Bressan. At Oranienbaum this man found a pretty painter's widow, Madame Grooth. It took a few days to persuade her, with I know not what promises, and then to instruct her on what was wanted of her and what she should do. Then Bressan was charged with introducing His Imperial Highness to this young, lovely widow. I well saw that Madame Choglokova was very involved in some intrigue, but I did not know what until Sergei Saltykov finally returned from his voluntary exile and more or less informed me of the matter. Finally, after much effort Madame Choglokova achieved her objective, and when she was sure of the result, she notified the Empress that everything was going in accordance with her wishes. She hoped for great rewards for her pains, but in this she was mistaken, because she was given nothing. Nevertheless, she said that the empire owed her for it.

Immediately afterward we returned to the city. It was at this time that I persuaded the Grand Duke to break off negotiations with Denmark. I reminded him of the advice of Count de Bernis, who had already left for Vienna; he listened to me and ordered a stop to them without any agreement.

After a brief stay at the Summer Palace, we moved to the Winter Palace.* It seemed to me that Sergei Saltykov was growing less interested, that he became distracted, and sometimes smug, arrogant, and dissolute. I was angered by this and spoke to him about it; he gave me some poor excuses and claimed that I did not understand how extremely clever his conduct was. He was right, for I found it quite strange. We were told to prepare for the journey to Moscow, which we did. We departed on December 14, 1752, from Petersburg.† Sergei Saltykov remained there and did not come until several weeks after us. I left Petersburg with a few small signs of pregnancy. We traveled very quickly, night and day. At the last station before Moscow, the signs of pregnancy ended with painful contractions. Arriving in Moscow and seeing the turn things had taken, I suspected that I may well have had a miscarriage.

---

* October 20, 1752.

† They actually departed on December 16 and arrived on December 20, 1752.

1753

Catherine's rapprochement with Bestuzhev-Riumin; Choglokova's
encouragement of an affair so Catherine can produce an heir;
Catherine's second miscarriage; Peter's execution of a rat;
fire destroys palace and Elizabeth's wardrobe; Saltykov's ruse
to court Catherine revealed by Peter

Madame Choglokova had stayed in Petersburg because she had just had her seventh child, a girl. When she had recovered, she joined us in Moscow. Here we had been lodged in a wing constructed of wood, newly built that autumn, and as water seeped from the paneling, all the apartments were amazingly damp. This wing contained two rows of five or six large rooms each; those on the street were for me, and those on the other side were for the Grand Duke. My maids and ladies-in-waiting were lodged with their servants in the room meant to serve as my dressing room, so that there were seventeen girls and women lodged in one room that had only three large windows but no other outlets except my bedroom, through which they were obliged to pass for all kinds of needs, which was inconvenient for them and for me. The first ten days after my arrival in Moscow, we were obliged to tolerate this inconvenience, whose equal I have never seen. Moreover, their dining room was one of my antechambers. I was ill upon arriving. To remedy this inconvenience I had several large partitions put up in my bedroom and by this means divided it into three. But this was of almost no help because the doors opened and closed continually, which was unavoidable. Finally on the tenth day the Empress came to see me, and seeing the continual traffic, she went into the other room and said to my ladies, "I will have you made another exit that does not go through the Grand Duchess's bedroom." But what did she do? She ordered that a partition be built that blocked one of this room's windows, never mind that seventeen people lived there with difficulty. With this the room was narrowed to gain a hallway, the window on the street was opened, a stairway was built to it, and in this way my ladies were obliged to exit via the street. Toilets were placed for them under their windows. When they went to eat, they again had to walk along the street. In a word, this whole arrangement was worthless, and I know not how these seventeen women, crammed together and sometimes ill, did not come down with some putrid fever in these corridors next to my bedroom, which was so full of all kinds of vermin that I could not sleep.

Finally Madame Choglokova recovered from her confinement and arrived in Moscow, and a few days later Sergei Saltykov arrived. As Moscow is very large and everyone is very spread out there, he used this advantageous locale to conceal at court the waning of his insincere or real affection. To tell the truth, I was hurt; however, he gave me such good and worthwhile reasons that as soon as I saw him and had spoken to him, my suspicions vanished. We agreed that to reduce the number of his enemies, I would have a few remarks made to Count Bestuzhev to give him the hope that I was less hostile to him than before. I entrusted this message to a man named Bremse, who was employed in the Holstein Chancery of Monsieur Pechlin. When he was not at court, this man often went to Chancellor Count Bestuzhev's home. He undertook this with great eagerness and told me that it had warmed the Chancellor's heart and that he had said that he was at my disposal anytime that I judged it necessary. If he could be useful to me, he begged me to indicate a sure channel by which we could communicate with each other as we saw fit. I liked his idea and told Bremse that I would think about it. I repeated this to Sergei Saltykov, and it was immediately resolved that he himself would go to the Chancellor's house under the pretext of a social call, since he had only just arrived. The old man received him marvelously, took him aside, and spoke to him of the inner world of our court and the stupidity of the Choglokovs, telling him, among other things, "I know that, although you are their most intimate friend, you view them as I do because you are an intelligent boy." Then he spoke to him about me and my situation as if he lived in my room. Then he said, "In gratitude for the goodwill that the Grand Duchess deigns to show me, I am going to do her a little service, for which I think she will be grateful to me. I will make Madame Vladislavova as sweet as a lamb, and the Grand Duchess will do as she wants with her. She will see that I am not the werewolf that I have been made out to be." Eventually Sergei Saltykov returned, delighted with this commission and this man, who personally gave him several pieces of advice that were as wise as they were useful. He became very intimate with us without a living soul knowing anything about it.

Meanwhile, Madame Choglokova, who always had her favorite project in mind, which was to ensure the succession, took me aside one day and said, "Listen, I must speak to you very seriously." I kept my eyes and ears open as one might expect. She began with a long disquisition, as was her wont, about her devotion to her husband, about her virtue, about what must and must not be done to love each other and to promote or support conjugal bonds, and then she pushed on, saying that there were sometimes situations of major consequence that should be exceptions to the rule. I let her say everything she wanted without interrupting, not knowing where she was going with this, a bit astonished, and not knowing if she was setting a trap for me or if she spoke sincerely. As I was having these private reflections, she said, "You are going to see how much I love my country and how sincere I am. I do not doubt that you fancy someone. You are free to choose between S.S. and L.N. If I am not mistaken, it is the latter." At this I cried out, "No, no, not at all." Then she said, "Well then, if it is not him, it is the other no doubt." I did not say a word, and she continued, "You will see that I will not make difficulties for you." I played dumb to the point where she scolded me many times, both in the city and eventually in the country, where we went after Easter.[*]

It was at or around this time that the Empress gave the estate of Liubertsy and several others fourteen or fifteen versts from Moscow to the Grand Duke. But before going to reside in these new possessions of His Imperial Highness, the Empress celebrated the anniversary of her coronation in Moscow. It was April 25. It was announced to us that she had ordered that the proceedings be conducted exactly as they had been organized on the actual day of the ceremony. We were very curious to see what would happen. The day before, she slept at the Kremlin. We stayed in the Sloboda at the wooden palace and we received the order to come to mass at the cathedral. At nine in the morning we left the wooden palace in ceremonial style with the servants proceeding on foot. We crossed all Moscow bit by bit; it was a seven-verst journey, and we stepped out in front of the church. A few moments later the Empress arrived with her cortege, the little crown on her head and the imperial mantle carried by

---

[*] From "Meanwhile, Madame Choglokova" to "after Easter" left out of the Russian Academy edition (1907) of Catherine's works.

the chamberlains as was customary. She went to sit in her usual place in the church, and as yet there was nothing in all this that was extraordinary or not done at all the other great celebrations of her reign. There was a damp cold in the church such as I have never felt in my life. I was completely blue and I froze from the cold in a court dress that left my throat uncovered. The Empress told me to put on a sable stole, but I did not have one with me. She had them bring hers, took one, and put it around her neck. I saw another one in the box; I thought that she was going to send it to me to put on, but I was mistaken. She sent it back; it seemed to me that this was a rather marked sign of ill will. Madame Choglokova, who saw that I was shivering, got from someone a silk kerchief, which I put around my neck. When the mass and the sermon were over, the Empress left the church. We prepared to follow her, but she had us told that we could return to the house. It was then that we learned that she was going to dine all alone on the throne, and in this way the ceremony would be as it was the very day of her coronation, when she had dined alone. Excluded from this meal, we returned as we had come, with great ceremony, our servants on foot, making the fourteen-verst round-trip through the city, and we were chilled to the bone and dying of hunger. The Empress had appeared to us to be in very bad humor during the mass, and we were dismissed by her no more kindly, with a very disagreeable lack of attention to say the least. At the other grand ceremonies, when she dined on the throne we had the honor of eating with her. This time she dismissed us publicly. On the way back, alone in a carriage with the Grand Duke, I told him what I thought of this; he told me that he would complain about it. Back at the palace, half dead from the cold and exhausted, I complained to Madame Choglokova about having gotten chilled. The following day there was a ball at the wooden palace. I said that I was sick and did not go.* The Grand Duke actually had the Shuvalovs told something about this, and they replied something that satisfied him, and that was the end of it.

Around this time, we learned that Zakhar Chernyshev and Colonel Nikolai Leontiev had quarreled over gambling debts at the home of Roman Vorontsov, that they had fought with swords and that Count Zakhar Chernyshev had a serious wound to the head. It was so bad that they had not been able to transport him from Count Roman Vorontsov's

---

* *Journal of the Court Quartermasters*, 1753: "April 29. Her Imperial Highness the Grand Duchess deigned to be absent because of illness."

house to his own. He remained there and was doing very badly, and there was talk of trepanning* him. I was very upset by this because I liked him a great deal. Leontiev was arrested by order of the Empress. This fight had the whole city talking because of the very numerous relations of both combatants. Leontiev was the son-in-law of Countess Rumiantseva, a very close relation of the Panins and of the Kurakins. The other man also had his relations, friends, and protectors. The whole thing had happened in Count Roman Vorontsov's house; the wounded man was at his home. Finally, when the danger passed, the affair blew over and things went no further.

During the month of May, I had new signs of pregnancy. We went to Liubertsy, the Grand Duke's country estate twelve or fourteen versts from Moscow. The stone house there, which had been built long ago by Prince Menshikov, was falling into ruins. We could not live in it. To remedy this, tents were set up in the courtyard. I slept in a kibitka;† at three or four in the morning my sleep would be interrupted by ax blows and the noise made by the construction of a wooden wing to the house, which they were rushing to build two steps, so to speak, from our tents, so that we would have a place to reside the rest of the summer. The rest of the time we would go hunting or on walks. I did not ride anymore, but went around in a cabriolet. Toward the feast of St. Peter we returned to Moscow, and I felt so weary that I slept every day until noon, and it was difficult to awaken me for dinner. The feast of St. Peter was celebrated in the usual manner. I got dressed, attended mass, and went to lunch, to the ball, and to supper. On the following day, I felt pains in my lower back. Madame Choglokova sent for a midwife, and she predicted a miscarriage, which in fact I had the following night. I may have been two to three months pregnant. I was in great danger for thirteen days, and it was suspected that part of the afterbirth had not been expelled. This was kept from me. Eventually, on the thirteenth day, it came out on its own, without pains or effort. I was made to rest for six weeks in my room because of this complication, during an intolerable heat wave. The very day that I fell ill, the Empress came to see me and seemed troubled by my state. During the six weeks that I stayed in my room, I was bored to death. My only companions were Madame Choglokova, although she came rather

* To drill a hole in the skull to relieve pressure.
† Nomad's tent or covered wagon.

infrequently, and a little Kalmuck girl, whom I liked because she was kind. I often cried out of boredom.

As for the Grand Duke, most of the time he was in his room, where a Ukrainian chamber valet named Karnovich, who was as much a fool as a drunk, did his best to entertain him, providing as many toys, as much wine, and other strong liquors as he could, unbeknownst to Monsieur Choglokov, who in any event was deceived and mocked by everyone. But in the Grand Duke's secret, nocturnal bacchanals with his servants, among whom were several Kalmuck boys, the Grand Duke often found himself poorly obeyed and served, for being drunk, they did not know what they were doing and forgot that they were with their master and that this master was the Grand Duke. His Imperial Highness would resort to blows from his stick or the flat of his sword. Despite this, his entourage obeyed him badly, and more than once he came to me, complaining of his servants and begging me to make them see reason. Then I would go to his residence and would berate them, reminding them of their duties, and immediately they would straighten up. This made the Grand Duke say to me more than once, and repeat as well to Bressan, that he did not know how I dealt with his servants, that while he thrashed them and could not make himself obeyed, I obtained what I wanted with a word.

One day, when I went into His Imperial Highness's apartment for this purpose, my eyes were struck by a large rat that he had had hanged with all the ceremony of an execution in the middle of a small room that he had had made with a partition. I asked what this meant. He said that this rat had committed a criminal act and merited the ultimate punishment according to military laws, that it had climbed atop the ramparts of a cardboard fortress on a table in this room and eaten two papier-mâché sentries standing watch on one of the bastions, and that the Grand Duke had had the criminal judged according to the laws of war. His setter had caught the rat, which had immediately been hanged as I saw it, and it would stay there exposed to the eyes of the public for three days as an example. I could not keep myself from bursting with laughter at the extreme folly of the thing, but this displeased him very much in light of the importance he gave to it. I withdrew and took refuge in my ignorance, as a woman, of military laws; nevertheless he remained angry because of my laughter. It could at least be said in the rat's defense that it had been hanged without anyone having asked or heard its defense.

During the court's stay in Moscow, it happened that a court lackey went mad and even became violent. The Empress ordered her chief doctor, Boerhave, to take care of this man. He was put in a room near the apartment of Boerhave, who resided at the court. Moreover, chance had it that several people lost their minds that year. When the Empress was informed of this, she brought them to the court and had them lodged near Boerhave, so that a little insane asylum was created at court. I remember that the most important patients were a major in the Semenovsky Guards, Chaadaev, a Lieutenant Colonel Leutrum, a Major Choglokov, a monk from Ascension Monastery, who had cut off his genitals with a razor,* and several others. Chaadaev's madness consisted in thinking that Shah-Nadir, also known as Tahmasp Kuli Khan, the Persian usurper and tyrant, was God himself.† When the doctors were unable to cure him of his delusion, he was put in the hands of priests; they persuaded the Empress to have him exorcised. She herself attended the ceremony, but Chaadaev remained as mad as he appeared to be. However, there were people who doubted his madness, because he was rational about all other matters but Shah-Nadir. His old friends even went to consult him about their affairs, and he gave them very sensible advice. Those who did not think him mad found the cause for this affected mania in a bad situation from which he could extricate himself only with this ruse. Since the beginning of the Empress's reign, he had been employed in the tax service. He had been accused of misappropriation of public funds and was supposed to be tried; out of fear he acquired this fantasy that got him through the affair.

In mid-August, we returned to the country. On September 5, the Empress's name day, she went to Ascension Monastery. While she was there, lightning struck the church. Fortunately, Her Imperial Majesty was in a chapel next to the main church. She learned of the event only because of the fright of her courtiers. However, no one was injured or killed in this accident. A short time later she returned to Moscow, where we also went from Liubertsy. Upon our return to the city, we saw the Princess of Courland kiss the Empress's hand publicly for the permission granted her to marry Prince Georgy Khovansky. She had fallen out with her first fiancé, Peter Saltykov, who for his part immediately married Princess Solntseva.

---

* This was the practice of members of the religious sect called *Skoptsy*.

† Shah-Nadir (1688–1747), Shah of Persia (r. 1736–47), known as the Persian Napoleon or the Second Alexander, served Tahmasp II (1704–40) and took the name Tahmasp Kuli Khan, or "Tahmasp's slave."

At three in the afternoon on November 1 of that year, I was in Madame Choglokova's apartment when her husband, Sergei Saltykov, Lev Naryshkin, and several other gentlemen of our court left the room to go to Chamberlain Shuvalov's apartment to congratulate him on his birthday, which was that day. Madame Choglokova, Princess Gagarina, and I chatted together. After hearing some noise in a little chapel that was near the apartment where we were, we saw a couple of these gentlemen return. They told us that they had been prevented from passing through the halls of the palace because there was a fire. I immediately went into my room, and crossing an antechamber, I saw that the balustrade in the corner of the great hall was on fire. It was twenty steps from our wing. I entered my rooms and found them already full of soldiers and servants, who were removing the furniture and carrying what they could. Madame Choglokova followed me closely, and as there was nothing more to do in the house but wait for it to catch fire, Madame Choglokova and I went out. Outside the door we found the carriage of the chapel master Araya, who had come for a concert in the Grand Duke's apartment and whom I myself warned that the house was burning. She and I got into the carriage, the street being covered in mud because of the continual rains that had fallen for a few days, and there we watched both the fire and the way in which the furniture was carried from all directions out of the house. Then I saw a singular thing. It was the astonishing number of rats and mice that descended the staircase in a line, without even really hurrying. They could not save this vast wooden house because of a lack of equipment, and because the little there was, was located precisely under the burning hall. This hall was more or less at the center of the buildings around it, all of which may have measured two or three versts in circumference. I left precisely at three, and at six no vestige of the house remained. The heat of the fire became so great that neither I nor Madame Choglokova could tolerate it anymore, and we had our carriage go into the field several hundred feet away. Finally, Monsieur Choglokov came with the Grand Duke and told us that the Empress was going to her house at Pokrovskoe and that she had ordered us to go to Monsieur Choglokov's house, which stood on the first corner to the right of the main street of the Sloboda. We went there immediately. There was a salon in the middle of this house and four rooms on each side. It is hardly possible to be more uncomfortable than we were there. The wind blew in from all directions, the windows and doors were half rotted, the floor was split with cracks two or three inches wide. Moreover, the vermin had the run of the house. The children and servants were living there when we arrived. They were sent out, and we were lodged in this horrible house, which was devoid of furniture.

The second day of my stay in this house, I learned what a Kalmuck nose is. The little girl whom I had in my service told me as I awoke, while pointing at her nose, "I have a hazelnut in here." I touched her on the nose and found nothing, but the whole morning this child kept repeating that she had a hazelnut in her nose. She was a child of four or five. No one knew what she meant by saying she had a hazelnut in her nose. Around noon, she fell while running and bumped her head against the table, which made her cry, and while crying she pulled out her handkerchief and blew her nose. As she wiped it, the hazelnut fell out of her nose, which I myself saw, and at this I understood that a hazelnut, which could not fit into any European nose without one noticing it, could fit in the cavity of a Kalmuck nose, which is sunk into the head between two fat cheeks.

Our clothes and everything we needed had stayed in the mud in front of the burned palace and were brought to us that night and the following day. What pained me most were my books. At the time, I was finishing the fourth volume of Bayle's *Dictionnaire.** I had devoted two years to it. Every six months I finished a volume, and from this, one can imagine in what solitude I spent my life. Finally they were brought to me. Among my clothes were those of Countess Shuvalova. Out of curiosity Madame Vladislavova showed me this woman's underskirts, which were all lined in back with leather because ever since her first confinement she had been incontinent, and the odor of urine permeated all her underskirts. I sent them back to their owner as quickly as possible.

In that fire, the Empress lost everything in her immense wardrobe that had been brought to Moscow. She did me the honor of telling me that she had lost four thousand outfits and that of all of them, she regretted losing only the one made of the cloth I had given her, which I had received from my mother. She lost other precious things too in the fire, among them a bowl covered with engraved stones that Count Rumiantsev had bought in Constantinople for eight thousand ducats. All these possessions had been placed in a room above the hall in which the fire had started. This hall

---

* *Dictionnaire historique et critique* 2 vol. (1697) by Pierre Bayle (1647–1706); 8 ed., 4 vol. (Amsterdam, 1740).

served as the entrance hall to the palace's great hall. At ten in the morning the stokers had come to heat this entrance hall. After putting the wood in the stove, they lit it as usual. This done, the room filled with smoke. They thought that it was escaping through a few imperceptible holes in the stove and began to cover the spaces between the stove tiles with clay. The smoke grew thicker, and they began to look for cracks in the stove; not finding any, they realized that the crack was inside the apartment's walls, which were only made of wood. They went to look for some water and extinguished the fire in the stove. But as the smoke grew thicker, it filled the antechamber, where there was a sentry from the horse guards. Thinking he would suffocate, and not daring to budge from his post, he broke a window and began to shout, but when he saw that no one heard him or came to his aid, he shot his rifle out the window. This shot was heard in the main guardhouse opposite the palace. Guards ran to him and upon entering found thick smoke everywhere, from which they pulled the sentry. The stokers were put under arrest. They had believed that they could extinguish the fire or else prevent the smoke from spreading without warning anyone. They had struggled earnestly for five hours. This fire led to a discovery by Monsieur Choglokov. In his apartment, the Grand Duke had many very large dressers. When they were carried from his room, a few open or badly closed drawers revealed their contents to the spectators. Incredibly, these drawers contained nothing but a huge number of wine and hard liquor bottles. They served as His Imperial Highness's wine cellar. Choglokov spoke to me about this. I told him that I was unaware of this situation, and I was telling the truth. I knew nothing of it, but very often, almost daily, I saw the Grand Duke drunk.

After the fire, we stayed at the Choglokovs' house for about six weeks, and when we went out we would often pass a wooden house, situated in a garden near the Saltykov bridge, which belonged to the Empress and was called the bishop's house because the Empress had bought it from a bishop. We decided to ask the Empress, unbeknownst to the Choglokovs, to allow us to reside in this house, which seemed to us and was said to be more livable than the one we were in. Finally, after many exchanges, we received permission to go live in the bishop's house. It was a very old wooden house without a view. It was built over a stone cellar and as a result was more elevated than the one we had just left, which had only a ground floor. The stoves were so old that when they were lit, one could see the fire in the furnace, so numerous were its cracks, and smoke filled the rooms. We all had headaches and sore eyes. We risked being burned alive in this house. There was only one wooden staircase, and the windows were high. Fire did in fact break out there two or three times during our stay, but they were extinguished. I came down with a sore throat and a very high fever. The same day that I fell ill, Monsieur de Bretlach, who had returned to Russia to represent the Viennese court, was supposed to come and have a farewell supper at our house, and he found me with red, swollen eyes. He thought that I had been crying, and he was not mistaken. The boredom, illness, and discomfort, both physical and mental, of my situation had made me very melancholy all day long. I had spent the day alone with Madame Choglokova, waiting for visitors who had not come. She repeatedly said, See how they abandon us. Her husband was dining out and had taken everyone with him. Despite all of Sergei Saltykov's promises to slip away from this luncheon, he only returned with Choglokov. All this put me in a foul mood.

Finally, a few days later, we were allowed to go to Liubertsy. Here we believed ourselves in paradise. The house was completely new and quite well furnished. We danced every evening, and our entire court was assembled there. During one of these balls, we saw the Grand Duke earnestly speaking into Monsieur Choglokov's ear for a long time, after which the latter appeared upset, distracted, and more withdrawn and sullen than usual. Seeing this, and because Choglokov gave him an especially cold shoulder, Sergei Saltykov went to sit with Mademoiselle Marfa Shafirova and tried to find out from her the reason for this unusual intimacy between the Grand Duke and Choglokov. She told him that she did not know, but that she suspected what it might be because the Grand Duke had said to her several times, "Sergei Saltykov and my wife are utterly deceiving Choglokov. Choglokov is in love with the Grand Duchess, and she cannot stand him. Sergei Saltykov is Choglokov's confidant. He makes Choglokov think that he is lobbying my wife on his behalf, when instead he is wooing her for himself, and she is happy to tolerate Sergei Saltykov, who is amusing. She uses him to deceive Choglokov as she pleases, and deep down she is toying with them both. I must open this poor devil Choglokov's eyes because I pity him. I must tell him the truth and then he will see who is his true friend, my wife or I." As soon as Sergei Saltykov learned of this dangerous talk and the scandal that could follow from it, he repeated it to me and then went to sit with Choglokov and asked him what was wrong. At first Choglokov did not want to explain and did nothing but sigh. Then he began to moan about how difficult it was to find faithful friends. Finally Sergei Saltykov brought him round and extracted a confession from him about the conversation that he had just had with the Grand Duke. Certainly one could not have predicted what they had said to each other unless one had been told. His Imperial Highness had poured forth solemn declarations of friendship to Choglokov, telling him that it was only in life's most demanding situations that one could distinguish true from false friends. To prove the sincerity of his friendship, he was going to give him striking proof of his honesty. He knew without doubt that Choglokov was in love with me. He said that he did not condemn him for this, that I might well seem loveable to him, and that we are not the masters of our hearts. But he had to warn him that he chose his confidants poorly, that Choglokov might well believe that Sergei Saltykov was his friend, and that he was wooing me on Choglokov's behalf, while Saltykov acted only for himself, and the Grand Duke suspected him of being Choglokov's rival, and that for my part, I was deceiving both Saltykov and Choglokov, but that if he, Choglokov, wanted to follow the Grand Duke's advice and confide in him, then he would see that he, the Grand Duke, was his true and only friend. Monsieur Choglokov thanked the Grand Duke profusely for his friendship and protestations of friendship, but deep down he considered the rest a chimera of the Grand Duke's imagination. It is easy to believe that in any case Choglokov did not care to have a confidant who was by nature and character equally feckless and useless. Once Choglokov had said all this, Sergei Saltykov had little trouble in reestablishing calm and tranquility in his mind, since Choglokov was not accustomed to attaching much importance or paying much attention to the discourse of a man who had no judgment and was known for it. When I learned of all this, I admit that I was outraged with the Grand Duke. And in order to prevent him from repeating this accusation, I made him understand that I was not unaware of what had occurred between him and Choglokov. He blushed, said not a word, and went away and ignored me, and the matter ended there.

Back in Moscow, we were moved from the bishop's house into the apartments of what was called the Empress's summer house, which had not caught fire. The Empress had had new apartments built in the space of six weeks. To this end, beams had been removed from the house at Perova, from that of Count Hendrikov, and from the house of the princes of Georgia, and transported there. She finally moved in toward the new year.

1754

Choglokova's infidelity and Choglokov's illness and death;
Catherine's pregnancy; Elizabeth's talk with Catherine; Count
Alexander Shuvalov replaces Choglokov; birth and baptism of heir,
Paul; Elizabeth's neglect of Catherine and miserable gift; a spell on
the royal bed; Saltykov's departure; Catherine sees her son;
her melancholy and reading

The Empress celebrated the first day of January 1754 in this palace, and the Grand Duke and I had the honor of dining with her in public under the dais. During the meal, Her Imperial Majesty appeared very gay and talkative. At the foot of the throne, tables were set for several hundred people of the highest ranks. During dinner the Empress asked who this very skinny and ugly person with a crane's neck, as she put it, was whom she saw seated there (she indicated the seat). She was told that it was Marfa Shafirova. She burst out laughing, and, speaking to me, she said that this reminded her of the Russian proverb шейка долга на виселница годна, "A long neck is good only for the hangman's noose." I could not keep myself from smiling at this imperial mischief and sarcasm, which did not go unnoticed and which the courtiers spread by word of mouth so that, as I rose from the table, I found several people already informed of it. As for the Grand Duke, I do not know if he heard it, but he certainly did not breathe a word of it, and I was careful not to mention it to him.

No years had ever seen more fires than 1753 and 1754. More than once I saw two, three, four, and up to five fires at a time in different parts of Moscow, from the windows of my apartment in the Summer Palace. During carnival the Empress ordered different balls and masquerades in her new apartment. During one of these, I saw that the Empress had a long conversation with General Matiushkin. He did not want his son to marry Princess Gagarina, my maid of honor, but the Empress persuaded the mother, and Princess Gagarina, who was well into her thirty-eighth year, was given permission to marry Monsieur Dmitry Matiushkin. She was very pleased about this, and I was too; they married for love. At the time, Marinshkin was very handsome. Madame Choglokova did not come to live with us in the summer apartments. Under different pretexts she stayed with her children in her house, which was very near the court. But the truth was that this virtuous woman, who had loved her husband so much, had conceived a passion for Prince Peter Repnin and a quite marked aversion for her husband. She believed that she could not be happy without a confidante, and I seemed the most trustworthy person. She showed me all the letters she received from her lover. I kept her secret very faithfully, with scrupulous care and prudence. She would see the Prince very secretly. Despite this, the lady's husband conceived a few suspicions. An officer of the horse guard, Kamynin, had given rise to them. By nature, this man was jealousy and suspicion personified. He was an old acquaintance of Choglokov's. The latter confided in Sergei Saltykov, who sought to reassure him. I was careful not to tell Sergei Saltykov what I knew, for fear of some involuntary indiscretion. Finally the husband mentioned something to me too. I played dumb, acted astonished, and was silent.

In the month of February, I had signs of pregnancy. On Easter Day itself, during mass, Choglokov fell ill with dry colic. He was given many medicines, but his illness only worsened. During Easter week the Grand Duke went riding with the gentlemen of our court. Sergei Saltykov was among them. I stayed at the house because they feared letting me out given my state and because I had already had two miscarriages. I was alone in my room when Choglokov asked me to come into his. I went there and found him in bed. He made a thousand complaints to me about his wife, told me that she was seeing Prince Repnin, who went to her house on foot, that during carnival, he had gone there during a court ball dressed as a Harlequin, and that Kamynin had had him followed. In the end, God knows all the details he told me. At the moment he was most worked up, his wife arrived. He launched into a thousand reproaches against her in my presence, saying that she was abandoning him in his illness. They were very suspicious and narrow-minded people. I was dying of fear that the wife would believe it was I who had betrayed her in many of the details that he recounted about her trysts. The wife told him that it would not be strange if she punished him for his conduct toward her, that, at least, neither he nor anyone else could reproach her for having failed him up until now in any way, and she finished by saying that it was unbecoming of him to complain. Both of them continually appealed to me as judge and arbiter of what they were saying. I was silent out of fear of offending one or the other or both, or of being compromised; my face flushed with anxiety. I was alone with them.

At the height of the dispute, Madame Vladislavova came to tell me that the Empress had come to my apartment. I ran there immediately, and Madame Choglokova left with me, but instead of following me she stopped in a corridor where there was a staircase that led into the garden, where she sat down, according to what I was later told. I entered my room completely out of breath and indeed I found the Empress there. As she saw me out of breath and a bit flushed, she asked me where I had been. I told her that I was coming from the apartment of Choglokov, who was sick, and that I had hurried back as quickly as possible, having learned that she had deigned to come to my apartment. She did not ask me any more questions, but it seemed to me that she was considering what I was saying and that it seemed odd to her. Nevertheless, she continued to speak with me. She did not ask where the Grand Duke was, because she knew he had gone out. During the Empress's entire reign, neither he nor I dared go into the city nor out of the house without sending to ask her permission. Madame Vladislavova was in my room. The Empress addressed her several times and then me, speaking of indifferent matters; then she left after about half an hour, telling me that because of my pregnancy, she excused me from appearing in public on April 21 and 25. I was surprised that Madame Choglokova had not followed me. When the Empress had gone, I asked Madame Vladislavova what had become of her. She told me that she had sat down on the stairs, where she had wept. As soon as the Grand Duke returned, I recounted to Sergei Saltykov what had happened to me during their ride, how Choglokov had sent for me, what had been said between husband and wife, my apprehension, and the Empress's visit. Then he said, "If this is the case, I think that the Empress came to see what you do in your husband's absence and to make sure that you were completely alone in both your apartment and Choglokov's. Since we are covered in mud from head to toe, I am going to take all of my comrades to Ivan Shuvalov's house." The Grand Duke having already retired, Sergei Saltykov went with all who had gone riding with the Grand Duke to the home of Ivan Shuvalov, who resided at the court. When they arrived there, Shuvalov asked for details about their ride, and Sergei Saltykov later told me that from his questions it appeared that he had not been mistaken.

Thereafter, Choglokov's illness only worsened. By April 21, my birthday, the doctors had lost all hope for his recovery. The Empress was informed, and as was her custom, she ordered the sick man transported to his own house so that he would not die at court, because she was afraid of the dead. I was very distressed as soon as I learned of Monsieur Choglokov's state. He was dying just when, after several years of trouble and effort, we had succeeded in making him not only less mean and wicked, but also tractable. One could even dominate him if one studied his character. As for his wife, she sincerely loved me at the time, and she had changed from a harsh and malevolent Argus into a staunch, devoted friend. Choglokov lived on in his house until April 25, the day of the Empress's coronation, when he died in the afternoon. I was immediately informed, as I sent for information almost every hour. I was truly grieved and I cried a great deal. His wife was also sick in bed during the last days of her husband's illness. He was on one side of the house, she on the other. Sergei Saltykov and Lev Naryshkin were in the wife's room at the moment of the husband's death. The windows of the room were open. A bird flew in and landed on the ceiling cornice opposite Madame Choglokova's bed. Seeing this, she said, "I am convinced that my husband has just given up the ghost. Find out if this is so." Someone came to say that he was indeed dead. She said that this bird was the soul of her husband. They wanted to prove to her that this was an ordinary bird, but could not find it again. She was told that it had flown away, but since no one had seen it, she remained convinced that it was her husband's soul come to find her. As soon as Monsieur Choglokov's funeral was over, Madame Choglokova wanted to come to my apartment. Seeing her cross the long bridge over the Yauza, the Empress sent someone to tell her that she excused her from her duties in my service and that she should return to the house. Her Imperial Majesty found it improper that a widow should go out so soon.

That same day, she named Monsieur Alexander Ivanovich Shuvalov to take up the late Monsieur Choglokov's duties in the Grand Duke's service. Now Monsieur Alexander Shuvalov was the terror of the court, the city, and the whole empire, not because of who he was but because of the position he occupied. He was head of the tribunal for crimes against the state, which was then called the Secret Chancery. His duties, it was said, had given him a sort of convulsive movement, which seized the entire right side of his face from the eye to the base of his jaw each time he was affected by joy, anger, fear, or apprehension. It was astonishing that one could have chosen to place a man with such a hideous grimace in the constant presence of a pregnant young woman. If I had given birth to a child who had this unfortunate tic, I think the Empress would have been very upset. Yet this could have happened, as I saw him all the time, never willingly and most of the time with an involuntary wave of repugnance because his servants, his relatives, and his office, as one might well suspect, could not increase the pleasure of his company. But this was only the beginning of the joys that were in store for us and principally for me.

The following day I was told that the Empress was once again going to place Countess Rumiantseva in my service. I knew that she was the sworn enemy of Sergei Saltykov, that she hardly liked Princess Gagarina any better, and that she had done much to harm my mother in the Empress's opinion. When I learned this, I lost all patience. I began to cry bitterly and I said to Count Alexander Shuvalov that if Countess Rumiantseva were placed with me, I would regard this as a very great misfortune, that in the past this woman had wronged my mother, that she had blackened her in the Empress's mind, and that at present she would do the same to me, that she had been feared like the plague when she had been at our residence, and that this arrangement would make many people unhappy if he did not find a way to avert it. He promised to work on this and tried to calm me, fearing above all for my condition. In fact, he went to the Empress's residence, and when he returned, he told me that he hoped that the Empress would not place Countess Rumiantseva with me. Indeed, I heard no more talk of this, and from then on we were occupied only with the departure for Petersburg.

It was decided that we would journey for twenty-nine days. In other words, we would do only one relay per day. I was scared to death that Sergei Saltykov and Lev Naryshkin would be left in Moscow, but I do not know how it happened that the Empress deigned to place them in our entourage. Finally we left on May 10 or 11 from the Moscow palace. I was in a carriage with Count Alexander Shuvalov's wife, a conceited woman who was the dullest thing imaginable, Madame Vladislavova, and the midwife, whom it was claimed we could not do without, because I was pregnant. I was bored to death in the carriage and did nothing but cry. Finally Princess Gagarina—who personally did not like Countess Shuvalova, because the Countess's daughter, who was married to Golovkin, the Princess's cousin, was insufficiently considerate toward her husband's family—found a moment when she could approach me to say that she was trying to make Madame Vladislavova well disposed toward me, because she and everyone else feared that the melancholy I felt due to my situation would harm both me and the child I was carrying. As for Sergei Saltykov, he dared not come anywhere near me because of the oppressive and continual presence of the Shuvalovs, husband and wife. In fact, Princess Gagarina succeeded in making Madame Vladislavova see reason. She deigned to alleviate somewhat the state of discomfort and perpetual oppressiveness that was the true source of this melancholy, which it was no longer in my power to master. It required so little effort, only a few moments of conversation; in the end she succeeded.

After twenty-nine days of such tedious travel, we arrived in Petersburg at the Summer Palace. There the Grand Duke immediately reinstated his concerts. This gave me some opportunity for conversation, but my melancholy had become such that at every moment and with every remark, I had tears in my eyes and a thousand worries passed through my head. In a word, I could not rid my mind of the thought that everything pointed to Sergei Saltykov's removal. We went to Peterhof. There I walked a lot, but despite this my worries followed at my heels.

In the month of August, we again returned to the city to reside in the Summer Palace. For me it was an almost mortal blow when I learned that the apartment being prepared for my confinement connected to and was part of the Empress's. Alexander Shuvalov took me to see it. I found two rooms like all those in the Summer Palace: sad, with only one exit, poorly decorated with crimson damask, and with almost no furniture or any kind of comfort. I saw that I would be isolated there without any company, very unhappy and absolutely alone. I told Sergei Saltykov and Princess Gagarina, who, although they did not like each other, nevertheless had their friendship for me in common. They saw what I saw, but it was impossible to remedy the situation. On Wednesday I was supposed to move into this apartment, which was very far from the Grand Duke's. I went to bed Tuesday evening and awoke in the night with pains. I awakened Madame Vladislavova, who sent for the midwife, who confirmed that I was going into labor. The Grand Duke, who was sleeping in his room, was awakened, as was Count Alexander Shuvalov. At around two in the morning, he sent to the Empress's residence, and she did not delay in coming. I was in a very bad way. Finally, toward noon of the following day,

September 20, I bore a son.* As soon as he was swaddled, the Empress had her confessor come in and he gave the child the name Paul, after which the Empress immediately had the child taken by the midwife and told the midwife to follow her. I stayed on my sickbed. Now, this bed was placed opposite a door through which I could see daylight. Behind me there were two large windows that closed poorly, and to the right and left of this bed, two doors, one of which opened onto my dressing room and the other onto that occupied by Madame Vladislavova. As soon as the Empress had left, the Grand Duke also went his way, as well as Monsieur and Madame Shuvalov, and I did not see anyone again until the stroke of three. I had perspired a great deal. I asked Madame Vladislavova to change my linen and put me to bed. She told me that she did not dare. Several times she sent someone to look for the midwife, but she did not come. I asked to drink, but again I received the same response. Finally, after three hours, Countess Shuvalova arrived in all her finery. When she saw me still lying in the same place where she had left me, she exclaimed that this could kill me. This was a great consolation for me, as I had already been in tears from the moment I gave birth, especially because of the negligent way in which I had been poorly and uncomfortably put to bed after a difficult and painful labor, between doors and windows that closed poorly, with no one daring to carry me to my bed, which was two steps away, and I had not the strength to drag myself to it. Madame Shuvalova left immediately, and I think that she sent for the midwife, because she came a half hour later and told us that the Empress was so occupied with the child that she had not let her go for a single moment.† No one had a thought about me. I was hardly flattered by this forgetfulness and neglect. Meanwhile I was dying of fatigue and thirst. Finally I was put in my bed and I did not see a living soul the whole day, nor was anyone even sent to find out how I was. For his part, His Imperial Highness did nothing but drink with those whom he found around him, and

---

* *Journal of the Court Quartermaster*, 1754: "September 20. Toward morning Her Imperial Highness Her Majesty Grand Duchess Ekaterina Alekseevna successfully gave birth. God has sent His Imperial Highness Grand Duke Paul Petrovich. In the eleventh hour, in the presence of Her Imperial Majesty, Grand Duke Paul Petrovich was brought from the chambers of Their Imperial Highnesses to the inner chambers of Her Imperial Majesty, and the successful birth is announced to the whole court through the raising of banners in the city and cannonades from all fortresses" (728).

† In a dispatch from July 27, 1757, L'Hôpital notes "the love of the Empress for the son of the Grand Duchess, which they say belongs to Monsieur Saltykov" (quoted in Böhme 2:177).

the Empress busied herself with the child. In the city and in the empire, the joy over this was so very great.

On the following day I began to feel an unbearable, rheumatic pain from the hip down along the thigh of my left leg. This pain kept me from sleeping, and I also came down with a high fever. Despite this, on the following day the consideration shown to me was about the same. I saw no one, and no one asked for news of me. However, the Grand Duke did come into my room for a moment and then left, saying that he did not have the time to stay. I did nothing but cry and moan in my bed, and only Madame Vladislavova was with me in my room. Deep down she felt sympathy for me but could not remedy the situation. Moreover I did not like to be pitied, nor to complain. I had too proud a soul, and the very idea of being unhappy was intolerable to me. Until now I had done everything I could not to appear so. I could have seen Alexander Shuvalov and his wife, but they were such insipid and boring creatures that I was always delighted when they were not there.

On the third day, someone came on behalf of the Empress to ask Madame Vladislavova if a blue satin cape that Her Imperial Majesty had worn the day that I gave birth, because it had been very cold in my room, had not been left behind in my apartment. Madame Vladislavova searched everywhere for this cape and finally found it in a corner of my dressing room, where it had not been noticed, because since my confinement few had entered this room. Having found it, she sent it back immediately. This cape, as we learned a little later, had given rise to a rather unusual incident. The Empress had no fixed hour for either going to bed, waking up, having dinner or supper, or dressing. One afternoon during the three days in question, she lay down on a sofa, where she had had a mattress and cushions placed. Lying down, she asked for this cape because she was cold. They looked everywhere and did not find it, because it had been left in my room. Then the Empress ordered them to look under the cushions at the head of her bed, believing that they would find it there. The sister of Madame Kruse, the Empress's favorite lady-in-waiting, passed her hand under Her Imperial Majesty's headboard and withdrew it, saying that the cape was not under the headboard but that there was a packet with hair or something like it. She did not know what it was. The Empress immediately got up, had the mattress and the cushions removed, and to their surprise, they saw a piece of paper in which some hairs were twisted around a few vegetable roots. The Empress's ladies and she herself said that these were surely charms or amulets, and they all speculated about what this could mean, and who could have had the audacity to place this packet under the Empress's headboard. One of the ladies whom Her Imperial Majesty liked best was suspected. She was known by the name of Anna Dmitrievna Domasheva, but not long before, this woman, having become a widow, had gotten remarried to one of the Empress's chamber valets. The Shuvalovs did not like this woman, who opposed them, because thanks to her merit and the Empress's trust, which she had enjoyed since her youth, she was quite capable of devising schemes to greatly diminish the Shuvalovs' favor. As the Shuvalovs did not lack allies, they too began to view the affair as a criminal act. The Empress herself was quite receptive to this view because she believed in charms and amulets. Consequently she ordered Count Alexander Shuvalov to arrest this woman, her husband, and her two sons, one of whom was an officer in the guards, the other a chamber page for the Empress. Two days after being arrested, the husband asked for a razor to shave his beard, and he cut his throat with it. As for the wife and children, they were under arrest for a long time, and she confessed that she had used these charms so that the Empress's favor toward her would continue, and that she had put a few grains of salt burned on Holy Thursday in a glass of Hungarian wine that she had presented to the Empress. This affair ended with the exile of the woman and her children to Moscow. Afterward, the rumor was circulated that a fainting spell, which the Empress had had shortly before my confinement, was the result of these drinks that the woman had given her. But the fact is that she had never given her more than two or three grains of salt burned on Holy Thursday, which certainly could not harm the Empress. In this matter, only this woman's audacity and superstition were reprehensible.

Eventually the Grand Duke, who in the evening was bored without my maids of honor, toward whom he made advances, came to suggest spending evenings in my bedroom, whereupon he courted the absolutely ugliest of my ladies; she was Countess Elizabeth Vorontsova. On the sixth day, my son's baptism took place; he had already almost died of thrush. I could get news of him only furtively because asking after him would have been seen as a lack of faith in the Empress's care for him and would have been very badly received. Indeed, she had taken him into her room, and as soon as he would cry, she would run to him herself, and he was literally smothered by her care. He was kept in an extremely hot room, swaddled in flannel, and laid in a crib lined with black fox fur. He was covered with a satin quilt lined with cotton wadding, and over this was placed another of pink velvet lined with black fox. Later I myself saw him lying like this many times, sweat pouring from his face and whole body, the result being that when he was older the slightest draft chilled him and made him ill. Moreover, he was surrounded by a great number of old matrons, who thanks to their misguided care and lack of common sense inflicted infinitely more physical and mental harm than good.

On the same day as the baptism, the Empress came into my bedroom after the ceremony and brought me, on a gold plate, an order directing her cabinet to send me one hundred thousand rubles. To this she had added a little jewelry box, which I opened only when she had left. This money came to me at the right time, because I did not have a cent, and was overwhelmed by debts. As for the box, when I had opened it, it did not have much effect on my mood. It contained a very poor little necklace with earrings and two pitiful rings that I would have been ashamed to give to my ladies-in-waiting. In the entire box there was not a single stone worth a hundred rubles; the workmanship and taste did not stand out either. I was silent and had the imperial jewelry box locked. Apparently they were aware of the real stinginess of this present, because Count Alexander Shuvalov came to tell me that he had been ordered to find out how I liked the box. I replied to him that I was accustomed to regarding everything that came to me from Her Imperial Majesty's hands as priceless. Hearing this compliment, he left with a pleased expression. He brought up the subject again when he saw that I never wore this lovely necklace and especially the miserable earrings, telling me to put them on. I replied that for the Empress's celebrations I was accustomed to wearing my finest jewelry and that the necklace and earrings were not in this category. Four or five days after I had been brought the money that the Empress had given me, Baron Cherkasov, her cabinet secretary, asked me in the name of God to lend this money to the Empress's cabinet because she wanted money and there was not a cent. I sent his money back to him, and he returned it to me in the month of January. Having learned of the present that the Empress had given me, the Grand Duke went into a terrible rage because she had not given him anything. He spoke vehemently to Count Alexander Shuvalov, who went to speak to the Empress. She immediately sent the Grand Duke a sum equal to what she had given me, and for this the money was borrowed from me. To tell the truth, in general the Shuvalovs were the most cowardly creatures, and it was by this defect that they could be manipulated; but at that time these wonderful qualities had not yet been fully discovered.

After the baptism of my son, there were parties, balls, illuminations, and fireworks at court, while I was still in bed, ill and suffering great boredom. To cap it all, the seventeenth day of my confinement was chosen to inform me of two very unpleasant pieces of news. The first was that Sergei Saltykov had been named to deliver the news of my son's birth to Sweden. The second was that Princess Gagarina's marriage had been set for the following week. That is, in plain language, I was immediately going to be separated from the two people I loved most in my entourage. I sank more than ever into my bed, where I did nothing but grieve. In order to stay there, I pretended to have new pains in my leg that prevented me from getting up, but the truth is that I neither could nor wanted to see anyone, because I was despondent.

During my confinement the Grand Duke also had a serious ordeal when Count Alexander Shuvalov came to tell him that an old huntsman of the Grand Duke, Bastian, whom the Empress had ordered several years before to marry Madame Schenk, my former chambermaid, had informed him that he had heard from someone that Bressan wanted to give something or other to the Grand Duke to drink. Now, this Bastian was a great rogue and a drunk who drank from time to time with His Imperial Highness, and having fallen out with Bressan, whom he believed more in the Grand Duke's favor than himself, he thought to play a dirty trick on him. The Grand Duke loved them both. Bastian was put in the fortress; Bressan was almost put there as well, but he got off with a scare. The huntsman was banished from the country and sent back to Holstein with his wife, and Bressan kept his position because he spied on everyone.

After a few delays arising from the fact that the Empress signed her name neither often nor easily, Sergei Saltykov departed. In the meantime Princess Gagarina was married on the appointed day.* When the forty days of my confinement had passed, the Empress came into my bedroom a second time for the churching ceremony.† I had risen from the bed to receive her, but when she saw me so weak and haggard, she had me sit during the prayers that her confessor read. My son had been brought into my

---

* November 6, 1754.

   † A religious ceremony marking the end of a woman's ritual impurity after childbirth, after which she is again allowed to go to church.

room. It was the first time I had seen him since his birth. I found him very beautiful, and the sight of him raised my spirits a little, but at the very moment that the prayers were over, the Empress had him taken out, and she left. The first of November was chosen by Her Imperial Majesty for me to receive the customary congratulations after the six weeks of confinement. For this purpose, very rich furnishings were put in the room next to mine, and there everyone came to kiss my hand while I was seated on a bed covered with pink velvet embroidered in silver.* The Empress came too, and from my apartment she went to the Winter Palace, and we were ordered to follow her there two or three days later.

We were lodged in the apartment that my mother had occupied and that, to be precise, composed part of the Iaguzhinsky house and part of the Raguzinsky house; the other half of the latter was occupied by the College of Foreign Affairs. At that time they were building the Winter Palace toward the main square. I moved from the Summer Palace to the winter residence firmly resolved not to leave my room as long as I did not feel myself strong enough to overcome my melancholy. At the time, I was reading *History of Germany* and Voltaire's *L'Histoire universelle.*† After that, I read as many Russian books that winter as I could procure for myself, among others two immense volumes by Baronio, translated into Russian.‡ Then I came across *The Spirit of the Laws* by Montesquieu, after which I read the annals of Tacitus, which produced a revolution in my thinking.§ Perhaps my despondent frame of mind at the time contributed in no small way to this. I began to see more things with a black outlook and to seek the causes that really underlay and truly shaped the different interests in the affairs that I observed.

* *Journal of the Court Quartermaster,* 1754: "November 1. Tuesday, Her Imperial Highness Grand Duchess, on the occasion of the six weeks since Her Highness successfully gave birth, while seated on her bed, deigned to accept the humble congratulations of resident distinguished persons of both sexes, from ambassadors and other foreign ministers of the second rank" (728).

† Voltaire's *Annales de l'Empire depuis Charlemagne,* 2 vols. (1753), *Abrégé de l'Histoire universelle depuis Charlemagne jusqu'à Charles V,* 2 vol. (1753), and *Histoire universelle,* 2 vol. (Paris, 1754); *Essai sur l'histoire universelle,* or in its final form, *Essai sur les moeurs et l'esprit des nations* (1769); in 1765 he published the introduction separately as *La philosophie de l'histoire, par feu l'Abbé Bazin,* which he dedicated to Catherine. Catherine was reading Barre's *History of Germany* in 1749 too.

‡ Cesare Baronio (1538–1607), *Secular and Ecclesiastical History* (1588–1607), *Annales ecclesiastici,* in Russian translation *Deianiia tserkovnye i grazhdanskie ot r. Khr. do XIII stoletii* (1719) (in Böhme 2:184).

§ Montesquieu, *L'esprit des lois* (1748) and Publius Cornelius Tacitus (55–117), *The Annals* (109 A.D.), an important 100-year history of Rome, beginning with Caesar Augustus.

I gathered my forces to appear in public at Christmas. I actually attended the divine service, but in church I was seized by shivering and pains throughout my body, so that back in my apartment, I undressed myself and lay on my bed, which was nothing but a chaise longue that I had placed in front of a blocked-off door. It seemed to me that no draft penetrated through it, because along with a portiere lined with wool there was also a large screen, but in fact I believe this door gave me all the colds that afflicted me that winter. The day after Christmas, my fever was so high that I was delirious. When I closed my eyes, I saw only the poorly drawn figures on the tiles of the stove that was at the foot of my chaise longue, the room being small and narrow. As for my bedroom, I hardly went into it because it was very cold due to the windows that opened to the east and north over the Neva River. The second reason I was exiled from my bedroom was the proximity of the Grand Duke's apartment, where during the day and part of the night there was always a racket similar to that of barracks. Moreover, as he and his entourage smoked a great deal, there was the unpleasant smoke and odor of tobacco. The entire winter I therefore remained in this miserable, narrow little room, which had two windows and a *trumeau,* and in total may have been seven or eight arshins long by four wide, with three doors.*

---

* A *trumeau* is a mirror having a painted or carved panel above or below the glass in the same frame.

1755

*Catherine's troubles with Saltykov and offensive against the
Shuvalovs; she sees her son a third time; Peter's Holstein troops at
Oranienbaum; Catherine's gardener predicts her great future; the
arrival of Sir Charles Hanbury-Williams and Count
Poniatowski, who courts her; Catherine's pregnancy;
a secret night out with friends*

Thus began the year 1755. From Christmas to Lent there were nothing but celebrations at the court and in the city. The birth of my son continued to be the occasion. By turns everyone vied with everyone else to give the most beautiful dinners, balls, masquerades, illuminations, and fireworks possible. I attended none of these, under pretext of illness. Toward the end of carnival Sergei Saltykov returned from Sweden. During Saltykov's absence, all his news and the dispatches from Count Panin, at the time the Russian envoy to Sweden, were sent to me by Grand Chancellor Count Bestuzhev through Madame Vladislavova, who received them from her son-in-law, the Grand Chancellor's head clerk, and I sent them back by the same channel. I also learned by this same channel that as soon as Sergei Saltykov returned, it had been decided to send him to Hamburg as the Russian minister to replace Prince Alexander Golitsyn, who was being sent to the army. This new arrangement did not diminish my sorrow. When Sergei Saltykov had returned, he sent Lev Naryshkin to tell me that I should indicate, if I could, a way for him to see me. I spoke about this to Madame Vladislavova, who consented to this interview. He was supposed to go to her residence and from there to mine. I waited for him until three in the morning, but he did not come. I was in mortal agony over what could have kept him from coming. I learned the following day that he had been dragged by Count Roman Vorontsov to a meeting of Freemasons. He claimed that he had not been able to get away without causing suspicion. But I questioned and probed Lev Naryshkin so much that I saw clear as day that he had failed to come due to a lack of enthusiasm and consideration for me, without any regard for what I had suffered for so long solely out of affection for him. Lev Naryshkin himself, although his friend, found little or no excuse for him. In truth, I was very angry. I wrote him a letter in which I complained bitterly about his conduct. He replied and came to my residence. It was not hard for him to appease me, because I was very willing to be appeased. He persuaded me to appear in public.

I followed his advice and I appeared on February 10, the Grand Duke's birthday and Shrovetide.* For this day I had made a superb outfit of blue velvet embroidered in gold. As I had had much time for reflection in my solitude, I resolved to make those who had caused me so many sorrows understand that they were answerable to me, that no one mistreated me with impunity, and that cruel conduct would not gain my affection or approbation. Consequently I never failed to show the Shuvalovs how they had disposed me in their favor. I treated them with bitter scorn, I made others aware of their nastiness, their stupidity, I ridiculed them, and everywhere I could, I always had some barb to throw at them, which would then race through the city, and provide malicious amusement at their expense. In a word, I avenged myself on them in every manner I could devise. In their presence I never failed to praise those whom they disliked. As there were a great many people who hated them, I did not lack for loyal allies. The Counts Razumovsky, whom I had always loved, were more flattered than ever. I redoubled my compliments and politeness toward everyone except the Shuvalovs. In a word, I drew myself up and walked with my head high, more like the leader of a very large faction than a humiliated or oppressed person. The Shuvalovs never knew on which foot to dance. They huddled together and resorted to courtiers' ruses and intrigues.

During this time a gentleman from Holstein, Monsieur Brockdorff, who had once before tried to enter the country, appeared in Russia, having previously been turned back at the Russian border by the Grand Duke's advisers at the time, Brümmer and Bergholz, because they knew

---

* Shrovetide, or *Maslenita*, is the Orthodox equivalent of Carnival, and lasts the week just before Lent.

him to be a man of very bad character and given to intrigue.* This man appeared at exactly the right moment for the Shuvalovs. As a duke of Holstein with a chamberlain's key from the Grand Duke, he had access to the residence of His Imperial Highness, who in any case was favorably disposed to every clod who came from that country. This man found his way into Count Peter Shuvalov's entourage, and here is how. In the inn where he lodged, he met a man who only left the inns of Petersburg to go to the home of three rather pretty German girls named Reiffenstein. One of these girls enjoyed the support of Count Peter Shuvalov. The man in question was called Braun. He was some kind of shady dealer in all manner of things. He brought Brockdorff to the girls' home, where he met Count Peter Shuvalov. Shuvalov made solemn declarations of devotion to the Grand Duke and eventually got around to complaining about me. At the first opportunity Monsieur Brockdorff reported all this to the Grand Duke, who was urged to bring his wife back to her senses, so to speak.

To this end, one day after we had had lunch, His Imperial Highness came into my room and told me that I was becoming intolerably haughty and that he knew how to bring me back to my senses. I asked him what he meant by haughty. He told me that I held myself very erect. I asked him if to please him, one had to keep one's back bent like some great master's slave. He grew angry and told me that he well knew how to bring me back to my senses. And I asked him, how? At this he put his back against the wall and drew his sword halfway out and showed it to me. I asked if this meant he wished to fight me. In that case, I would need one too. He put his half-drawn sword back into its scabbard and told me that I had become dreadfully nasty. I asked him, "In what way?" He stammered, "Well, with the Shuvalovs." I replied that this was only recrimination and that he

* In 1760, Catherine made notes about this visit: "At the end of 1754, seeing that his affairs were in a state that threatened widespread bankruptcy, the Grand Duke decided to give me the task of putting things in order. At first I did not want to take this on, foreseeing the difficulty of remedying this hopeless situation, as well as the jealousy and envy that this would earn me, but I finally decided to agree to it; I could no longer refuse without offending the Grand Duke. She takes us through his accounts. "I then put into writing all of Brockdorff's contradictory actions for and against the Shuvalovs, his accusations, and I gave this text to the Grand Duke. Brockdorff induced his master to reveal its contents to Count Alexander Shuvalov, who, trusting Brockdorff, believed me the author of everything against the Shuvalovs. They detested Chancellor Bestuzhev; these suspicions, and the fear that my relations with him might become harmful to them one day, hastened his fall. At that time they could not imagine that a consistent policy was the product of a woman's mind, that this woman already had all of the small and great affairs of her husband in hand, that this woman would not tolerate any embezzlement, insinuations, injustice, etc." (621–24)

would do well not to speak of what he did not know or understand. He continued, "You see what happens when you do not trust your true friends—you regret it. If you had trusted me, you would have benefited." I said to him, "But trust you how?" Then he began to say things that were so extravagant and nonsensical that I, seeing that he talked nonsense pure and simple, let him speak without responding and exploited what seemed to me an auspicious pause to advise him to go to bed because I saw clearly that wine had addled his reason and completely stupefied any common sense. He followed my advice and went to bed. At that time he was already beginning to smell almost continually of wine mixed with smoking tobacco, which was literally intolerable for those who went near him.

That same evening, while I was playing cards, Count Alexander Shuvalov came to convey from the Empress that she had forbidden the ladies to include in their finery many kinds of ribbon and lace as specified in the decree. To show him how His Imperial Highness had chastened me, I laughed in his face and told him he could have dispensed with notifying me of this decree because I never wore any ribbons or lace that displeased Her Imperial Majesty, that besides, I did not make beauty or finery the source of my merit, for when one was gone, the other became ridiculous, and only character endured. He listened to the end, twitching his right eye as was his habit, and left with his usual grimace. I pointed this out to those who were playing with me by imitating him, which made the group laugh.

Some days later the Grand Duke told me that he wanted to ask the Empress for money for his dealings in Holstein, which continued to get worse and worse, and that Brockdorff advised him to do this. I saw clearly that this was bait set for him by the Shuvalovs to raise his hopes. I said to him, "Is there no other way to handle this?" He replied that he would show me what the Holsteiners were reporting to him about the situation. This he in fact did, and after seeing the documents he showed me, I told him that it seemed to me that he could manage without begging for money from Madame his aunt, who had given him one hundred thousand rubles less than six months before and might again refuse him, but he held to his position and I to mine. It is certain that for a long time he was made to hope he would get it and he received nothing.

After Easter we went to Oranienbaum.* Before we left, the Empress allowed me to see my son for the third time since his birth. I had to pass

* May 23, 1755.

through all of Her Imperial Majesty's apartments to arrive at his bedroom, I found him suffocating from the heat, as I have already recounted. Upon arriving at the Oranienbaum estate, we saw something extraordinary. His Imperial Highness's Holstein retinue continually preached to him about the deficit, and he was told by everyone to cut down this useless retinue, which in any case he could see only furtively and in small groups. He suddenly decided and made so bold as to have an entire detachment of Holstein troops come. This was again a scheme of that miserable Brockdorff, who pandered to this Prince's dominant passion. He had made it known to the Shuvalovs that in granting their tacit approval to the Grand Duke for this plaything or bauble, they would assure themselves of his favor forever, that they would keep him occupied and would be sure of his approval for everything else that they would undertake. The Empress detested Holstein and everything that came from it, and had seen that such military playthings had undone the Grand Duke's father, Duke Karl Friedrich, in the eyes of Peter I and of the Russian public.* It seems that at first the affair was kept hidden from her or that she was told it was a minor matter that was not worth discussing, and besides, Count Alexander Shuvalov's presence alone was enough to keep things from getting out of hand. Sailing from Kiel, the detachment landed at Kronstadt and came to Oranienbaum. The Grand Duke, who during the time of Choglokov had worn the Holstein uniform only in his room and somewhat furtively, was already wearing this uniform every day but court days, though he was a lieutenant colonel in the Preobrazhensky regiment and in addition had a regiment of cuirassiers in Russia. On Monsieur Brockdorff's advice, the Grand Duke kept the transport of these troops completely hidden from me. I admit that when I learned of it, I shuddered at the terrible impression that the Grand Duke's action would make on the Russian public, and indeed, on the mind of the Empress, since I was not at all unaware of her sentiments. Monsieur Alexander Shuvalov watched this detachment pass the balcony of Oranienbaum twitching his eye; I was next to him. Personally he disapproved of what he and his relatives had agreed to tolerate. The Oranienbaum castle was guarded alternately by the Ingerman regiments and that of Astrakhan. I

---

* The opposite is probably true. With his toy soldiers and play regiments, Peter III followed the practice of Peter the Great, who as a young man had toy boats and regiments at his estate outside Moscow in Kolomenskoe.

learned that when they saw the Holstein soldiers pass by, they had said, "These cursed Germans have all been sold to the King of Prussia. A troop of traitors has been brought to Russia." In general the public was shocked by their arrival. The most devoted subjects shrugged their shoulders, the most moderate found the affair ridiculous. Basically it was a very imprudent bit of childishness. For my part, I held my tongue, and when it was mentioned to me, I clearly implied that I did not at all approve, that in fact no matter how I looked at it, I regarded it as thoroughly harmful to the Grand Duke's well-being, for what other opinion could one have after examining the matter? His pleasure alone could never compensate for the harm that this would do him in public opinion. But His Imperial Highness, full of enthusiasm for his troops, went to lodge with them in the camp he had had set up and did nothing but drill them thereafter. They had to be fed, and no one had even thought of this. However, the matter was pressing and there were a few arguments with the Marshal of the Court, who was not prepared to meet the request. Finally he gave in, and court lackeys along with castle guards from the Ingerman regiment were employed to carry food from the palace kitchen to the camp for the new arrivals. This camp was not very close to the household, and nothing was given to either the lackeys or the soldiers for their trouble. One can imagine the fine impression that such a wise and prudent arrangement must have made. The soldiers of the Ingerman regiment said, "Here we are, the valets of these cursed Germans." The court servants said, "We are employed to serve a bunch of worthless peasants." When I saw and learned of what was happening, I very firmly resolved to keep myself as far away as I could from this dangerous child's game. The gentlemen of our court who were married had their wives with them. This made for a rather large group, and the gentlemen had nothing to do with the Holstein camp, from which His Imperial Highness no longer budged. As I was therefore amid this group of people from the court, I would go for walks with them as often as I could but always in a direction away from the camp, to which we gave a wide berth.

At the time, I took it into my head to make a garden at Oranienbaum, and since I knew that the Grand Duke would not give me an inch of land for this, I asked Princess Golitsyna to sell or give me a piece of uncultivated land, two hundred yards in length and long abandoned, which they owned, right next to Oranienbaum. This land belonged to eight or ten people in their family, and they gave it to me willingly, asking nothing to boot. I thus began to draw up plans for building and planting, and as this was my first foray into plants and buildings, it became an enormous project. I had an old French surgeon named Guyon, who, seeing this, said, "What good is all this? Remember what I say. I predict that one day you will abandon this project." His prediction came true, but at the time, I needed an amusement, and this was one that exercised the imagination. At first, I employed the gardener of Oranienbaum, Lamberti, to plant my garden. He had served the Empress when she was still a Princess on her estate of Tsarskoe Selo, from which she had him moved to Oranienbaum. He dabbled in predictions, and among others, one about the Empress had come true. He had predicted to her that she would ascend to the throne. This same man said to me and repeated as often as I wished that I would become Sovereign Empress of Russia, that I would see sons, grandsons, and great-grandsons, and I would die at a grand old age of more than eighty. He did more. He set the year of my ascension to the throne six years before it occurred. He was a very curious man who spoke with an assurance that nothing could deter. He claimed that the Empress wished him ill because he had predicted what had happened to her and that she had sent him from Tsarskoe Selo to Oranienbaum because she feared him, with no throne anymore to promise her.

I believe that on Pentecost we were taken from Oranienbaum to the city. It was around this time that the Ambassador from England, Sir Williams, came to Russia. In his entourage he had Count Poniatowski, the son of the Poniatowski who had belonged to the faction of Charles XII, King of Sweden.* After a short stay in the city, we returned to Oranienbaum, where the Empress ordered the celebration of the Feast of St. Peter. She did not come herself, because she did not want to celebrate my son Paul's first name day, which falls on the same day. She stayed at Peterhof. There she sat herself at a window, where apparently she remained all day, because all those who came to Oranienbaum said that they had seen her at this window. A great many people came. We danced in the salon at the entrance to my garden and then we had supper. The ambassadors and foreign ministers came. I remember that the Ambassador from England, Sir Hanbury-Williams, was my neighbor at supper and that we had a conversation as pleasant as it was merry. As he had great wit and

* Sir Charles Hanbury-Williams arrived June 12, 1755, and Count Stanislaw Poniatowski arrived at the end of the month.

knowledge and was familiar with all of Europe, it was not difficult to have a conversation with him. Later I learned that at this supper he had been as amused as I and that he spoke of me with praise, which I always elicited from those minds or wits that squared with mine, and at that time I had fewer people who were envious of me, so I was generally spoken of with a fair amount of praise. I was known for having intelligence, and many people who knew me more intimately honored me with their confidences, trusted me, and asked me for advice and benefited from what I told them. The Grand Duke had long been calling me Madame Resourceful, and however upset or sulky he was toward me, if he found himself in any distress, he ran as fast as he could, as was his habit, to my apartment to get my opinion, and as soon as he had got it, he ran away again as fast as his legs could carry him.

I still recall that at this celebration of the Feast of St. Peter at Oranienbaum, while watching Count Poniatowski dance, I spoke with Sir Williams about the Count's father and about the harm that he had done to Peter I. The English Ambassador told me many good things about the son and confirmed what I knew, to wit, that at the time, his father and his mother's family, the Czartoryskis, made up the Russian faction in Poland and that they had sent this son to Russia and had entrusted him to the English Ambassador so as to nourish in him the parents' sentiments for Russia, and that he hoped that this young man would succeed in Russia. He might have been twenty-two or twenty-three at the time. I replied that in general I thought that for foreigners Russia was like a touchstone for their merit and that he who succeeded in Russia could be sure of succeeding in all of Europe. I have always considered this observation infallible because nowhere are people more skillful than in Russia at noticing the weakness, ridiculousness, or faults of a foreigner. One can be assured that nothing will get past a Russian, because every Russian naturally, viscerally, dislikes all foreigners. Around this time I learned that Sergei Saltykov's conduct had been as indiscreet in Sweden as in Dresden, and in addition, in both countries he had wooed every woman whom he had met. At first I did not want to believe any of it, but in the end I heard it repeated from so many sides that even his friends could not exculpate him.

During this year I formed a closer friendship than ever with Anna Nikitichna Naryshkina. Lev, her brother-in-law, contributed greatly to this. He was almost always with us, and his antics were endless. At times he would say, "To the one who behaves the best, I promise a jewel for which you will thank me." We let him talk and were not even curious to ask him what this jewel was. In autumn, the Holstein troops were sent back to sea, and we returned to the city and went to reside in the Summer Palace. During this time, Lev Naryshkin fell ill with a severe fever during which he wrote me letters that I saw clearly were not by him. I replied to him. In his letters he asked me at times for sweetmeats, at other times for similar trifles, and then thanked me for them. These letters were perfectly well written and quite pleasant; he said that he employed his secretary to write them. Finally I learned that this secretary was Count Poniatowski, that he had become intimate with the house of Naryshkin, and that he did not budge from their residence.

At the beginning of winter we were moved from the Summer Palace to the new Winter Palace that the Empress had built from wood on the site where the Chicherins' house presently stands.* This palace occupied the entire neighborhood up to the house of Countess Matiushkina, which at the time belonged to Naumov. My windows were opposite this house, which was occupied by the maidens of the court. Upon arriving there, I was quite struck by the height and size of the apartments that were assigned to us. Four large antechambers and two rooms with an alcove had been prepared for me and the same for the Grand Duke. My apartment was rather well situated, so that I did not have to bear the proximity of those of the Grand Duke. This was a great advantage. Count Alexander Shuvalov noticed my contentment and immediately went to tell the Empress that I had greatly praised the beauty, the size, and the number of the rooms that had been assigned to me. He later told me this with a kind of satisfaction, accented by his twitching eye and accompanied by a smile.

During this period and for a long time thereafter, the Grand Duke's principal toy in the city was an excessive number of little toy soldiers made of wood, lead, papier-mâché, and wax, which he arranged on very narrow tables that occupied an entire room. One could barely move between these tables. He had nailed thin strips of brass along the length of these tables. Strings were attached to these brass bands, and when one pulled them, the brass strips made a noise that according to him imitated the running fire of rifles. With great frequency, he celebrated court ceremonies by making these troops shoot their rifles. In addition, every day the guard was changed, which meant that the figures who were supposed

---

* November 10, 1755.

to mount the guard were taken from each table. The Grand Duke attended this parade in uniform with boots, spurs, high collar, and scarf, and those servants admitted to this lovely exercise were obliged to dress in the same manner.

Toward winter that year I believed that I was pregnant again; I was bled. I had, or rather thought I had, gumboils under both my cheeks, but after suffering for a few days, four wisdom teeth appeared in the four corners of my mouth. As our apartments were very spacious, the Grand Duke instituted a weekly ball on Thursdays and concerts on Tuesdays. The only ones who came to these were our maids of honor and the gentlemen of our court, with their wives. These balls could be interesting depending on the people who came to them. I very much liked the Naryshkins, who were more sociable than others. I include in their number Mesdames Seniavina and Izmailova, sisters of the Naryshkins, and the wife of the elder brother, whom I have already mentioned. Lev Naryshkin, always crazier than before and regarded by everyone as a man of no importance, which indeed he was, had gotten into the habit of running continually from the Grand Duke's room to mine without stopping anywhere for long. When entering my room he had the habit of meowing like a cat in front of my door, and when I replied, he would enter.

On December 17, between six and seven in the evening, he announced himself in this way at my door. I told him to enter. He began by giving me regards from his sister-in-law, telling me that she was not doing very well, and then he said, "But you should go see her." I said, "I would do so willingly, but you know that I cannot go out without permission and that I will never be permitted to go to her house." He replied, "I will take you there." I retorted, "Have you lost your mind? What do you mean, go with you? You will be put in the fortress, and God knows what trouble I will be in." "Oh," he said, "no one will know about it. We will take our precautions." "How's that?" Then he said, "I will come to get you an hour or two from now. The Grand Duke will be eating supper" (for a long while I had been keeping to my room under the pretext of not wanting supper), "he will be at table for a good part of the night, will only leave very drunk, and will go to bed." Since my confinement, he had been sleeping in his room most of the time. "To be on the safe side, dress as a man and we will go to Anna Nikitichna's together." The adventure was beginning to tempt me. I was always alone in my room with my books and without any company. Finally, after debating with him this plan, which was itself mad and which had seemed so to me from the first, I began to find it plausible and agreed so as to give myself a moment of amusement and pleasure. He left. I called for a Kalmuck hairdresser who was in my service and told him to bring me one of my men's outfits and everything that went with it because I needed to make a present of it to someone. This boy never opened his mouth, and it was more difficult to make him talk than it is to make others be quiet. He promptly carried out my commission and brought me everything I needed. I pretended to have a headache and went to bed earlier than usual. As soon as Madame Vladislavova had put me to bed and withdrawn, I got up and dressed from head to toe in the man's outfit. I arranged my hair as best I could. I had been doing this for a long time and was not clumsy at it. At the appointed time Lev Naryshkin came through the Grand Duke's apartment and meowed at my door, which I opened for him. We passed through a little antechamber into the vestibule and got into a carriage without anyone seeing us, laughing like fools at our escapade. Lev was living with his brother and sister-in-law in the same house, which was also occupied by their mother. When we arrived, Anna Nikitichna, who suspected nothing, was there. We found Count Poniatowski there too. Lev introduced me as one of his friends and asked them to receive me well, and the evening passed in the merriest manner one can imagine. After visiting for an hour and a half, I left, and returned to the palace the happiest person in the world without meeting a living soul. At the morning court and the evening ball on the following day, the Empress's birthday, none of us who shared the secret could look at one another without bursting with laughter at the previous day's madness. A few days later Lev proposed a second visit that would take place in my residence, and as before he escorted his group into my room so that no one caught wind of this.

1756

The Seven Years' War with Prussia begins; Elizabeth's frequent illness; Peter courts Mme. Teplova; Catherine's miscarriage; her riding lessons; Count Poniatowski, Count Horn, and her little Bolognese dog; her quarrel with Peter over his mistresses; the Franco-Austrian faction defeats Bestuzhev-Riumin's Anglo-Prussian party

So began the year 1756. We took a singular pleasure in these furtive gatherings. Not a week went by without one, two, or three of them, alternating between different people's houses, and when someone in the group was sick, we were sure to go to that person's house. Sometimes at the theater, although we were in different loges and some of us were in the orchestra, each of us knew in a flash where to go by certain agreed-upon signs without speaking to one another, and there was never a misunderstanding among us, except that it happened twice that I had to return to the palace on foot, which meant a walk.

At the time, there were preparations for war against the King of Prussia. Under her treaty with the house of Austria, the Empress was supposed to give thirty thousand men in assistance. This was the opinion of Grand Chancellor Bestuzhev, but the house of Austria wanted Russia to assist with all its might. Count Esterhazy, the Ambassador from Vienna, schemed for this with all his might wherever he could and often through different channels. The faction opposed to Count Bestuzhev was Vice Chancellor Count Vorontsov and the Shuvalovs. At the time, England was allied with the King of Prussia and France with Austria.* That was when Empress Elizabeth began to fall ill frequently. At first no one understood what this was, and they attributed it to the tapering off of her menstrual periods. The Shuvalovs often seemed distressed and deep in

* On January 16, 1756, in a surprise move, Frederick the Great signed the Whitehall Treaty with England, and on May 1, 1756, his spurned ally France signed the Versailles Treaty with Austria, which, by the end of the year, Russia signed too. The war began with Frederick the Great's invasion of Saxony on August 18, 1756.

intrigue, heavily fawning over the Grand Duke from one moment to the next. The courtiers who pored among themselves that Her Imperial Majesty's illness was more serious than was believed. Some called it hysteria, while others called it fainting, convulsions, or bad nerves. This lasted the entire winter of 1755 and 1756. Finally, in the spring, we learned that Marshal Apraksin was leaving to command the army that was supposed to invade Prussia. His wife came to our residence with her youngest daughter to take her leave of us. I spoke to her of the worries that I had about the Empress's health and said that I was upset that her husband left at a time when I thought I could not expect much from the Shuvalovs, whom I regarded as my personal enemies and who were terribly angry with me because I preferred their enemies, namely the Counts Razumovsky, to them. She repeated all this to her husband, who was as happy with my inclination toward him as was Count Bestuzhev, who did not like the Shuvalovs and was allied with the Razumovskys, his son having married one of their nieces.* Marshal Apraksin was able to be a useful intermediary between all the interested parties because of his daughter's liaison with Count Peter Shuvalov.† It was claimed that this liaison was known to the mother and father. In addition, I understood perfectly and saw clear as day that the Shuvalovs employed Monsieur Brockdorff more than ever to distance the Grand Duke from me as much as they could. Despite this, he instinctively trusted me even then. To a singular degree, he almost always maintained this trust, which he himself neither perceived, suspected, nor distrusted.

For the moment, he had fallen out with Countess Vorontsova and was in love with Madame Teplova, a niece of the Razumovskys. When he wanted to see the latter, he consulted me on how to decorate the room and showed me that to please the lady more he had filled the room with rifles, grenadiers' hats, swords, and bandoliers, so that it had the air of an arsenal. I let him do as he wished and went my way. In addition, he also brought a little German singer, whom he supported and who was named Leonore, to have supper with him in the evening. It was the Princess of Courland who had put the Grand Duke on bad terms with Countess Vorontsova. To tell the truth, I do not quite know how. At the time, the Princess of Courland played a special role at court. To begin with, she was then a girl of around

---

* Count Andrei Alekseevich Bestuzhev-Riumin married Evdokia Danilovna Razumovkaia on May 5, 1747.

† His daughter is Princess Elena Stepanovna Kurakina.

thirty years old, small, ugly, and hunchbacked, as I have already said. She had been able to arrange for herself the protection of the Empress's confessor and of several of Her Imperial Majesty's old ladies-in-waiting, so that she got away with everything she did. She lived with Her Imperial Majesty's maids of honor. They were under the iron rule of a Madame Schmidt, who was the wife of a court trumpeter. This Madame Schmidt was of Finnish nationality, prodigiously large and stout. Moreover, she was a formidable woman who had retained perfectly the coarse peasant manner of her former station. Nevertheless, she played a role at court and was under the immediate protection of the Empress's old German, Finnish, and Swedish ladies-in-waiting and consequently under that of Marshal of the Court Sievers, who was himself Finnish and who had married the daughter of Madame Kruse, the sister of one of the most beloved ladies, as I have already said. Madame Schmidt ruled the domestic affairs in the residence of the maids of honor with more strictness than intelligence, but never appeared at court. In public, the Princess of Courland was at their head, and Madame Schmidt had tacitly entrusted their conduct at court to her. In their residence, they all lived in a row of rooms that led at one end to that of Madame Schmidt and at the other to that of the Princess of Courland. They were two, three, and four to a room, each with a screen around her bed and all the rooms with exits only into one another. At first glance it therefore seemed that with this arrangement the apartment of the maids of honor was impenetrable because one could enter it only by passing through the room of either Madame Schmidt or the Princess of Courland. But Madame Schmidt was often ill with indigestion from all the greasy patties and other delicacies that the relatives of these maidens sent her. Consequently there remained only the passage through the Princess of Courland's room. Malicious gossip had it that to pass through here into the other rooms, it was necessary to pay a toll one way or another. What could be verified about this was that the Princess of Courland arranged and broke the engagements of the Empress's maids of honor, promised and unpromised them over several years as she saw fit. I have the story of the toll from the mouths of several people, among others Lev Naryshkin and Count Buturlin, which they themselves claimed did not in their case have to be paid in money. The love affair between the Grand Duke and Madame Teplova lasted until we went to the country. Here it was interrupted because His Imperial Highness found that this woman was intolerable during the summer, when she claimed that since he was unable to see her, he should write to her once or twice a week. To engage him in this correspondence, she began by writing him a four-page letter. As soon as he received it he came into my room with a very irritated look, holding Madame Teplova's letter in his hand, and with vehemence and in an angry tone said rather loudly, "Imagine, she writes me a full four-page letter and claims that I should read it and, what is more, respond, I who have to go drill" (he had again had his troops from Holstein come), "then eat dinner, then shoot, then watch the rehearsal for an opera and the ballet that the cadets are going to dance in. I will tell her very firmly that I do not have the time, and if she gets upset, I will break off with her until winter." I replied that this was surely the easiest path. I think that the traits I am disclosing are characteristic of him and therefore not out of place.

Here is the crux of how the cadets appeared at Oranienbaum. In the spring of 1756, the Shuvalovs believed that they had found a very diplomatic way to detach the Grand Duke from his Holstein troops by persuading the Empress to give His Imperial Highness command of the cadet infantry corps, which at the time was the only cadet corps that existed. Melgunov, the intimate friend and confidant of Ivan Ivanovich Shuvalov, had been placed under the Grand Duke. This man was married to one of the Empress's German maids of honor and favorites. Thus the Shuvalovs had one of their most devoted intimates in the Grand Duke's entourage, able to speak to him at all hours. Under the pretext of the Oranienbaum opera ballets, a hundred cadets were thus brought there, and Monsieur Melgunov and the officers attached to the corps, who were his closest intimates, came with them. These were so many spies for Shuvalov.

Among the instructors who came to Oranienbaum with the cadets was their riding master Zimmermann, who was said to be the best horseman in Russia at that time. As my supposed pregnancy of the previous autumn had disappeared, I decided to take formal lessons from Zimmermann to handle my horse properly. I spoke of this to the Grand Duke, who made no objections to it. For a while now all the old rules introduced by the Choglokovs had been neglected, forgotten, or ignored by Alexander Shuvalov, who in any case did not enjoy any or even a little respect. We made fun of him, his wife, his daughter, and his son-in-law practically in their presence.* They invited this because one never saw more horrible, petty people. Madame Shuvalova had received from me the epithet "pillar of

* His son-in-law was Count Gavril Ivanovich Golovkin.

salt." She was thin, small, and rigid. Her miserliness was perceptible in her dress. Her skirts were always too tight and one panel fewer than was necessary and than those of the other ladies. Her daughter, Countess Golovkina, dressed in the same manner. Their headwear and their cuffs were meager and always smacked of stinginess. Although these were very rich people and comfortably off, their taste ran to everything that was small and constrained, which painted a true picture of their minds. As soon as I began to take formal lessons in horseback riding, I again gave myself passionately to this exercise. I awoke at six in the morning, dressed in a man's outfit, and went into my garden. There I had had an outdoor area prepared that served as my riding ground. I made such rapid progress that Zimmermann often ran to me from the center of this manège with a tear in his eye and kissed me on the boot with an uncontrollable enthusiasm. Other times he declared, "Never in my life have I had a student do me so much honor and make such progress in so little time." At these lessons only my old surgeon, Guyon, a lady-in-waiting, and some servants were present. As I had put much effort into my lessons, which I took every morning except Sundays, Zimmermann rewarded my labors with silver spurs, which he gave me according to the riding school custom. After three weeks, I was familiar with all the riding styles, and toward autumn, Zimmermann had a steeplechaser brought that he wanted me to ride. But the day before I was to ride it, we received the order to return to the city. The outing was therefore postponed until the following spring.

During this summer Count Poniatowski went to make a tour of Poland, from which he returned with his diplomatic credentials as minister from the King of Poland. Before leaving he came to Oranienbaum to take leave of us. He was in the company of Count Horn, whom the King of Sweden had sent to Russia under the pretext of announcing the death of his mother, my grandmother, to Petersburg so as to protect the Count from the persecutions of the French faction, called the Hats, against the Russian faction, the Caps.* This persecution became so great in Sweden that at the Diet of 1756, almost all the leaders of the Russian faction had their

* Duchess Albertine Friederike von Holstein-Gottorp died on December 22, 1755. Defeated by Russia in the Great Northern War (1700–21), Sweden retreated militarily, until in a backlash in the 1730s, Swedish nobles (the Hats) accepted French support against Russia. Their opponents (the Nightcaps, or Caps) looked to England, and after 1748, to Russia, for support; their dependence on Russia and a failed coup in 1755, by King Adolf Friedrich and his Prussian wife to restore an absolutist monarchy, weakened their position.

heads cut off. Count Horn himself told me that if he had not come to Petersburg, he would certainly have joined them. Count Poniatowski and
Count Horn stayed at Oranienbaum for two days. The first day, the
Grand Duke treated them very well, but on the second they bored him
because he had a huntsman's wedding on his mind, where he wanted to go
drink, and when he saw that Counts Poniatowski and Horn were staying,
he walked out on them, and it was I who stayed to honor our guests and
show them around. After lunch, I took the group that had stayed with me
and was not very large to see the Grand Duke's and my private apartments. When we arrived in my study, a little Bolognese dog that I owned
ran up to us and began to bark loudly at Count Horn, but when it noticed
Count Poniatowski, I thought the dog would go mad with joy. As the
study was very small, no one saw this except Lev Naryshkin, his sister-in-
law, and I, but Count Horn was not deceived, and while crossing the
apartment to return to the salon, Count Horn grabbed Count Poniatowski by the coat and said to him, "My friend, there is no worse traitor
than a little Bolognese dog. The first thing I always did with the women I
loved was give them one, and it was from these dogs that I always knew if
there was someone more favored than I. This rule is sure and certain. You
see, the dog wanted to eat me, whom it did not know, whereas it only rejoiced when it saw you again, for this is surely not the first time it has seen
you here." For his part, Count Poniatowski treated all this as nonsense,
but could not dissuade him. Count Horn only replied to him, "Fear not.
You are dealing with a discreet man." The following day they left. Count
Horn said that when he went so far as to fall in love, it was always with
three women at once. He put this into practice before our eyes in Petersburg, where he courted three of the Empress's maids of honor at the same
time.

Count Poniatowski left two days later for his country. During his absence, the English Ambassador, Sir Williams, told me through Lev
Naryshkin that Grand Chancellor Bestuzhev was mounting a conspiracy
so that Count Poniatowski's nomination would not go through, and that it
was through Williams that Bestuzhev had attempted to dissuade Count
Brühl, at the time minister and favorite of the King of Poland, from this
nomination. Williams had taken care not to fulfill this commission, although he had not declined it, for fear that the Grand Chancellor would
give it to someone else who would have carried it out more conscien-
tiously perhaps, and in this way would have undermined Williams's

friend, who hoped above all to return to Russia. Sir Williams suspected that Count Bestuzhev, who for a long while had had the Saxon and Polish ministers at his disposal, wanted to nominate someone from among his closest henchmen for this position. However, Count Poniatowski obtained it and returned toward winter as the envoy from Poland, and the Saxon mission remained under the immediate direction of Count Bestuzhev.

Sometime before leaving Oranienbaum, we saw the Prince and Princess Golitsyna arrive, accompanied by Monsieur Betskoi. They were going abroad for their health, especially Betskoi, who needed distraction from the profound grief he still felt over the death of the Princess of Hessen-Hamburg, née Princess Trubetskaia, mother of Princess Golitsyna, who had been born from the first marriage of the Princess of Hessen with the Hospodar of Walachia, Prince Kantemir.* As Princess Golitsyna and Betskoi were old acquaintances, I tried to receive them at Oranienbaum as best I could, and after we walked around quite a while, Princess Golitsyna and I got into a cabriolet, which I drove myself, and we went for a ride in the environs of Oranienbaum. Along the way, Princess Golitsyna, who was quite odd and very narrow-minded, began to make remarks by which she gave me to understand that she believed that I had a grudge against her. I told her that I had none and did not know what this grudge could be about, never having argued with her over anything. At this, she said she was worried that Count Poniatowski had lowered her in my esteem. I almost fell off my seat at these words and replied to her that she was absolutely imagining this and that he was not even in a position to discredit her with me, since he had left a long while ago and I knew him only by sight and as a stranger. I did not know where she got this idea. Back at my house, I called for Lev Naryshkin and recounted this conversation, which to me seemed as stupid as it was impertinent and indiscreet. He replied that the previous winter Princess Golitsyna had moved heaven and earth to woo Count Poniatowski, that out of politeness and so as not to slight her, he had been somewhat attentive toward her. She had made all sorts of

---

* Ivan Ivanovich Betskoi (1704–95) was the illegitimate half brother of the Princess of Hessen-Hamburg; their father was Prince Ivan Iurevich Trubetskoi (1667–1750). The Princess of Hessen-Hamburg's first husband was Prince Dmitry Antiokhovich Kantemir (1663–1723); their daughter Princess Ekaterina Dmitrievna Golitsyna (1720–61) married (in 1751) Prince Dmitry Mikhailovich Golitsyn (1721–93). Hospodar was the title given to princes and governors of Moldavia and Walachia (today Romania).

advances toward him, and as one might imagine, he had not responded much because she was old, ugly, stupid, foolish, and almost crazy. Seeing that he barely responded to her ardor, she had apparently formed a suspicion that he was still with Lev and his sister-in-law and at their house.

During Princess Golitsyna's short stay at Oranienbaum, I had a terrible quarrel with the Grand Duke about my maids of honor. I remarked that they were always either confidantes or mistresses of the Grand Duke and that on numerous occasions they had neglected their duty as well as the regard and respect they owed me. One afternoon I went to their apartment and reproached them for their conduct, reminded them of their duty and what they owed me, and said that if they continued, I would complain to the Empress. A few were alarmed, others were angered, and others cried. But as soon as I had left, they could not wait to repeat to the Grand Duke what had just occurred in their room. His Imperial Highness became furious and immediately ran to my apartment. As he entered he began by saying that I had become impossible to live with, that every day I was becoming prouder and haughtier, that I was asking for respect and regard from the maids of honor and was spoiling their life, that they cried rivers all day long, that they were well-born girls whom I treated like servants and that if I complained about them to the Empress, he would complain about me, my pride, my arrogance, my cruelty, and God knows what else he said to me. I listened not without irritation myself, and replied that he could say all he liked about me, that if the affair were to be brought before Madame his aunt, she would easily judge it most reasonable to dismiss the girls who misbehaved, who by their gossip put her nephew and niece on bad terms, and that assuredly Her Imperial Majesty, to reestablish peace and union between him and me, and to avoid hearing repeatedly about our disagreements, could make no other decision but that one, and that she would do this without fail. At this he softened his tone and, because he was very suspicious, imagined that I knew more of the Empress's intentions regarding these girls than I let on, and that they truly could be dismissed over this matter. He said, "Tell me then, do you know something about this? Are people talking about it?" I replied to him that if the matter came to the point of being brought before the Empress, I did not doubt that she would dispose of it in a very decisive manner. He began to pace around the room, reflecting on this, and calmed down, then left sulking only a little more than usual. That same evening I recounted word for word to those maids who seemed the most sensible to me the scene that their imprudent tattling had earned me, which put them on their guard against taking things to such an extreme that they might become the victims.

During the autumn we returned to the city. A short while later, Sir Williams returned to England on leave.* He had failed to achieve his objective in Russia. The day following his audience with the Empress, he had proposed a treaty of alliance between Russia and England. Count Bestuzhev had the permission and the power to conclude this treaty, and indeed, the treaty was signed by the Grand Chancellor and the Ambassador, who was overjoyed with his success. The following day, Count Bestuzhev informed him in a note of Russia's participation in the agreement signed at Versailles between France and Austria.† This was a great blow to the English Ambassador, who had been outwitted and deceived in this affair by the Grand Chancellor, or so it seemed. But at the time, Count Bestuzhev himself was no longer able to do as he pleased. His enemies began to gain the upper hand over him, and they intrigued, or rather others intrigued around them, to draw them into the Franco-Austrian faction, which they were very inclined to join. The Shuvalovs and above all Ivan Ivanovich fervently loved France and everything that came from there, and were supported by Vice Chancellor Count Vorontsov. For this service, Louis XV had furnished the mansion that Vorontsov had just built in Petersburg with old furniture that had begun to bore the Marquise de Pompadour, his mistress, and that she had therefore sold at a profit to the King, her lover. Aside from profit, the Vice Chancellor had another motive, which was to discredit his rival Count Bestuzhev and seize his position. As for Peter Shuvalov, he was planning to establish a monopoly in Russian tobacco and sell it in France. Toward the end of the year, Count Poniatowski returned to Petersburg as a minister of the King of Poland.‡

---

* He departed in early November 1757.

† The treaty between Russia and England of September 19/30, 1755, was ratified on February 1, 1756. Russia then signed the Treaty of Versailles with France and Austria on December 20/31, 1756.

‡ He arrived on December 23 and presented his papers as minister on December 31, 1756.

1757

*Holstein intrigues; Catherine alerts Elizabeth to bad influences
around Peter; Catherine lectures him on proper governance of
Holstein and future duties in Russia; Peter's lies and tall tales;
Lev Naryshkin's arranged marriage into Razumovsky family
to thwart Shuvalovs; Russian successes against Prussia;
Catherine's talk with Elizabeth about Peter; Elizabeth's
illness creates turmoil at court and the front*

During that winter at the beginning of 1757, we led the same life as the previous winter, same concerts, same balls, same cliques. Soon after our return to the city, where I observed things more closely, I noticed that Monsieur Brockdorff was gaining influence over the Grand Duke's mind with his intrigues. He was aided in this by a rather large number of Holstein officers, whom he had encouraged His Imperial Highness to keep in Petersburg that winter. The group of at least twenty were continually with and around the Grand Duke, without counting a couple of Holstein soldiers, who served in his room as errand boys and chamber valets, and were used as flunkies. Basically, all these men served as so many spies for master Brockdorff and company. I awaited a favorable moment that winter to speak seriously to the Grand Duke and tell him sincerely what I thought of those around him and of the intrigues I observed. One such moment presented itself and I did not miss it. One day the Grand Duke himself came into my apartment to tell me that he was being told it was absolutely necessary for him to send a secret order to Holstein to arrest a man named d'Elendsheim, who by both his office and his merit was one of the country's most important people. Of bourgeois origins, he had achieved his position through study and skill. I asked what the grievances were that he had against this man and what he had done that would lead the Grand Duke to arrest him. He replied, "You see, they say that they suspect him of embezzlement." I asked who his accusers were. He clearly believed himself fully justified and said, "Oh, there are no accusers, because everyone in the country fears and obeys him, and for this reason I must have him arrested, and after that, I am assured that there will be more than enough accusers." I shuddered at what he said and retorted, "But if one acts in this manner, there will be no more innocent people in the world. All it takes is one jealous person to spread publicly whatever vague rumor pleases him, at which they will arrest whomever they want, saying that the accusers and the crimes will appear later. It is like the song 'Barbarie, mon ami.' You are being advised to act without regard either for your glory or your justice. Will you permit me to ask who is giving you such bad advice?" My Grand Duke was a bit sheepish at my question and said, "You always want to know more than the others." Then I responded that I was not speaking to seem clever but because I hated injustice and did not believe that he would in any way commit one willingly. He began to pace around the room, then left more irritated than sullen. A short while later he returned and said, "Come to my apartment. Brockdorff will speak with you about the d'Elendsheim affair and you will see and be persuaded that I have to have him arrested." I replied to him, "Very well, I will follow you and listen to what he says, since you wish it." I did indeed find Monsieur Brockdorff in the room of the Grand Duke, who said to him, "Speak to the Grand Duchess." Monsieur Brockdorff, somewhat taken aback, bowed to the Grand Duke and said, "Since Your Imperial Highness orders me, I will speak about it to Madame the Grand Duchess...." Here he paused and then said, "This is an affair that must be treated with great secrecy and prudence...." I listened. "The entire country of Holstein is full of rumors about d'Elendsheim's embezzlement and misappropriations. It is true that there are no accusers, because he is feared, but when he is arrested, then there will be as many as one could want." I asked him for the details about this embezzlement and misappropriation, and I learned that there could not be embezzlement since he did not have the Grand Duke's money in hand, but that as the head of the justice department, he was thought to be embezzling, because after every trial, one of the litigants complained of injustice and said that the other party had won only because of a handsome payoff to the judges. But despite all the eloquence and knowledge Monsieur Brockdorff displayed, he did not persuade me. I continued to maintain to Monsieur Brockdorff in the Grand Duke's presence that they were trying to lead His Imperial Highness to commit a gross injustice by persuading him to expedite an arrest warrant for a man against whom there existed neither a formal complaint nor an accusation. I said to Brockdorff that by this logic the Grand Duke could have him locked up at any moment, that the crimes and accusations would come later, and that as concerned affairs of justice it was not difficult to understand why those who lost their cases always claimed that they had been wronged. I added that the Grand Duke more than anyone should be on his guard against such proceedings, because experience had already taught him, at his expense, what the persecution and hatred of factions could produce, since it had been two years at most since the Grand Duke, after my intercession, had released Monsieur de Holmer. This man had been kept in prison six or eight years to make him confess about his dealings during the Grand Duke's tutelage and during the administration of his guardian, the Royal Prince of Sweden, to whom M. de Holmer had been devoted and whom he had followed to Sweden, from where he had not been able to return until after the Grand Duke signed and dispatched a formal approval of, and general pardon for, everything that had been done during his minority. Despite this, the Grand Duke had been persuaded to have Monsieur de Holmer arrested and to name a commission to investigate what had been done during the Prince of Sweden's administration. This commission, after at first acting with great energy and opening its doors wide to informers, nevertheless had found no informers and fallen into inactivity for lack of evidence. Meanwhile, however, Monsieur de Holmer languished in a narrow prison cell, which neither his wife, children, friends, nor relatives were permitted to visit. Finally the whole country cried out against the blatant injustice and tyranny displayed in this affair. It would not even have ended quickly had I not advised the Grand Duke to cut the Gordian knot by dispatching an order to release Monsieur de Holmer and abolish a commission that had, moreover, rather drained the coffers, which were quite empty in the Grand Duke's hereditary domain. But I cited this striking example in vain. I think the Grand Duke listened to me while musing on something else, and Monsieur Brockdorff, hardened by his cruel heart, very narrow-minded and stubborn as a mule, let me go on, having no more arguments for me. When I had left, he told the Grand Duke that all I had said sprang from no other source than my desire to dominate and that I disapproved of all measures I had not recommended, that I understood nothing of political affairs, that women always wanted to meddle in everything, that they spoiled all they touched, and that above all decisive actions were beyond their ken. In the end, he said and did what was needed to prevail over my advice, and the Grand Duke, persuaded by him, had the order for Monsieur d'Elendsheim's arrest drawn up, signed, and sent off. A certain Zeitz, the Grand Duke's secretary, an intimate of Pechlin and a son-in-law of the midwife who had served me, informed me of this. In general, the Pechlin faction did not approve of this violent and uncalled-for measure, with which Monsieur Brockdorff made them and the entire land of Holstein tremble.

As soon as I learned that Brockdorff's machinations had prevailed in such an unjust cause over me and all that I had argued to the Grand Duke, I firmly resolved to make Monsieur Brockdorff feel the brunt of my indignation. I said to Zeitz and I had it reported to Pechlin that from this moment I regarded Brockdorff as a plague that we must avoid and remove from the Grand Duke's presence if possible. I myself would go to any lengths to see this through. Indeed, I made a point of showing on every occasion, both public and private, the disgust and horror that this man's conduct had inspired in me. There was no kind of ridicule to which he was not subjected, and when the occasion presented itself, I left no one unaware of what I thought of him. Lev Naryshkin and other young people of our court assisted me in this. When Monsieur Brockdorff passed through the room, everyone cried out after him, "Баба птица, баба птица" which was his epithet,* since this bird was the most hideous known, and Monsieur Brockdorff was as hideous on the outside as on the inside. He was tall, with a long neck and a thick, flat head. He had red hair and wore a wig of brass wire. His eyes were small, set back in his head and almost without lids or brows. The corners of his mouth drooped toward his chin, which always gave him a miserable, nasty look. As for his inner qualities, I refer to what I have already said. But I will also add that he was so full of vice that he took money from whoever wanted to give it to him. To keep his august master from ever reprimanding him for his misappropriations, he persuaded the Grand Duke, who he knew was always in need of money, to do the same. He acquired as much money as he could for him by selling Holstein orders and titles to whoever wanted to pay for them, or by having the Grand Duke make appeals, or by promoting all kinds of deals in the different regions of the empire and in the senate. These deals were often unjust and sometimes even onerous for the empire, such as the monopolies and other grants that otherwise would never

---

* "Baba Ptitsa" means pelican; it is a bird ("ptitsa") that looks like a "baba," an old woman.

have passed because they broke Peter I's laws. In addition, Monsieur Brockdorff immersed the Grand Duke more than ever in drink and villainy, having surrounded him with a pack of fortune hunters and people drawn from the guard corps and taverns of both Germany and Petersburg, who had no morals, and did nothing but drink, eat, smoke, and speak coarsely about nonsense. Seeing that despite all I said and did against Monsieur Brockdorff to weaken his standing he maintained himself in the Grand Duke's favor and was more in favor than ever, I resolved to tell Count Alexander Shuvalov what I thought about him, adding that I regarded this man as one of the most dangerous creatures one could possibly place with a young Prince, heir to a great empire, and that in good conscience I found myself obliged to speak to him in confidence so that he could warn the Empress or take such measures as he saw fit. He asked if he might quote me. I said yes, and that if the Empress asked me herself, I would not mince words but say what I knew and saw. Count Alexander Shuvalov twitched his eye, listening to me very seriously, but he was not a man to act without the advice of his brother Peter and cousin Ivan. For quite a while he did not contact me. Then he let me know that the Empress might want to speak with me.

Meanwhile, one fine morning I saw the Grand Duke skip into my room and his secretary Zeitz run after him with a paper in his hand. The Grand Duke said to me, "Take a look at this devil of a man. I drank too much yesterday. I am still completely hung over today, and here he is bringing me a sheet of paper and it is only the accounts register that he wants me to finish. He even follows me into your room." Zeitz said to me, "Everything I have here is only a simple matter of yes or no. It will only take fifteen minutes." I said, "But let us see now, perhaps you will finish sooner than you think." Zeitz began to read, and as he spoke, I myself said yes or no. This pleased the Grand Duke, and Zeitz said to him, "You see, my lord, if you consented twice a week to do this, your affairs would not come to a halt. These are only trifles, but they must be taken care of, and the Grand Duchess has finished this with six yes's and as many no's, more or less." From that day on, His Imperial Highness decided to send Zeitz to me every time that he had yes's or no's to ask about. After some time, I told him to give me a signed order concerning what I could or could not decide without his permission, which he did. Only Pechlin, Zeitz, the Grand Duke, and I knew of this arrangement, which delighted Pechlin and Zeitz. When it came to signing, the Grand Duke signed according to what I had decided. The d'Elendsheim affair remained under Brock-dorff's supervision. But as d'Elendsheim had been arrested, Monsieur Brockdorff was in no rush to conclude the affair, because this was more or less what he had wanted, that is, to distance this man from governmental affairs and to show those in Holstein his standing with his master.

I chose a day on which I found the occasion, or moment, favorable to tell the Grand Duke that though he found the affairs of Holstein so boring to manage and regarded them as a burden, nevertheless they were only a small sample of what he would one day have to manage when the Russian empire passed to him. I thought that he ought to envisage that moment as a much greater weight. He again repeated what he had said to me many times. He felt that he had not been born for Russia, that he did not suit the Russians nor the Russians him, and that he was convinced that he would die in Russia. On this subject I too told him what I had told him many times before, to wit, that he must not give in to this fatalistic idea, but do his best to make himself loved by every Russian and ask the Empress to put him in a position where he could learn about the Empire's affairs. I even urged him to request a place in the conferences that served as the Empress's council.* He did speak about this to the Shuvalovs, who urged the Empress to admit him to this conference every time she herself attended. This was the same as saying he would not be admitted, because she went with him two or three times and then neither of them went anymore.

The advice I gave the Grand Duke was generally sound and beneficial, but he who advises can do so only according to his own mind and own manner of conceiving and handling matters. Now the great defect of my advice to the Grand Duke was that his way of acting and managing was entirely different from mine, and as we grew older, it became more so. Always and in all matters I tried to get as close as possible to the truth, while he distanced himself from it daily, to the point that he became an inveterate liar. As the manner in which this happened was quite singular, I am going to speak about it. Perhaps this will advance human understanding of this phenomenon and in that way serve to prevent this vice or correct it in whoever has a penchant for lying. The first lie that the Grand Duke dreamed up came in order to make himself appealing to some young woman or girl. Counting on her ignorance, he told her that while he was

* Elizabeth first established a council in March 1756 to prepare for war with Prussia.

still at his father's house in Holstein, his father had placed him in charge of a squad of his guards and had sent him to capture a troop of Egyptians who prowled in the environs of Kiel and committed, so he said, ghastly acts of robbery. He recounted these acts in detail, as well as the ruses that he had employed to pursue, surround, and combat them once or several times, during which he claimed to have accomplished great feats of skill and valor, and then to have captured the Egyptians and taken them to Kiel. At first he took the precaution of recounting all this only to people who knew nothing about the matter. Little by little he grew bold enough to recount his tale before those whose discretion he could trust would keep them from refuting him. But when he began to try this tale out in my presence, I asked him how long before his father's death it had taken place. Without hesitating, he replied, "Three or four years." Well then, I said, you began to accomplish your feats of arms very young, because three or four years before the death of your father the Duke you were only six or seven, since at age eleven you were left by your father in the guardianship of my uncle, the Royal Prince of Sweden. What astonishes me equally, I said, is that your father, having you as his only son and your health having always been delicate in your youth, as I have been told, sent you to fight these robbers, and what is more, at the age of six or seven. The Grand Duke got terribly angry with me for what I had just said and told me that I wanted to make him look like a liar in front of everyone and that I was discrediting him. I told him that it was not I but the almanac that discredited what he was recounting, that I would let him judge for himself if it was humanly possible to send a little child of six or seven, an only son and hereditary Prince, his father's entire hope, to capture Egyptians. He fell silent and I did too, and he was angry with me for a very long time, but when he had forgotten my reproach, even in my presence he did not stop spinning this tale, which he varied endlessly. After this he made up another one, infinitely more shameful and harmful to him, which I will relate when the time comes. It would be impossible for me to tell at present of all the fantasies he often imagined and presented as facts and which did not have a shadow of truth. I think this example suffices.

One Thursday toward the end of carnival, when there was a ball at our residence, while I was sitting between Lev Naryshkin's sister-in-law and her sister, Madame Seniavina, we watched Marina Osipovna Zakrevskaia, the Empress's maid of honor and a niece of the Counts Razumovsky, dance the minuet. She was graceful and light-footed then, and it was said that Count Horn was very much in love with her, but as he was always in love with three women at the same time, he was also courting Countess Maria Romanovna Vorontsova and Anna Alekseevna Khitrova, also a maid of honor to Her Imperial Majesty. We found that Countess Vorontsova danced well and was rather pretty; she danced with Lev Naryshkin. As for Lev Naryshkin, his sister-in-law and sister told me that his mother spoke of marrying him to Mademoiselle Khitrova, a niece of the Shuvalovs by her mother, who was a sister of Peter and Alexander and had been married to Mademoiselle Khitrova's father. This man often came to the Naryshkins' house and managed to plant the idea of this marriage in the mind of Lev Naryshkin's mother. Neither Madame Seniavina nor her sister-in-law cared at all to be related to the Shuvalovs, whom they did not like, as I have said. As for Lev, he did not even know that his mother was thinking about marrying him off. He was in love with Countess Maria Vorontsova, of whom I have just spoken. Hearing this, I said to Mesdames Seniavina and Naryshkina that we had to prevent this marriage with Mademoiselle Khitrova that the mother was negotiating. No one could tolerate her, because she was scheming, gossipy, and slanderous, and I said that to dispel such notions, we had to give Lev a woman to our liking and for this purpose choose the aforementioned niece of the Counts Razumovsky, who were also friends and allies of the house of Naryshkin. Moreover, Count Kirill Razumovsky was much loved by these two ladies and always in their house when they were not at his. The ladies strongly approved my idea. As there was a masquerade at the court the following day, I spoke to Marshal Razumovsky, who at the time was Hetman of Ukraine, and I told him clearly that he made a mistake in letting a match like Lev Naryshkin get away from his niece, that Lev's mother wanted to marry him to Mademoiselle Khitrova, but that Madame Seniavina, her sister-in-law Madame Naryshkina, and I agreed that his niece would be a more suitable match and that without wasting any time, he should go make the proposal to the interested parties. The Marshal approved of our plan and spoke about it with Teplov, his factotum at the time, who immediately went to discuss it with the elder Count Razumovsky, who consented. The following day, Teplov went to the Bishop of Petersburg's residence to purchase the permission or dispensation for fifty rubles. Having obtained this, Marshal Razumovsky and his wife went to the house of their aunt, Lev's mother, and there they handled things so deftly that they got the mother to consent to what she did not want. They came at exactly the right time, because that very day, she was supposed to give her word to Monsieur Khitrov. This done, Marshal Razumovsky, Mesdames Seniavina and her sister-in-law Naryshkina buttonholed Lev and persuaded him to marry the one whom he had not even considered. He consented though he loved another woman, but she was practically promised to Count Buturlin. As for Mademoiselle Khitrova, he did not care for her at all. Having obtained this agreement, the Marshal had his niece come to his house, and she found the marriage too advantageous to refuse. On the following day, Sunday, the two Counts Razumovsky requested the Empress's consent for this marriage, which she gave immediately. Messieurs Shuvalov were astonished by the way in which Khitrov and they too had been thwarted, learning of the affair only after the Empress's consent had been obtained. The affair resolved, no one could get over how Lev, who was in love with one maiden, and whose mother wanted him to marry another, married a third, about whom neither he nor anyone else had been thinking three days earlier. Lev Naryshkin's marriage linked me more strongly than ever in friendship with the Counts Razumovsky, who were truly grateful to me for having procured such a good and advantageous match for their niece, nor were they at all upset to have gotten the upper hand over the Shuvalovs, who were not even able to complain about it and were obliged to conceal their humiliation. This was yet one more advantage that I had obtained for them.

The Grand Duke's affair with Madame Teplova was on its last legs. One of the greatest obstacles to this affair was the difficulty they had in seeing each other. It was always furtively, and this annoyed His Imperial Highness, who liked these difficulties no more than he liked responding to the letters he received. At the end of carnival, their love affair became a matter of factional politics. The Princess of Courland informed me one day that Count Roman Vorontsov, the father of two young maidens at the court, and who I should say in passing was the bête noire of the Grand Duke and also of his own five children, was making immoderate remarks about the Grand Duke. Among other things, he was saying that if he so desired, he could easily put an end to the hatred that the Grand Duke bore him and change it into favor; he had only to offer a meal to Brockdorff, give him English beer to drink, and, when he left, put six bottles in his pocket for His Imperial Highness, and then he and his youngest daughter would rank first in the Grand Duke's favor. At the ball this same evening I noticed much whispering between His Imperial Highness and

Countess Maria Vorontsova, the youngest daughter of Count Roman, and since this family was on very intimate terms with the Shuvalovs, at whose house Brockdorff was always quite welcome, I was not pleased to see that Mademoiselle Elizabeth Vorontsova might return to a position of favor. To help prevent this, I told the Grand Duke about her father's remark, which I have just described. He almost flew into a rage and asked me with great anger from whom I had heard this. I refrained from telling him for a long moment. He told me that since I could not name anyone, he supposed that it was I who had invented this story to undermine the father and his daughters. No matter how much I told him that I had never in my life made up such stories, I was obliged in the end to name the Princess of Courland. He told me that he was going to write her a note immediately to find out if I was telling the truth and that if there was the slightest variation between what she replied and what I had just told him, he would complain to the Empress about our schemes and lies. After this he left my room. Apprehensive about what the Princess of Courland would say to him and fearing that she would equivocate, I wrote a note to her and said, "In the name of God, tell the pure and simple truth about what you will be asked." My note was delivered immediately and arrived in time, because it preceded that of the Grand Duke. The Princess of Courland responded to His Imperial Highness with truthfulness and he found that I had not lied. For some time this restrained his liaisons with the two daughters of a man who had so little respect for him and whom he disliked anyway. But in order to put up yet one more obstacle, Lev Naryshkin persuaded Marshal Razumovsky to invite the Grand Duke very secretly to his house one or two evenings a week. It was almost a couples gathering because only the Marshal, Maria Pavlovna Naryshkina, the Grand Duke, Madame Teplova, and Lev Naryshkin were there. This lasted for part of Lent and gave rise to another idea. At the time, the Marshal's house was made of wood. The group assembled in his wife's apartment, and as both the Marshal and his wife loved to play cards, there was always a game going. The Marshal came and went and had his coterie in his own apartment when the Grand Duke did not come. But since the Marshal had been to my residence with my secret little coterie several times, he wanted this group to come to his house. For this purpose, what he called his hermitage, which comprised two or three apartments on the ground floor, was assigned to us. We all hid from one another because we did not dare go out, as I have said, without permission. So by this arrangement there were three or four groups in the house and the Marshal went from one to the other, and only I alone knew everything that was happening in the house, while no one knew that we were there.

Toward spring, Monsieur Pechlin, the Grand Duke's Minister for Holstein, died.* Grand Chancellor Count Bestuzhev, foreseeing his death, had advised that I ask the Grand Duke to name a certain Monsieur de Stambke, who was sent for to replace Monsieur Pechlin. The Grand Duke gave him signed permission to work with me, which he did. By this arrangement I had unfettered communication with Count Bestuzhev, who trusted Stambke. At the beginning of spring we went to Oranienbaum.† Here our lifestyle was as it had been in previous years, except that the number of soldiers from Holstein and fortune hunters who were stationed there as officers increased from year to year, and as lodging could not be found for this crowd in the little village of Oranienbaum, where at first there had been only twenty-eight huts, these troops were made to set up camp, their number never exceeding thirteen hundred men. The officers ate dinner and supper at the court. But as the number of women from the court and of gentlemen's wives did not exceed fifteen or sixteen, and as His Imperial Highness passionately loved grand meals, which he frequently gave both in his camp and in all the nooks and crannies at Oranienbaum, he invited not only the female singers and dancers from his opera to these meals, but many very vulgar, bourgeois women, who were brought to him from Petersburg. As soon as I learned that the singers etc. would be invited to these meals, I refrained from going, at first under the pretext that I was taking the waters, and most of the time I ate in my room with two or three people. Later I said to the Grand Duke that I was afraid that the Empress would find it improper for me to appear in such mixed company, and in truth, I never went when I knew that the hospitality was indiscriminate, so that when the Grand Duke wanted me to come, only the ladies from the court were invited. I went to the masquerades that the Grand Duke gave at Oranienbaum only in very simple outfits, without jewelry or finery. This made a very good impression on the Empress, who neither liked nor approved of these parties at Oranienbaum, where the meals became veritable bacchanalia, but nevertheless she tolerated them or at least did not forbid them. I learned that Her Imperial Majesty said,

* January 29, 1757.
† May 6, 1757.

"These parties please the Grand Duchess no more than they do me. She goes there dressed as simply as she can and never has supper with all who come." At the time, I busied myself at Oranienbaum with building and planting what was called my garden, and the rest of the time I took walks, went riding, or drove in a cabriolet, and when I was in my room, I read.

In the month of July we learned that Memel had agreed to surrender to Russian troops on June 24. And in the month of August we received the news of the battle of Gross Jägerndorf, won by the Russian army on August 19. The day of the Te Deum* I gave a large banquet in my garden for the Grand Duke and all of the most important people at Oranienbaum, and at it the Grand Duke and the entire company seemed as joyful as they were satisfied. This momentarily diminished the pain that the Grand Duke felt over the war that had just been declared between Russia and the King of Prussia, of whom he had been extremely fond since childhood. What was at first in no way excessive degenerated into mania later on.[†] The public joy over the Russian military's success at that time forced the Grand Duke to dissimulate his true thoughts, because he regretted the defeat of the Prussian troops, whom he had regarded as invincible. I had a roast ox given to the masons and workers at Oranienbaum on that day.

A few days after this banquet, we returned to the city, where we went to reside in the Summer Palace. Here Count Alexander Shuvalov came to tell me one evening that the Empress was in his wife's room and was summoning me there to speak with her as I had desired the previous winter. I immediately went to Count and Countess Shuvalov's apartment, which was at the end of my apartment. I found the Empress there alone. After I had kissed her hand and she had kissed me as was her custom, she did me the honor of telling me that having learned that I wished to speak with her, she had come today to learn what I wanted to say. Now, at that time it had been eight months and more since my conversation with Alexander Shuvalov about Brockdorff. I replied to Her Imperial Majesty that the previous winter, seeing Monsieur Brockdorff's conduct, I had believed it indispensable to speak about it with Count Alexander Shuvalov, so that he could inform Her Imperial Majesty. He had asked me if he

---

* A religious service held to mark a victory.

† According to Poniatowski, the Prussian King Frederick the Great said: "I am his Dulcinea; he has never seen me, and like Don Quixote, he has fallen in love with me." *Mémoires du roi Stanislas-Auguste Poniatowski*, 2 vols. (St. Petersburg, 1914), 1:172.

could quote me, and I had said to him that if Her Imperial Majesty wished it, I would repeat to her myself everything I had said and knew. Then I recounted the story of d'Elendsheim as it had happened. She appeared to listen to me with great coldness, then asked me for details about the Grand Duke's private life and his entourage. With the greatest truthfulness I told her everything I knew. When I gave her several details concerning the affairs of Holstein that made her see that I knew them quite well, she said, "You seem well-informed about this country." I replied simply that it was not difficult to be informed, the Grand Duke having ordered me to learn about it. I saw from the Empress's face that this confession made an unpleasant impression on her. In general she seemed to me to be extremely reserved the entire conversation, during which she questioned me so as to make me speak and hardly said a word, so that this interview seemed to me more a kind of interrogation on her part than a confidential conversation. Finally she dismissed me as coldly as she had received me, and I was perplexed by my audience, which Alexander Shuvalov suggested I keep very secret, and I promised him this. In any case there was nothing to boast about. Back in my apartment, I attributed the Empress's coldness to the antipathy that the Shuvalovs had provoked in her against me, about which I had long been warned. We will see later the detestable use, if I may say so, that she was persuaded to make of this conversation between her and me.

Sometime later we learned that Marshal Apraksin, far from taking advantage of his successes after the capture of Memel and the victory at the battle of Gross Jägerndorf and advancing, withdrew with such speed that this retreat resembled a rout because he discarded and burned his equipment and spiked his cannons. Nobody understood the reasons for this operation. Even his friends did not know how to defend him, and as a result people looked for the hidden motives. Although I myself do not know exactly how to explain the Marshal's precipitous and incoherent retreat, having never seen him again, nevertheless I think that the cause could have been that he received quite precise news about the Empress's health, which was going from bad to worse, from his daughter, Princess Kurakina, still linked by politics though not by inclination to Peter Shuvalov; from his son-in-law, Prince Kurakin; and from his friends and relatives. At the time most people had begun to believe that every month she was regularly having very strong convulsions, that these convulsions visibly weakened her organs, and that after each convulsion she was in such a state of weakness, diminished mental ability, and abnormal drowsiness for two, three, or four days that during this time no one could talk or discuss anything at all with her. Marshal Apraksin, perhaps believing that the danger was more pressing than it was, had not judged it the right moment to drive farther into Prussia, but had believed he should fall back to be nearer the Russian border under the pretext of a lack of provisions, foreseeing that in the event of the Empress's death this war would end immediately. It is difficult to justify Marshal Apraksin's actions, but such may have been his views, especially since he believed himself needed in Russia, as I said earlier in discussing his departure. Count Bestuzhev sent Stambke to tell me about the way Marshal Apraksin had conducted himself; the Imperial Ambassador and the French Ambassador were complaining loudly about it. Bestuzhev begged me to write the Marshal as his friend and to join my entreaties to his own to make him turn his march around and put an end to a retreat that his enemies were interpreting in an odious and sinister way. I did indeed write a letter to Marshal Apraksin in which I warned him of the harmful rumors in Petersburg and how his friends had had great trouble in defending the speed of his retreat, begging him to turn his march around and to fulfill the orders he had from the government. Grand Chancellor Count Bestuzhev sent him this letter. Marshal Apraksin did not reply to me.

Meanwhile, we saw the Empress's director general of construction, General Fermor, leave Petersburg and take his leave of us. We were told that he was departing to take a post in the army. He had formerly been the quartermaster general for Marshal Münnich. General Fermor's first request was to retain the brigadiers Riazanov and Mordvinov, his employees or superintendents of construction, and with them he left for the army. They were military men who had done almost nothing but execute building contracts. As soon as he arrived, he was ordered to take command from Marshal Apraksin, who was recalled, and when he returned, he found an order at Triruki to remain there and await the Empress's orders. These were a long time in coming because his friends, his daughter, and Peter Shuvalov did everything in the world they could, moving heaven and earth, to calm the Empress's anger, which had been fomented by the Vorontsovs, Count Buturlin, Ivan Shuvalov, and others, who were pushed by the ambassadors from the courts of Versailles and Vienna to bring Apraksin to trial. Finally a commission was named to investigate him. After the first interrogation, Marshal Apraksin was seized by a bout of apoplexy, from which he died within about twenty-four hours.* General Lieven must certainly have been involved in this trial as well. He was Apraksin's friend and confidant. I would have been grieved even more at this because Lieven was very sincerely devoted to me. But whatever friendship I felt for Lieven and Apraksin, I can swear that I was perfectly unaware of the reason for their conduct, and of their conduct itself, although some tried to spread the rumor that it was to please the Grand Duke and myself that they had retreated instead of advancing. At times Lieven made quite singular shows of his devotion to me. For example, one day when the Ambassador from the Viennese court, Count Esterhazy, was giving a masquerade, which the Empress and the entire court attended, Lieven saw me cross the room and said to his neighbor, who at that moment was Count Poniatowski, "There is a woman for whom an honest man would suffer a few blows of the knout without regret." I heard this anecdote from Count Poniatowski himself, since made King of Poland.†

* August 6, 1758.
† May 1764.

1758

Lev Naryshkin forsakes Catherine for her enemies; Prince Charles of Saxony visits Russia; Catherine's pregnancy; her elaborate party for Peter; her punishment of Naryshkin; Russian losses against Prussia; Elizabeth's convulsions; birth and baptism of Anna

As soon as General Fermor had taken command, he hastened to carry out his instructions to advance, which were precise, for despite the harsh weather he seized Königsberg, which capitulated and sent deputies to him on January 18, 1758.*

During that winter I suddenly noticed a great change in Lev Naryshkin's behavior. He started to become uncivil and crude. He came to see me only reluctantly and made remarks that showed that someone was filling his head with ill will against me, his sister-in-law, his sister, Count Poniatowski, and all those in my circle. I learned that he was almost always at Monsieur Ivan Shuvalov's home and I easily guessed that he was being turned against me to punish me because I had prevented him from marrying Mademoiselle Khitrova, and they would surely do everything to elicit indiscretions from him that could become harmful to me. His sister-in-law, his sister, and his brother were as angry with him as I was, and he literally behaved like a fool and willingly offended us as much as he could, and did this while I was furnishing, at my expense, the house where he was supposed to live after his marriage. Everyone accused him of ingratitude, while he said that he did not have a self-serving nature. In short, he had no reason to complain in any way, and people saw clearly that he served as an instrument for those who had taken control of him. He paid his respects to the Grand Duke more regularly than ever and amused him as much as he could and urged him more and more to do what he knew I disapproved of. Sometimes he carried his incivility to the point that when I spoke to him he would not reply to me. To this day I do

---

* January 10, 1758.

not know what bee he had in his bonnet, when I had literally showered him with presents and friendship, along with all his family, ever since I had known them. I think that he also took to cajoling the Grand Duke because of the advice of the Shuvalovs, who told him that the Grand Duke's favor for him would always be more valuable than mine because the Empress and Grand Duke disapproved of me, that neither liked me, that he would undermine his prospects if he did not disassociate himself from me, that as soon as the Empress was dead the Grand Duke would put me in a convent, and other similar remarks, which the Shuvalovs made and were reported to me. Moreover, they raised the prospect of his receiving the Order of St. Anna as a token of the Grand Duke's esteem for him. With the help of these arguments and promises, they had all the little betrayals they wanted from this weak and feckless mind, and they pushed him as far as they wanted him to go, and even further, although at times he had small pangs of regret. As we will see later, at the time, he applied himself as much as he could to distancing the Grand Duke from me, so that the Grand Duke ignored me almost without interruption and was again on familiar terms with Countess Vorontsova.

Toward spring of that year, word spread that Prince Charles of Saxony, son of King August III of Poland, was going to come to Petersburg. This did not please the Grand Duke for various reasons, the chief one being that he feared this visit would inconvenience him because he did not want the life that he had arranged for himself to be in the least disturbed. The second reason was that the House of Saxony was aligned against the King of Prussia. The third reason may have been that he feared to lose out in comparison.* He was being very modest, to say the least, because this poor Prince of Saxony was nothing without his title and had no education at all. Except for hunting and dancing, he knew nothing, and he told me himself that he had never held a book in his hands in his life, except for prayer books given to him by the Queen, his mother, who was a very sanctimonious Princess.† Prince Charles of Saxony indeed arrived on April 5 of that year in St. Petersburg, where he was received with much ceremony and a great display of magnificence and splendor. His entourage was very large. Many Poles and Saxons accompanied him, among whom were a Lubomirski, a Potocki, Pizarc, Count Rzewuski, who was called

---

* Prussia and Saxony were the most powerful German states.
† Maria Josepha was the oldest daughter of Emperor Joseph I.

"The Handsome," two Princes Sulkowski, a Count Sapieha, the Count Branicki, since made Grand General, a Count Einsiedel, and many others whose names I no longer remember. He had a kind of assistant tutor with him, named Lachinal, who managed his conduct and his correspondence. The Prince of Saxony was lodged in Chamberlain Ivan Shuvalov's recently finished house, into which the master of the house had poured all his taste, despite which the house was tasteless and quite ugly, though very richly appointed. There were many paintings, but most were copies. One room had been decorated with chinar wood, but since chinar does not shine, it had been covered with varnish, from which it became yellow, but an unpleasant yellow that made the room look ugly. To remedy this the room was covered in a very heavy and richly carved wood painted silver. The exterior of the house was imposing, but was so heavily decorated that its ornamentation resembled ruffles of Alençon lace. Count Ivan Chernyshev was named to attend Prince Charles of Saxony, and he was served and provided everything at the expense of the court and waited on by the court servants. The night before Prince Charles came to our residence, I came down with such severe colic and diarrhea that I had to go to the toilet more than thirty times. Despite this and the fever that seized me, I dressed the following day to receive the Prince of Saxony. He was taken to the Empress's residence around two in the afternoon, and after leaving her, he was brought to my residence, where the Grand Duke was supposed to enter a moment after him. For this meeting, three armchairs had been placed against the same wall. The one in the middle was for me, the one to my right for the Grand Duke, and the one to my left for the Prince of Saxony. It was I who led the conversation because the Grand Duke hardly wanted to speak and Prince Charles was not talkative. Finally, after half a quarter hour of conversation, Prince Charles rose to present his immense entourage to us. I believe he had more than twenty people with him to whom that day were added the envoy from Poland and that of Saxony, who resided at the Russian court with their employees. After a half hour of conversation, the Prince left, and I undressed to get in bed, where I remained for three or four days with a very high fever, after which I had new signs of pregnancy.

At the end of April we went to Oranienbaum.* Before our departure we learned that Prince Charles of Saxony would join the Russian army as

* May 30, 1758.

a volunteer. Before leaving for the army, he went with the Empress to Peterhof and was feted there and in the city. We did not attend these festivities, but stayed at our country house, where he took leave of us on July 4 The Grand Duke was almost always very ill-tempered with me, and I knew of no other reason for this than that I would receive neither Monsieur Brockdorff nor Countess Elizabeth Vorontsova, who again had become the favorite of his harem. I decided to throw a party for His Imperial Highness in my garden at Oranienbaum in order to calm his anger, if this were possible. Any party was always appreciated by His Imperial Highness. Therefore, in a remote spot I had an Italian architect, Antonio Rinaldi, whom I had in my service at the time, build a large wooden cart on which one could place an orchestra of sixty musicians and singers. I had verses composed by the court's Italian poet and music by the choirmaster Araya. We placed decorative illuminations in the garden's grand avenue, which we hid behind a curtain, across from which the dinner table was set up. At dusk on July 17, His Imperial Highness, everyone at Oranienbaum, and numerous spectators from Kronstadt and Petersburg went to the garden, which they found illuminated. We sat at the table, and after the first course the curtain that hid the grand avenue was raised and we saw arriving in the distance the rolling orchestra, pulled by twenty oxen decorated with garlands and surrounded by all the male and female dancers I was able to find. The avenue was illuminated so brightly that one could see everything in it. When the cart stopped, chance had it that the moon hung precisely over the cart, which made an admirable impression and greatly astonished the whole company. Moreover, the weather was the finest it could have been. Everyone jumped up from the table to enjoy the beauty of the symphony and the spectacle up close. When it was over the curtain was lowered and we returned to the table for the second course. At the end of this we heard trumpets and drums, and a mountebank cried out, "Gentlemen and ladies, come, come see me, you will find in my booths free lottery tickets." On either side of the large curtain, two small curtains were raised and we saw two brightly lit booths, one of which distributed free tickets for the porcelain lottery, which this booth contained, and the other tickets for flowers, ribbons, fans, combs, purses, gloves, sword knots, and other finery of that sort.* When

---

* A sword knot is a looped strap, ribbon, etc., attached to the hilt of a sword as a support or ornament.

the booths were empty we went to eat dessert, after which we danced until six in the morning. To top it all off, no scheming or ill will interfered with my party, and His Imperial Highness and everyone else were ecstatic and did nothing but praise the Grand Duchess and her party. Indeed, I had spared no expense. My wine was found delicious, my banquet the best possible, everything was at my own expense, and the banquet cost me between ten and fifteen thousand rubles. Note that I had only thirty thousand per year. But this party ended up costing me much more dearly because on July 17, having gone out in a cabriolet with Madame Naryshkina to see the preparations, when I wanted to get out of the cabriolet and my foot was already on the step, the horse jerked and made me fall to the ground on my knees; I was four or five months pregnant.* I acted as if nothing had happened and stayed until the end of the party, doing the honors. Nevertheless I greatly feared a miscarriage. However, nothing happened to me and I got off with a scare. For several days, the Grand Duke, all those in his entourage, all his Holsteiners, and even my fiercest enemies did not stop singing praises for me and my party. There was neither a friend nor an enemy who had not taken away some bauble to remember me by, and at this party, which had been masked, there were a great many people of all stations and the company in the garden was very mixed. Among others there were, moreover, many women who did not appear at court, and in my presence all these women boasted and displayed my gifts, which were basically trifles, for I think that there were not any that cost more than a hundred rubles. But they were given by me, and people were very happy to say, "This was given to me by Her Imperial Highness, the Grand Duchess. She is kindness itself, she gave presents to everyone, she is charming, she looked at me affably with a laugh on her face. She took pleasure in having us dance, eat, and promenade. She found seats for all those who had no place to sit. She wanted us to see what there was to see. She was joyful." In short, on that day people discovered qualities in me that they had not known I possessed, and thus I disarmed my enemies. This was my goal, but it did not last long, as we will see later.

After this party Lev Naryshkin again began to visit me. One day, wanting to use my study, I found him there impertinently lying on a couch and singing a song that made no sense. Seeing this, I left, closing the door be-

---

* In a dispatch from July 27, 1757, L'Hôpital writes: "They say that the Grand Duchess is recently pregnant by Count Poniatowski" (quoted in Böhme 2:239).

hind me, and I immediately went to find his sister-in-law, to whom I said that we had to go get a good handful of nettles and whip this man who had behaved with such insolence toward us for so long, so as to teach him respect. His sister-in-law agreed heartily and we immediately had sturdy sticks wrapped in nettles brought to us. We were accompanied by a widow, Tatiana Iurevna, who was among my ladies, and all three of us went to my study, where we found Lev Naryshkin singing his song at the top of his lungs. When he saw us he tried to escape, and we gave him so many blows with our nettle sticks that his legs, hands, and face swelled up for two or three days, so that on the following day he could not go to Peterhof with us for a day of court, but was obliged to remain in his room. Moreover, he took care to keep quiet about what had just happened to him because we assured him that at the slightest impolite act, or if he gave us any reason to complain about him, we would recommence the same operation, seeing as this was the only way to get through to him. All this was treated as a pure joke and without anger, but our man felt it sufficiently to remember it and did not invite it again, at least not to the degree that he had previously.

In the month of August, we learned at Oranienbaum that on the fourteenth of August the battle of Zorndorf had occurred, one of the bloodiest of the century; each side counted more than twenty thousand men killed and lost. Our loss among officers was considerable and numbered more than twelve hundred. We were told that this battle was a victory for us, but it was whispered that the loss was equal on both sides, that for three days neither of the two armies had dared to claim victory, and that finally on the third day the King of Prussia in his camp, and Count Fermor on the battlefield, had both had the Te Deum sung. The Empress's sorrow and the city's consternation were great when we learned all the details of that bloody day, on which many people lost family, friends, and acquaintances. For a long time one heard only laments. Many generals were killed, wounded, or taken prisoner. Eventually it was conceded that Count Fermor's conduct had been anything but skillful and military. The army detested him and had no confidence in him. The court recalled him, and General Count Peter Saltykov was named to command the army in Prussia in General Fermor's place. To this end, Count Saltykov was brought from Ukraine, where he was in command, and in the meantime command of the army was given to General Frolov-Bagreev, but with a secret order to do nothing without Lieutenant Generals Count Rumiantsev and

Prince Alexander Golitsyn, the brother-in-law of Rumiantsev. The accusation was made that Rumiantsev had been a short distance from the battlefield with a corps of ten thousand men on heights from which he heard the cannonade, and that it had been up to him to make the attack more decisive by advancing against the rear of the Prussian army while it was engaged with ours. Count Rumiantsev did not do this, and when his brother-in-law Prince Golitsyn came to his camp after the battle and recounted to him the butchery that had occurred, Rumiantsev took it very badly, said all kinds of harsh things to him and afterward did not want to see him, treating him like a coward, which however, Prince Golitsyn was not. The entire army is more convinced of the courage of the latter than that of Count Rumiantsev, despite his present glory and his victories.

At the beginning of September the Empress was at Tsarskoe Selo, where on the eighth of the month, the day of the Nativity of the Virgin, she went on foot from the palace to the parish church, which is only a stone's throw from the north gate, to hear mass.* The divine service had only just begun when the Empress, feeling unwell, left the church, descended the little flight of steps that lead at an angle toward the palace, and, having reached the bend at the corner of the church, fell unconscious onto the grass in the middle of, or rather, surrounded by, the crowd of people who had come from all the surrounding villages to hear mass for the feast day. No one in the Empress's entourage had followed her when she left the church, but having been quickly alerted, the ladies of her entourage and her most trusted intimates ran to her aid and found her still and unconscious in the middle of the crowd, which was looking at her without daring to approach. The Empress was very tall and strong, and the sudden fall alone must have hurt her badly. She was covered with a white shawl, and doctors and a surgeon were sent for. The surgeon arrived first and could do no better than bleed her there on the ground amid and in the presence of all these people. But she did not wake up. The doctor took a long time in coming, being sick himself and unable to walk. He had to be carried in a chair. He was the late Kondoïdi, of Greek nationality, and the surgeon was Fousadier, a French refugee. Finally screens were brought from the court and a sofa, upon which she was placed, and by virtue of medicine and ministrations she somewhat came to, but upon opening her eyes she did not recognize anyone and asked almost unintel-

* September 8, 1757.

ligibly where she was. All this lasted more than two hours, at the end of which the decision was made to carry Her Imperial Majesty on the sofa into the palace. One can imagine the consternation of all those who were attached to the court. The publicity of the affair added even more to the anxiety. Up until now, her state of health had been kept very secret, and in this one moment the illness had become public. The following morning I learned of these circumstances at Oranienbaum from a note that Count Poniatowski sent to me. I immediately went to tell the Grand Duke, who knew nothing of it, because everything was always kept from us with the greatest care, and more particularly, anything regarding the Empress personally. It was usual, however, that when we were not in the same location as the Empress, every Sunday one of the gentlemen from our court was sent to inquire about her state of health. We did not fail to do this the following Sunday and we learned that for several days the Empress had not recovered full use of her tongue and that she continued to speak with difficulty. It was said that during her fainting attack, she had bitten her tongue. All of this made us think that her weakness was due more to convulsions than to fainting.

At the end of September we returned to the city. As I began to grow heavy because of my pregnancy, I appeared no more in public, believing that I was closer to giving birth than I really was. This annoyed the Grand Duke, because when I did appear in public, very often he claimed to be unwell so as to stay in his apartment, and since the Empress too appeared rarely, the court days, parties, and balls at the court fell to me. But when I was not there, His Imperial Highness was harassed to go so that someone could fulfill the official duties. His Imperial Highness therefore resented my pregnancy and, one day in his room in the presence of Lev Naryshkin and several others, got it in his head to say, "God knows where my wife gets her pregnancies. I really do not know if this child is mine and if I ought to recognize it." Lev Naryshkin ran to my room to share this remark with me immediately. I was naturally alarmed and said, "You are all impudent fools. Make him swear that he has never slept with his wife and tell him that if he makes this oath, you will go immediately to share it with Alexander Shuvalov and the grand inquisitor of the empire." Lev Naryshkin indeed went to His Imperial Majesty and asked him for this oath, to which he received the response, "Go to the devil and do not speak to me anymore about this." The Grand Duke's remark, made so imprudently, angered me greatly, and from that moment I saw that I had a choice among three equally dangerous paths: *primo,* to share the Grand Duke's fortune, whatever it might be; *secondo,* to be exposed constantly to everything it might please him to devise for or against me; *tertio,* to take a path independent of all events. To put it more clearly, it was a question of perishing with him, or by him, or else of saving myself, my children, and perhaps the state from the disaster that all this Prince's moral and physical faculties promised. This last choice seemed to me the surest. I therefore resolved to continue, as much as I could, to give him all the advice I could summon for his well-being, but never to be stubborn to the point of angering him as I had done before when he did not follow my advice; to open his eyes to his true interests every time the occasion would present itself, and the rest of the time, to shut myself up in a very dull silence, and at the same time to cultivate my reputation with the public so that it would see in me the savior of the commonweal if the occasion arose.

In October I received notice from Bestuzhev that the King of Poland had sent letters of recall to Count Poniatowski. Count Bestuzhev had a heated argument about this with Count Brühl and the Saxon cabinet and was angered that he had not been consulted as previously about this matter. He finally learned that it was the Vice Chancellor Count Vorontsov and Ivan Shuvalov who, through Monsieur Prasse, the resident minister of Saxony, had plotted the whole affair. Indeed, this Monsieur Prasse often seemed informed about numerous details, which astonished people, who wondered where he had learned them. Several years later the channel was discovered. He was the very secret and very discreet lover of the wife of the Vice Chancellor Count Vorontsov, Countess Anna Karlovna, née Skavronskaya. She was very close to the wife of the master of ceremonies, Samarin, and it was at the wife's home that the Countess would see Monsieur Prasse. Chancellor Bestuzhev seized the letters of recall that had been sent to Count Poniatowski and sent them back to Saxony under the pretext that certain formalities had not been observed.

In the night of December 8 to 9, I began to feel labor pains. I sent Madame Vladislavova to inform the Grand Duke as well as Count Alexander Shuvalov, so that he could inform the Empress. After some time, the Grand Duke came into my room dressed in his Holstein uniform, in boots and spurs, with a sash around his waist, with an enormous sword at his side, and immaculately groomed. It was about half past two in the morning. Quite amazed by this costume, I asked him the reason for such exquisite finery. He replied that it was only in times of need that one knew one's true friends, that in this outfit he was ready to act according to his duty, that the duty of an officer of Holstein was to defend according to his oath the ducal house against all its enemies, and that as I found my self in difficulty, he had run to my aid. One might have thought that he was joking, but not at all; what he said was very serious. I easily understood that he was drunk and I advised him to go to bed so that the Empress, when she came, would not have the double displeasure of seeing him drunk and armed from head to toe in his Holstein uniform, which I knew she detested. I had a great deal of trouble making him leave, but Madame Vladislavova and I persuaded him with the help of the midwife, who assured him that I would not give birth quite yet. Finally he left, and the Empress arrived. She asked where the Grand Duke was. We told her that he had just left and would certainly return. When she saw that the labor pains were coming less often and the midwife said that this could last for several more hours, she returned to her apartment and I went to bed, where I slept until the following day. I got up at my usual time, here and there feeling labor pains, after which I would be without pains for whole hours. Toward dinner time I was hungry and had some dinner brought to me. The midwife was seated next to me, and seeing my voracious appetite, she said, "Eat, keep eating. This dinner will bring us good luck." Indeed, having finished the meal, I arose from the table, and the very moment that I got up, I was seized by such a pain that I let out a great cry. The midwife and Madame Vladislavova seized me under the arms and put me on the sickbed, and we sent for the Grand Duke and the Empress. They had hardly entered my room when I gave birth on December 9 between ten and eleven at night to a girl, and I begged the Empress to permit us to give the child her name.* But she decided that the child would have the name of Her Imperial Majesty's older sister, the Duchess of Holstein Anna Petrovna, the Grand Duke's mother. He seemed very happy about the birth of this child. In his apartment, he had grand celebrations for it and had others held in Holstein, and received all the congratulations that were made to him with shows of happiness. Six days later the Empress held this child over the baptismal font, and she brought me an order to the cabinet to give me sixty thousand rubles. She sent the same amount to the Grand Duke, which increased his satisfaction even more.

* Grand Duchess Anna Petrovna (December 9, 1757, to March 8, 1759). Catherine has the year wrong.

After the baptism, the celebrations began. It is said that there were some very beautiful ones. I did not see any of them. I was in my bed all alone, without a living soul for company, except for Madame Vladislavova, because as soon as I had given birth, not only had the Empress this time, like the last time, taken the infant into her apartment, but also under the pretext of the rest that I needed, I was left abandoned like a poor wretch. No one set foot in my apartment, nor even asked or sent to ask how I was doing. Like the first time, I suffered greatly from this abandonment. This time I had taken all possible precautions against the drafts and the room's other drawbacks, and as soon as I had given birth, I got up and went to lay down in my own bed. Since no one dared to come see me except secretly, here too I did not lack forethought. My bed was almost in the center of a rather long room. The windows were to the right of the bed. To the left of it there was a side door that led to a kind of wardrobe that also served as an antechamber and was quite packed with screens and chests. Between my bed and this door I had set up an immense screen that hid the prettiest alcove that I could have imagined, given the locale and the circumstances. In this alcove there were a sofa, mirrors, portable tables, and a few chairs. When the curtain on that side of my bed was drawn, one saw nothing at all; when it was open, one saw the alcove and those who were in it. Those who entered the room saw only the large screen. When someone asked what was behind the screen, we would say the commode. But in fact this was within the screen itself, and no one was curious to see it, and we could have shown them the commode without revealing the alcove that this screen covered.

1759

*Poniatowski's recall to Poland; Catherine's private party; triple
wedding; arrest of Bestuzhev-Riumin endangers Catherine;
his plan for succession after Elizabeth's death includes Catherine;
her secret communications with Bestuzhev-Riumin discovered;
she burns her papers; she fears her removal; her letter to Elizabeth;
her philosophical self-portrait; removal of Mme. Vladislavova;
she sends for her confessor to plead her cause with Elizabeth;
her two conversations with Elizabeth*

On January 1, 1759, the court's celebrations ended with a very grand fireworks display between the ball and dinner.* As I was still confined, I did
not appear at court. Before the fireworks, Count Peter Shuvalov decided to
come to my room to show me the plan for the fireworks display. A short
time before they were set off, Madame Vladislavova told him that I was
sleeping, but that nevertheless she would go to see. It was not true that I
was asleep, only that I was in my bed and had my usual very small circle,
which was at the time, as before, Mesdames Naryshkina, Seniavina, Izmailova, and Count Poniatowski. Since his recall he had been claiming to
be ill, but was coming to see me, and these women liked me well enough
to prefer my company to the balls and parties. Madame Vladislavova did
not know exactly who was with me, but she had much too good a nose not
to suspect that there was someone. I had told her early in the evening that
I was going to bed out of boredom, and thereafter she had come in no
more. After the arrival of Count Peter Shuvalov, she came to knock on my
door. I drew my curtain on the screen side and told her to come in. She entered and gave me Count Peter Shuvalov's message. I told her to have him
come in. She went to find him, and meanwhile my friends behind the
screen nearly died laughing at the utter outrageousness of this scene,
where I was going to receive the visit of Count Peter Shuvalov, who would

---

* The events Catherine assigns to this year in fact occurred in 1758. Catherine also wrote
"1759," the wrong year, in the margin.

be able to swear that he had found me alone in my bed when there was only a curtain that separated my merry little circle from this personage, so important at the time, the oracle of the court, who possessed the Empress's trust to an eminent degree. Finally he entered and brought me his plan for the fireworks display; he was at the time the grand master of artillery. I began by making him my excuses for having made him wait, having only, I said, just woken up. I rubbed my eyes a little, saying that I was still quite sleepy. I lied so as not to contradict Madame Vladislavova, after which we had a conversation that was rather long, so much so that he seemed to me eager to leave so as not to make the Empress wait for the beginning of the display. Then I dismissed him and he left, and I again opened my curtain. My company was beginning to get hungry and thirsty from laughing. I said, "Very well, you will have something to drink and eat. It is fair that for your indulgence in keeping me company, you should not die either of hunger or of thirst in my home." I again closed my curtain and I rang. Madame Vladislavova came, and I told her to bring me supper, that I was dying of hunger and there should be at least six good dishes. When the meal was ready, it was brought. I had everything put next to my bed and told the servants to leave. Then my famished friends behind the curtain came out to eat what they found. The gaiety added to their appetite. I admit that this soiree was one of the maddest and most joyful that I have had in my life. When dinner had been gobbled up, I had the leftovers taken away in the same way the food had been brought. I think my servants were rather amazed at my appetite. Toward the end of the court supper my group withdrew, also very pleased with the soiree. Count Poniatowski always wore a blond wig and a cloak to go out, and when the guards asked him "who goes there," he said he was a musician of the Grand Duke. On that day this wig made us laugh a great deal. This time, after the six weeks' confinement, my churching ceremony was held in the Empress's little chapel, but except for Alexander Shuvalov, no one attended it.

Toward the end of carnival, all the celebrations in town ended and there were three weddings at the court: that of Count Alexander Strogonov with Countess Anna Vorontsova, daughter of the Vice Chancellor, was the first, and two days later that of Lev Naryshkin with Mademoiselle Zakrevskaia, which was on the same day as that of Count Buturlin with Countess Maria Vorontsova.* These three young ladies were the

* Buturlin married on February 15, Strogonov on February 18, and Naryshkin on February 22, 1758.

Empress's maids of honor. On the occasion of these three weddings a bet was made at the court between the Hetman Count Kirill Razumovsky and the Minister from Denmark, Count d'Osten, about which of the three grooms would be cuckolded first, and it happened that those who had bet it would be Strogonov, whose new wife seemed the ugliest at the time, the most innocent and the most infantile, won the bet.

The day before the weddings of Lev Naryshkin and Count Buturlin was a day of unfortunate events. For a long while already it had been whispered that Grand Chancellor Bestuzhev's position was shaky, that his enemies were gaining the upper hand. He had lost his friend General Apraksin. Count Razumovsky the elder had long supported him, but since the Shuvalovs' favor had begun to grow, he hardly got involved in anything anymore except to ask, when the occasion presented itself, for some little favor for his friends or relatives. The Shuvalovs and Mikhail Vorontsov were also spurred on in their hatred for the Grand Chancellor by the ambassadors from Austria, Count Esterhazy; and France, the Marquis de l'Hôpital. The latter believed Count Bestuzhev more favorable toward Russia's alliance with England than with France. The Austrian ambassador conspired against him because Bestuzhev wanted Russia to respect its treaty of alliance with the Court of Vienna and to give aid to Maria Theresa, but did not want Russia to act as the main warring party against the King of Prussia. Count Bestuzhev thought as a patriot and was not easy to manipulate, whereas Mikhail Vorontsov and Ivan Shuvalov were in the pocket of the two ambassadors to the point that fifteen days before Grand Chancellor Count Bestuzhev was disgraced, the Marquis de L'Hôpital, Ambassador from France, went to the home of Vice Chancellor Vorontsov with a dispatch in hand and said to him, "Monsieur Count, here is a dispatch from my court that I have just received, which says that if in fifteen days' time the Grand Chancellor has not been replaced by you, I must address myself to him and deal only with him henceforth." This inflamed the Vice Chancellor, and he went to Ivan Shuvalov's home, and they made it seem to the Empress that her glory was suffering because of Count Bestuzhev's great stature in Europe. She ordered that a meeting be held that very evening and that the Grand Chancellor be called to it. He sent word that he was ill. Whereupon, this illness was viewed as disobedience and he was told to come without delay. He came and was arrested in the middle of the meeting, all his functions, titles, and orders were stripped from him without a living soul being able to articulate for what crimes or misdeeds the first personage of the empire was being so despoiled, and he was sent back to his mansion as a prisoner.* As all this had been prepared in advance, a company of grenadiers from the guard had been ordered to come. While they had been marching along the Moika, where Counts Alexander and Peter Shuvalov had their houses, the soldiers had said, "Thank God we are finally going to arrest those cursed Shuvalovs, who do nothing but increase their monopolies." But when the soldiers saw that it was about Count Bestuzhev, they showed their displeasure, saying, "It is not he but the others who trample the people."

Although Count Bestuzhev was arrested in the very palace where we occupied a wing, not very far from our apartments, they were so careful to hide everything that was happening from us that we learned nothing about it that evening. On the following day, Sunday, when I awoke, I received a note from Lev Naryshkin that Count Poniatowski sent me through him, a channel that had already been suspect for quite a while. The note began with these words: "Man is never without resources. I am using this channel to warn you that yesterday evening Count Bestuzhev was arrested and stripped of his functions and titles, and with him your jeweler Bernardi, Elagin, and Adadurov." I was bowled over by these lines, and after reading them I told myself that I must not delude myself into thinking that this affair did not concern me more directly than it seemed. Now, to understand this a commentary will be necessary. Bernardi was an Italian jewel merchant who did not lack intelligence and whose profession gave him entrée to all the best houses. I think that there was not a single one that did not owe him something and to which he did not render some small service or other. As he came and went everywhere continually, he was also sometimes charged with commissions between houses. A message in a note sent with Bernardi arrived more quickly and more surely than with servants.† Thus Bernardi's arrest concerned the whole city because he had commissions from everyone including me. Elagin was the former adjutant of the Grand Master of the Hunt Count Razumovsky who had had the guardianship of Beketov. He had remained devoted to the house of Razumovsky and through them to Count Bestuzhev. He had become the friend of Count Poniatowski. He was a trustworthy man of

* February 14, 1758.

† Poniatowski writes: "There was a Venetian jeweler who often took the Grand Chancellor's and my letters to the Grand Duchess and brought the replies." *Mémoires* 1:319.

integrity. When one gained his affection one did not easily lose it. He had always shown devotion to and an obvious liking for me. Adadurov had formerly been my Russian language teacher and had remained very devoted to me. I had recommended him to Count Bestuzhev, who had begun to trust him only two or three years earlier and who in the past had not liked him, because Adadurov had formerly been in the service of the procurator, Prince Nikita Iurevich Trubetskoi, Bestuzhev's enemy. After reading this note and after the thoughts that I have just described, a flood of ideas, each more unpleasant and sadder than the last, arose in my mind. With a dagger in my heart, so to speak, I got dressed and went to mass, where it seemed to me that most of those whom I saw had faces as long as mine. No one said a word to me that day, and it was as if people were unaware of the event. I did not say a word either. The Grand Duke had never liked Count Bestuzhev. He seemed to me rather joyful that day, but discreetly kept his distance.

That evening we had to go to the wedding. I got dressed again and attended the blessing of the marriages of Count Buturlin and Lev Naryshkin, then went to supper and the ball. During this I went up to the marshal of the wedding, Prince Nikita Trubetskoi, and under the pretext of examining the ribbons on his marshal's baton, I said to him in a low voice, "What are these fine things? Have you found more crimes than criminals or do you have more criminals than crimes?" At this he said to me, "We have done what we were ordered to do, but as for the crimes, we are still looking for them. So far what we have uncovered does not bode well." When I finished speaking with him, I went to speak with Marshal Buturlin, who said to me, "Bestuzhev has been arrested, but at present we are looking for the reason why." Thus spoke the two head commissioners, named with Count Alexander Shuvalov by the Empress to examine the arrested men. At this ball I saw Stambke from a distance and thought he appeared to be suffering and discouraged. The Empress did not appear at either of these two weddings, neither at the church nor at the banquet.

The following day Stambke came to see me and told me that he had just been given a note from Count Bestuzhev, who wrote Stambke to tell me to have no worries about what I knew, that he had had time to throw everything in the fire and that he would inform Stambke about his interrogations by the same channel when he underwent them. I asked Stambke what this channel was. He told me that a hunting-horn player of the Count had given him this note, and that it was agreed that in the future, they would place their communications to each other in a marked spot among some bricks not far from Count Bestuzhev's house. I told Stambke to be very careful that this sensitive correspondence not be discovered, but though he seemed to me to be in great anguish himself, nevertheless he and Count Poniatowski continued to communicate. As soon as Stambke left, I called Madame Vladislavova and told her to go to the home of her son-in-law Pugovishnikov and give him the note I was writing. In this note there were only these words: "You have nothing to fear, there was time to burn everything." This calmed him, for it seemed that since the Grand Chancellor's arrest he had been more dead than alive.

Here is the reason for his fear, and what Count Bestuzhev had had time to burn. The Empress's sickly state and frequent convulsions could not fail to turn all eyes toward the future. Because of both his position and intelligence, Count Bestuzhev was certainly not among the last to reflect on this situation. He knew of the antipathy against him that had long been cultivated in the Grand Duke. He was very aware of the feeble capacities of this Prince, born the heir to so many crowns. It is natural that this statesman, like any other, felt the desire to maintain his position. It had been several years since he had seen me throw off the bad impressions of him that had been instilled in me. Moreover, since then he had regarded me personally as perhaps the only individual in whom the public could place its hope when the Empress passed away. This and other similar reflections led him to form the plan whereby upon the Empress's death, the Grand Duke would be declared the rightful Emperor and at the same time, I would be declared as sharing the government with him. All public offices were to be maintained, and Bestuzhev would be appointed lieutenant colonel of the four guard regiments and president of the three Colleges of the Empire, that of Foreign Affairs, the College of War, and the admiralty. His ambitions were therefore excessive. He had sent me the draft of this manifesto written in Pugovishnikov's hand via Count Poniatowski, with whom I had agreed to reply to Bestuzhev orally that I thanked him for his good intentions toward me, but that I regarded the affair as difficult to execute. He had had his draft written and revised several times, had changed it, expanded it, and shortened it. He appeared very busy with it. To tell the truth, I regarded his plan as rambling nonsense and as bait that the old man threw me to gain more and more of my affection. But I did not take this particular bait, because I saw it as harmful to the empire, which would have been torn apart with each domestic dispute between me and my husband, who did not love me. However, as I did not yet see the need arising, I did not want to contradict an old man who was persistent and uncompromising when he had taken something into his head. And so he had had time to burn his plan and had informed me so as to calm those of us who knew about it.

Meanwhile, my chamber valet, Shkurin, came to tell me that the captain who was guarding Count Bestuzhev was a man who had always been his friend and who dined at his house every Sunday after leaving the court. I said to him that if matters were thus and he could count on this man, he should try to sound him out to see if he would be willing to have secret contacts with his prisoner. This had become all the more necessary since Count Bestuzhev had communicated to Stambke by his channel that they should inform Bernardi to tell the pure truth at his interrogation and let Bestuzhev know what Bernardi was asked. When I saw that Shkurin had voluntarily undertaken to find some way to reach Count Bestuzhev, I told him to try to establish communication with Bernardi also, to see if he could not win over the sergeant or some other soldier who was guarding Bernardi in his quarters. The same day, Shkurin told me toward evening that Bernardi was guarded by a sergeant of the guards named Kolyshkin, with whom he would have a meeting the following day. However, Shkurin had sent to the home of his friend the captain, who was at Count Bestuzhev's residence, to ask if he could see him. The captain had told Shkurin that if he wanted to talk to him, he should come to his house. But one of the captain's underlings, whom Shkurin also knew and who was his relative, had told him not to go, because if he went, the captain would have him arrested; the captain had already boasted privately of this, and would improve his standing at Shkurin's expense. Shkurin therefore ended contact with his so-called friend, Monsieur the captain. On the other hand, Kolyshkin, whom I ordered to act in my name, told Bernardi all that we wanted him to, and since he only had to tell the truth, both were happy to go along with this.

A few days later, very early one morning, Stambke entered my room quite pale and haggard and told me that his correspondence and that of Count Poniatowski with Count Bestuzhev had just been discovered, that the little horn player had been arrested and that there was every indication that their latest letters had had the misfortune of falling into the hands of Count Bestuzhev's guards. He himself expected to be dismissed, if not arrested, at any moment, and he had come to tell me this and take his leave of me. What he said hardly put me at ease. I consoled him as best I could and sent him away, not doubting that his visit would do nothing but increase, if this was possible, the totality of bad feeling against me, and that people were perhaps going to abandon me like someone who is wanted by the government. Nevertheless I was deeply convinced that as concerned the government, I had nothing to reproach myself. Aside from Mikhail Vorontsov, Ivan Shuvalov, the two ambassadors from Vienna and Versailles, and those whom they made believe what they wanted, the public in general, everyone in all Petersburg, great and small, was convinced that Count Bestuzhev was innocent, and that he was not responsible for any crime or offense.

It was known that the day after the evening of his arrest, a group had worked on a manifesto in Ivan Shuvalov's chambers and that Master Volkov, Count Bestuzhev's former head clerk and now first secretary of the commission, had had to write it. In 1755, Volkov had fled from his home and after wandering in the woods, had turned himself in. They wanted to publish this manifesto to inform the public of the reasons that had obliged the Empress to act as she had against Grand Chancellor Count Bestuzhev. Thus this secret conventicle, racking its brain to find offenses, conspired to say that the crime was lèse-majesté, because Bestuzhev had sought to sow discord between Her Imperial Majesty and Their Imperial Highnesses.* Without an indictment or judgment, on the day following his arrest they wanted to send him to one of his estates and strip him of the rest of his possessions. But there were those who thought that it was extreme to exile someone without evidence of a crime or a judgment, and that despite the expectation of finding crimes they nevertheless had to be sought, and that whether they were discovered or not, it was still necessary to have the prisoner, who had been stripped of his functions, titles, and orders for reasons unknown, undergo the judgment of the commissioners.† Now these commissioners, as I have already said, were Marshal Buturlin, Procurator General Prince Trubetskoi, General Count Alexander Shuvalov, and Master Volkov, the secretary. The first thing that the commissioners did was order, through the College of Foreign Affairs, the Russian ambassadors, envoys, and employees at foreign courts to send copies of the dispatches that Count Bestuzhev had written them since he had been in

---

* A conventicle is a small, clandestine meeting, in a pejorative sense.
† By the manifesto of February 27, 1758.

charge of foreign affairs. This was so as to find incriminating evidence in his dispatches. It was said that he wrote only what he wanted, and things contradictory to the orders and wishes of the Empress. But as Her Imperial Majesty neither wrote nor signed anything, it was difficult to act against her orders, and as for verbal orders, Her Imperial Majesty was hardly in the position to give any to the Grand Chancellor, who went entire years without having the opportunity to see her. Strictly speaking, verbal orders delivered by a third party could be misinterpreted, and were as vulnerable to bad delivery as they were to miscomprehension. But nothing came of all this except the order that I mentioned, because I think that none of the employees took the trouble to go through their twenty-year-old archive and copy it to look for crimes by the man whose instructions and directions these same employees had followed, since they might thereby find themselves implicated, with the best intentions in the world, in what might be found reprehensible in this correspondence. Moreover, the sending of such archives alone would cost the crown considerably, and once they arrived in Petersburg, there would have been enough to try the patience of a good number of people over several years in order to find and disentangle something that was perhaps not even there. Once sent, this order was never carried out. The affair itself grew tiresome and was brought to an end after a year by the manifesto they had begun to compose the day following the Grand Chancellor's arrest.*

The afternoon of the day that Stambke had come to see me, the Empress told the Grand Duke to send Stambke back to Holstein, because his secret contacts with Count Bestuzhev had been discovered and he deserved to be arrested. But out of consideration for His Imperial Highness and as his minister, he remained free on the condition that he be dismissed at once. Stambke was sent away immediately, and with his departure my handling of the affairs of Holstein ended.† The Grand Duke was made to understand that the Empress did not judge it right that I was involved in them, and His Imperial Highness was himself rather partial to this opinion. I do not remember very well whom he chose afterward to replace Stambke, but I think it was a certain Wolff. Then the Empress's Minister formally asked the King of Poland for the recall of Count Poniatowski, one of whose notes to Count Bestuzhev had been found. In truth it was

* Manifesto of April 5, 1759.
† April 7, 1758.

quite innocent, but nevertheless addressed to a so-called prisoner of the state. As soon as I learned of Stambke's dismissal and Count Poniatowski's recall, I did not foresee anything positive for me, and here is what I did. I called my chamber valet, Shkurin, and told him to gather all my account books and everything among my effects that might even resemble a document and bring it to me. He executed my order with zeal and precision. When everything was in my room, I dismissed him. When he had left, I threw all these books and papers into the fire, and when I saw them half consumed, I again called for Shkurin and said to him, "Witness that all my accounts and papers are burned, so that if you are ever asked where they are, you can swear to have seen them burned here by me." He thanked me for the consideration that I showed him and told me that a quite extraordinary change had just occurred in the prisoners' guard. Since the discovery of Stambke's correspondence with Count Bestuzhev, he was being watched more closely, and to this end Sergeant Kolyshkin had been moved from Bernardi's home and had been put in the room and near the person of the former Grand Chancellor. When Kolyshkin realized this, he requested that he be given some of the soldiers attached to him when he was guarding Bernardi. And so the most trustworthy and intelligent man that Shkurin and I had was placed in Count Bestuzhev's room, moreover without having lost all his secret contacts with Bernardi. Meanwhile, the interrogation of Count Bestuzhev was under way. Kolyshkin introduced himself to Count Bestuzhev as a man entirely devoted to me, and in fact he rendered him a great many services. Like me, he was deeply convinced that the Grand Chancellor was innocent and the victim of a powerful cabal; the public was convinced too.

I saw that the Grand Duke had been frightened and that he had been made to suspect that I was not unaware of Stambke's correspondence with the prisoner of the state. I saw that His Imperial Highness hardly dared talk to me and avoided coming into my room, where I was moreover completely alone, not seeing a living soul. I myself avoided having people come, for fear of exposing them to some misfortune or trouble. At court, fearing that I would be avoided, I refrained from approaching all those who I thought might be implicated. During the last days of carnival, there was going to be a Russian play at the court theater. Count Poniatowski begged me to come because the rumor was beginning to circulate that they were preparing to send me away to prevent me from appearing in public, and I know not what else. Each time I did not appear at the theater or at court, everyone was intrigued to know the reason for it, perhaps as much out of curiosity as out of the concern they had for me. I knew that Russian theater was one of the things His Imperial Highness liked least and that to speak of going to it was enough to greatly displease him. But this time the Grand Duke joined to his dislike of the national theater another motive and minor personal objective. He was not yet seeing Countess Elizabeth Vorontsova in his apartment, but since she stayed in the antechamber with the other maids of honor, His Imperial Highness had conversations with or courted her there. If I went to the theater, these maidens were obliged to follow me, which would upset His Imperial Highness, who would find no other recourse than to go drink in his apartment. Without regard for his situation, as I had decided that day and given my word to go to the theater, I told Count Alexander Shuvalov to order my carriages. Count Shuvalov came to see me and told me that my plan to go to the Russian play did not please the Grand Duke. I replied to him that as I did not count among His Imperial Highness's company, I thought it would not matter to him whether I was alone in my room or in my loge at the theater. He left twitching his eye as he always did when he was bothered by something. Sometime later the Grand Duke came into my room. He was terribly angry, shrieking like a banshee, saying that I enjoyed upsetting him and that I had decided to go to the theater because I knew he did not like this kind of spectacle. I explained to him that he was wrong not to like it. He told me that he would forbid them to give me my carriage. I told him that I would go on foot, and that I could not guess what pleasure he took in making me die of boredom alone in my room, where I had my dog and my parrot as my only company. After we had both argued for a long while and spoken very loudly, he left angrier than ever, and I persisted in going to the theater. As the hour of the play neared, I sent to ask Count Shuvalov if the carriages were ready. He came to see me and told me that the Grand Duke had forbidden them to be given to me. At this I got good and angry, and I said that I was going on foot and that if the ladies and gentlemen were prohibited from following me, I would go all alone, and that moreover, I would complain in writing to the Empress about both the Grand Duke and him. He said to me, "And what will you say to her?" "I will tell her," I said, "the manner in which I am treated and that you, in order to arrange a rendezvous with my maids of honor for the Grand Duke, encourage him to prevent me from going to the play, where I may have the happiness of seeing Her Imperial Majesty, and moreover, I will beg her to send me back to my mother's home because I am sick and tired of the role that I am playing, alone and abandoned in my room, hated by the Grand Duke and not at all loved by the Empress. I desire only my rest, and I no longer want to be a burden to anyone, nor to bring misfortune to whomever approaches me and especially my poor servants, so many of whom have already been exiled because I wished them well or was good to them. You should know that I am going to write to Her Imperial Majesty straight away and then I will see whether or not you take my letter to her yourself." The man was frightened by the determined tone I took.

He left and I began to write my letter to the Empress in Russian, making it as moving as I could. I began by thanking her for all the favors and kindness with which she had showered me since my arrival in Russia, saying that unfortunately, events proved that I had not merited them, because I had incurred the Grand Duke's hatred and the very marked disfavor of Her Imperial Majesty. Seeing my misfortune and that I was withering with boredom in my room, where I was deprived of even the most innocent pastimes, I begged her to put an immediate end to my unhappiness by sending me away to my family in whatever manner she judged fitting. Since I did not see my children, although I lived with them in the same household, it made no difference to me whether I was in the same place they were or a few hundred leagues away. I knew that her care for them surpassed what my feeble abilities would permit me to give them. I dared to ask her to continue to care for them, and trusting in this, I would spend the rest of my life with my family, praying to God for her, the Grand Duke, my children, and all those who had done me good and ill. But because of sorrow, my health was reduced to such a state that I had to do what I could to at least save my life, and to this end I was beseeching her to allow me to take the waters and from there go to my family's home. Having written this letter, I sent for Count Shuvalov, who upon entering told me that the carriages that I had asked for were ready. I told him, while giving him my letter for the Empress, that he could tell the ladies and gentlemen who did not want to follow me to the theater that I excused them. Count Shuvalov received my letter twitching his eye, but since it was addressed to the Empress, he was utterly obliged to take it. He also relayed my words to the maidens and gentlemen, and it was His Imperial Highness himself who decided who should go with me and who should stay with him. I passed through the antechamber, where I found

His Imperial Highness ensconced with Countess Elizabeth Vorontsova, playing cards in a corner. He rose and she too when he saw me, something that he never did, moreover. I responded to this formality with a very deep curtsy and went my way. I went to the theater, where the Empress did not appear that day. I think that my letter prevented her. Upon returning from the theater, Count Shuvalov told me that Her Imperial Majesty informed me that she herself would have an interview with me. Apparently Count Shuvalov gave an account both of my letter and of the Empress's response to the Grand Duke, for though from that day on he did not set foot in my room again, nevertheless he did everything he could to be present at the interview that the Empress was having with me, and it seemed that they could not refuse him. I waited calmly in my apartment. I was deeply convinced that if they had been thinking of sending me back or frightening me with the possibility, the step that I had just taken completely disrupted the Shuvalovs' plan. In any case, this plan would meet the most resistance in the mind of the Empress herself, who was not at all inclined toward such blatant acts. Moreover, she still remembered the former disagreements in her family and would certainly not have wished to see them rekindled in her lifetime. There could only be a single mark against me, which was that her nephew did not seem to me to be the most lovable of men, just as I did not seem to him to be the most lovable of women. The Empress felt exactly as I did about her nephew, and she knew him so well that for many years already she had not been able to pass a quarter hour with him anywhere without feeling disgust, anger, or sorrow. In her room, when conversation turned to him, she spoke either through bitter tears about the misfortune of having such an heir or else while showing her contempt for him, and would often give him epithets that he deserved only too well. I have had proofs of this in hand, having found among her papers two notes written in the Empress's hand to I know not whom. One appeared to be for Ivan Shuvalov and the other for Count Razumovsky, and in them she cursed her nephew and sent him to the devil. In one there was this expression: "Проклятой мой племеник сегодня так мне досадил как нельзя более"; and in another she said, "Племенник мой урод, черть ево возми."*

---

* "Today my damned nephew irritated me as never before" and "My nephew is a monster, the devil take him." The spelling irregularities may be Catherine's transcription or Elizabeth's original notes.

In any case my decision was made, and I viewed my being sent home or not with a very philosophical eye. In whatever situation it should please Providence to place me, I would never find myself without those resources that intelligence and talent give to each according to his natural abilities, and I felt the courage to rise and fall without my heart and my soul feeling either pride or vanity or, in the opposite case, shame or humiliation. I knew that I was human, and therefore a limited being incapable of perfection. My intentions had always been honest and pure, as I had understood from the very beginning that to love a husband who was not amiable, nor took any pains to be so, was a difficult thing, if not impossible. At least I had given both to him and his interests the sincerest devotion that a friend and even a servant could give to his friend and master. My advice had always been the very best I could devise for his welfare. If he did not follow it, this was not my fault but that of his judgment, which was neither sound nor just. When I came to Russia, and during the first years of our union, had this Prince shown the least desire to make himself bearable, my heart would have been opened to him. When I saw that of all possible objects I was the one to whom he paid the least attention, precisely because I was his wife, it is not at all strange that I found this situation neither pleasant nor to my taste, and that it bothered and perhaps even pained me. This latter sentiment, that of pain, I suppressed infinitely more than all the others. My soul's natural pride and mettle made the idea of being unhappy intolerable to me. I would say to myself, "Happiness and misery are in the heart and soul of everyone. If you feel misery, rise above it, and act so that your happiness does not depend on any event." I had been born with this turn of mind and endowed with very great sensitivity, and an appearance that was at the least very interesting and pleasing at first sight, without art or affectation. My disposition was naturally so accommodating that no one was ever with me a quarter of an hour without falling comfortably into conversation, chatting with me as if they had known me for a long time. Naturally indulgent, I easily won the trust of those who dealt with me, because everyone felt that the strictest probity and goodwill were the impulses that I most readily obeyed. If I may dare to use such terms, I take the liberty to assert on my own behalf that I was an honest and loyal knight,* whose mind was infinitely more male than female. But for all that, I was anything but man-

---

* Chevalier, a knight of an order (not a cavalier, or gentleman).

nish, and in me others found, joined to the mind and character of a man, the charms of a very attractive woman. May I be pardoned this description in recognition of the truth of this confession, which my self-esteem makes without covering itself with false modesty. Besides, this writing itself should prove what I say about my mind, my heart, and my character.

I have just said that I was attractive. As a result, I was already halfway along the road to temptation, and it is the essence of human nature that in such a situation the other half will not go untraveled. For to tempt and to be tempted are very close to each other, and despite the finest moral maxims engraved in the mind, when sensibility joins in, by its very presence, one is already infinitely further from these maxims than one thinks. Even now I still do not know how one can prevent sensibility from appearing. Perhaps flight alone can remedy this. But there are cases, situations, circumstances where flight is impossible, for how can one flee, avoid, or turn one's back in the middle of a court? The very action would cause gossip, but if you do not flee, there is nothing as difficult in my opinion as escaping what profoundly pleases you. Everything that they will tell you to the contrary will only be prudishness, and not drawn from the human heart. No one holds his heart in his hand and restrains or releases it by closing or opening his hand at will.*

I return to my narrative. The day after the play, I declared that I was unwell and did not go out anymore, waiting calmly for Her Imperial Majesty's decision about my humble request. However, the first week of Lent I judged it fitting to attend services to show my devotion to the Greek Orthodox faith.† The second or third week of Lent brought me another bitter disappointment. One morning after I had risen, my servants informed me that Count Alexander Shuvalov had sent for Madame Vladislavova. This seemed somewhat strange to me. I waited anxiously for her return, but in vain. Around one in the afternoon, Count Alexander Shuvalov came to tell me that the Empress had seen fit to remove Madame Vladislavova from my service. I burst into tears and replied to him that Her Imperial Majesty was certainly free to remove from me or place with me whomever she pleased, but that I regretted seeing more and more that all those who came near me were as many victims doomed to the disfavor of Her Imperial Majesty. So that there would be fewer un-

* From "I have just said" to "hand at will" left out of the Russian Academy edition (1907) of Catherine's works.
† March 7, 1758.

fortunates, I begged and beseeched him to appeal to Her Imperial Majesty to put an end as soon as possible to the state to which I was reduced, in which I only made others miserable, by sending me home to my family. I assured him again that Madame Vladislavova would not be of any use in shedding light on anything, because neither she nor anyone else was in my confidence. Count Shuvalov wanted to speak, but seeing my sobs, he began to weep with me and told me that the Empress would speak to me personally on the subject. I begged him to hasten the moment, which he promised to do. Then I went to tell my attendants what had just happened and told them that if any duenna I happened to dislike took the place of Madame Vladislavova, she should be prepared to receive from me every imaginable mistreatment, including even blows. I begged them to repeat this to whomever they pleased, so as to repulse all those that they might want to place in my service from rushing to accept the position, for I was tired of suffering. Seeing that my mildness and patience had brought about nothing but to make everything around me go from bad to worse, I was consequently going to change my behavior thoroughly. My servants did not fail to repeat what I told them to.

That evening, after I had cried much and eaten very little, I was walking up and down in my room quite agitated in both body and mind, when I saw one of my ladies-in-waiting, named Katerina Ivanovna Sharogorodskaia, enter my bedroom, where I was alone as always. With tears and great affection, she said, "We all fear that you will succumb to the state in which we see you. Permit me to go today to my uncle, who is your own confessor as well as the Empress's. I will talk to him and tell him everything you order me to, and I promise you that he will be able to speak to the Empress in a manner that you will be happy with."* Seeing her good-will, I recounted to her very clearly the state of things, what I had written to the Empress, and everything else. She went to her uncle, and after speaking to him and disposing him in my favor, she returned around eleven o'clock to tell me that the confessor, her uncle, advised me to declare during the night that I was ill and to ask to make my confession, and for this purpose have him sent for, so that he would be able to tell Her Imperial Majesty what he heard from my own mouth. I very much approved

---

* Fedor Iakovlevich Dubiansky was married to Maria Konstantinovna Sharogorodskaia, the daughter of Konstantin Fedorovich Sharogorodsky (d. 1735), who had also been Elizabeth's confessor (Böhme 2:271).

of this idea and promised to carry it out, and then dismissed her, thanking both her and her uncle for the devotion they were displaying. As planned, I rang between two and three o'clock in the morning; one of my ladies entered. I told her that I felt so ill that I wanted to make my confession. Instead of the confessor, Count Alexander Shuvalov came running into my room, and in a weak and broken voice I repeated to him my request to have my confessor summoned. He sent for the doctors. I told them that I needed spiritual aid, that I was suffocating. One felt my pulse and said it was weak. I said that my soul was in danger and my body no longer needed doctors. Finally the confessor arrived and we were left alone. I had him sit next to my bed and we had a conversation for at least an hour and a half. I described and recounted to him the past and present state of affairs, the Grand Duke's conduct toward me, mine toward His Imperial Highness, the Shuvalovs' hatred, and how they were bringing Her Imperial Majesty's disfavor down on me, and finally the continual exile or dismissal of many of my servants, and always those who were most devoted to me, and then where matters stood at present, which had brought me to write the Empress the letter by which I requested my dismissal. I begged him to obtain a prompt response to my plea. I found he had the best intentions in the world for me and that he was less stupid than he was said to be. He told me that my letter was having, and would have, the desired effect, that I should persist in asking to be dismissed, and that I would certainly not be sent away, because they could not justify this dismissal in the eyes of the public, whose attention was on me. He agreed that I was being treated cruelly and that the Empress, having chosen me at a very tender age, was abandoning me to the mercy of my enemies. She would do much better to dismiss my rivals, above all Elizabeth Vorontsova, and to rein in her favorites, who had become leeches on the people through all the monopolies that the Shuvalovs were constantly establishing. Moreover, everyone was crying out at their injustice: witness the affair of Count Bestuzhev, of whose innocence the public was convinced. He ended this interview by telling me that he would go to the Empress's apartment immediately, where he would await her awakening to speak to her and hasten the interview that she had promised me, which was going to be decisive, and that I would do well to remain in my bed. He would say that sorrow and pain could kill me if a swift remedy was not applied and I was not rescued, one way or another, from the state I was in, alone and abandoned by everyone. He kept his word, and described my state to the Empress with such vivid and immediate colors that Her Imperial Majesty summoned Count Alexander Shuvalov and ordered him to see if I was in a state to come and talk to her the following night. Count Shuvalov came to tell me this. I told him that for this purpose I would gather all my remaining strength.

Toward evening I was getting up when Alexander Shuvalov came to tell me that after midnight he would come to accompany me to the Empress's apartment. Through his niece, the confessor also informed me that things were going rather well and that the Empress would speak to me the same evening.* I therefore got dressed toward ten o'clock in the evening and lay down fully dressed on a couch, where I fell asleep. At around half past one, Count Alexander Shuvalov came into my room and said that the Empress was asking for me. I got up and followed him; we crossed the antechambers, where there was no one. Arriving at the door of the gallery, I saw that the Grand Duke was crossing the opposite doorway and that just like me, he was going to see Her Imperial Majesty. I had not seen him since the day of the play. Even when I had said that my life was in danger, he had neither come nor sent to ask how I was doing. I learned afterward that on that same day he had promised Elizabeth Vorontsova that he would marry her if I happened to die, and that they both greatly rejoiced at my state. Finally, having reached Her Imperial Majesty's apartment, where I found the Grand Duke, as soon as I saw the Empress I threw myself at her knees and begged her with tears to immediately send me back to my family. The Empress wanted to make me get up, but I stayed at her feet. She seemed to me to be more pained than angry, and said to me with tears in her eyes, "Why do you want me to send you back? Remember that you have children." I said, "My children are in your hands and could not be better off. I hope that you will not abandon them." Then she said, "But what shall I tell the public is the reason for sending you back?" I replied, "Your Imperial Majesty will tell them, if she sees fit, the reasons that I have incurred your disfavor and the hatred of the Grand Duke." The Empress said, "And what will you live on at your family's home?" I replied, "On that which I lived before you did me the honor of choosing me." At this she said, "Your mother is in exile. She was obliged to withdraw from her home and went to Paris."† At this I

* April 13, 1758.

† Princess Johanna was in Hamburg; she arrived in Paris in July 1758, a refugee (because of her ties with Russia) from Prussia's Seven Years' War with Russia.

said, "I know this. She was believed to be too devoted to the interests of Russia, and the King of Prussia drove her away." The Empress told me a second time to get up, which I did, and she walked away from me a little, in thought. The room we were in was long and had three windows, between which there were two tables with the Empress's gold toiletries. There was no one in the apartment aside from her, the Grand Duke, Alexander Shuvalov, and me. Across from the windows there were large screens before which a sofa had been placed. From the first, I suspected that Ivan Shuvalov was certainly behind these screens, and perhaps also Count Peter, his cousin. I learned later that I had guessed correctly in part and that Ivan Shuvalov was there. I stood next to the dressing table closest to the door by which I had entered and noticed that in the basin there were some folded letters. The Empress came toward me again and said to me, "God is my witness how much I cried when you were deathly ill upon your arrival in Russia, and if I had not loved you, I would not have kept you here." Now with this, in my opinion, she was excusing herself after what I had said about incurring her disfavor. I responded by thanking Her Imperial Majesty for all the favors and kindness that she had shown me, then and later, saying that their memory would never be effaced from my mind, and that I would always consider having incurred her disfavor as the greatest of misfortunes. Then she came even closer to me and said, "You are extremely proud. Remember that at the Summer Palace I approached you one day and asked you if your neck hurt, because I saw that you hardly bowed to me and that it was out of pride that you greeted me with only a nod." I said to her, "My God, Madame, how can you believe that I wanted to affect pride toward you? I swear to you that it never even crossed my mind that this question you posed to me four years ago could have meant such a thing." At this she said, "You imagine that no one is more intelligent than you." I replied, "If I did believe this, nothing would more thoroughly disabuse me than my present state and this very conversation, because I see that out of stupidity I have not understood until now what you deigned to say to me four years ago." While the Empress was speaking to me, the Grand Duke whispered with Count Alexander Shuvalov. She noticed this and approached them. They were both standing in the middle of the room. I did not hear too well what they said among themselves. They did not speak too loudly, and the room was large. At the end, I heard the Grand Duke say, raising his voice, "She is terribly wicked and very stubborn." Then I saw that he was speaking of me, and addressing myself to the Grand Duke, I said to him, "If you are speaking of me, I am quite happy to tell you in the presence of Her Imperial Majesty that in truth I am spiteful toward those who advise you to commit injustices, and that I have become stubborn ever since I saw that my acts of kindness bring me nothing but your enmity." He said to the Empress, "Your Imperial Majesty herself sees how wicked she is by what she says." But my remarks made a different impression on the Empress, who had infinitely more intelligence than the Grand Duke. I saw clearly that as the conversation continued, although it had been recommended to her or she herself had resolved to be harsh with me, her mind was gradually softening in spite of herself and her resolutions. However, she turned toward him and said, "Oh, you do not know everything she has said to me against your advisers and Brockdorff regarding the man whom you had arrested." To the Grand Duke, this must have seemed a formal act of treason on my part. He did not know a word of my conversation with the Empress at the Summer Palace, and now he saw his Brockdorff, who had become so dear and so precious to him, accused before the Empress and by me. This therefore put us more at odds than ever and perhaps made us irreconcilable and deprived me forever of the Grand Duke's trust. I almost fell over hearing the Empress recount to the Grand Duke in my presence what I had told her for the well-being of her nephew, and seeing it turn into a lethal weapon against me. The Grand Duke, utterly astonished by this secret, said, "Ah, here is a nice little story that I did not know. It proves her wickedness." I thought to myself, God knows whose wickedness it proves.

With a brusque transition the Empress went from Brockdorff to the uncovered connection between Stambke and Count Bestuzhev, and said to me, "I leave you to consider how having contact with a prisoner of the state could be excusable." As my name did not appear in this affair and as there had been no mention made of me, I was silent, taking this as a remark that did not concern me. At this the Empress approached me and said, "You meddle in many things that do not concern you. I would not have dared to do as much during Empress Anna's reign. How, for example, did you dare to send orders to Marshal Apraksin?" I said to her, "Me! The thought of sending him orders never entered my head." "How," she said, "can you deny having written to him? Your letters are there in this basin." She pointed at them. "You are forbidden to write." Then I said, "It is true that I transgressed this prohibition and I beg your pardon for it.

But since my letters are there, these three letters can prove to Your Imperial Majesty that I never sent him orders, but that in one I told him what was being said of his conduct." Here she interrupted me, saying, "And why did you write him this?" I replied, "Quite simply because I took an interest in the Marshal, whom I liked a great deal. I asked him to follow your orders. The two other letters contain only congratulations on the birth of his son and best wishes for the new year." At this she said, "Bestuzhev says that there were many others." I replied, "If Bestuzhev says this, he is lying." "Well then," said she, "since he is lying about you I will have him put to torture." She thought to frighten me with this. I replied to her that she was the sovereign mistress and could do what she judged fitting, but that I had certainly only written these three letters to Apraksin. She fell silent and appeared to gather her thoughts.

I am reporting the most striking details of this conversation that have remained in my memory, but it would be impossible for me to remember everything that was said during the at least one and a half hours that it lasted. The Empress walked about the room, alternately addressing herself to me, her nephew, and even more often Count Alexander Shuvalov, with whom the Grand Duke was in conversation most of the time while the Empress spoke to me. I have already said that I observed in Her Imperial Majesty less anger than worry. As for the Grand Duke, in all of his remarks during this interview he showed a great deal of venom, animosity, and even rage toward me. He sought to anger the Empress against me as much as he could. But as he went about this stupidly and showed more passion than justice, he missed his mark, and the Empress's intelligence and perspicacity brought her to my side. She listened with particular attention and a kind of instinctive approbation to my firm and moderate responses to the immoderate remarks that Monsieur my husband made and in which one saw clear as day that he sought to clear out my position to have his mistress of the moment placed there, if he could. But this could not be to the Empress's liking, nor would Messieurs Shuvalov scheme to make the Counts Vorontsov their masters. But this lay beyond the powers of judgment of His Imperial Highness, who always believed what he wished and who brushed aside all ideas contrary to the one that dominated him. And he carried on so much that the Empress approached me and said to me in a low voice, "I will have many more things to say to you, but I cannot speak because I do not want to put you two more at odds than you already are," and with her eyes and head she showed me that it was because of those present. Seeing this sign of intimate goodwill that she gave me in such a critical situation, I was deeply touched, and I too said very quietly, "And I too cannot speak, as pressing as my desire is to open my heart and my soul to you." I saw that what I had just said to her made a very vivid and favorable impression on her. Tears had come to her eyes, and to hide that she was moved, and to what extent, she dismissed us, saying that it was very late. In truth, it was almost three in the morning. The Grand Duke left first; I followed him. At the moment that Count Alexander Shuvalov wanted to pass through the door after me, the Empress called him, and he stayed in her room. The Grand Duke kept walking with long strides. I did not hurry this time to follow him. He went back into his rooms and I into mine. I began to undress to go to bed when I heard knocking at the door through which I had just entered. I asked who it was. Count Alexander Shuvalov said that it was he, asking me to open, which I did. He told me to dismiss my ladies; they left. Then he said to me that the Empress had summoned him, and after speaking to him some time, she had asked him to present her compliments to me, and to beg me not to be distressed, and that she would have a second conversation with me alone. I bowed deeply before Count Shuvalov and told him to present my very deepest respects to Her Imperial Majesty and to thank her for her kindness toward me, which had brought me back to life, and that I would wait for this second conversation with the keenest impatience and that I begged him to hasten the moment. He told me not to speak of it to a living soul and namely to the Grand Duke, whom the Empress regretted seeing so angry with me. I promised this. I thought, But if she is upset that he is angry, why therefore anger him even more by recounting to him the conversation at the Summer Palace about the people who made him behave stupidly? Nevertheless this unforeseen return of intimacy on the part of the Empress made me very happy.

The following day I told the confessor's niece to thank her uncle for the exceptional service he had just rendered me in obtaining this conversation with the Empress. She returned from her uncle's home and told me that the confessor knew the Empress had said that her nephew was an idiot, but that the Grand Duchess had much intelligence. This remark was repeated to me by more than one source, as was the fact that Her Imperial Majesty did nothing but boast of my abilities among her intimates, often adding, "She loves truth and justice. She is a woman with much intelligence, but my nephew is an idiot." I shut myself up in my apartment as before, under the pretext of ill health. I remember that, at the time, I was reading the first five volumes of the *Histoire des voyages* with the map on the table, which amused and instructed me.* When I was tired of this reading, I leafed through the first volumes of the *Encyclopédie*.† I waited for the day when it would please the Empress to invite me for a second conversation. From time to time I repeated my request to Count Shuvalov, telling him I greatly wished for my fate to be decided at last.

As for the Grand Duke, I did not hear any more talk of him at all. I knew only that he was waiting for my dismissal with impatience and that he was planning for sure to marry Elizabeth Vorontsova in a second wedding. She came to his apartment and already played the hostess there. Apparently her uncle, Vice Chancellor Count Vorontsov, who was a hypocrite if ever there was one, learned of the plans that were perhaps his brother's or more likely his nephews', who were only children at the time, the eldest being barely twenty years old or thereabouts. Fearing that his newly restored favor with the Empress would suffer from this plan, he requested the task of dissuading me from requesting my dismissal. For here is what happened. One fine morning it was announced to me that Vice Chancellor Mikhail Vorontsov was asking to speak to me on behalf of the Empress. Utterly astonished by this extraordinary delegation, though not yet dressed, I had Monsieur the Vice Chancellor enter. He began by kissing my hand and squeezing it with great affection, after which he wiped his eyes, from which flowed a few tears. As at the time I had been somewhat warned against him, I did not put much faith in this prelude, which was supposed to signal his zeal, but I let him perform what I regarded as a kind of playacting. I asked him to sit down. He was a bit out of breath because of a kind of goiter from which he suffered. He sat down with me and told me that the Empress had asked him to speak with me and to dissuade me from insisting on being sent home. Her Imperial Majesty herself had ordered him to beg me on her behalf to give up this idea, to which she would never consent. In particular, he begged and beseeched me to give

---

* Abbé Prévost (1697–1763), et al., ed. *Histoire générale des voyages; ou, Nouvelle collection de toutes les relations de voyages par mer et par terre, qui ont été publiées jusqu'à présent dans les différentes langues de toutes les nations connues ... pour former un système complet d'histoire et de géographie moderne, qui representera l'état actuel de toutes les nations: enrichi de cartes géographiques ...*, 20 vols. (Paris: Chez Didot, 1746–92).

† Denis Diderot and Jean d'Alembert, *Encyclopédie ou Dictionnaire raisonné des sciences, des arts et des métiers*, 58 vols. (1751–72).

him my word not to talk about it anymore. This plan truly pained the Empress and all honorable people, among whose number he assured me that he counted. I replied to him that there was nothing that I would not do willingly to please Her Imperial Majesty and honorable people, but I believed my life and my health were in danger from the kind of life to which I was exposed. I only made people miserable, all those who drew near me were continually exiled and dismissed, the Grand Duke was poisoned against me to the point of hatred, and moreover he had never loved me. Her Imperial Majesty as well gave me almost continual signs of her disfavor, and seeing myself a burden to everyone and dying from boredom and sorrow myself, I had asked to be sent home so as to free everyone of this person who was such a burden and was wasting away from sorrow and boredom. He spoke to me of my children. I told him that I did not see them, and that since my churching ceremony I had not yet seen the youngest and could not see them without an express order from the Empress, two rooms from whom they resided, their apartment being part of hers. I did not doubt that she took excellent care of them, but being deprived of the satisfaction of seeing them, it did not matter to me whether I was a hundred steps or a hundred leagues from them. He told me that the Empress would have a second conversation with me, and he added that it was to be sincerely hoped that Her Imperial Majesty would be reconciled with me. I replied by asking him to hasten this second conversation and said that for my part, I would neglect nothing that could expedite his wish. He stayed in my room for more than an hour and spoke a long time and about many different things. I noticed that his improved favor had given him something attractive in his speech and his bearing that he did not have before, when I had considered him indistinguishable from everyone else. One day at the court, unhappy with the Empress, with political affairs, and with those who possessed Her Imperial Majesty's favor and trust, seeing that the Empress spoke at length with the Ambassador of the Empress Queen of Hungary and Bohemia while he and I and everyone were standing around bored to death, he had said to me, "What do you want to bet that she is mouthing nothing but empty phrases?" Laughing, I replied, "My God, what are you saying?" He replied in Russian with this catchphrase: "Она с природой фадайзница," "she is by her nature a speaker of empty phrases." Finally he left, assuring me of his zeal, and he took leave of me by kissing my hand once again. For the time being I was sure not to be sent away, because I was being asked not even to speak of it. But I judged it fitting not to appear in public and to continue to stay in my room, as if I expected the decision about my fate only in the second conversation that I was supposed to have with the Empress.

I waited for this conversation a long time. I remember that April 21, my birthday, I did not go out. While having dinner, the Empress informed me through Alexander Shuvalov that she was drinking to my health. I thanked her for deigning to remember me on the day, I said, of my unfortunate birth, which I would curse if on the same day I had not received baptism.* When the Grand Duke learned that the Empress had sent this message to me that day, he decided to send me the same message. When they came to give me his compliments, I got up and with a very deep bow, I expressed my thanks. After the parties for my birthday and the Empress's coronation day, which were four days apart, I again remained in my room without going out until Count Poniatowski sent me notice that the French Ambassador, Marquis de L'Hôpital, highly praised my firm conduct and said that this decision to not leave my apartment could only turn to my advantage. Taking this remark as devilish praise from an enemy, I then decided to do the opposite of what he praised, and one Sunday, when it was least expected, I dressed myself and left my private apartment. At the moment that I entered the apartment in which the ladies and gentlemen were, I saw their astonishment at seeing me. A few minutes after my appearance, the Grand Duke arrived. I saw his astonishment too, displayed on his physiognomy, and as I spoke to the group, he participated in the conversation and addressed a few remarks to me, to which I responded in a natural tone.

Meanwhile, on April 17, Prince Charles of Saxony came to Petersburg for the second time. The Grand Duke had received him the first time he had been to Russia in a sufficiently gentlemanly style. But this second time, His Imperial Highness believed himself justified in behaving without any manners toward him, and here is why. It was not a secret to the Russian army that at the battle of Zorndorf, Prince Charles of Saxony had been one of the first to flee. It was even said that he had continued this flight without stopping until Landsberg. Now, having heard this, His Imperial Highness decided that as the man was an avowed coward, he would not speak to him, nor did he want anything to do with him. There is every indication that the Princess of Courland, the daughter of Biron, of whom

---

* Princess Sophie was baptized on April 23, 1729.

I have already often had occasion to speak, contributed more than a little to this, because at the time, people had begun to whisper that the plan was to make Prince Charles of Saxony a Duke of Courland, which greatly angered the Princess of Courland, whose father was still held at Yaroslavl.* She conveyed her animosity to the Grand Duke, over whom she had maintained some influence. At the time, this Princess was promised for the third time, to Baron Alexander Cherkasov, whom she in fact married the following winter.†

Finally, a few days before going to the country, Count Alexander Shuvalov came to say on behalf of the Empress that I should request through him to see my children that afternoon and that afterward, leaving their room, I would have this second, long-promised interview with the Empress.‡ I did as I was told, and in the presence of many people I told Count Shuvalov to ask Her Imperial Majesty for permission to see my children. He left, and when he returned, he said that at three o'clock I could. I was very punctual. I stayed with my children until Count Alexander Shuvalov came to tell me that the Empress was available. I went to her room. I found her all alone, and this time there was no screen in the room. She and I could therefore speak freely. I began by thanking her for the audience that she was according me, telling her that the very gracious promise of it that she had deigned to make had in itself brought me back to life. After this, she said to me, "I demand that you tell me the truth about everything I shall ask you." I replied by assuring her that she would hear only the most exact truth from my mouth and that I asked no more than to open my heart to her without any restriction of any kind. Then she asked me again if truly there had been only these three letters written to Apraksin. I swore this to her with the greatest truthfulness, for indeed it was so. Then she asked me for details about the Grand Duke's life.

* Prince Charles became Duke of Courland on November 16, 1758, and was invested on January 8, 1759.

† Catherine dedicated part 2 of her middle memoir to him.

‡ May 23, 1758.

CATHERINE'S OUTLINE, 1756–59

Return to town. The chevalier W[illiams] departs. Count P[oniatowski] returns as the minister from Pol[and] toward the **end of 1756.** The assignations continue on the same footing. The intrigues of Brockdorff and the Holstein entourage, a number of officers from this country in the Grand Duke's chambers. What he thinks of Russia, his lies; the Elendsheim affair, my opposition to his arrest; he is arrested just as Holmer had been, without evidence, with neither an accuser nor an accusation; my views on this subject. **Beginning in 1757.** Continuation of the Grand Duke's affairs with Madame Teplova, with Countess Vorontsova, with the Princess of Courland, the danger she risked; Marshal Razumovsky's affair with Madame Naryshkina; Lev N[aryshkin's] promise, how they wanted to marry him off and how he . . . How we went one day . . . to Marshal Razumovsky's home one day during Lent, and how . . . Departure for the country, Pechlin's death, Stambke's arrival. In the month of July news of the capture of Memel by the treaty of June 24th. In the month of August, news of the battle of Gros Jägerndorf, which had occurred on the 19th of the same month. I held a party in my garden on the day of the Te Deum, which consisted of a large dinner, and a roast ox for my garden workers and for the masons, who were building a man-made mountain. In the autumn, conversation with the Emp[ress] at the Summer Palace. Retreat of Marshal Apraksin, which has the appearance of flight. Why. Sinister explanation. His difficulties, my letters at the request of the Grand Chancellor. The Marshal does not answer. **Winter of 1757. Beginning of 1758,** the dispatch of Fermor, capture of Königsberg on January 18th. Marshal Apraksin is taken to Triruki. His trial, his death. General Lieven, mixed up in this affair. His devotion to me, what he says about this to Count Pon[iatowski] at Count Esterhazy's masked ball. Arrival of Prince Charles of Saxony. New pregnancy. How he was received, the Grand Duke barely honors him, hardly talks to him; the Princess of Courland's part in this. Prince Charles joins the army. Departure for Oranienbaum, the party that I give there for . . . the effect of this party.* His Imperial Highness reattaches himself to Countess Vorontsova, he increasingly shuns me; the party I give at Oranienbaum, the effect of this party. How Lev turns his back on me in the spring of this year, how he attaches himself to the Grand Duke, how his sister-in-law and I whipped him. The Empress's suffering over the Battle of Zorndorf; it is declared won; the truth was that both sides were beaten, the Te Deum is not sung until the third day, our troops however sang it on the battlefield. The Emp[ress] on the Battle of Zorndorf. *Count Schwerin, the adjutant general of the King of Prussia is taken prisoner. Fermor gives Lieutenant Captain Grigory Orlov the order to take this prisoner of war to Petersburg.*† The Empress goes from Peterhof to Tsarskoe Selo; what happens to her on September 8th, the day of the Virgin's Nativity, how I learn about it.‡ Return to town. I do not appear in public, believing that I am close to giving birth; I am off by a month; what Lev N[aryshkin] comes to tell me about my pregnancy in October. Why I had my big bed removed and thereafter only slept in my little bed and this in another room. October, news of the recall of Count P[oniatowski]. Count Bestuzhev's anger about this, my delivery in December,§ celebrations of this, fireworks on **January 1st, 1759.** How Peter Shuvalov brings me the plan for the fireworks, where I hide my company and how I receive him. During carnival three weddings at court, disastrous weddings of L[ev] N[aryshkin], of Strogonov, and of B[uturlin];** bets about these, who of the three would first be cuckolded. Arrest of Count Bestuzhev,†† of my jeweler Bernardi, of Elagin, Adadurov; Shkurin's secret contacts, which fail. The Grand Duke no longer comes into my chambers. Discovery of Stambke's and Count Pon[iatowski's] secret contacts with Count Bestuzhev, dismissal of Stambke; the affairs of Holstein are taken from me, someone named Wolff is brought in, they are given to him. The Grand Duke is made to fear speaking to me during the Bestuzhev affair. How I wanted to go to the Comédie Russe and how they wanted to keep me from going there, how I wanted to write to the Emp[ress] about why they wanted to keep me from going. I am warned that there is talk of dismissing me, my decision concerning this. I demand to be dismissed. I write of this to the Empress, what this letter contained; I say that I am sick and no longer go out. I am

---

* June 17, 1757.

† Catherine crossed out what she used in the memoir. Whatever she did not cross out is in italics.

‡ Elizabeth has a stroke on September 8, 1757.

§ December 9, 1757. Her daughter, Anna Petrovna, died on March 8, 1759; she never mentions her daughter's death anywhere.

** February 18 and 22, 1758.

†† February 14, 1758.

alone in my chambers, I read five volumes of the *Histoire des voyages* with the map on the table and the *Encyclopédie* for my amusement. The Empress has me informed that she wants to speak to me. The Grand Duke learned of this, he became jealous of it and demands to be present at this conversation. How this conversation took place.* The Empress's conduct, her words, her actions, the Grand Duke's conduct on this occasion, mine, how I began upon entering. What the Empress said to me while approaching her toiletry table, what I replied to her. She dismisses us, what Alexander Shuvalov comes to tell me on her behalf. How I reply. How she sends Count Vorontsov to me a short time later. The Prince of Saxony returns to Petersburg after the Battle of Zorndorf,† how he had fled to Landsberg; because of his cowardice, the Grand Duke does not speak to him, nor does he wish to have anything to do with him. There is talk of making Prince Charles Duke of Courland, the Princess of Courland makes the Grand Duke angry at Prince Charles; third engagement of the Princess of Courland with Cherkasov. *How the Grand Duke wanted to go to Holstein, what he did to this end, what was done, how I was told about it; what I said, what Count Vorontsov told me about it, this should be put at the **end of 1759**. Departure for the country;‡ before this second conversation with the Emp[ress] in private, the Empress's decision about my situation.§ This was the day following Prince Charles's visit to our residence, what Count P[oniatowski] said to me rather loudly upon departing was heard, I think, by Brockdorff, who was quite near us. I take the waters, where I stay. How Count P[oniatowski] is arrested leaving my residence.** Brockdorff speaks of killing him. Lev N[aryshkin] advises giving him to Count Ale[xander] Sh[uvalov], who hands him to his son-in-law and leaves for Peterhof. Ivan Sh[uvalov] advises him to have him released, which he does. Ale[xander] Sh[uvalov] comes the following day to tell me what happened overnight, I knew nothing of it, the Grand Duke comes to my chambers, speaks to me, they had appeased him because they did not want any rupture, ~~he proposes that I see~~, demands that I see Countess Eliz[abeth] V[orontsova]. She comes to my chambers, I remain in bed all day, quite overcome. The evening of the following day, I receive from Alex[ander] Sh[uvalov] a note from the Empress, written in the hand of Ivan Sh[uvalov] and signed Eli[zabeth], in which she begs me not to be distressed and to come to Peterhof for the feast of St. Peter as if nothing had happened. I reply to this and show her my heartfelt gratitude. I go to Peterhof. During the St. Peter's day ball, Count Rzewuski says to me: my friend asked me to tell you that by the channel of La Grelée and that of Count Branicki, everything is arranged and that this evening he hopes to have the pleasure of seeing you in the Grand Duke's chambers. Now, he had never been there. I replied to Count Rzewuski: tell your friend that I find this conclusion*

---

* April 13, 1758.
† August 14, 1758 (n.s.).
‡ May 30, 1758.
§ May 23, 1758.
** June 25/July 6, 1758.

*completely ridiculous and that [a mountain has given birth to a mouse].** *Back from [supper]
I went to bed without hearing discussion of anything. Between two and three in the morning
I heard the curtain of my bed being drawn and I awoke with a start, it was the Grand Duke,
who told me to get up and follow him; whom I find in his chambers.† There we all are, the best
friends in the world. How until Count P[oniatowski's] departure, the Grand Duke spent two
and three evenings per week in my circle and drunk my English beer; so that as a result of this
episode and that of the following winter there was no trust to be had in His Imperial High
ness in anything, and things took such a turn* that it was necessary to perish with him,
by him, or else to try to save oneself from the wreckage and to save my children,
and the state.‡

---

* Horace, *Ars Poetica*, 1. 139.
† In his memoirs (1: 327–31), Poniatowski describes how the Grand Duke and his drunken
party met him as he arrived at Oranienbaum to see Catherine. After snide comments by his
mistress, the Grand Duke had him detained as he was leaving. The Grand Duke "first asked me
in clear terms whether I had . . . his wife. I told him no." The Grand Duke brought in Alexander
Shuvalov as head of the Secret Chancery, to whom Poniatowski said, "I believe that you understand, Monsieur, that it is absolutely crucial for the honor of your own court that all of this end
with as little fuss as possible and you get me out of here as soon as possible." Shuvalov agreed,
and gave Poniatowski a carriage to leave. Two days later he received a note from Catherine,
indicating "that she had taken several steps to win over her husband's mistress." Catherine told
him to meet her at Peterhof, where she would be with the court for St. Peter's Day, June
29/July 11, 1758. That evening Catherine finds Poniatowski in the Grand Duke's chamber.
‡ This passage appears in final memoirs before what should be the end of 1757 (before the
birth of her daughter), but which Catherine mistakenly thinks is 1758. Here it comes after the
middle of 1758, or what Catherine thinks is 1759.

Appendices

GENEALOGICAL TABLE, THE HOUSE OF ROMANOV*

Maria Dolgorukova (d. 1626) = **Michael I** (1596–1645, r. 1613–45) = Evdokia Streshneva (d. 1645) 10 children; 4 outlived her

Maria Miloslavskaia (1625–69) = **Alexei** (1629–76, r. 1645–76) = Natalia Naryshkina (1651–94)

2. **Ekaterina Skavronska** (**Catherine I, 1684–17   , r. 1725–27**)

Peter² (1704?)
Paul² (1705?)
Ekaterina (1706–8)

Peter I, "the Great," (1672–1725, r. 1682–1725) = 1. Evdokia Lopukhina (1669–1731);
Natalia (1673–1716) Charlotte of Brunswick-Wolfenbüttel (1694–1715) = Alexei (1690–1718)
Feodora (1674–78)   Alexander (1691–92)
                                                                           Paul² (1692?)

Natalia (1714–28)
Peter II (1715–30, r. 1727–30) /
Ekaterina Dolgorukaia

Karl Friedrich of Holstein = Anna (1708–28)
(1700–39)

Elizabeth I (1709–61, r. ■41–61)
Maria (1713–15)
Margarita (1714–15)
Peter (1715–19)
Paul (1717)
Natalia (1718–25)

Dmitry (1649–51)
Evdokia (1650–1712)
Marfa (1652–1707)
Alexei (1654–70)
Anna (1655–59)
Sophia (1657–1704) / Vasily Golitsyn (d. 1713)
Ekaterina (1658–1718)
Maria (1660–1723)
Fedor III (1661–82, r. 1676–82) = 1. Agafia Grushchetsky (d. 1681)
Feodosia (1662–1713)   2. Marfa Apraksina (1664–1715)
Simeon (1665–69)
Ivan V (1666–96, r. 1682–96) = Praskovia Salrykova (1664–1723)
Evdokia (1669)   Maria (1689–92)
                                           Feodosia (1690–1)
                                           Ekaterina (1692–1733)
Karl Leopold of Mecklenburg =   **Anna Ivanovna** (1693–1740, r. 1730–40) = Friedrich Wilhelm of Kurland (1692–1711)
                                           Praskovia (1694–1731)

Anton Ulrich of = Anna Leopoldovna (1718–46,
Brunswick-Wolfenbüttel │ **Regent 1740–41**
(1714–74)   │ (Anna Karlovna, Elisabeth-Katharina)

Ivan VI (1740–64, r. 1740–41)
Ekaterina (1741–1807)
Elizaveta (1743–82)
Peter (1745–98)
Alexei (1746–87)

Catherine II (the Great), (1729–96, r. 1762–96) = **Peter III** (1728–62, r. 1761–62)
Count Stanislaw Poniatowski / **Paul I** (1754–1801, r. 1796–1801) = 1. Natalia Alexeevna (1755–76)
Count Grigory Orlov /   (Wilhelmina of Hessen-Darmstadt)
                          Anna (1757–59)   2. Maria Fedorovna (1759–1828)
                          Count Alexei Bobrinsky   (Sophie Dorothea Auguste of Würtemburg)
                          (1762–1813)

Elizaveta Alexeevna (1779–1826) = **Alexander I** (1777–1825, r. 1801–25)
(Louise Maria of Baden–Baden)   Konstantin (1779–1831) = 1. Anna Fedorovna (Juliane of Sachsen-Ko▨urg)
Alexandra Fedorovna (1798–1860) = **Nicholas I** (1796–1855, r. 1825–55)   2. Countess Johanna Grudzinska
(Charlotte of Prussia)   **Alexander II** (1818–81, r. 1855–81) = 1. Maria Alexandrovna (1823–89)
Duke of Leichtenberg = Maria (1819–76)   (Marie of Hessen-Darmstadt)
King of Würtemburg = Olga (1822–92)   2. Countess Iurevskaia (1849–▨22)

---

*Russians often refer to their rulers by name and patronymic; Eliz-
abeth I is Elizaveta Petrovna. See LeDonne, "Ruling Families,"
260–61; *Memoiren*, trans. Böhme, vol.2; Hughes, *Peter the Great,* xxi;
http://members.surfeu.fi/thaapanen/index.html. Symbols:
= marriage/lower.

GENEALOGICAL TABLE, THE HOUSE OF SCHLESWIG-HOLSTEIN-GOTTORP*

Prince Christian Albrecht (1641–94, r. 1659–94) = Friederike Amalie of Denmark (1649–1704)

Friedrich IV (1671–1702, r. 1695–1702) = Hedwig Sophie of Sweden (1681–1708)

Karl Friedrich (1700–39, r. 1702–8) = Anna Petrovna of Russia (1708–28)

Karl Peter Ulrich (Peter III, 1728–62, r. 1761–62) = Sophie Auguste Friederike of Anhalt-Zerbst (Catherine II)

Christian August (1673–1726) = Albertine Friederike of Baden-Durlach (1682–1755)

Hedwig Sophie Auguste (1705–64)
Karl August (1706–27) = Elizaveta Petrovna of Russia (Elizabeth I, 1709–61)
Friederike Amalie (1708–31)
Anna (1709–68) = Wilhelm of Sachsen-Gotha
Adolf Friedrich (King of Sweden, 1710–71, r. 1751–71) =
Luise Ulrike of Prussia (1720–82)
August Friedrich (1711–85, Duke of Oldenburg 1775–77) =
Friederike of Hessen-Kassel | Peter Friedrich Wilhelm
Johanna Elisabeth (1712–60)   Luise
Friederike Sophie (1713)   Hedwig Sophie Charlotte
Wilhelm Christian (1716–19)
Friedrich Konrad (1718)
Georg Ludwig (1719–63) = Sophie of Schleswig-Holstein-Sonderburg-Beck

Gustav III of Sweden (1746–92)
Charles XIII of Sweden (1748–1818)
Friedrich Adolf
Sophie Albertine

Marie Elisabeth (1678–1755)

Prince Christian August of Anhalt-Zerbst (1690–1747, r. 1742–47) =

1. Karoline Wilhelmine Sophie of Hessen-Kassel
2. Friederike Auguste Sophie of Anhalt-Bernburg

Sophie Auguste Friederike (1729–96)
(Catherine II, 1762–96)
Wilhelm Christian Friedrich (1730–42)
Friedrich August (1734–93, r. 1747–93) =

Auguste Christiane Charlotte (1736)
Elisabeth Ulrike (1742–45)

Friedrich (1751–52)
Wilhelm (1753–74)
Peter Friedrich Ludwig (1755–1829, Grand Duke of Oldenburg, 1823–29) =
Friederike of Würtemberg (1765–85)

Prince Friedrich of Hessen-Kassel = Alexandra (1825–44)
    (née Ekaterina Dolgorukaia) |
Nikolai (1831–91)   3 children
Mikhail (1832–1903)   8 children, including
Maria Fedorovna (1847–1928) = Alexander III (1845–94, r. 1881–94)
    (Dagmar of Denmark) |
Alexandra Fedorovna (1872–1918) = Nicholas II (1868–1918, r. 1894–1917)
    (Alisa of Hessen-Darmstadt) |5 children

Sophie Amalie (1670–1710) =
August Wilhelm of Brunswick-Wolfenbüttel

---

*Catherine's and Peter's genealogies
can be found in *Memoiren*, trans.
Böhme, vol. 2; Alexander, *Catherine
the Great*, 18; and http://www
.ThePeerage.com.

TABLE OF RANKS AND CHIVALRIC ORDERS

In the eighteenth century, Russian noble status depended on the combination of family, noble title, service rank, profession, wealth, and education. The importance of these factors that accorded prestige was for the most part unspoken, yet essential for understanding individuals and their relationships. This brief note explains the nature of noble rank, a phenomenon that is central to the personal and political maneuvering described in Catherine's memoirs. Although Catherine's familiar tone gives the impression that she is quite like us, at the same time, the terms in which she thought of herself and others were utterly different.

Throughout the eighteenth and nineteenth centuries, the Russian nobility comprised a mere 1.5 percent of the population, ranging from titled landowners to impoverished, landless civil servants, and distinguished as an estate by legal privileges.[1] In 1722, in his drive to modernize Russia, Peter the Great instituted the Table of Ranks to create a sufficient and able bureaucracy and army. He forced the nobility to serve the state in order to acquire service rank (*chin*), which became the determining factor of social identity. He also allowed non-nobles to attain noble ranks through their service. The importance of service rank is apparent in the fact that a nobleman without it was technically a minor, though still a noble. After 1762, even though nobles no longer had to serve, most did in order to gain rank.

There were fourteen ranks in the military, civil service, and the court, which remained in effect from 1722 until 1917. Fourteen was the lowest rank and one was the highest. Given equal ranks, military rank was superior to court rank, which in turn was superior to the civil service, and the jobs assigned to ranks changed greatly over time. All ranks in the military and classes eight to one in the civil service endowed individuals with either personal or hereditary nobility.

With rare exceptions, women did not serve in positions in the military or government that accorded them service rank, and therefore historians of the Russian nobility generally ignore noblewomen. A noble woman's rank derived first from her father's rank and then from her husband's, and her rank was in relation to her mother and later to other wives. However, in the Russian court that comprises the world of Catherine's memoirs, noblewomen could acquire their own rank through serving in the personal courts of Empress Elizabeth and Grand Duchess Catherine.[2]

Service rank visibly upheld the privileges of the nobility and distinguished nobles from non-nobles, in a period when nobility no longer depended solely on birth. The rules on rank governed all aspects of the appearance of nobles in public, from forms of address, access to events, and precedence, to clothing, carriages, and livery, with fines for acting or dressing above one's rank.[3] Only certain informal occasions were declared rank-free, and Catherine composed her "Rules" to describe proper conduct at such a gathering. Otherwise, rank shaped all ceremonial activity at the court. In the memoirs, once Catherine becomes Grand Duchess, she supersedes her mother in rank, which creates friction between them. As Catherine explains in the final memoir, "My mother, whom I had always obeyed, did not see without displeasure that I preceded her, which I avoided everywhere that I could, but which was impossible in public." According to both Catherine's early and middle memoirs, the day after their arrival in Moscow on February 9, 1744, Empress Elizabeth I presented first Catherine and then her mother, Princess Johanna, with the Order of St. Catherine (41, 449). In contrast, the account that Princess Johanna wrote for her husband stresses that the Empress presented the order "to me first together with the star and afterward to my daughter."[4] Status was integral to noble identity, especially at court, for women as well as men.

Beginning in 1699, upon his return from the Grand Embassy to Europe (1697–98), Peter the Great instituted chivalric orders, modeled on European orders, as rewards for service to the state. Like rank, orders were meant to connote individual merit through service, and to supplant a system of precedence through noble birth. The symbol of an order was a medal with a motto; the addition of diamonds and a wide, colored ribbon signified the highest degrees of these orders, with the first degree a ribbon worn over the shoulder, and the second degree a ribbon around the neck. Most orders had uniforms, anniversary gatherings, dues, pensions, charters that limited the number of members, and a chief knight. With the exception of the Order of St. Catherine, which was for women only (although Catherine I had awarded it to her favorite, Alexander Menshikov), with rare exceptions, all the orders were for men. Unlike rank, orders did not confer privileges, but orders correlated with ranks and thus might be accompanied by promotions in rank and position. In the memoirs, Catherine hints that her opponents have bought Lev Naryshkin's loyalty with the inducement of getting the Order of St. Anna.

Details of Catherine's coup in 1762 reveal the symbolic power of orders. On the eve of Catherine's coup, the rumor that Peter III had presented his mistress, Elizabeth Vorontsova, with the Order of St. Catherine added urgency to Catherine's decision to seize power. As Princess Ekaterina Dashkova (née Vorontsova, sister of Elizabeth) writes in her memoirs, the Order of St. Catherine could "be given only to members of the Imperial family and to princesses of foreign ruling houses, unless a woman had saved the ruler's person or rendered a notable service to the nation."[5] In other words, it signaled that Peter was preparing to depose Catherine and force her into a convent or prison, and make Elizabeth his consort. During the coup, as Catherine dressed to meet the guard regiments, she removed the Order of St. Catherine, which she then presented to Dashkova, who meanwhile procured for Catherine the blue ribbon of the Order of St. Andrei from Count Nikita Panin, which she then wore over her guard's uniform. Again Dashkova explains that "the blue ribbon was not worn by the Emperor's wife." Thus it indicated that Catherine now ruled. Such details in portraits of the Russian nobility and royalty clearly had important state functions. Thus in the final memoir, in a verbal self-portrait, Catherine calls herself "an honest and loyal knight," for she was a knight of the orders of St. Catherine, St. Andrei, St. George, and St. Vladimir.

Stepping outside this well-developed system of elite status, we find the undistinguished masses in three groups: merchants, clergy, and peasants and serfs. In the opening maxim of the memoir translated here, Catherine refers to the "common herd." Her term in French, *le vulgaire*, refers to a traditional notion, the Greek *hoi polloi*, the Latin *profanum* or *ignobile vulgus* and *mobile vulgus*, or Shakespeare's "beast with many heads."[6] In this memoir, she illustrates her highly restricted view of society when she writes:

> One of the masked balls was for the court alone and those whom the Empress deigned to admit; the other was for all the titled people in the city to the rank of colonel and those who served as officers in the guards. Sometimes the entire nobility and the wealthiest merchants were also permitted to come. The court balls did not exceed 150 to 200 people and those that were called public, 800 maskers.

In contrast to our understanding of the term "public" today, for Catherine it was limited to those who had the right to appear at court. It is worth remembering that when Catherine was writing these memoirs, French citizens had beheaded Louis XVI and American electors had elected their first president with 69 out of 138 votes. Catherine's memoirs belong to a world of status and rank whose foundations were crumbling elsewhere, but which survived in Russia until 1917, and arguably survives there to the present day. Catherine's era truly was the golden age of the nobility.

TABLE OF RANKS

The laws governing the Table of Ranks were periodically modified, and the simplified chart below represents the positions by class over the course of the eighteenth century.[7] Nineteen additional points to the Table of Ranks detail ranks for women, privileges, responsibilities, and punishments. Military ranks here correspond to those in the army. At the end of the eighteenth century, the complete table breaks down military ranks in the following order: guards (foot soldiers and cavalry), army (foot soldiers and cavalry), dragoons, Cossacks, artillery, and navy.[8] For example, the rank of major in the guards was two classes above that in the army (class 6 and class 8, respectively). Laws limited advancement by the number of places in each class and the minimum number of years someone had to spend in a class. It was possible to occupy a class above or below one's profession, or service rank, and advance despite restrictions.

Class	Military	Civil Court	Men[9]	Women[10]
1	Field Marshal	Chancellor	——	——
2	General in Chief	Vice Chancellor Actual Privy Counselor	Chief Chamberlain Chief Marshal Chief Steward Chief Cup-Bearer Chief Master of the Hunt Chief Equerry	Chief Stewardess
3	Lieutenant General	Procurator General Privy Counselor	Marshal Steward Master of the Hunt Equerry Chief Master of Ceremonies	Actual Lady-in-Waiting Stewardess
4	Major General	Actual State Counselor	Chamberlain	Lady-in-Waiting
5	Brigadier	State Counselor	Master of Ceremonies Gentleman of the Bedchamber	Maid of the Bedchamber
6	Colonel	Collegiate Counselor	Purveyor of the Bedchamber	Court Maid of Honor / Maid of Honor
7	Lieutenant Colonel	Court Counselor	——	——
8	Major	Collegiate Assessor	——	——

Class	Military	Civil Court	Men	Women
9	Captain	Titular Counselor	Court Purveyor	———
10	Lieutenant Captain	Collegiate Secretary	———	———
11		Naval Secretary	———	———
12	Lieutenant	Government Secretary	———	———
13	Second Lieutenant	Provincial Secretary	———	———
14	Standard-Bearer	Collegiate Registrar	———	———

CHIVALRIC ORDERS

The orders are listed according to the general hierarchy of their importance; the complete list would include the degrees of each order in relation to each other.[11] Russia also added several foreign orders, some of which dated to the Crusades.

Order (year founded, Russianized)	Color of ribbon	Motto[12]
St. Andrei (1699)	Blue	For truth and loyalty
St. George (1769)	Orange/black stripes	For service and bravery
St. Vladimir (1782)	Red/black stripes	Usefulness, honor, and bravery
St. Catherine (1714)	Red, silver edge	For love and fatherland
St. Alexander Nevsky (1725)	Red	For deeds and fatherland
Foreign orders		
St. Anna (1736, 1742)[13]	Red, yellow edge	Lover of truth, virtue, and loyalty
White Eagle (1325, 1831)	Light blue	For truth, czar, and law
St. Stanislav (1765, 1831)	Red, double white edge	Reward and encourage
St. John/Knights of Malta (1098, 1797)	Black	Honor and kindness

NOTES

1. Privileges included (1) the right to own land occupied by serfs (until their emancipation in 1861), (2) the right not to serve in the government or military (from 1762 to 1874, when universal military conscription became law) and preference in service for those who did serve, (3) freedom from corporal punishment (until 1863), (4) exemp-

tion from the poll tax (until 1883), (5) the right to be judged by peers (given to all Russians in judicial reforms of 1864, together with due process for life, status, and property), and (6) the right to travel abroad (restricted under Nicholas I). Paul I suspended the second and third privileges from 1796 to 1801, which led to his murder in 1801.

2. In 1725, at Peter the Great's funeral, Catherine I's ladies-in-waiting preceded the wives of men of the first eight ranks. Hughes, *Russia in the Age of Peter the Great,* 194.

3. Ibid., 180–85. Sumptuary laws regulated, for example, the type of fabric and the width of lace, a luxury item, nobles of each rank were allowed to wear.

4. Anthony, *Memoirs,* 81.

5. Princess Dachkova, *Mon histoire: mémoires d'une femme de lettres russe à l'époque des Lumières,* ed. Alexander Woronzoff-Dashkoff, Catherine Le Gouis, and Catherine Woronzoff-Dashkoff (Paris: L'Harmattan, 1999), 44.

6. Barbara Ann Kipfer, ed., *Roget's International Thesaurus,* 6th ed. (New York: Harper-Collins, 2001), 444 (606.2).

7. "Tabel' o rangakh," no. 3890, January 24, 1722, *Polnoe sobranie zakonov Rossiiskoi Imperii, 1649–1913,* vol. 6 (St. Petersburg, 1830–1916), 486–93. The most recent full discussion of the Table of Ranks is L. E. Shepelev, *Chinovnyi mir Rossii: XVIII-nachalo XIX v.* (St. Petersburg: Iskusstvo-SPB, 2001). In English, Smith, *Love and Conquest,* 403–4; Paul Dukes, trans. and ed., *Russia Under Catherine the Great,* vol. 1 (Newtonville, Mass.: Oriental Research Partners, 1978), 4–14.

8. Shepelev, *Chinovnyi mir,* 150.

9. Ibid., 399–401. There is little information about the actual ranks of men's and women's court titles by the end of the eighteenth century, although the Table of Ranks lists positions for all men's ranks.

10. Ibid., 410–11. The Table of Ranks initially included additional titles, which were simplified over the course of the century. In the eighteenth century, a total of eighty-two women held these positions. Maids of honor were not married, and had the privilege of being given in marriage with a dowry by the Empress; most came from court families, while a third were from the titled nobility. Once married, they retired from the court, though they retained the right to appear at court. Ladies-in-waiting and above were usually wives of important men in the military or civil service, and were also knights of the Order of St. Catherine. The most extensive information on women at the Russian court is P. F. Karabanov, "Stats-damy i freiliny russkago dvora v XVIII i XIX stoletiiakh," *Russkaia starina* 2 (1870): 443–73; 3 (1871): 39–48, 272–82, 457–73; 4 (1871): 59–67, 379–404.

11. Shepelev, *Chinovnyi mir,* 346.

12. Ibid., 341–42.

13. In 1736, the Duke of Holstein-Gottorp established the Order of St. Anna in honor of his wife, Anna Petrovna, and it was added to Russian orders by Empress Elizabeth I, Anna's younger sister, in 1742.

BIBLIOGRAPHY

Alexander, John T. "Catherine II (Ekaterina Alekseevna), 'The Great,' Empress of Russia." *Early Modern Russian Writers: The Late Seventeenth and Eighteenth Centuries*, edited by Marcus C. Levitt, 43–54. Dictionary of Literary Biography. Vol. 150. Detroit: Bruccoli Clark Layman and Gale Research, 1995.

———. *Catherine the Great: Life and Legend*. New York: Oxford University Press, 1989.

———. "Ivan Shuvalov and Russian Court Politics, 1749–63." *Literature, Lives, and Legality in Catherine's Russia*, edited by A. G. Cross and G. S. Smith, 1–13. Nottingham, England: Astra Press, 1994.

Anisimov, Evgenii. *Elizaveta Petrovna*. Moscow: Molodaia gvardiia, 1999.

———. *Empress Elizabeth: Her Reign and Her Russia, 1741–1761*. Translated and edited by John T. Alexander. Gulf Breeze, Fla.: Academic International Press, 1995.

Babich, I. V., M. V. Babich, and T. A. Lapteva, eds. *Ekaterina II: Annotirovannaia bibliografiia publikatsii*. Moscow: ROSSPEN, 2004.

Beasley, Faith. *Revising Memory: Women's Fiction and Memoirs in Seventeenth-Century France*. New Brunswick, N.J.: Rutgers University Press, 1990.

Bil'bassov, Vasilii A. "The Intellectual Formation of Catherine II." *Catherine the Great: A Profile*, edited by Marc Raeff, 21–40. New York: Hill and Wang, 1972.

———. *Istoriia Ekateriny vtoroi*. Vols. 1–2. St. Petersburg, 1890–91; Vol. 12. Berlin, 1896.

Buckley, Veronica. *Christina, Queen of Sweden*. London: Fourth Estate, 2004.

Catherine II. *Correspondance de Catherine Alexéievna, Grande-Duchesse de Russie, et de*

Sir Charles H. Williams, Ambassadeur d'Angleterre, 1756 et 1757. Edited by Serge Goriaïnow. Moscow, 1909.

———. *Correspondence of Catherine the Great with Sir Charles Hanbury-Williams and Letters from Count Poniatowski.* Translated and edited by Earl of Ilchester and Mrs. Langford-Brooke. London: Thornton Butterworth, 1928.

———. *Katharina II in ihren Memoiren.* Translated and edited by Dr. Erich Böhme. 1920. Reprint, Frankfurt am Main: Suhrkamp, 1972.

———. *Memoiren der Kaiserin Katharina II.* Translated by Erich Böhme. 2 vols. Leipzig, 1913.

———. Memoirs. Secret Packet. Fond 1, catalog 1, documents 20–23. Russian State Archive of Ancient Documents (RGADA), Moscow.

———. *Memoirs of Catherine the Great.* Translated by Katharine Anthony. New York: Alfred A. Knopf, 1927.

———. *Sochineniia Imperatritsy Ekateriny II.* Edited by A. N. Pypin. 12 vols. St. Petersburg: Imperial Academy of Sciences, 1901–7.

———. *Two Comedies by Catherine the Great, Empress of Russia.* Translated and edited by Lurana Donnels O'Malley. Amsterdam: Harwood Academic Publishers, 1998.

Christina, queen of Sweden. "La Vie de la Reine Christine faite par Elle-même, dédiée à Dieu." *Mémoires concernant Christine, reine de Suède,* edited by Johann Arckenholtz. Vol. 3. Amsterdam and Leipzig: P. Mortier, 1759.

Cross, Anthony. "Catherine the Great: Views from the Distaff Side." *Russia in the Age of the Enlightenment: Essays for Isabel de Madariaga.* Edited by Roger Bartlett and Janet Hartley, 203–21. New York: St. Martin's Press, 1990.

d'Alembert, Jean Le Rond. *Oeuvres complètes de d'Alembert.* Vol. 2. Geneva: Slatkine Reprints, 1967.

———. *Oeuvres et correspondances inédites de d'Alembert.* Edited by Charles Henry. Geneva: Slatkine Reprints, 1967.

d'Encausse, Hélène Carrère, ed. *L'Impératrice et l'Abbé: Un duel littéraire inédit entre Catherine II et l'Abbé Chappe d'Auteroche.* Paris: Fayard, 2003.

———. *Catherine II: Un âge d'or pour la Russie.* Paris: Fayard, 2002.

Dashkova, Princess Ekaterina. *The Memoirs of Princess Dashkova.* Translated and edited by Kyril Fitzlyon. London: John Calder, 1956. Reprint, with an introduction by Jehanne M. Gheith, Durham, N.C.: Duke University Press, 1995.

———. *Mon histoire: mémoires d'une femme de lettres russe à l'époque des Lumières.* Edited by Alexander Woronzoff-Dashkoff, Catherine LeGouis, and Catherine Woronzoff-Dashkoff. Paris: L'Harmattan, 1999.

Dawson, Ruth. "Perilous Royal Biography: Representations of Catherine II Immediately After Her Seizure of the Throne." *Biography* 27.3 (Summer 2004): 517–34.

DeJean, Joan. "Classical Reeducation: Decanonizing the Feminine." *The Politics of*

Tradition: Placing Women in French Literature, edited by Joan DeJean and Nancy K. Miller. Yale French Studies, no. 75, 26–39. New Haven, Conn.: Yale University Press, 1988.

Diderot, Denis. *Diderot: Édition critique et annotée.* 25 vols. Paris: Hermann, 1975– .

Dixon, Simon. *Catherine the Great.* New York: Longman, 2001.

———. "The Posthumous Reputation of Catherine II in Russia, 1797–1837." *Slavonic and East European Review* 77.4 (October 1999): 646–79.

———. "Catherine the Great and the Romanov Dynasty: The Case of the Grand Duchess Mariia Pavlovna (1854–1920)." *Russian Society and Culture and the Long Eighteenth Century: Essays in Honour of Anthony G. Cross,* edited by Roger Bartlett and Lindsey Hughes, 195–208. Münster, Germany: LIT Verlag, 2004.

Dukes, Paul. *Russia under Catherine the Great.* 2 vols. Newtonville, Mass.: Oriental Research Partners, 1977.

Eidel'man, N. Ia. "Memuary Ekateriny II—odna iz raskrytykh tain samoderzhaviia." *Voprosy istorii* 1 (1968): 149–60.

Ezell, Margaret J. M. *Social Authorship and the Advent of Print.* Baltimore: Johns Hopkins University Press, 1999.

Fainshtein, M., and F. Göpfert, eds. *Katharina II: Eine russische Schriftstellerin,* FrauenLiteraturGeschichte, vol. 5. Wilhelmshorst: Verlag F. K. Göpfert, 1996.

Fedorchenko, V. *Imperatorskii dom: Vydaiushchiesia sanovniki.* 2 vols. Moscow: Olma-Press, 2000.

Frederick II. *L'Histoire de mon temps.* Vol. 1, *Oeuvres posthumes de Frédéric II, Roi de Prusse.* Berlin, 1788.

Gavrilova, L. M. "Istochniki 'Zapisok kasatel'no rossiiskoi istorii' Ekateriny II." *Vspomogatel'nye istoricheskie ditsipliny* 20 (1989): 164–74.

Golitsyn, Prince N. N. *Bibliograficheskii slovar' russkikh pisatel'nits.* 1889. Reprint, Leipzig: Zentralantiquariat der Deutschen Demokratischen Republik, 1974.

Goodman, Dena. *The Republic of Letters: A Cultural History of the French Enlightenment.* Ithaca, N.Y.: Cornell University Press, 1994.

Goodman, Dena, ed. *Marie-Antoinette: Writing on the Body of a Queen.* New York: Routledge, 2003.

Gossman, Lionel. "Marginal Writing." *A New History of French Literature,* edited by Denis Hollier, 381. Cambridge, Mass.: Harvard University Press, 1989.

Greenleaf, Monika. "Performing Autobiography: The Multiple Memoirs of Catherine the Great (1756–96)." *The Russian Review* 63 (July 2004): 407–26.

Griffiths, David M. "Castéra-Tooke: The First Western Biographer(s) of Catherine II." *Study Group on Eighteenth-Century Russia Newsletter* 10 (1982): 50–62.

Gukovskii, Grigorii A. "The Empress as Writer." *Catherine the Great: A Profile,* edited by Marc Raeff, 64–89. New York: Hill and Wang, 1972.

Hays, Mary. "Catherine II." *Female Biography; or, Memoirs of Illustrious and Celebrated Women, of all Ages and Countries,* 2:247–404, 3:1–271. London, 1803.

Heldt, Barbara. *Terrible Perfection: Women and Russian Literature.* Bloomington, Ill.: University of Illinois Press, 1987.

Holmgren, Beth, ed. *The Russian Memoir: History and Literature.* Evanston, Ill.: Northwestern University Press, 2003.

Hughes, Lindsey. *Russia in the Age of Peter the Great.* New Haven, Conn.: Yale University Press, 1998.

Jones, W. Gareth. "Biography in Eighteenth-Century Russia." *Oxford Slavonic Papers* 22 (1989): 58–80.

———. "The Russian Language as a Definer of Nobility." *A Window on Russia: Papers from the V International Conference of the Study Group on Eighteenth-Century Russia, Gargnano, 1994,* edited by Maria Di Salvo and Lindsey Hughes, 293–98. Rome: La Fenice Edizioni, 1996.

———. "The Spirit of the Nakaz: Catherine II's Literary Debt to Montesquieu." *Slavonic and East European Review* 76.4 (October 1998): 658–71.

Kamenskii, Aleksandr. *"Pod seniiu Ekateriny": Vtoraia polovina XVIII veka.* St. Petersburg: Lenizdat, 1992.

———. *Rossiiskaia imperiia v XVIII veke: traditsii i modernizatsii.* Moscow: Novoe literaturnoe obozrenie, 1999.

———. *Zhizn' i sud'ba Imperatritsy Ekateriny Velikoi.* Moscow: Izdatel'stvo Znanie, 1997.

Karabanov, P. F. "Stats-damy i freiliny russkago dvora v XVIII i XIX stoletiiakh," *Russkaia starina* 2(1870): 443–73; 3(1871): 39–48, 272–82, 457–73; 4(1871): 59–67, 379–404.

Khrapovitskii, A. V. *Dnevnik A. V. Khrapovitskogo, 1782–1793.* St. Petersburg, 1874.

Kornilovich, O. "Zapiski Imperatritsy Ekateriny II." *Zhurnal Ministerstva narodnogo prosveshcheniia* 37 (January 1912): 37–74.

LeDonne, John P. *Absolutism and Ruling Class: The Formation of the Russian Political Order, 1700–1825.* New York: Oxford University Press, 1991.

———. "Ruling Families in the Russian Political Order, 1689–1825." *Cahiers du Monde russe et soviétique* 28.3–4 (July–December 1987): 233–322.

———. *Ruling Russia: Politics and Administration in the Age of Absolutism, 1762–1796.* Princeton, N.J.: Princeton University Press, 1984.

Leonard, Carol S. *Reform and Regicide: The Reign of Peter III of Russia.* Bloomington, Ind.: Indiana University Press, 1993.

Levitt, Marcus C. "Catherine the Great." *Russian Women Writers,* edited by Christine D. Tomei, 1:3–27. New York: Garland Publishing, 1999.

Lopatin, V. S., ed. *Ekaterina II i G. A. Potemkin. Lichnaia perepiska, 1769–1791.* Moscow: Nauka, 1997.

Madariaga, Isabel de. "Catherine II and Enlightened Absolutism." *Politics and Culture in Eighteenth-Century Russia.* New York: Longman, 1998.

———. "Catherine and the *philosophes.*" *Politics and Culture in Eighteenth-Century Russia.* New York: Longman, 1998.

———. *Catherine the Great: A Short History.* New Haven, Conn.: Yale University Press, 1990.

———. "The Role of Catherine II in the Literary and Cultural Life of Russia." *Politics and Culture in Eighteenth-Century Russia.* New York: Longman, 1998.

———. *Russia in the Age of Catherine the Great.* New Haven, Conn.: Yale University Press, 1981.

Marcus, Leah S., Janel Mueller, and Mary Beth Rose, eds. *Elizabeth I: Collected Works.* Chicago: University of Chicago Press, 2000.

Margadant, Jo Burr, ed. *The New Biography: Performing Femininity in Nineteenth-Century France.* Berkeley: University of California Press, 2000.

Mazour, Anatole G. *Modern Russian Historiography.* Westport, Conn.: Greenwood Press, 1975.

Montefiore, Simon Sebag. *Prince of Princes: The Life of Potemkin.* New York: St. Martin's Press, Thomas Dunne Books, 2001.

Mueller, Janel and Leah S. Marcus, eds. *Elizabeth I: Autograph Compositions and Foreign Language Originals.* Chicago: University of Chicago Press, 2003.

Novikov, Nikolai. *Opyt istoricheskogo slovaria o rossiskikh pisateliakh.* St. Petersburg, 1772.

Ottomeyer, Hans, and Susan Tipton, eds. *Katharina die Grosse.* Eurasburg, Germany: Edition Minerva, 1997.

Pavlenko, N. I. *Ekaterina Velikaia.* Moscow: Molodaia gvardiia, 2003.

Pekarskii, P. *Materialy dlia istorii zhurnal'noi i literaturnoi deiatel'nosti Ekateriny II,* Prilozhenie k III-mu tomu Zapisok Imperatorskoi Akademii nauk. Vol. 6. St. Petersburg, 1863.

Piotrovsky, Mikhail B., ed. *Treasures of Catherine the Great.* London: Thames & Hudson, 2000.

Plutarch. *Plutarch's Lives.* Translated by John Dryden. 2 vols. New York: Random House, 2001.

Poniatowski, Stanislaw August. *Mémoires du roi Stanislas-Auguste Poniatowski.* Vol. 1. Edited by A. S. Lappo-Danilevskii, S. M. Gorianov, and S. F. Platonov. St. Petersburg: Imperial Academy of Sciences, 1914.

Redford, Bruce. *The Converse of the Pen: Acts of Intimacy in the Eighteenth-Century Familiar Letter.* Chicago: University of Chicago Press, 1986.

Rulhière, Claude C. de. *A History, or Anecdotes of the Revolution in Russia, in the Year 1762.* 1797. Reprint, New York: Arno Press and *The New York Times,* 1970.

Sacke, Dr. Georg. "Die Pressepolitik Katharinas II von Russland." *Zeitungswissenschaft* 9 (1934): 570–79.

Safonov, M. M. " 'Seksual'nye otkroveniia' Ekaterina II i proiskhozhdenie Pavla I." In *Reflections on Russia in the Eighteenth Century,* edited by Joachim

Klein, Simon Dixon, and Maarten Fraanje, 96–111. Cologne: Böhlau Verlag, 2001

Saint-Simon, Duc de. *Mémoires complète et authentiques du Duc de Saint-Simon sur le siècle de Louis XIV et la régence.* Vol. 1. Paris: Hachette, 1882.

Sbornik Imperatorskogo russkogo istoricheskogo obshchestva. 148 vols. St. Petersburg, 1867–1926.

Scharf, Claus. *Katharina II: Deutschland und die Deutschen.* Mainz, Germany: Verlag Philipp von Zabern, 1995.

———. *Katharina II, Russland und Europa: Beiträge zur internationalen Forschung.* Mainz, Germany: Verlag Philipp von Zabern, 2001.

Ségur, Louis-Philippe de. *Mémoires ou souvenirs et anecdotes.* 2nd ed., vol. 3. Paris, 1826.

Shchebal'skii, P. K. "Ekaterina II, kak pisatel'nitsa: literaturnaia perepiska Ekateriny." *Zaria* 2 (1869): 99–146; 3 (1869): 100–127; 5.3 (1869): 31–50; 6 (1869): 1–19; 8 (1869): 68–111; 9 (1869): 68–101; 3 (1870): 1–38; 6.2 (1870): 1–40.

Shepelev, L. E. *Chinovnyi mir Rossii: XVIII–nachalo XIX v.* St. Petersburg: Iskusstvo-SPB, 2001.

Siebigk, Ferdinand. *Katharina der Zweiten Brautreise nach Russland, 1744–1745. Eine historische Skizze.* Dessau, Germany, 1873.

Smith, Douglas, ed. *Love and Conquest: Personal Correspondence of Catherine the Great and Prince Grigory Potemkin.* DeKalb, Ill.: Northern Illinois University Press, 2004.

Stegnii, P. V. *Razdely Pol'shi i diplomatiia Ekateriny II: 1772, 1793, 1795.* Moscow: Mezhdunarodnye otnosheniia, 2002.

Tartakovskii, A. G. *Russkaia memuaristika XVIII-pervoi poloviny XIX v.* Moscow: Nauka, 1991.

Thyrêt, Isolde. *Between God and Tsar: Religious Symbolism and the Royal Women of Muscovite Russia.* Dekalb, Ill.: Northern Illinois University Press, 2001.

Tooke, William. *The Life of Catharine II, Empress of Russia.* 3rd ed., vol. 1. London, 1799.

Voltaire. *Voltaire's Correspondence.* Edited by T. Besterman. 107 vols. Geneva: Institut et Musée Voltaire, 1953–65.

Wachtel, Andrew. *An Obsession with History: Russian Writers Confront the Past.* Stanford, Calif.: Stanford University Press, 1994.

Whittaker, Cynthia Hyla. *Russian Monarchy: Eighteenth-Century Rulers and Writers in Political Dialogue.* DeKalb, Ill.: Northern Illinois University Press, 2003.

Wortman, Richard. "Texts of Exploration and Russia's European Identity." *Russia Engages the World, 1453–1825,* edited by Cynthia Hyla Whittaker, 90–117. Cambridge, Mass.: Harvard University Press, 2003.

———. *Scenarios of Power: Myth and Ceremony in Russian Monarchy.* Vol. 1. Princeton, N.J.: Princeton University Press, 1995.

Zaionchkovskii, P. A. *Istoriia dorevoliutsionnoi Rossii v dnevnikakh i vospominaniiakh.* 5 vols. Moscow, 1976.

INDEX*

Adadurov, Vasily Evdokimovich, privy
   counselor, senator (1709–80), 10, 23,
   189–90, 214
Adlerfelt, Gustavus (1671–1709), 4n
Adlerfelt, Karl Emanuel Johann,
   chamberlain, 3
Adolf Friedrich, Prince of Holstein,
   Bishop of Lübeck, King of
   Sweden, guardian of Peter,
   Catherine's maternal uncle
   (1710–71, r. 1751–71), lii, lxviii
   n.146, 3, 4, 5, 6, 21, 24, 25, 155,
   162, 166
Aksakov, Elizabeth's fool, 74
Albertine Friederike of Baden-Durlach,
   Catherine's maternal grandmother
   (1682–1755), xiv, 5, 155

d'Alembert, Jean Le Rond (1717–83),
   xxvi, lv, lix n.30, 208n
Alexander I, Emperor Alexander
   Pavlovich (1777–1825, r. 1801–25), x,
   xxiii, xxxiv, lvii n.4
Alexander II, Emperor Alexander
   Nikolaevich (1818–81, r. 1855–81),
   xxiii, xxxv
Alexei Petrovich, tsarevich, Peter the
   Great's son (1690–1718), xvi, xvii, lix
   n.27, 38
Anna, Duchess of Courland, Empress
   Anna Ivanovna (1693–1740, r. 1730–
   40), xvii, lxxxvi, 16n, 38, 48, 73, 81, 92
Anna Leopoldovna, Princess of
   Mecklenburg, Regent (1718–46,
   r. 1740–41), xvii, 81, 87

---

* This name index is based on the annotated indexes to Catherine's memoirs by Pypin (1907)
and Böhme (1913), who based his on Pypin's index too, while adding dates and more accurate
spellings of foreign names, especially for Germans. In addition, to give a fuller sense of the status of noblewomen at court, I have added all titles for those in Karabanov's "Ladies-in-Waiting
and Maids of Honor of the Russian Court" (1870–71) and give the number for their entry. Family connections can be traced through maiden and married names, and Russian middle names,
which are patronymics that indicate the father's first name.

ABOUT THE TRANSLATORS

MARK CRUSE has a Ph.D. in French literature from New York University and is assistant professor of medieval French literature at Arizona State University. He translated *Blue: The History of a Color* by Michel Pastoureau.

HILDE HOOGENBOOM received her Ph.D. in Russian literature from Columbia University and teaches Russian and translation at State University of New York at Albany. She has published widely on life writing by Russian women writers and is completing a book on gender, nobility, and aesthetics in nineteenth-century Russian literature.

A NOTE ON THE TYPE

The principal text of this Modern Library edition
was set in a digitized version of Janson, a typeface that
dates from about 1690 and was cut by Nicholas Kis,
a Hungarian working in Amsterdam. The original matrices have
survived and are held by the Stempel foundry in Germany.
Hermann Zapf redesigned some of the weights and sizes for
Stempel, basing his revisions on the original design.

MODERN LIBRARY IS ONLINE AT
WWW.MODERNLIBRARY.COM

MODERN LIBRARY ONLINE IS YOUR GUIDE
TO CLASSIC LITERATURE ON THE WEB

THE MODERN LIBRARY E-NEWSLETTER

Our free e-mail newsletter is sent to subscribers, and features sample
chapters, interviews with and essays by our authors, upcoming books,
special promotions, announcements, and news. To subscribe to the Modern
Library e-newsletter, visit **www.modernlibrary.com**

THE MODERN LIBRARY WEBSITE

Check out the Modern Library website at
www.modernlibrary.com for:

- The Modern Library e-newsletter
- A list of our current and upcoming titles and series
- Reading Group Guides and exclusive author spotlights
- Special features with information on the classics and
  other paperback series
- Excerpts from new releases and other titles
- A list of our e-books and information on where to buy them
- The Modern Library Editorial Board's 100 Best Novels and
  100 Best Nonfiction Books of the Twentieth Century written in
  the English language
- News and announcements

Questions? E-mail us at **modernlibrary@randomhouse.com**.
For questions about examination or desk copies, please visit
the Random House Academic Resources site at
www.randomhouse.com/academic.

Printed in the United States
by Baker & Taylor Publisher Services